ORALITY AND PERFORMANCE IN EARLY FRENCH ROMANCE

Evelyn Birge Vitz

D. S. BREWER

First published 1999
D. S. Brewer, Cambridge

ISBN   0 85991 538 7

T

D. S. Brewer is an imprint of Boydell & Brewer Ltd
PO Box 9, Woodbridge, Suffolk IP12 3DF, UK
and of Boydell & Brewer Inc.
PO Box 41026, Rochester, NY 14604–4126, USA

A catalogue record for this book is available
from the British Library

Library of Congress Cataloging-in-Publication Data
Vitz, Evelyn Birge.
    Orality and performance in early French romance / Evelyn Birge
Vitz.
      p.   cm.
    Includes bibliographical references and index.
    ISBN 0–85991–538–7 (hc. : alk. paper)
    1. French poetry – To 1500 – History and criticism.   2. Romances –
History and criticism.   3. Oral tradition – France.   I. Title.
PQ205.V58   1999
841'.109–dc21   98–36154

This publication is printed on acid-free paper

Printed in Great Britain by
St Edmundsbury Press Ltd, Bury St Edmunds, Suffolk

Orality and Performance in Early French Romance

CONTENTS

ACKNOWLEDGEMENTS

This book has been some years in the making, and many friends and colleagues have made generous contributions to it. My special thanks to Nancy Regalado for her support and encouragement from the very start. I am also deeply grateful for the help of many others who have given me valuable feedback at one stage or another of the elaboration and refinement of this argument: Benjamin Bagby, Michel Beaujour, Michael T. Clanchy, Thomas O. Clancy, Joyce Coleman, Mark Cruse, Peter F. Dembowski, Joseph J. Duggan, Karen Duys, Elizabeth Emery, Maureen Gillespie, Peter Kardon, Marilyn Lawrence, Kathleen Loysen, Michelle Magallanez, Joseph Nagy, Judith Nolan, Walter J. Ong, Thomas Pavel, Roger Pensom, Laurie Postle-wate, Robert Raymo, Edward Roesner, Margaret Switten, Katherine Talarico, Jane H.M. Taylor, Kenneth Varty, Linda Marie Zaerr, Michel Zink and the late Paul Zumthor. I do not wish to imply that all these scholars agree with my positions, but I have certainly benefited from their learning and at various points they have helped me extract my foot from my mouth. I also thank Glyn Burgess, the reader for Boydell and Brewer, for his valuable suggestions, and my editor Caroline Palmer for her good advice and her encouragement. Finally, my thanks to my husband, Paul C. Vitz, and all our children for their multiple contributions to this "performance."

Preliminary versions of Chapters 1 and 2 were published in *Romanic Review* 77:4 (1986) and 78:3 (1987), respectively. An early version of Chapter 3 appeared in *Poétique* 81 (1990) under the title: "Chrétien de Troyes: clerc ou ménestrel?: Problèmes des traditions orale et littéraire dans les Cours de France au XIIe siécle" and an abridged translation of an early form of Chapter 6 appeared as "*Romans Dir et Contar*: Réflexions sur la performance des romans médiévaux" in *Cahiers de littérature orale* 36 (1995). Permission to reprint is gratefully acknowledged.

For MJ and TTR

FOREWORD: THE ARGUMENTS OF THIS BOOK

This book proposes a major revision of our understanding of early French romance, and of the "birth of French literature" as a whole. It puts forth two arguments. The first – the more modest of the two – is that early verse romance shows evidence of having been, to a significant degree, a blend of oral and written cultures. (These terms and concepts, and others introduced below, will of course require reflection, careful definition, and in some cases, repeated discussion.) Romance was, apparently from a very early period, a mixed, indeed an ambivalent, genre, containing within its implicit definition – its "poetics" – important features both of minstrelsy and of clerkliness. Thus, for example, romance poets invariably speak to "listeners" and their "authors" typically use verbs like "make" or "tell" to refer to their work. But romances also generally show the stamp of the literary and clerical traditions in their references to "the book" and other written documents, their interest in literate characters, their recourse to classical allusions, and the like. Thus, virtually all romances represent some blend of the minstrel and the clerkly traditions. Oral and literary poetic practices and conceptualizations of romance co-existed in general and even within individual works.

The blend of these traditions in romance does not appear to have been merely "accidental," and therefore temporary or short-lived, but was of a significant and fairly enduring character: it lasted from the mid-twelfth century through the thirteenth and well into the fourteenth century; to some degree it can still be seen at the very end of the medieval period. Thus, we are not simply dealing with a brief moment in the transition from the oral to the written, or looking at a one-way street toward the modern and the literary. Rather, the blend of oral and written elements in medieval romance seems to be an expression of the nature of court life in the period. In court settings we find, on the one hand, the delights provided by minstrels and minstrelsy: the pleasures of music, story-telling and other forms of entertainment. But we also see the important – and the rising – presence and prestige of clerks, books, and documents. (The many studies of the phenomenon called "The Twelfth Century Renaissance" have made this clear.) Both the written/clerical tradition and that of minstrelsy and *jonglerie* exerted a strong magnetic pull; both were perceived as having "authority." It is worth restating this point in terms of human interaction rather than abstract principles: clerks and minstrels knew each other, they influenced each other, they borrowed strings from each other's bow; they may even have collaborated at times.

But while I will show that romance was a blended tradition – and one that allowed for a wide range of options – my second and more fundamental argument is that verse romances of the twelfth and thirteenth centuries were substantially more oral than is generally thought – or at least, than is commonly emphasized in literary studies today. The "learned" or "literary" character of early romance is virtually a *topos* of modern criticism. What needs to receive far greater emphasis is romance's orality – an orality relating not merely to one or two features, but existing on a range of dimensions including the poetic form in which romances were composed; the non-literate vs. literate status of the poets who "made" them; the modes in which romances were composed, transmitted and preserved; thematic contents and plot structures; the nature of the impact of romances on their medieval audiences; and the social functions of romance. Throughout this book I will emphasize an array of oral and performed features as being strongly characteristic of much early French romance.

One might think in terms of a multi-stranded counter, or abacus, with several wires running horizontally, and one or two beads on each wire. (I refrain from attempting to construct such an abacus visually.) One end of the abacus might be taken to signify more-or-less "pure orality" on these various dimensions; the more fully written tradition would be at the other end. We will, however, return to the fact that, in medieval France – unlike certain primitive cultures – the oral is never purely oral, due to the presence of books (in particular, the Bible), and clerks and other churchmen. And *no* culture, however advanced, can be entirely written.

In any event, this book will have as one of its primary purposes to slide French medieval romance down closer to the oral side of the abacus: to move the beads farther over in that direction. While I do not deny the blend of oral and written in romance, and while I recognize a considerable range of possibilities (some works being strongly oral, others predominantly written), the general oral/written center of gravity of romance needs to be substantially shifted.

These two fundamental arguments come together in – indeed throughout – this book. Part I focuses on the complex combination of oral and written elements in early romance, but emphasizes the importance of orality and the surprisingly oral quality of several important early romances. Part II takes up broad issues of performance – recitation from memory, public reading, and private reading – but focuses particularly on the oral and dramatic performance of romances and emphasizes the importance of such considerations for audience response.

Within Part I, Chapter 1 focuses on the poetic form in which romances were composed – the octosyllabic rhymed couplet, or "octo" – and argues that this form was not originally "literary," as has been claimed. Rather, octo was a traditional vernacular story-telling form. I also point out, however, that in the early- to mid-twelfth century, octo became a form attractive to clerks, and that much of its development has a written cast: thus, for example, reference is often made to written sources and the status of the work as a "book" may be emphasized.

Chapter 2 lays out, on a variety of dimensions, some of the different sorts of developments that octo compositions could receive, from the strongly oral to the markedly clerical and text-centered. This discussion will focus on three late-twelfth century treatments of the Tristan story: those by Béroul, Thomas and Marie de France. (The first two are generally called "romances" – though there are dissenting voices in this generic assignment; Marie wrote short poetic narratives called "lais.") We will see that even the most oral version recognizes the authority of written texts, while the written treatments acknowledge their debt to oral traditions. Moreover, it is not clear that "literary" is a useful word to use with regard to the texted versions: the lure of written letters lay in their authority – and their durability – rather than in any perceived esthetic superiority over oral story-telling traditions.

Henceforth, our focus is almost exclusively on romance since, among narrative genres, it may be said to present the most interesting and complex blend of the oral and the written, the minstrel and the clerical. Moreover, it offers the strongest challenges to my theory, in light of its highly clerical reputation. Chapters 3 and 4 argue that two early major *romanciers* – the anonymous poet of the *Roman de Thèbes* and Chrétien de Troyes – may well have been, not clerks, as is commonly believed, but rather *ménestrels* and *trouvères*: makers and performers of romance; both belonged to a significant degree to an oral culture. In these chapters, however, I also emphasize the refined and knowledgeable way in which such romance poets speak. And I point out in Chapter 3 that another of the earliest romance poets, Benoît de Sainte-Maure, author of the *Roman de Troie*, is unquestionably a clerk. The world of romance does not present a simple picture with regard to matters of literacy.

Differences between Anglo-Norman England and France turn out to be significant with regard to oral vs. written configurations: the Anglo-Norman monarchs – for whom Wace and Benoît de Sainte-Maure wrote their romances, and to whom Marie de France dedicated her lais – made early and highly political use of vernacular reading and writing. Courts in France appear to have remained more generally oral and text-less longer.

The issues addressed in Chapters 3 and 4 could have been continued by an entire series of chapters taking up the status of particular medieval poets with respect to matters of minstrelsy and clerkliness, orality and literacy. I will reserve this task for another time, perhaps for a series of articles. But for the moment, the fundamental point is established: oral traditions and minstrelsy – as broadly defined – played an important role in the birth of romance.

We turn, in Part II, to issues of performance – for no matter what sort of poets composed those early romances, or how they "made" them, all these works were intended to be heard. Chapter 5 takes up the role played by voice in medieval romance – voice being understood in a very concrete (or, rather, audible) sense, rather as one might study the use of voice in "radio theatre."

The romances can be seen as scripts that encode a dramatic and varied use of the human voice (and sometimes animals' "voices"). Primary examples here are taken from the romances of Chrétien de Troyes, but many other narrative poets also made dramatic use of voice.

Chapter 6 pushes the point made in Chapter 5 one large step further. There is substantial evidence that many romances were recited from memory – indeed played and sung – by minstrels and *jongleurs* in the twelfth and thirteenth centuries. We examine this evidence and look in considerable detail at what is known about performance of romance. This chapter defines the term "performance" broadly enough to include the practice of reading, and discusses romance-reading; this practice, however, appears to have been surprisingly rare until well into the fourteenth century.

Chapter 7 addresses the issue of memory in performance, asking how romances can have been performed "par cuer"; it focuses on a wide variety of features that make verse romances what I call "memory-friendly" as regards both the substance of the plot and the words and lines themselves. Here again the works of Chrétien de Troyes are taken as exemplary.

This book argues that early French romance was rooted in oral culture, that it was frequently performed in strongly dramatic fashion, and that, as performed, it filled major social functions. We cannot, then, just study romances as though they were books intended for private readers. Rather, we need new approaches that can help us take into account the oral and performed features of early romance. Chapter 8 presents the advantages of a performance-oriented approach to romance, especially as regards the important issue of audience response; this chapter also presents the view that medieval romances can and should be performed today.

None of this is to say that we should simply abandon more strictly literary or historical approaches to romance: many early romances were, as I noted earlier, involved in the prestige of the written and made use of knowledge that came from books; a few early romances (and related works) were indeed produced by "writers" and conceived as "textual objects." And romance certainly *became* an increasingly written genre. Different approaches to romance can inform and enrich each other.

A final note. The central argument of this book will seem, to some, radical; to be sure, it goes against a good deal of received academic wisdom. But to the extent that it does seem extreme, I believe this is primarily because, as the saying goes, "History is written by the winners." In the case of the "History of French Literature," the saying is doubly true. First, the writers ultimately won out over the oral poets and performers: verbal eloquence, songs and stories became "Literature"; such cultural transformations are seen as "progress." Second, the histories that we read to learn about the development of French "literature" were all themselves written by readers and writers, to whom oral culture was generally a closed book.

Today's academics are the intellectual heirs to the clerical culture of the Middle Ages, and we cannot help but project the "literary" tastes, habits and prejudices of our caste back onto that part of the medieval situation with which we can identify. In short, it is very difficult for any of us to overcome our double bias against – or at least our blindness and deafness toward, and incomprehension of – the oral culture of the Middle Ages.

Finally, whatever one's "sympathy" with oral tradition (and some have romanticized it), it is an obvious fact that this culture, as it existed, and even thrived, in the Middle Ages, has long since disappeared, leaving little trace. Or, rather, it has left few but *written* traces. (It also has, to be sure, some useful analogues in parts of the world where oral cultures are still to be found.)

It is the purpose of this book at least to open discussion of these complex issues.

Part I

ORALITY AND LITERACY

CHAPTER ONE

The Orality of the Octosyllabic Rhymed Couplet

Part of the essential professional lore that budding French medievalists have learned at their mentor's knee for several generations now is the dichotomy between the oral and written (or literary) traditions; and, first corollary to that axiom, that in early vernacular "literature"[1] the oral narrative tradition is represented by the formulaic epic, the written tradition by the octosyllabic rhymed couplet – understood to have been an essentially literary form, even perhaps a clerical invention. In their *Histoire de la littérature française*[2] Bédier and Hazard said of the anonymous author of the *Roman d'Enéas*:

> Une dizaine d'années plus tard [que le *Roman de Thèbes*], vers l'an 1160, un autre poète traite Virgile comme Stace venait d'être traité [dans le *Thèbes*]. Clerc tout imbu des doctrines de l'école, habile à dessiner des portraits selon les formules enseignées, rompu à tous les procédés de la rhétorique, l'auteur du *Roman d'Enéas* imite excellemment l'auteur du *Roman de Thèbes*. Il adopte le mètre nouveau, l'octosyllabe à rimes plates inauguré par son devancier. (I, p. 24)

The octosyllabic rhymed couplet was thus a "new meter," launched by the clerical author of the *Roman de Thèbes* around mid-century.

Even Paul Zumthor, who in the last decades of his life became virtually the champion of the oral tradition, which he generally referred to as "vocal poetry," spoke of the octosyllabic rhymed couplet as an "innovation" in his *Essai de poétique médiévale*.[3] In any event, this form, like the romance genre in which it was used, has long been thought of as inherently written, even clerical.

---

1 I use this word in quotation marks here (following Paul Zumthor's frequent practice) to highlight the problem of how to speak of works that are not reliably written. But on the whole I will abandon the quotation marks, only returning to them when the issue needs to receive particular emphasis.

2 Full references to all items will be provided in the Bibliography.

3 P. 339. In *Histoire littéraire de la France médiévale* he referred to the octosyllable as being "d'origine sans doute latine," p. 131. While in the *Introduction à la poésie orale* and his other subsequent work Zumthor did not explicitly revise his earlier view of the octo, he increasingly viewed romance – along with all medieval literature – as "vocal poetry." See the discussions of his work in Part II. See also Vitz, "Paul Zumthor and Medieval Romance."

I will argue here that there is little evidence for the common assumption that the octosyllabic rhymed couplet – henceforth, for the sake of brevity, "octo" – is a literary creation, or that it emerged along with the written vernacular. On the contrary, there is good reason to believe that octo is a *pre*-literary form. This hypothesis, if accepted, will force us to rethink our understanding of the birth and early development of French literature, and of romance in particular. Indeed this book as a whole is the result of just such a rethinking.

The oral origins of the octosyllabic rhymed couplet – preliminary evidence

Let me begin with the issue that led me to this view of octo. It concerns the story-telling tradition – what we might very loosely term the "folktale": all that old narrative material that has been so popular throughout the world, throughout the centuries, and that was certainly popular in medieval Europe where legends, myths, and tales abounded. The question that puzzled me is this: in what poetic or literary form(s) was story-telling material known in France, around the time of the emergence of vernacular literature, and especially *before* its emergence in writing? – let's say in the eleventh and early twelfth centuries. Now to some degree, and to some people, this material – these stories – must have been known in textual form; that is, in Latin, if we are speaking of the period before the existence of vernacular texts. But surely we do not believe that it is only, or even mainly, in Latin that such stories were transmitted! Latin, quite clearly, offers a texted and "respectable" rendering of material commonly told in the vernacular.[4] One important feature of the folktale tradition is that it is a mixed tradition: partly, occasionally, written, but more often, oral; the written seems like the tip of a great invisible (and indeed largely lost) iceberg of orality. This is above all a story-telling tradition, in which each new teller has felt free to adapt and modify a story he heard (or read, or had read to him) to appeal to a new audience or provide a new "take" on the story. But the question concerning me was: in what poetic form or forms did story-tellers tell these stories, in the pre-literary vernacular?

This is a question that folklorists seem rarely to ask, being more concerned with other sorts of issues. They talk of genres, motifs, and themes; of sources and analogues; of archetypes. They may speak about context and performance. But they rarely address issues of poetic form. Their concerns tend to be more those of the anthropologist or ethnologist than of the literary historian or critic – which should come as no particular surprise. Literary historians, perhaps more surprisingly, have almost exclusively asked questions about the content of the tales and legends being transmitted – "Where does a particular *matière*

---

4   See, for example, Ziolkowski, *Talking Animals*, pp. 31–32, 46, 64, 129, 236.

come from?'' – and little about the form in which the stories circulated. I will return to the oral theorists, but most of the French medievalists among them have been almost solely preoccupied with the *chanson de geste* and the particular problems that it presents. The work of oral theory generalists is extremely useful. In particular, scholars like Walter J. Ong and Ruth Finnegan have focused our attention on broad differences of content, style, and mind-set between oral and written traditions, as well as on variability within the oral and performed tradition.

To return to our question: in what form did the stories circulate orally? Hypothetically, there are numerous possibilities, for historically a great many different poetic forms have been utilized by story-tellers (and in oral poetry in general).[5] But, first, can it have been in prose – at least in ''non-verse,'' as it were[6] – that these stories were told in pre-literary France? But we know that vernacular prose does not emerge in France, and in French, as a ''literary'' form until the end of the twelfth century. The rare exceptions and early models[7] indicate that prose arose in French from the learned, clerical tradition – initially perhaps from within historiography.[8] There is no evidence that it had any connection with popular or folktale-type material. Moreover, pure prose is rarely the vehicle for oral composition and performance, as it is less ''memorable.'' (This is not to imply that ordinary conversation was conducted in verse, only that compositions with any poetic pretentions, or in which performance-skill was an issue, are likely to have borne the marks of prosody.) Verse, rhyme, etc. are all powerful mnemonic aids; we will return to such issues in Chapter 7.

In short, it is probable that the folktale was transmitted in some poetic form – poetic in the sense of versified, rhymed and embellished with other kinds of

5   See, for example, *The Penguin Book of Oral Poetry*, ed. by Ruth Finnegan.

6   The definition of prose and the distinctions between prose and verse are extremely complex. For example, just how rhythmic and how rhymed – how marked by regular prosodic elements – can prose be before it ceases to be prose and becomes poetry? In ''The Poetic and the Everyday,'' Ruth Finnegan says that she used to transcribe as prose many discourses that she would now transcribe as (free) verse; p. 10. See also Finnegan, *Oral Poetry*, pp. 25ff; Dell Hymes, *Ethnography, Linguistics, Narrative Inequality*, Chapter 6, pp. 121–41, 219; Dennis Tedlock, *Finding the Center*. These scholars have been concerned with the poetry and internal patterning within the narrative ''prose'' of myths and tales.

7   Such examples would include early sermons, translations from the Bible and chronicles. On this general issue see Godzich and Kittay, *The Emergence of Prose*.

8   See Zumthor, *Histoire*, p. 131. Both Peter F. Dembowski and Jeannette Beer have shown that in early prose works, such as those of Robert de Clari and Villehardouin, the style of the *chanson de geste* can be detected; Dembowski, *La chronique de Robert de Clari*, esp. p. 115; Beer, *Villehardouin – Epic Historian*, pp. 31–56; and *Early Prose in France*, p. 136. The situation was different in England – that is, in English: vernacular history-writing was done in prose from an early period; recourse to verse for the writing of history was apparently the result of Anglo-Norman influence.

repetition. The line was probably fairly short – easier to retain, obviously, than a long one.

While a good many forms are thus hypothetically possible as the vehicle for pre-literary French folktale and popular narrative material, clearly the most likely candidate is octo: it is historically attested – indeed, massively so; it was a frequent vehicle for precisely the sort of material of which we are speaking; and it offers a short poetic line.

Moreover, other oral traditions which still exist today, or for which we have firm evidence from the past, have also frequently had recourse to lines of 8 syllables. In their classic work, *The Growth of Literature*, H.M. and N.K. Chadwick discuss a great many oral traditions. In many parts of Indo-European heroic tradition a long poetic line – like the decasyllable – has been favored. But in many cases, such as the French tradition, the decasyllable is fundamentally broken by a strong caesura into two shorter lines: a 4-syllable and a 6-syllable line (occasionally, the reverse: 6 + 4 syllables). Some long heroic lines seem to be "decomposable" into more or less 8-syllable units. In the South Slavic tradition, the *bugarstica* (a form of epic narrative) is most commonly, at least in modern times, decasyllabic. But among the many older (and still variant) forms, is one in which the line is longer, with, commonly, 8 syllables after the caesura, and between 6 and 9 syllables in the first half.[9] David E. Bynum, for example, states that in the South Slavic epic tradition, the long line was a "mirage," and was "metrically speaking, never really a 'long line' at all, but only a couplet of lines" – that is, a pair of couplets run together. The "dominant schema" within the couplets was 4 + 3 // 4 + 4 and the "recessive schema" was 4 + 4 // 5 + 3 = 3 + 5.[10] In short, the lines had strong octosyllabic tendencies. Bynum documents the general tendency toward the octosyllabic line in the South Slavic epic tradition.

Shorter lines, including 8-syllable lines, have also been common. For example, in Russian heroic poems, or *byliny*, the Chadwicks note that "different localities favour different lengths of line. Poems obtained to the east of Lake Onega . . . are generally composed in short lines of 5 or 6 syllables, whereas the same poem to the west of the lake is generally in long lines of 8 or 9."[11]

In non-heroic, story-telling forms, 8-syllable lines are also common (though I would not wish to claim that they were standard). For example, again in northern Russia, tales, or *skaza* "generally consisted of seven, eight, or nine

9 In "Bugarscice: A Unique Type of Archaic Oral Poetry," Josip Kekez states: "The bugarstica verse line varies from thirteen to nineteen syllables, but lines of fifteen and sixteen syllables occur most often . . .," p. 211.

10 Chadwicks, *Growth*, II, p. 304; Bynum, "Oral Epic Tradition in South Slavic," esp. pp. 315, 320, 328.

11 Chadwicks, *Growth*, II, p. 20.

feet.''[12] In Romania, epic songs are today generally ''trochaic verses of seven or eight syllables.''[13] In any event, we can say that lines of 8 syllables are common in oral tradition. Calvert Watkins believes that there was in Indo-European poetics a basic 7-syllable – 4 + 3 – line, one of whose variants was a 5 + 3 line.[14]

The success of 8-syllable and similarly short lines may well be linked to a phenomenon studied by Benoît de Cornulier, in *Théorie du vers: Rimbaud, Verlaine, Mallarmé*. Basing himself on psycholinguistic and psychometric research, Cornulier states that: ''en français, la perception instinctive et sûre du nombre syllabique exact est limitée, selon les personnes, à huit syllabes, ou à moins.''[15] Thus the longest verse unit that can be perceived as such by a listener is an 8-syllable line; for some people, it is less. Cornulier restricts himself to French, and essentially to issues of perception, but the same phenomenon – the number 8 as an outer perceptual limit – has been shown to be quite general and to affect learning and memory as well. (We will return to such issues in Chapter 7.) The early French octosyllable had a further advantage of being decomposable into two highly regular 4-syllable halves: Stephen Guthrie, in ''Meter in Performance in Machaut and Chaucer,'' showed that the early narrative octosyllable, as exemplified by *Gormont et Isembart*, had strong caesura at the fourth syllable, and was thus composed of two even shorter lines.[16]

Let me make it clear that my purpose in this discussion has not been to find ''universals'' but rather to show that short lines, like the octo *line*, have been common in – attractive to – oral traditions.

In this framework, we return to the situation in Old French. Is not octo precisely the sort of form that we are looking for? Let us note a few of the immediate advantages that the hypothesis presents to us – aside perhaps from relief at the prospect of being spared yet another asterisked – ''unattested'' – form: we may not have to believe that there was some ancient vernacular form in which stories were told, but that disappeared, leaving no trace.

If octo was indeed a pre-literary form – if it was there already when French literature began to emerge, if it did not have to be ''invented'' by early vernacular writers – this will allow us to account for one of the most extraordinary and under-discussed phenomena of the twelfth century, namely the remarkably rapid and widespread appearance of octo in almost every genre of early vernacular literature. If the octo form really was a literary invention – *trové* in a particular place and milieu – one would expect to see it radiate out

---

[12] Chadwicks, *Growth*, II, p. 250.

[13] Beissinger, ''Text and Music in Romanian Oral Epic,'' p. 296.

[14] See Watkins, *How to Kill a Dragon*, p. 20.

[15] P. 90; see also pp. 32ff.

[16] P. 76. Guthrie argues that later poets did more complicated things with the octosyllable and increasingly varied the rhythmic patterns.

over time toward other parts of France and Anglo-Norman England; one would expect some time to have elapsed before octo was established as the "up-and-coming form" – a viable, indeed on some criteria the most attractive, vehicle for narrative and other discourse. But such is not the case. At the very dawn of French "literature" – from our earliest known texts – the octo form had *already* imposed itself in most narrative genres, and indeed in almost every sort of discourse, throughout the French-speaking world. Indeed, aside from the *chanson de geste* and the lyric, almost all vernacular literature of the twelfth century was composed in octo: the list of works *not* in octo in this century is very short. Octo is indeed the standard narrative form for non-epic works – the form from which others are seen, by contemporaries, as "different": thus, the *Roman d'Alexandre*, rewritten (from an earlier, octo version) at the end of the twelfth century into 12-syllable lines, provides the name for the rare "alexandrine" line.

There are no literary masters of such widely acknowledged authority early in the twelfth century that this factor can account for the rapid predominance of octo. It is difficult to avoid the impression that the octo form was there at the very beginning of French "literature" – already fully familiar both to storytellers and their audiences.

Where did octo originate?

If octo was not "invented" by early vernacular writers, where did it come from? Where and how did it arise? There are, I think, three general possibilities. First is that octo is the French form of the Latin iambic dimeter form. This hypothesis can be subdivided into a learned and a non-learned form. According to the former, octo would be the translation – as Georges Lote saw it, the "transcription"[17] – of the iambic dimeter. Now, medieval Latin poets did indeed use this form, and it does bear a marked resemblance to octo. A few examples may prove useful. A number of medieval hymns are composed entirely of lines which look and sound like a double octo line. An "abecedarian" hymn (stanzas begin with the letters of the alphabet in order, starting with "A"), traditionally attributed to St. Columba (521–596), has as its first stanza:

> Altus prosator, vetustus   dierum et ingenitus
> erat absque origine   primordii et crepidine,
> est et erit in saecula   saeculorum infinita;
> cui est unigenitus   Christus et Sanctus Spiritus

---

[17] Lote did not consider octo an invention, but viewed it as the "simple transcription en roman du dimètre iambique latin," appearing at the end of the 10th century: *Histoire du vers français*, Vol. II, p. 58.

coaeternus in gloria   deitatis perpetua.
Non tres deos depromimus,   sed unum Deum dicimus.[18]

The hymn is similarly rhymed in all stanzas. It looks very much like Latin octo. (That is, each line breaks up into a pair of rhymed couplets: Altus prosator, vetus*tus/* dierum et ingeni*tus*.)

Another example comes from the Venerable Bede (672–735). His hymn to the Holy Innocents does not rhyme throughout, but the opening lines of its first stanza certainly show what one might call the "pull" of rhyme; it too is in iambic dimeter:

> Hymnum canentes martyrum
> Dicamus innocentium,
> Quos terra flentes perdidit,
> Gaudens sed aethra suscipit.
> Vultum patris per saecula
> Quorum tuentur angeli,
> Eiusque laudant gratiam,
> Hymnum canentes martyrum.[19]

The first two couplets are rhymed. The last line repeats, therefore rhyming with, the first. The refrain effect occurs in all stanzas, each of which contains at least some other irregular rhyme as well.

An anonymous twelfth century hymn to "Christ, Son of the Virgin, Spouse of Virgins" is composed of four-line iambic dimeter stanzas, some of which rhyme throughout, but some of which are rhymed couplets – as in the closing stanza:

> Paranymphi secretales
> Et amici speciales;
> Ante sacrosanctum thorum,
> Cantant cantum canticorum.[20]

But though rhymed iambic dimeter couplets can be found in medieval Latin poetry, there are two problems with viewing octo as the translation or transcription of this Latin form. First, medieval Latin poetry knew a great variety of forms, among which the iambic dimeter is far from common. Indeed, in consulting anthologies of medieval Latin verse, I have found only a small handful of poems in this form.[21] Moreover, Latin narrative was commonly written in prose. Yet when Latin narrative in any of its various forms,

---

[18] *Poésie latine chrétienne du Moyen Age*, ed. by Henry Spitzmuller, p. 172.
[19] K.P. Harrington, ed., *Medieval Latin*, pp. 89–91.
[20] Spitzmuller, *Poésie latine*, pp. 1358–60.
[21] Aside from collections by Spitzmuller and Harrington, see also *The Oxford Book of Medieval Latin Verse*, edited first by Stephen Gaselee, then later by F.J.E. Raby.

including prose, was "turned" into French in the twelfth and early thirteenth centuries, it was almost invariably put into octo. The modest popularity of use of the iambic dimeter does not square with the overwhelming dominance of octo. We seem to be picking up something else.

Second problem: early "translations" of Latin works into French in question rarely correspond to what we today understand by the term. The word "translation" referred almost exclusively to the moving of the relics of a saint to a new place of burial, a new altar. What we mean by the word was generally expressed by the expression "mettre en roman." Early vernacular *mises en roman* are not word-for-word, highly text-dependent translations, but generally quite free retellings. The translator – or "rimeur" – often adds details that interest him, or that he feels will interest his listeners, and he cuts what he perceives as *longueurs* (by whatever criteria). While the work being translated and adapted is often given as a Latin text, the substance is typically recast into an oral, story-telling mode, and into verse. There is, moreover, no guarantee that the translator himself actually knew the Latin work *as* a text: it may already have been told to him in the vernacular before he retold it, in turn, in his version. Verse translations of the Bible were, for example, more often paraphrases and adaptations – retellings – than actual translations (and they generally presented single books of the Bible, the most common being Genesis and the Psalter). We should also note that the word "roman" did not simply mean "French," nor did it reliably mean "romance." The word commonly referred to the rhymed vernacular, mostly – though not always – the French octo.[22] It is specifically into this French form that most translation was done. In short, we are not simply dealing with translations from Latin texts.

Now to the *non*-learned form of the argument for Latin origins – or at least Latin analogues. Though octo does not appear to make sense as the translation of the iambic dimeter, both of these forms may correspond to centuries-old popular lyric and narrative traditions. Though we tend to think of Latin as representing the "learned" tradition, it too was long a spoken language in France as elsewhere in the Romance world; it too was a language with both popular and learned, oral and written, forms. In short, the iambic dimeter may have been a popular Latin form – its very "popularity" working against high poetic status. The fact that we find the iambic dimeter most often in hymns – poems intended to be sung – is itself suggestive.

It is, moreover, worth remembering that the influence between the Latin

---

22 In *From Latin to Modern French*, Mildred K. Pope explains that "romans" comes from Late Latin (Gallo-Roman) "loqui romanice" (p. 11). She emphasizes the meaning of "romans" as meaning French (as opposed to Latin), but her examples make it clear that much of the time it refers to French *verse*, especially octo. Both Godefroy and Tobler-Lommatzsch in their dictionary entries on the topic give a range of meanings for the word, from the French language, to verse narrative (especially in octo, apparently), to any sort of narrative, etc.

and the vernacular – especially Romance vernaculars – was by no means a one-way street: always from the former to the latter. As Elizabeth Salter has said, speaking of the lyric but expanding its "lessons" to other genres:

> . . . vernacular lyric forms pre-dated, and coexist with, Latin: only in the case of the most exact translation can we ever be sure that the flow of influence is one way, not two. What has been described [by Peter Dronke] as a "total situation . . . shared by 'chevalier et clerc et lai' '' embraces all kinds of composition.[23]

Medieval Latin may well, then, show the influence of un-written vernacular forms, such as octo or its analogues and ancestors. Even churchmen had a mother tongue and spent their earliest years within the verbal folds – in the lap – of vernacular lyric, story-telling and proverbial traditions. And tropes, for example, are, precisely, oral, performed amplifications of official, written texts; hymns are works not to be read, but to be sung. (One thinks in this context of the late tenth–early eleventh century rhymed octosyllabic tropes produced at St. Martial of Limoges.)

But, in short, though recourse to Latin as a learned language cannot explain the great popularity of octo or its widespread dominance, the remarkable success of octo may nonetheless be related to the existence of an octo-esque form with a strong investment in oral performance or recitation – and with a strong predisposition toward rhyme – in the late Latin or early medieval Latin period.[24]

Can other linguistic and cultural traditions have played an important role in the historical emergence of octo? What of Romanized Celtic influence – that of the Welsh and Breton traditions? Heroic Welsh poetry, as preserved in manuscripts dating from the twelfth century (such as the *Black Book of Carmarthen*) and later, did use couplets, as well as triads, connected by rhyme.[25] This poetry exists in a wide variety of meters, in which 7-syllable lines were favored.[26] And Celtic – or, more accurately, Brythonic – poets are certainly very much present in the early flowering of octo – as in the case of the apparently Breton poet Bréri, to whom (as we will see) Thomas defers in his *Tristan*. Brythonic subject-matter – the "Matter of Britain" – predominates in early octo compositions, not merely in the story of Tristan and Iseut, but also in the legends of King Arthur, and in the *Voyage de saint Brendan* (one of the first surviving

---

23 "The Mediaeval Lyric," p. 454. (Salter's quotation is from Peter Dronke, *Medieval Latin*, p. 56.) Salter states further: "When we find expressions and attitudes common to Latin, English, French, and German poetry, it is only necessary to remember that the contacts between various classes of mediaeval poets and singers were lively and continuous. Minstrel, cleric, and courtier met naturally at ecclesiastical or royal court, at cathedral school or university."

24 Chadwicks, *Growth*, I, pp. 36, 60–61.

25 Chadwicks, *Growth*, I, p. 43.

26 Chadwicks, *Growth*, I, pp. 36, 43.

works produced in octo). All these early octo works focus heavily on adventure, which is a major feature of Welsh tradition as well.[27] Against these factors on the plus side of the Celtic ledger stands the negative fact that there is no evidence for verse narrative in the Welsh tradition; tales were told in prose.[28] It is therefore difficult to imagine how Welsh can have influenced the emergent French poetic narrative tradition. As to potential Irish connections: There are interesting similiarities between medieval Irish narrative forms and octo. In particular, medieval Irish poets favored a metre called "deibide," composed of four-line stanzas of two couplets each, with seven syllables to the line. Although this form seems to have been widely used in story-telling primarily from the twelfth century on, it was employed around 700 for the translation of the Infancy Gospels into Irish. Calvert Watkins has traced the roots of this form to the 7-syllable Indo-European line referred to earlier.

If Celtic influence is questionable at best, that of the Germanic traditions is still less likely. Teutonic poetry, like modern English, is accent- or stress-based, rather than quantitative (based on the number of syllables). Moreover, Germanic oral tradition strongly favored alliteration, but not rhyme. Nothing here resembles or can account for the special features of octo. The likelihood is, then, that octo is a more-or-less indigenous and popular development within the Romance – possibly the larger Indo-European – tradition.

A brief historical survey of the emergence of octo

We need to review briefly the emergence of the octo form and its early development through the end of the twelfth century. How far back does this tradition go? We are, of course, woefully lacking in documentation. (This is precisely what it means to be in a period before vernacular writing – and before anthropologists with notebooks and camcorders.) For the period before the second quarter of the twelfth century, we have little more than fragments. But a northern French *Passion* dating from the beginning of the tenth century and a *Vie de Saint Léger* (perhaps from the Walloon region) dating from the close of that century have come down to us. They are suggestive of what octo may have looked like in this early period. Both works are composed in octosyllabic couplets. The couplets are not rhymed but are, rather, assonanced, and are grouped into short stanzas: two pairs per stanza for the *Passion*, three pairs for the *Saint Léger*. Both works are short: 516 lines for the earlier work, 240 for the later one. As for the eleventh century, we have extant only fragments of *Gormont et Isembart* (which may in fact date from the early twelfth century), on which more below.

Our first surviving text composed in full-fledged octo – that is, not merely

---

[27] Chadwicks, *Growth*, I, p. 42.
[28] See Sioned Davies, "Storytelling in Medieval Wales," pp. 231, 242.

in the octosyllable but in non-stanzaic, rhymed couplets – is the Anglo-Norman *Voyage de Saint Brendan*, by Benedeit, who wrote it apparently in the 1120s (or perhaps even earlier: at the very beginning of the century), at the court of Henry I. Many years ago, E.G.R. Waters commented on certain peculiarities of Benedeit's versification but added: "yet the technical perfection attained by the author indicates that he was using a well-established form" – this though Benedeit's is the first extant work we have in octo form.[29] The next work to consider is the first vernacular version of the often-retold story of Alexander the Great; it dates from about 1130, and was produced by Alberic de Pisançon. This work, extant only in fragmentary form – 105 lines remain, telling part of Alexander's childhood – is Franco-Provençal in origin; thus, it comes from a region far from the Anglo-Norman and Norman territory in which much of the early octo material is found. This work is composed in octo-syllables, the lines being organized into fairly regular laisses, mostly of 6 to 8 lines. One interesting feature of various early surviving works in octosyllables is that there seems little clear distinction among different narrative forms that use the 8-syllable line: that is, between laisses, strophes and continuous narrative (such as that found in rhymed couplet sequences).

Also from around 1130, or slightly earlier, dates the *Bestiaire* by the Anglo-Norman Philippe de Thaon; it was begun in hexasyllables and completed in octo. (He had already written a *Comput* – a treatise on how to calculate the date of feasts – in hexasyllables.) It may also be Philippe who wrote an alphabetically-organized lapidary – and that is surely a literary idea. Or more precisely, it is one that demonstrates a strong desire to foreground matters of literacy – for example, of letters as the components of words. It too is in octo. (One of the few surviving examples of vernacular prose in this century is a prose translation of the same Latin source that was used in the octo lapidary – a work by a major figure, the "authoritative" eleventh century writer Marbod of Rennes.) Both bestiaries and lapidaries are learned works, in that they deal with "scholarly" lore on the natural world. But many of them appear to have been written to be read aloud to unlettered nobles; they "speak" to listeners.

It is striking that the first octo works to be written down are those devoted to "lofty" subject matter: material of a pious, learned, or royal nature. Works that are thought of as worth saving get written down. The only vernacular productions that, in this early and tentative period, could compete with the intrinsic value of Latin – with its claims to learning, indeed to eternity – and thus be worthy of redaction, were works of high seriousness. That these vernacular works were not simply left in Latin – that they were translated into French, that they were written down in the vulgar tongue at all – presumably tells us that there was now an audience of nobles (and perhaps some wealthy

---

[29] E.G.R. Waters, ed., *The Anglo-Norman Voyage of St. Brendan by Benedeit*, pp. xxix ff.

bourgeois, especially in northern France?) interested not merely in knowing about science and desirous of "hearing" about it from the lips of a clerk, but in having it read aloud or recited to them from a *book*. One must assume that they had acquired the desire to have books produced under their patronage; to own books; to have libraries or book-cupboards (often called "aumoires"). This does *not*, however, mean that these men and women could, or even desired to, actually *read* books by or for themselves: on the important issue of the long-term "aural" presentation of books in the Middle Ages, I refer my reader to the fundamental new study by Joyce Coleman, *Public Reading and the Reading Public in Late Medieval England and France*. Coleman's basic point is that, even at the end of the medieval period (and well beyond), public reading was a great deal more common than private reading. And I will attempt to show that in the earlier period, which concerns us, recitation from memory was far more common than reading of any kind.

From before 1150 dates the *Histoire des angleis*, composed in octo by the Anglo-Norman Geffroi Gaimar. Of this work a 6,000-line fragment remains. Geffroi's sources are primarily the Latin works of William of Malmesbury and Geoffrey of Monmouth, but he had other sources as well and the first 800 lines of his "history" are devoted to the Scandinavian legend of Haveloc. The anonymous *Roman de Thèbes*, composed in octo (10,230 lines) in Normandy, dates from around 1150 or shortly thereafter. Wace, a clerk under the patronage of Henry II, finished a *Roman de Brut* (a translation and paraphrase of Geoffrey of Monmouth's *Historia regum Britanniae*) in 1155. His *Roman de Rou*, presented as a continuation of the *Brut*, was begun around 1160 but was still being worked on in the 1170s. Wace's first *roman* is entirely in octo (15,300 lines). In the second, he began with octo, then briefly switched to – experimented with? – alexandrine monorhymed laisses, then reverted to octo for the last 11,500 lines. Wace also composed several hagiographical works (perhaps before his vernacular chronicles), all in octo.

From around (or even before) 1160 date the *Roman de Troie* and the *Roman d'Enéas*, both in octo, the former (a massive work: 30,316 verses) composed at the Anglo-Norman court by Benoît de Sainte-Maure, the latter – a mere 10,156 lines – in Normandy by an anonymous poet. From here on out, the numbers of texts composed in octo and extant in manuscripts multiply rapidly, and there are dozens of works composed in octo before the end of the century: the Béroul and Thomas versions of the Tristan material; the romances of Chrétien de Troyes; *Floire et Blancheflor*, in two versions; two romances – *Eracle* and *Ille et Galeron* – by Gautier d'Arras; the *Lais, Fables*, and *Espurgatoire saint Patrice* of Marie de France; the little *Piramus et Tisbé*; *Partonopeus de Blois*; *Florimont*; *Le Roman des sept Sages*; *Robert le Diable*; Robert de Boron's version of the Grail material – and this list is not exhaustive. We also have the beginnings – the first dozen branches or so – of the Renart story, and the first surviving fabliau, *Richeut*. In hagiography – aside from the *Brendan*, Marie's *Espurgatoire* and the saints' lives of Wace – we have, in octo, Guernes de Pont

Sainte Maxence's *Thomas Becket*, composed between 1172 and 1174. (He says he has frequently read it aloud to pilgrims at the saint's tomb.) We also have quite a number of other works, all dating from before the end of the twelfth century. Then there are the earliest dramatic texts: the *Jeu d'Adam*, c.1150, and Jean Bodel's *Jeu de saint Nicolas* from the end of the century, both in octo. Also translations from the Bible (there are some in prose as well, and in other poetic forms). There were octo sermons too (some were also done in prose and in other verse forms).

We close this rapid survey at the end of the twelfth century, as we are primarily concerned with the emergence and early development of octo. We have seen some poetic development of the octo form. But what we have seen perhaps even more clearly is the development of vernacular *writing*: the rise in frequency of the *redaction* of vernacular works. Initially, only certain kinds of works – ''distinguished'' works – were considered worth saving. Increasingly, a wider array of things were written down and preserved. It may simply be that once the principle had been established that ''vulgar'' productions were worth the redaction, manuscript production spread fairly quickly and spontaneously. Perhaps the emerging reading public for vernacular works constituted a market for books. (On this issue, however, see Chapter 6.) Perhaps we are already witnessing the early constitution of princely libraries and competition among book-collecting magnates. All these factors may help to account for the rapid increase in vernacular manuscript production.

But the fact that many of our earliest extant texts tend to be more-or-less learned may not mean any more than that they are the first octo compositions to get written down and preserved. It does not mean that nothing else was composed and recited in this period. Presumably, works composed for a religious community – perhaps even commissioned by it – would be written down and kept. The same goes for a court – especially one like the glory-hungry Anglo-Norman court. Compositions that redounded to the glory of God, of the monastery (or its patron), of King Arthur (and his anti-Saxon heirs such as the Plantagenets!), of the lord (or the lady or their dynasty), would tend to be preserved. By contrast, works composed on more mundane or secular themes, or for a less exalted and well-heeled public were clearly more ephemeral – truly ''winged words.'' The very availability of scribes in certain milieux – e.g., monastic, royal, archival – is an important consideration. We should remember that the survival of texts does not give us a reliable indication of what was produced in the period. It is not just that many texts have disappeared, but that many works presumably never got written down at all. In numerous medieval works we hear reference to heroes whose names alone have come down to us, but whose stories are lost. (We will meet up with some of these, in passing, in the coming chapters.) Some of the references appear to be to epics, others to romances. It may be that these manuscripts – these physical objects – have indeed been lost, but there is no guarantee that the stories in question ever existed or circulated in written form at all.

15

This general argument – that octo antedates its early written exemplars and was an oral form – is hardly more than putting two and two together. We normally expect there to be some correspondence between the form in which stories were originally told in a particular language and the form in which they have come down to us. While the *chansons de geste* were no doubt transformed to some degree by being written down, we have generally assumed that what we have in our written texts corresponds to a substantial degree to what was sung, at least as concerns poetic form. If there were no such correspondence, we could not hope to have any idea of what the ancient or medieval epic looked like – yet we do believe we have some idea. We should, I think, be prepared to make the same assumption about other narrative material – in particular, octo narrative – and to consider that it too has come down to us in more or less the same form as that in which story-tellers told it before the development of a written vernacular.

Is octo an "oral form"?

Are we, then, to think of octo as having been, like the decasyllabic epic *laisse*, an "oral form"? But, first, what do we mean when we use the words "orality," and "oral tradition"? The oral tradition has been defined by Parry and Lord, and by the many whose work was primarily inspired by theirs, as being purely, totally oral; as being not merely orally performed but also orally composed. That is, it was improvised, during the performance itself by non-literate poets using formulaic language. The basic paradigm of orality for all these scholars is the traditional but still-living Yugoslav formulaic epic, sung by an illiterate bard who improvises his song. This model was then extrapolated back to Homer, and generalized elsewhere, as to the French *chanson de geste*.

But, as I have already suggested, there does appear to be *another* oral tradition – albeit a broader and, as it were, a messier one. This is the vast tradition in which we find the folk tale and a great many other things as well: oral and semi-oral forms, such as the sermon, that do not fit the South Slav model of epic orality.

There are today two major groups of oral theorists. First, those whom we might call the purists, and for whom the oral tradition is almost synonomous with the formulaic epic: if it isn't formulaic and an epic, it isn't oral. (This phenomenon is particularly common in the discipline of French; less so elsewhere.)

But there is another school of thought, best represented for our purposes here by Ruth Finnegan, which is more open-ended in its definitions of oral tradition. (Perhaps it is simply that scholars such as Finnegan have been concerned with material that does not fit well into established categories –

16

material similar to that which concerns us here.) In a seminal paper entitled "What is Oral Literature Anyway?," and then in several books – in particular, *Oral Poetry, Its Nature, Significance and Social Context* and *Literacy and Orality: Studies in the Technology of Communication* – Finnegan put into question many of the fundamental principles of the oral traditionalists, pointing out that, in the African tradition on which she has worked – and in some other cultures that she cited – the "oral formulaic" model for recognizing and defining "orality" does not hold up; thus, such "rules" cannot function universally as criteria. For example, sometimes oral poetry is not composed during the performance, but, rather, is composed ahead of time, the poet either being alone or in a group that helps him to refine and retain in memory what he has composed. Such oral works are not, then, necessarily composed and mastered formulaically, but are learned in a more set, fixed way; that is, they are essentially memorized (anathema to many oral purists).[30] Moreover, the dichotomy between purely oral and written does seem to hold in the African context. Literacy and textuality have not killed off the oral tradition (as Lord considered that they would[31]). Rather, in the African tradition, many orally performed poems show in some way the clear impact of texts – for example, the influence of the literacy brought by Christian missionaries, or of earlier Islamic literacy, or recently the impact of radio and other electronic media. Finally, not all poets who work in the traditional oral forms are themselves illiterate: some can and do read and write, yet continue to compose and perform orally.

Our understanding, then, of what constitutes oral culture is far from perfect, and is still subject to serious debate.[32] In any event, the situation in twelfth century France resembles in intriguing ways that of twentieth century Africa. In both cases, we have a largely but by no means entirely non-literate population, being told stories by story-tellers who are themselves sometimes non-literate, sometimes literate. In most cases the story-tellers know their material by heart, but also feel free to modify it as the spirit moves them, or to satisfy a

---

[30] See, e.g., Finnegan, *Oral Poetry*, pp. 73ff, and Albert B. Lord, *The Singer of Tales*, p. 280.

[31] See, for example, *Singer of Tales*, Ch. 6: "Writing and Oral Tradition," pp. 124–38. Lord states: ". . . one cannot write song. One cannot lead Proteus captive; to bind him [in a text] is to destroy him" (p. 124; see also pp. 137–38). While Lord is, of course, speaking primarily of the epic, the very title of the chapter as well as the tenor of his remarks indicate that he extended the "lessons" of the epic to oral tradition in general; many other scholars have followed his lead.

[32] Many of the issues that concern me here have been addressed and debated in the journal *Oral Tradition* (though not much with regard to the French Middle Ages). In particular, numerous articles have taken up complex blends of oral and written traditions. For example, Lea Olsan, in "Latin Charms of Medieval England: Verbal Healing in Christian Oral Tradition," speaks of the orality of these charms as "a matter of degree," p. 138.

particular audience. It may be that the story-teller originally read the story – or had it read to him. His knowledge may have a textual origin. But now he knows it; it is his, and he retells it – in the French case, in octo.

But *is* this the oral tradition? Well, if it's not *the* Oral Tradition, it appears to be *an* oral tradition – that is, a tradition that thrived in a largely but not entirely pre-literate culture. Surely it is clear that, within the oral tradition as broadly defined, defined as "verbal performance in non- or semi-literate society," there can – indeed there must – have been many different genres, such as the tale, the proverb, the joke, the love song, the work-song, etc. The epic is not the only oral medieval genre but one of many – though they weren't all *purely* oral (but then, neither was the epic![33]). The epic may be, according to some tastes, the 'top of the line' within the oral tradition, but there are other powerful and impressive genres as well; also some that are perhaps humbler, homelier, but no less oral.

Octo between oral and written traditions; octo and the epic decasyllable

We can not just say that octo is an old oral story-telling form and be done with it; matters are by no means so simple. It is clear from much of the evidence I have adduced that the octosyllabic rhymed couplet began, early in the twelfth century, to receive a decidedly clerical handling – often, at least, a clerical *patina*. We must try to account for the literary development of octo while also examining ways in which it continued to function orally.

Octo received learned and literary development: we find it used in lapidaries and bestiaries, for chronicles and in saints' lives, as well as in romances which claim classical sources, deploy learned rhetoric and allegorical personifications, and even sometimes claim to be "books." All this might seem "natural" – even self-evident – were it not for the fact that, in this period, it is *only* in octo that these things occur. We do not find the same picture in the French "heroic" line: decasyllables[34] set in *laisses*. The epic form was never used in "learned" works or for didactic purposes; never for chronicles; only for saints' lives with truly epic plots or heroes. While sometimes a bookish source or a clerical author is claimed, *chansons de geste* are never said to be "books" themselves. The situation is, then, markedly different in the epic.

Why was octo so much more likely to receive learned and literary development – sometimes even heavy-handedly clerical treatment? Is this development to be accounted for by the nature of the octo form iself, or by the settings

---

[33] See the work of William Calin, e.g. *A Muse for Heroes: Nine Centuries of the Epic in France.*

[34] There is one surviving *chanson de geste* composed in octosyllables: *Gormont et Isembart*; its very uniqueness may perhaps be taken as evidence that the octo line was felt as "unsuitable" for epic material.

in which it was often produced? To the matter of context we will return in detail in Chapters 3 and 4 – for indeed, I think octo appears to have been practiced largely in and for noble courts, and this setting was an important meeting-place between the lay and the clerical worlds: the world of story-telling and minstrelsy on the one hand, and of learning and literacy on the other.[35]

But for the moment let us look at the intrinsic character of octo and at its poetic tradition, as compared with the epic line and tradition. Octo seems to have been an old story-telling and as one might say a "talking" form[36] – but it is never called a "song." By contrast, the French epic belongs to a *sung* tradition: these are, indeed, "*chansons* de geste" – *songs* of deeds. Many *chansons de geste* – *Le Couronnement de Louis*, *Le Charroi de Nîmes*, *La Prise d'Orange*, and dozens of others – are referred to in their opening lines as "songs." But narrators working in octo speak of themselves consistently as *telling*, never as *singing*, their stories. This is not to say that octo stories were not sometimes intoned or even sung by a *jongleur*, like epic. (There is evidence that they were; we will take this evidence seriously in Chapter 6.) But there is an important difference: the *chanson de geste had* to be sung by a skilled performer, whether professional or amateur. Octo compositions could be so performed, but they did not have to be. They could also be recited from memory without musical accompaniment, or read aloud. Some sorts of "performance" could be carried out by about anyone – literate or illiterate, trained or untrained; to perform certain kinds of works (such as translations from the Bible) it was enough to know how to read. Octo, then, could be put to use by many kinds of speakers and performers, from preachers to story-tellers to knights and ladies with a taste for reading. To perform octo apparently did not require so specialized a set of skills as to sing a *chanson de geste* – though, again, any material that became popular might well be taken into the professional *jongleur*'s repertory.

In some respects, the traditional French epic – like its oral counterparts elsewhere in the world – appears to be a narrowly specialized genre amid the almost riotous assortment of oral possibilities. (Many other oral genres have highly specific features or functions as well.) The epic appears to have been limited, by some strong if unarticulated poetic, in what it could talk about, and in how it could speak: it had to sing of war and warriors; it could not have lyric or other inserts; it could refer only to other epics (not to other sorts of works), and so on.

Chansons de geste did, of course, get copied into manuscripts – blessedly

---

[35] See Vitz, "Minstrel Meets Clerk in Early French Literature: Medieval Romance as the Meeting-Place between Two Traditions of Verbal Eloquence and Performance Practice."

[36] Jeffrey Kittay has referred to octo as the form for "represented speech": "On Octo (Response to 'Rethinking Old French Literature')."

so: that is how we know them. One might suspect that something more fundamental may have been felt to be lacking when the epic was written – read and
not sung – than was missing when octo was written.[37] Indeed, some octo was
probably produced through and even specifically *for* redaction. This is perhaps
why epics occur more frequently than other vernacular works in manuscripts
that have been called "manuscrits de *jongleurs*" because of their small size,
their limited contents (just one or two "songs"), their single-column format,
and, typically, their grubby condition.

Octo compositions too could be recited and even sung; but they could also
be read aloud to a group or read privately. In short, octo was both a more
flexible and "all-purpose" form, and its performance possibilities were
broader. One might think of octo works as "amphibians": at home in a variety
of composition and performance habitats.

But when we have said that octo lent itself – more readily, certainly, than the
French epic – to literary handling, we must be careful not to go too far: the fact
that octo productions could be, or become, texts, or could sound clerical or
literary, is not to say that they were originally so, or had to be so. Two facts
must be kept in mind. First, the mere fact that stories get written down does not
mean that the story-tellers themselves are doing the writing, or should be
thought of *as* writers. Throughout most of the medieval period, the act of
composing and the act of writing were seen as distinct activities, and were
commonly performed by two different persons. Most writing was done by a
scribe to whom a speaker dictated, and this practice remained true of
vernacular literature until well into the fourteenth century. Thus, the mere fact
that an octo work exists in manuscript form does not mean that the story-teller
wrote it down. Indeed there is no guarantee that the story-teller ever saw the
"text" of his work, or even knew that his work had *become* a text, or indeed
that he could read or write at all.

Despite the early learned development of octo, this form did not get cut off
from its oral and performed roots. I have evoked the suitability – the attractiveness – of octo for didactic works, histories and the like, and its appeal to clerks.
But it was no less popular for literarily unpretentious genres such as fabliaux.[38]

---

[37] Many manuscript compilations of both epics and romances have a strongly historical
purpose: the stories and songs were seen to constitute the history of certain dynasties and
regions. (Similarly historical principles can operate in compilations of hagiographical
narrative; see Vitz, "From the Oral to the Written in Medieval and Renaissance Saints'
Lives.")

[38] While most fabliaux date from the thirteenth century, the earliest surviving
specimens, e.g., "Richeut," date from the twelfth century. On the fabliau and its origins,
Peter Dronke has stated, in an article on "Profane Elements in Literature": "When we turn
to the sphere of satire and parody, determining the specific twelfth-century contributions
raises problems of a different kind. To begin with fabliau: here I believe we must recognize
that the commonest mode of existence of this genre in most periods and places is not literary
at all; rather, there is a continuing 'underground' tradition of telling fabliaux, which are

Some of these tales have courtly or clerical patina, and may well have been originally composed by clerks or other writers, but others are simple and crude, very much part of the old oral story-telling tradition. Fabliaux often survive in a variety of forms, having apparently been retold and modified by different performers (and writers, as well). T.B.W. Reid says, speaking of the transmission of fabliaux:

> Two copies of the same fabliau sometimes show substantial divergence not only in details of wording but even in rhymes, suggesting that at least one of the copies has been written down from memory, in some cases with a modification of dialectal features.[39]

Many fabliaux were, we know, performed from memory by minstrels and *jongleurs*. (Numerous fabliaux, such as "Les Trois Boçus," refer to such performance.) Octo was also the standard form used in the medieval theatre as it developed – or as it began to be written down – starting in the late twelfth century. It was in octo that characters invariably "talked" – though they might use lyric forms for lament or to express their love or their religious faith.

But these two octo genres – the fabliau and the theatre – raise an issue that we have, up to now, slid past with little comment: the performance of octo works. Chapter 6 will be entirely devoted to this issue, but we must at least point up its importance here, for the degree to which octo productions belong, or do not belong, to oral tradition can be seen as hinging largely on the ways in which they were *performed*. It can even be argued – Finnegan has done so compellingly – that the issue of performance is at the very heart of what we mean by oral tradition. What matters most is not, for example, whether or not poets, performers, or audiences knew how to read or write, or how works were transmitted – though we will certainly be concerned with these matters! – but how works were performed. Was a work read or recited? Performed from memory? Told or sung? Acted out? These are fundamental questions that we cannot simply sweep under the rug for the next couple of hundred pages.

One of the most significant – certainly one of the most vivid – pieces of evidence for a significant measure of octo performance, and in that particular sense octo orality, is the frequent insistence on the part of apparently non-literate minstrels and *jongleurs* that they know, and can sing or tell by heart,

---

seldom committed to writing, and even more rarely transmuted, by writers of unusual talent, into works of high art . . .," p. 579. On the orality of the fabliau tradition, see also Pierre-Yves Badel, *Le sauvage et le sot: Le fabliau de Trubert et la tradition orale*.

[39] Quoted in *Twelve Fabliaux*, p. xiv. Jean Rychner concurs, though his primary emphasis is on textual transmission of the fabliaux, thus viewed as "literature"; he speaks of "transmission mémorielle" as being the only explanation for the state in which we find some texts (*Contribution à l'étude des fabliaux*, p. 99). He also stresses the mixed status of the fabliaux as being sometimes literary, courtly – and sometimes more "humble," lower. But though the non-literary (semi-oral?) form may appear a "degradation," this does not make the work any less of a fabliau.

vast quantities of stories and songs. A brief look at "Les Deux Bourdeurs Ribauds"[40] will make the point amply. This is a thirteenth century octo work in which two minstrels compare their art, each claiming superiority. Each minstrel, as he lists all he "knows" – all that he can sing ("chanter") or tell about ("conter") – mentions not merely *chansons de geste* but also stories of the Round Table, *romans d'aventure*, stories about Renart, fabliaux, and so on. Each minstrel claims to know all this material "par memoire," "par cuer." For example, the first "bourdeur" (jokester) denigrates the other and praises himself saying:

> Tu ne sez dire nul bon mot
> Dont tu puisses en pris monter;
> Mais ge sai aussi bien conter
> Et en roumanz et en latin,
> Aussi au soir come au matin,
> Devant contes et devant dus,
> Et si resai bien faire plus
> Quant ge sui a cort ou a feste.
> Car ge sai de chançon de geste.
>   Chanteres el mont n'i a tel:
> Ge sai de Guillaume au Tinel,
> Si com il arriva as nés
> Et de Renouart au cort nés
> Sai ge bien chanter com ge vueil;
> Et si sai d'Aïe de Nantueil
> Si com ele fu en prison;
> Si sai de Garin d'Avignon,
> Qui moult estore bon romans; . . .
>   [further enumeration of chansons de geste, lines 74–80]
> Mais de chanter n'ai ge or cure.
> Ge sai des romanz d'aventure,
> De cels de la Reonde Table,
> Qui sont a oïr delitable.
> De Gauvain sai le malparlier,
> Et de Quex le bon chevalier;
> Si sai de Perceval de Blois;
> De Pertenoble le Galois
> Sai ge plus de .LX. laisses.
> Et tu, chaitis, morir te laisses
> De mauvaitie et de paresce:
> En tot le monde n'a proesce
> De quoi tu te puisses vanter;
> Mais ge sai aussi bien chanter
> De Blancheflor comme de Floire;
> Si sai encore moult bone estoire,

[40] Text in Edmond Faral, ed., *Mimes français*.

Chançon moult bone et anciene:
Ge sai de Tibaut de Viane.   lines 56–98

(You don't know how to say anything clever/ By which you could rise in worth;/ But I know how to tell stories/ Both in French and in Latin,/ In the evening, as in the morning,/ In front of counts and dukes,/ And I know how to do even more/ When I am at court or at a feast,/ For I know chansons de geste./ And there is not another such singer in the world:/ I know about Guillaume with his Big Stick,/ And how it landed on his nose,/ And about Rainouart with the short nose/ I know how to sing well, when I want:/ And I know about Aie de Nantueil/ How she was in prison;/ And I know about Garin d'Avignon,/ Which is a very good romance . . ./ But I don't care about singing right now./ I know adventure romances,/ The ones about the Round Table,/ Which are delightful to hear./ I know about Gauvain who talked so badly,/ And about the good knight Kei;/ And I know about Perceval of Blois,/ About Partonopeu the Welshman/ I know more than 60 laisses./ And you, wretch, let yourself die/ Of wickedness and laziness:/ In the entire world there is nothing of value/ That you can brag about;/ But I know how to sing/ About Blancheflor, and about Floire;/ And I know many a good story,/ Many a good and ancient song:/ I know about Tibaut de Vienne.)

There are joking and nonsense in their discourse – these are after all "bourdeurs"! – and they garble names and subject-matter. For example, Guillaume and Rainouart are reversed here: the former had the short nose, the latter the cudgel. So are Gauvain and Kei [Quex]: Kei is well-known for his rudeness and Gauvain for his chivalric excellence. Perceval and Pertenoble [Partonopeu] as well: the former is "le Galois," the latter from Blois. It should be Girard – not Tibaut – de Vienne, and so on. But the basic structure of the repertory seems reliable, in particular, its generic inclusiveness which we will see replicated in many similar texts, in Chapter 6. Minstrels and *jongleurs* are telling/singing both *chansons de geste* and romances – along with other things.

This text raises interesting questions, such as: were some minstrels really able to tell stories in Latin, as the first one claims he can, in line 58? My feeling is, why not? Whether or not a minstrel understood any Latin himself – and some began their careers as *clergeons* ("little clerks": students) – there is no reason to believe he couldn't learn by heart a story or song in Latin, or for that matter in any other language. And some minstrels no doubt performed before churchmen who might well have been edified or entertained by material presented in Latin. Was *all* this material sung? It is not quite clear here. The minstrel quoted above first speaks of songs, then says he does not want to talk about singing but about romances (lines 81–82) – but he says he knows how to sing the story of Floire and Blanchefleur, which is, in its various surviving versions, romance. In any event, one point is clear: octo productions were not merely read and preached; they were performed by minstrels and *jongleurs*.

Implications

The purpose of this chapter has been to demonstrate that the octosyllabic rhymed couplet was not a clerical invention, or simply the translation of a learned Latin form, but that it was rooted in French oral culture. Moreover, while it frequently received literary treatment at the hands of clerical authors, it long *remained* in important respects an oral form. Indeed, the development of vernacular prose, from the early thirteenth century on, may paradoxically have enhanced and prolonged the orality of the octo form. Until then, octo was the only vernacular form available for non-lyric, non-epic discourse; thus, for all that was "un-sung." It may be that prose took the pressure off octo, and romance in particular, to be a "serious" and "historical" form by filling these functions itself. Vernacular authors who sought a fully intellectual audience – even a "readership": readers instead of listeners – had henceforth only to have recourse to prose. Octo remained the standard form for recitation "by heart": for dramatic speech. It remained common in rhymed sermons and other devotional and catechetical works whose purpose was to touch the heart and remain fixed in memory.[41] And it was the form for story-telling and folktales: new narrative material continued to pour into short octo narrative, such as the *conte* and *fabliau*, and some romances, throughout the thirteenth century. Bible stories were also turned into octo – though, again, it is not accurate to think of most of them as "biblical translations," by any means. Rather, the stories often appear told from memory and are interspersed with oral (and semi-oral) legends from apocryphal traditions. What springs first to my mind is the strange mid-thirteenth century *Évangile de l'Enfance*,[42] an apocryphal account of Christ's childhood miracles, which belongs to an ancient, part-oral, part-written tradition. It is far, far closer to the folktale than it is to the Bible. This is

---

[41] It is quite true (as a reader has pointed out to me) that many sermons, in this period and later, were composed in prose. Many books on the history of preaching do not even mention verse sermons. Certainly, university and other "learned" sermons were typically in prose. But sermons whose purpose was to move hearts or which had a basic catechetical thrust were often in verse, and, when the verse form was not lyric (strophic) in nature, it was frequently octo. See, for example, Adgar, *Le gracial*; Brian Levy, *Nine Verse Sermons by Nicholas Bozon*; Cesare Segre, "Sermoni in versi" and "Cicli di sermoni in versi" (pp. 60–64). A good many (though by no means all) of these rhymed sermons are in octo. Many catechetical works, such as *Le manuel des péchés*, were also composed in octo. See Vitz, "The Impact of Christian Doctrine on Medieval Literature."

Octo was the standard form for mock-sermons (and often of other religious parodies); see Jelle Koopmans, *Recueil de sermons joyeux*, p. 64.

[42] This work has recently been edited by Maureen Boulton. See Vitz, "The Apocryphal and the Biblical, the Oral and the Written, in Medieval Legends of the Life of Christ: The Old French *Évangile de l'Enfance*." See also my review of Boulton's edition.

the work that originally put the flea in my ear about octo: "text" though it is, it is deeply rooted in oral traditions (and moreover appears to have been composed (I will not say "written"!) by a poet remarkably ignorant of Christian tradition – of the Bible in particular. Where octo and prose appear primarily to have competed was for "serious fiction," and for works intended to be read aloud.[43]

In any event, the primary purpose of this book will be to explore the implications of the orality of octo for the early development of French "literature" – orality set into "letters." We will see in many works a reflection of the tensions and the cooperation between oral culture and the world of the book.

[43] See, e.g., Coleman, *Public Reading*.

CHAPTER TWO

Oral and Written Traditions in the Early Tristan Material: Béroul, Thomas and Marie de France

The previous chapter argued that the octosyllabic rhymed couplet form, or "octo," was rooted in oral traditions, but noted that, from about the mid-twelfth century on, this form often received literary handling – as well as being increasingly written down. With regard to oral and written culture, octo was thus amphibious: at home in either habitat. But the very adaptability of this form creates problems. On the one hand, the fact that octo could function as a clerical vehicle does not mean that it was originally literary or learned, or that works produced in this form could only be so. But the converse is also true: even if octo had its origins in oral narrative traditions, not all works composed in this form were equally oral, or even necessarily oral in the same ways. We have no blanket certainties about octo works. We need to examine particular genres, even individual works, one by one.

But now the question arises: when we examine works for evidence of oral and written character, just what is it that we are looking for? How are we to discriminate between "oral" and "written"? What are the distinguishing features – the earmarks – of each? And what is the difference between "clerical," "written," and "literary"? (These latter two terms in particular are often used as though they were synonymous.) The purpose of this chapter will be to take a close preliminary look at a few seminal works, and to elaborate problematics and establish criteria that will serve us in subsequent chapters. What we will be looking for – and at – is the complex interactions of oral and written elements in early octo narrative.

We will take as examples here the three earliest surviving treatments of the story of Tristan in French: those of Béroul, Thomas, and Marie de France. They were all composed in octo. Our primary questions will be: 1) What can we tell about our narrators? For example, do they make claims to or display evidence of *clergie*[1] – or at least of vernacular literacy? To what sorts of "authority" and "literary status" do these narrators lay claim, and how? 2) Are

---

[1] I will devote lengthy discussions to the terms "clerc" and "clergie" in the next two chapters. For the moment, we can simply say that a *clerc* (which I will often anglicize as "clerk," despite the dangers of anachronism) is a person educated by the Church and at least in minor orders, and that *clergie* refers to clerical status and training.

there indications, within the work, that suggest the mode of performance? 3) What, if anything, do we know about the scribe, or about the writing down of the work? 4) What sort of public is addressed? Can we tell the difference between a literate and a non-literate audience?

Béroul's *Tristan*

We will begin with Béroul.[2] Even scholars who are inclined to think of *romanciers* as reliably literate and learned generally make an exception of Béroul, and call his work "primitive" or "unlearned": it is "commune." But what of its orality? Let us look at the profile of the characteristically oral work that Walter J. Ong, basing himself on a wide variety of research, provides in Chapter 3 of *Orality and Literacy, The Technologizing of the Word*. The Béroul *Tristan* is, for example, powerfully "agonistically toned": good guys vs. bad guys. The former include, of course, the lovers, but also God (who performs miracles to help and save them), and every positive character in the work; King Arthur is thrown in for good measure as someone who admires Iseut and can serve as an authoritative witness to her "innocence." The bad guys are, of course, the dwarf Frocin, and the three "felons" who betray the lovers to Mark (in a feudal understanding of things they are only doing their duty, but never mind: these are wicked creatures, motivated by "envy"). Béroul, deeply engaged in the story he is telling, intervenes frequently not just to tell his audience to listen – "Oyez!" – but to express his sorrow over the sufferings of the lovers, and to damn their enemies – those "felons que Dex cravent" (line 2754, "those felons, may God crush them").

This work is decidedly, in Ongian terms, "non-analytical": we are never invited to approach the moral issues logically and to think objectively about what the lovers are doing: treason, adultery, incest. Béroul's work is "empathetic": we are invited – indeed, we are compelled – to be, simply and absolutely, on the lovers' side. In case we should have any hesitation, Béroul forces our hand, making us react at the affective level – and in the proper way.

Béroul's *Tristan* is peopled with highly memorable figures: this is also a feature which, Ong notes, is characteristic of oral tradition. (We will return to issues of memory and memorability in Chapter 7.) The lovers, in Béroul's version, are "perfect" – or at least they are perfectly what they are. Iseut is the most beautiful woman in the world; Tristan is handsome, a great shot with an arrow and an amazing trainer of dogs – and Husdent, whom he teaches to hunt without barking, is an extraordinary dog. Most importantly, Tristan and Iseut are defined as The Greatest Lovers in the World: no one ever loved more, or

---

2 Béroul, *Le Roman de Tristan*, ed. Ernest Muret. The exact date of this work remains uncertain, with dates from the mid-twelfth century to "after 1191" having been proposed (some scholars have also hypothesized more than one narrator).

suffered more for love, than they. Their enemies are an ugly dwarf, and three felons – and even when one gets killed, there are still three of them. This use of numbers is common in oral and folk tradition. We find this even today in children's stories which constitute, in the West, one of our few surviving pockets of oral culture: the Three Bears and Three Billy Goats Gruff, the Seven Dwarves, the Twelve Dancing Princesses . . . Finally, the Béroul story is deeply episodic, with many episodes seeming curiously unrelated to each other (thus, we have a dramatic scene of repentance when the potion wears off; but soon Tristan and Iseut are again lovers and little seems to have changed).

Ong speaks fairly little of the style of orally composed works.[3] In particular, he does not strongly emphasize the issue of the formula, which has been, as noted earlier, so central to studies of medieval orality (thereby restricted, in the French case, to the epic). I would not be inclined to argue that Béroul's work is formulaic, however we define the formula (this is a thorny issue).[4] But one is struck by the presence in Béroul's work of other stylistic features associated with orality, such as repetition, at many different levels, and by the extremely limited, concrete – and reusable – vocabulary. In any event, Ruth Finnegan has shown in *Oral Poetry, Its Nature, Significance and Social Context* that orally composed works are not necessarily formulaic.

Does this mean that the work was "orally composed" – or in any case, composed without recourse to writing? If we assume that Béroul was a *jongleur* (a professional story-teller), and that he was not also a *clerc* – the text gives no indication whatsoever that he was – then we are forced to assume that Béroul composed his version "in his head" – and on his tongue. It would seem, then, that this was indeed, in some sense of the word, "orally composed." It may not have been composed at the very time that it was recited – but here again, Finnegan has shown that many an oral work is composed in advance and mastered largely through memorization.[5] Béroul never speaks of his work as a book, as a thing written – but always as a story that he is telling – *now*. And we do have texts, such as the *Deux Bourdeurs Ribauds*, discussed in Chapter 1, which make it clear that *jongleurs* claimed to know by heart vast quantities of narrative material, much of it presumably in octosyllables: the *Deux Bourdeurs* itself is composed in octo, as are many of the works cited. Why should we assume that such works couldn't be composed orally – that is, in the mind and on the tongue – if they could be mastered and performed orally, from memory? Do we really believe that minstrels and *jongleurs* had nothing to say or sing until clerks provided them with a repertory?

---

3 In important respects this has been a decided advantage. Scholarship has often been overly preoccupied with – even fixated on – the formula. Ong has significantly contributed to the opening of discussions of orality to non-formulaic works.

4 Perhaps as interesting – certainly as spirited! – an exchange on this vexed question as one could find is in the debate between William Calin and Joseph J. Duggan that appeared in *Olifant* 8.

5 *Oral Poetry*, pp. 73ff.

Now to the question: who was the scribe? For example, who wrote down our one surviving, mutilated copy, dating from the second half of the thirteenth century? H.J. Chaytor (in *From Script to Print: An Introduction to Medieval Literature*) and other scholars as well have pointed out that composing (or "making") and writing were two quite separate tasks throughout most of the medieval period. Typically, the "author" dictated, and a scribe took down the words. But not all works "needed" a scribe: a story, made to be told, did not "have" to be written down by a scribe at all; it required only someone's lips, not a pen. In a word, however necessary this scribe's activity was to *our* knowledge of this marvelous work – and let me take this opportunity to express my gratitude to all those medieval scribes – from the point of view of the work itself, this "writer" may have stumbled into the picture late in the game and (as it were) accidentally.

There are, however, a few passages which might make us think that Béroul could read and write, indeed that he was personally involved in the phenomena of literacy and text-production. First is the rather lengthy passage, extending for about three hundred lines (starting roughly at line 2350) involving an exchange of letters between the lovers and King Mark. First, Tristan and Iseut send a *brief*, or letter, written out by the hermit Ogrin, to the king. The letter is delivered to Mark by Tristan, acting as his own messenger or postman. When Marks finds it, he immediately sends for his chaplain to read it for him. We need not necessarily take this fact as an indication of illiteracy on the part of the king: great lords did not read things for themselves but had clerks who read missives and other written documents to them; on the other hand, this scene certainly does not indicate that Mark is represented as knowing how to read – especially since even the private reading of the letter is done to Mark by a clerk. After the letter is read privately to the king, the chaplain reads it again, aloud to the whole court. Mark replies to it with another letter, written by the chaplain, which he has hung on the Red Cross for the lovers to find. Tristan retrieves this letter and takes it to Ogrin.

In this passage we certainly see an interest on the part of Béroul and presumably his audience in the practice of letter-writing, for which this is one of our early vernacular examples. But let us have a closer look at these two letters, and at the processes of their composition and deciphering. The Cornish nobles call for the letter to be read aloud to the court: "Dam chapelain, lisiez le brief/ Oiant nos toz, de chief en chief" ("Lord chaplain, read the letter,/ In the hearing of all, from beginning to end").

> Levez s'en est li chapelains,
> Le brief deslie o ses deus mains,
> En piez estut devant le roi:
> "Or escoutez, entendez moi.
> Tristan li niés nostre seignor
> Saluz mande prime et amor
> Au roi et a tot son barnage:

"Rois, tu sez bien le mariage
"De la fille le roi d'Irlande.
"Par mer en fui jusqu'en Horlande,
"Par ma proece la conquis.
"Le grant sepent cresté ocis,
"Par qoi ele me fu donee.
"Amenai la en ta contree.
"Rois, tu la preïs a mollier.
"Si que virent ti chevalier. . . ."   lines 2549–64

(The chaplain has gotten up./ He unfolds the letter with his two hands,/ He stands before the king:/ "Now hear well, listen to me./ Tristan, our lord's nephew/ First sends greetings and love/ To the king and all his barony./ King, you know well about the marriage/ Of the daughter of the king of Ireland./ I went by sea as far as Holland./ By my prowess I conquered her./ I killed the great crested serpent/ For this she was given to me./ I brought her to your country/ King, you took her to wife./ As your knights saw. . . .)

The letter goes on to give a somewhat expurgated account of Tristan and Iseut's relationship: they are "innocent." Béroul is clearly interested in the visual and auditory drama of the scene – in what one might call the theatre of the disembodied, and lying, voice: the chaplain, standing before the king, pronounces words from Tristan's lips. At the end of the letter, and of the scene, Tristan offers to give the queen back:

"Ge m'en irai au roi de Frise;
"Jamais n'oras de moi parler,
"Passerai m'en outre la mer.
"De ce q'oiez, roi, pren consel.
"Ne puis mes soufrir tel trepel:
"Ou je m'acorderai a toi,
"Ou g'en merrai la fille au roi
"En Irlandë, ou je la pris.
"Roïnë ert de son païs."
Li chapelains a au roi dit:
"Sire, n'a plus en cest escrit."   lines 2610–20

("I will go away to the king of Frisia;/ Never again will you hear speak of me,/ I will go beyond the sea./ Concerning what you hear, king, take counsel./ I can no longer bear such distress:/ Either I will make peace with you,/ Or I will take the king's daughter/ Back to Ireland where I got her./ She will be queen in her own country."/ The chaplain said to the king:/ "Lord, there is nothing more in this text.")

There is little sense here of the epistolary rhetoric that would normally have been part of a real letter: of the formulas that were part of the art of letter-writing,

30

or "Ars dictaminis."[6] It is also of course likely that a letter of so formal and official a nature would have been written not in French at all, but in Latin.

The second letter is not read aloud in our presence. When Tristan has retrieved the "charte seelee" (line 2654) and brought it back to Ogrin, we are told:

> Li hermites la chartre a prise,
> Lut les letres, vit la franchise
> Du roi qui pardonne a Yseut
> Son mautalent, et que il veut
> Repenre la tant bonement;
> Vit le terme d'acordement.
> Ja parlera si com il doit
> Et com li hom qui a Deu croit:
> "Tristran, quel joie t'est creüe!
> Ta parole est tost entendue,
> Que li rois la roïne prent.
> Loé li ont tote sa gent;
> Mais ne li osent pas loer
> Toi retenir a soudeier,
> Mais va servir en autre terre
> Un roi a qui on face gerre,
> Un an ou deus. Se li rois veut,
> Revien a lui et a Yseut.
> D'ui en tierz jor, sanz nul deçoivre,
> Est li rois prest de lié reçoivre.
> Devant le Gué Aventuros,
> Est li plez mis de vos et d'eus.
> La li rendrez, iluec ert prise.
> Cist briés noient plus ne devise."   lines 2657–80

(The hermit took the letter [charter]./ He read the letters, he saw the generosity/ Of the king who forgave Yseut/ His wrath, and that he wanted/ To take her back graciously./ He [Ogrin] saw the terms of the agreement./ Now he will speak as he should/ And like a man who believes in God:/ "Tristan, how your joy is increased!/ Your words have been heard,/ That the king should take back the queen./ All his people have praised this solution./ But they do not dare suggest/ That he keep you as a vassal;/ But go serve in another land/ A king against whom war is being waged/ For a year or two. Then if the king wants it,/ Come back to him and to Yseut./ On the third day from now, without fail,/ The king is ready to receive her./ Before the Adventurous Ford,/ Is the meeting set between you and them./ Give her back to him; there she will be taken./ This letter says nothing more.")

6 For the "Arts dictaminis," see James J. Murphy, ed., *Three Medieval Poetic Arts*, pp. 1–25.

Thus, the hermit first reads the letter to himself, then explains the substance to the lovers as though it were an oral message. That is, we do not hear the "king's voice" as set into writing but are simply told what Mark wants. Here as before we get no sense of epistolary style or rhetoric. While this passage as a whole clearly reveals an interest in these *briefs*, or "letters," they both function primarily as oral messages. And it is the drama of their production and oral performance – the parchment and ink, the seal, the delivery or posting, the retrieval and "publication" – that appears primarily to draw Béroul's interest. This long passage also clearly expresses the conviction that literacy was an affair of the clergy, not of ordinary laymen. All the reading and writing are done by *clercs*, one a hermit, the other a chaplain.

Aside from Ogrin, the only character who is represented in the Béroul version as capable of writing, and who deals in letters, is the nasty and learned dwarf Frocin, of whom we are told that "Certes il set de maint latin" (line 610: "He certainly knows a lot of Latin"). It is worth noting that both Frocin's and Ogrin's "letters" *lie*. Indeed, Ogrin explicitly recommends that the lovers lie to Mark in their – his – letter: "Doit on un poi par bel mentir" (line 2354: "One must lie a little, cleverly"). In other words, we see here some fascination with literacy, but it is not clear whether Béroul has a very clear understanding of how written things work. He also appears to have misgivings about its moral status.

We now take up the second relevant passage. At one point Béroul assures us:

> . . . Ne, si conme l'estoire dit,
> La ou Berox le vit escrit,
> Nule gent tant ne s'entramerent
> Ne si griment nu compererent.   lines 1789–92

> (. . . Nor, as the story tells it/ There where where Béroul saw it written,/ Did any other couple ever love each other as much/ Or pay for it as dearly.)

Is this not a recognition of the status and authority of books rather than a claim that Béroul has read something himself? He does not actually say he has read such a text, but merely that he has "seen the story written." But even if we should be invited to construe this enigmatic remark as implying that Béroul is actually claiming to have read it, does anything induce us to believe him? Many a medieval narrator has lied on this score! Moreover Béroul, when referring to himself and his art as a story-teller, makes this telling claim:

> Li conteor dïent qu'Yvain
> Firent nïer, qui sont vilain.
> N'en savent mie bien l'estoire,
> Berox l'a mex en sen memoire.   lines 1265–68

> (Story-tellers say that they [Tristan and Governal]/ Had Yvain

> drowned, but they are mere peasants./ They do not know the
> story at all,/ Béroul has it better in his memory.)

This insistence on the accuracy of Béroul's story as linked to the power of his memory is clearly a claim that comes from the oral, not the written, tradition. It is not that memory "belongs" in some fundamental sense to oral tradition; by no means! (See, e.g., Mary Carruthers' *Book of Memory*.) But in the world of written works, the memory of fragile, mortal, humans is understood as needing to be projected onto texts for preservation; unless works are written down, they will perish, as human minds and unwritten words do. But, here, we are told that Béroul "has the work better in his memory." His memory – his head – is thus the reliable strongbox containing the story, and the soundness of his memory guarantees the authenticity of his version of the story. The emphasis is very different.

It is often said of Chrétien and other *romanciers* that the fact that they denigrate story-tellers (*conteors*) and entertainers (such as *jongleurs* or *ménestrels*) shows that they, in contrast, are "writers" and producers of "text." We will return to this issue in a later chapter. But in this context let us simply note that Béroul too criticizes "conteurs," the point being not that they are story-tellers and he a writer, but that their stories are not as *good* as his; they are ignorant churls: *vilains*.

Béroul does, however, see texts – and especially references to texts – as bearing authority. This is a highly important fact, in part because it means that any story-teller, even one working essentially within the oral tradition, can lay claim to the authority of written tradition by speaking of his "written source." This is not to suggest that all claims to written sources are lies: many are certainly true. But the very prevalence of such claims suggests not that all poets could read and write, but that they recognized the clout of the written word, and of "documents." And the very fact that such claims were so easy to make and so hard to verify – one could hardly demand that a performer physically produce the manuscipt he claimed as his source, and someone who went to seek it out might simply find it "lost" – made it inviting for poets and performers to lie on this score. Might we call this latter phenomenon "fictional" or "invented intertextuality"?

Thomas's *Tristan*

Thomas's version of the story of Tristan survives in 9 fragments, scattered among 6 manuscripts.[7] To make sense of the many differences between Béroul's and Thomas's versions of the story, the essential considerations to

---

[7] *Les Fragments du Roman de Tristan: poème du XIIe siècle*, ed. Bartina H. Wind. Since this work is made up of fragments, page numbers will be provided.

A new and important fragment of the Thomas *Tristan* was recently discovered; see

keep in mind are, first, the way in which Thomas represents himself, and the subtle and clerical – shall we call them "literary"? – ways in which he uses elements which seemed oral in Béroul's work.

True, Thomas, like Béroul – indeed, like virtually all twelfth century and most thirteenth century narrators – addresses his audience with the verb "oïr," inviting them to listen, reminding them of what they have heard and telling them what they will hear. But such expressions are substantially less common in Thomas than in Béroul. More importantly, Thomas only rarely solicits from his public any emotional involvement in the story, as for example approval for the lovers, indignation against their enemies, or amusement at the ways in which the lovers deceive and humiliate these enemies – all standard in Béroul. In Thomas's version the lovers really have no enemies other than themselves. (Or perhaps we might borrow a current idiom and say that they are "their own worst enemies.") This is, then, not an "agonistic" work (in Ongian terms): no good guys vs. bad guys. Nor is it "empathetic": Thomas distances us and himself in a number of respects from his story and his characters, such as by making it clear that he himself is not a lover. He says that he cannot tell whether Tristan, Iseut, Marc, or Iseut aux Blanches Mains suffered the most, or why, because he himself has never suffered in love: "I have never experienced this": "Por ce quë esprové ne l'ai" (v. 1088). Indeed, with regard to virtually all the features that, according to Ong, characterize orality, this work draws a blank. For example, the characters are quite unmemorable: there are too many of them, and they are *all* lovers (in this version, *everybody* loves); all of them are both good and bad; both Iseut and her double are beautiful, etc.

But let us return to Thomas, as narrator and as narrative voice. He is both present to and absent from his story and his public. We see this most vividly at the end, where Thomas speaks of his story as *sun escrit*: "his written text."

> Tumas fine ci sun escrit
> A tuz amanz salut i dit,
> As pensis e as amerus,
> As emvius, as desirus,
> A enveisiez e as purvers,
> A tuz cels qui orrunt ces vers.   p. 162, lines 820–25

(Thomas ends his written text ["writing"] here/ To all lovers he says greetings/ To the pensive and to those who are in love,/ To the envious, to those filled with desire,/ To those who are given over to sensual pleasure [vice] and to the perverted [or perverse],/ To all those who will hear these verses.)

This is surely rather an insulting greeting that Thomas extends to his

Benskin, Hunt, and Short, "Un nouveau fragment du *Tristan* de Thomas." As this new fragment raises no issues relevant to our concerns, it will not be discussed here.

audience! – to "cels qui orrunt ces vers." He associates their involvement in love with envy and cupidity ("as emvius"), with vice ("as enveisiez"), and with perversion or perversity ("as purvers"). He invites them to define, and thus to know, themselves in these terms: as sinners. He names himself – "Tomas" – and speaks in terms of an audience of listeners, but makes it clear that he, the writer, will not be there when they "will hear" these verses. (Presumably, they will hear his book recited or read aloud to them. More on these issues in Chapter 6.) The voice that they will hear is thus both his, and not his. Of course, such is always the case of works intended for reading aloud by readers other than the author. If Thomas is indeed offending his intended audience in the remarks just cited, it is surely safer to insult an audience when you are not yourself present before them as the performer!

There is, I believe, little doubt that Thomas was a clerk. It is certainly not because he "had never experienced love" that I think so: a clerk could, in the twelfth century, be in lower orders and still be married; he could certainly have been in love; and of course in all periods it has been possible to be a *clerc* and be unchaste! Nor is it because his work shows rhetorical excellence: the belief that the mastery of rhetoric and the presence of "figures" to which Latin or Greek names can be applied, provide adequate grounds for proving clerical training is, in my view, highly questionable. (We will return to the issue of rhetoric in greater detail in Chapter 4.)

His reference to his work as an "escript" (line 3127) is certainly important evidence for Thomas's *clergie*. It is, however, at least conceivable that an oral poet *cum* performer – for example, a *trouvère* who was also a minstrel or *jongleur* – might have been aware that his "work" was being, or had been, copied down by a scribe; he might, then, begin to speak of his work as an "escrit" – to lay some claim to writerly status, precisely because of the growing authority of the written word.

But aside from the word "escrit" (p. 162, line 820) and from other potentially clerical elements enumerated above, there are two other factors that convince me even more compellingly that he was a clerk and writer: that is, that Thomas had received a clerical formation.[8] The first is the strongly intellectual and analytical quality of his treatment of the story. His understanding of love and of lovers' frequently self-inflicted miseries seems to derive from a meditation on the sinfulness – the astonishing, almost ludicrous, fallenness –

---

8 Yet another interesting stone to bring to this strongly-clerical edifice has recently been provided by David Howlett in *The English Origins of Old French Literature*, pp. 125–26. Howlett argues that the closure of Thomas's *Tristan* conforms to biblical/ mathematical style, defined earlier in his book. Thomas's is the only octo romance discussed by Howlett, the two other romances which he takes up being *The Romance of Horn* by Mestre Thomas and Thomas of Kent's *Le Roman de Toute Chevalerie*, both composed in Alexandrine (12-syllable) lines; pp. 126–29.

of man. See for example, the long passage that relates, and reflects on, Tristan's marriage to Iscut of the White Hands. It begins:

> Oez merveilluse aventure,
> Cum genz sunt d'estrange nature,
> Que en nul lieu ne sunt estable:
> De nature sunt si changable,
> Lor mal us ne poent laissier,
> Mais le buen puent changer. . . .   pp. 43–44, lines 233–38

(Listen to an amazing adventure/ About how people are strange in nature,/ Since in no place are they ever stable:/ By nature they are so changeable,/ Their evil habits they cannot abandon,/ But they can change from [doing] good.)

The other, related, factor is Thomas's rather long-winded pedantry which I see as arising naturally from a certain kind of clerical training. Thomas does not know when to stop; he frequently has to say the same thing just one more time, in different terms. His analyses of words and issues can go on for hundreds of lines. One might argue that Thomas is a clerk first – a somewhat moralistically pedantic clerk – and a verbal or "literary" artist only second. In any event, no entertainer could allow himself to run on in this way.

But, in fact, what do we mean by the words "literary" and "literature" – as in expressions such as "literary gift," or "literary skill," or "the love of literature"? Do we mean, in the latter case for example, the love of eloquence, of beautiful words? (By this definition, "literary" is not opposed to "oral.") Or do we mean, more narrowly and specifically, the love of written texts, *qua* written – thus, for example, the love of written puns or intertextuality, as distinct from oral puns and echoes of other stories and songs? Or by "the love of literature" do we mean the love of the pleasure of reading? This meaning is really quite different – and I think very common today among educated people. I raise these issues because what we have seen so far is that Béroul and Thomas, despite their considerable differences, both speak of writing as bearing authority and as having what one might call some "thing-hood" (a book, an "escrit" is a thing, an object). Both poets respect the written word, but neither of them suggests that the world of letters – "literature" – has *beauty*: an esthetic character peculiar to it. The world of the written vernacular is not yet "lovable." We will have occasion to return to this important issue.

Even Thomas, and this despite his involvement in "écriture," has one foot firmly planted in oral tradition. At one point he dismisses other versions of the story, saying:

> Entre ceus qui solent cunter
> E del cunte Tristran parler,
> Il en cuntent diversement:
> Oï en ai de plusur gent.

36

> Asez sai que chescun en dit
> E ço qu'il unt mis en escrit,
> Mes sulun ço que j'ai oï,
> Nel dient pas sulun Breri
> Ky solt les gestes e les cuntes
> De tuz les reis, de tuz les cuntes
> Ki orent esté en Bretaigne.   p. 119, lines 841–51

(Among those who are used to telling stories/ And to talking about the story of Tristan,/ They tell it differently:/ I have heard it told by many people./ I well know what each one says about it/ And what they have put into writing,/ But, according to what I have heard,/ They don't tell it according to Bréri/ Who knew the stories [deeds? *chansons de geste*?] and the tales/ Of all the kings, of all the counts/ Who had been in Brittany.)

It is clear from this passage that in this period several different versions of the tale of Tristan and Iseut – some oral, some written – already exist, and that they compete for authority with regard to their "truthfulness." Thomas insists here on the authority of an oral source – the story-teller, Bréri, whose name is known to us – over and against inferior accounts, some of them written. In this competition for literary "authority," the oral tradition wins out over the written, at least in regard to material presented as "traditional."

There is yet another interesting passage where we see the pull of oral culture even on a clerk like Thomas. At one point, while the lovers were apart, Iseut was suffering greatly.

> Apruef si prist un vielur,
> Si li manda tote sa vie
> E sun estre, e puis li prie
> Qu'il li mant tut son curage
> Par enseingnes par cest message.
> Quant Tristran la novele sout
> De la reïne qu'il plus amout,
> Pensis en est e deshaitez . . .   p. 117, lines 772–79

(Then she got a vielle-player,/ She told him all about her life/ And her condition, and then begs him/ To tell him [Tristan] the state of her heart/ Through signs by this message./ When Tristan learned the news/ About the queen whom he loved the most,/ He was pensive and unhappy . . .)

This is the start of a new episode: Tristan will go in disguise to see Iseut. It is interesting that instead of sending him a *brief* or a trusted messenger, Iseut engages a *vielleur* to carry the message of her love to Tristan. The use of the word "*enseignes*" – "signs" – suggests that Iseut's message, as transmitted musically and poetically by the *vielleur*, is conceived as indirect and discreet: in code.

37

Marie de France's *Lais*

There can be little doubt that Marie was herself a lettered woman; she may have been a nun.[9] Moreover, she certainly wanted her audience to know that she was learned. Her "general prologue" makes her learned status apparent, with its numerous references to Priscian, to ancient books, to glossing the letter, and the like. But Marie, like Thomas, also makes it clear that her lais are meant to be *heard*, and she is pleased at the thought that hearing them will give the king pleasure. Again as in the case of Thomas, she herself will not be present when they are performed aloud. She presents the lais as making up some sort of "assemblage" or *recueil* (she does not use the word "livre") to be presented to the king and intended for public reading or recitation. Here is how she closes her prologue:

> En l'honur de vus, nobles reis,
> Ki tant estes pruz e curteis,
> A ki tute joie s'encline
> E en ki quoer tuz biens racine,
> M'entremis de lais assembler,
> Par rime fere, e reconter;
> En mon quoer pensoi e diseie,
> Sire, ke vos presentereie.
> Si vos les plest a receveir,
> Mult me ferez grant joie aveir,
> A tuz jurz mais en serrai lie.
> Ne me tenez a surquidie
> Si vos os fere icest present,
> Ore oëz le comencement.   lines 43–56[10]

(In your honor, noble king,/ Who are so hardy and courtly,/ Before whom all joy bows/ And in whose heart all good takes root,/ I have undertaken to assemble lais/ By making rhymes and telling stories;/ In my heart I thought and said,/ Lord, that I would present them to you./ If it pleases you to receive them,/ You will give me great joy,/ Forever will I be happy./ Do not think me too bold/ If I dare to make you this gift,/ And now listen to the beginning.)

It is in the short (118-line) lai of "Chevrefoil" that we see Marie's handling of the Tristan material. In this version of the story, the lovers are presented as able to read, and even to write. Indeed most of the lai is taken up, not just with

---

[9]   Thus, she would have been in an important sense, a member of the "clergie." If she was not a nun, but a learned laywoman, then her learning corresponds to highly interesting developments in lay learning, as discussed in Chapters 3 and 4.

[10]   Marie de France, *Les Lais*, ed. Jean Rychner.

the sending but the physical preparation of a written message, and with its retrieval: Tristan carves his words of love on a branch, leaving it in the path, where Iseut will see it:

> Une codre trencha par mi,
> Tute quarreie la fendi.
> Quant il a paré la bastun,
> De sun cutel escrit sun nun.
> Se la reïne s'aperceit,
> Que mut grant garde en perneit –
> Autre feiz li fu avenu
> Que si l'aveit aparceü –
> De sun ami bien conustra
> Le bastun, quant el le verra.
> Ceo fu la summe de l'escrit
> Qu'il li aveit mandé e dit
> Que lunges ot ilec esté;
> Et atendu et surjurné
> Pur espïer e pur saver
> Coment il la peüst veer,
> Kar ne poeit vivre sanz li.
> D'euls deus fu il tut autresi
> Cume del chievrefoil esteit
> Ki a la codre se perneit:
> Quant il s'i est laciez e pris
> E tut entur le fust s'est mis,
> Ensemble poënt bien durer,
> Mès ki puis les voelt desevrer,
> Li codres muert hastivement
> E li chievrefoilz ensement.
> "Bele amie, si est de nus:
> Ne vus sanz mei, ne jeo sanz vus."   lines 51–78

(He cut a hazelbranch in half,/ He cut it with square edges./ When he had prepared the stick,/ With his knife he wrote his name on it./ If the queen who was very attentive about such things/ Noticed it – This had happened once before/ And she had noticed –/ She will recognize the stick/ Of [made by] her lover, when she sees it./ This was the sum of the writing/ That he had sent and told to her,/ That he had been there for a long time;/ He had stayed and waited/ To spy out to know/ How he could see her,/ For he could not live without her./ For the two of them it was just as/ It was with the goatleaf/ Which attached itself to the hazelbranch:/ When it was fastened to it/ And was fixed all around the trunk/ They could survive together,/ But if anyone wants to cut them apart,/ The hazel immediately dies/ And the goatleaf as well./ "Fair friend, so it is with us:/ Neither you without me nor I without you.")

39

The queen does indeed notice the stick and decipher the message:

> La reïne vait chevauchant.
> Ele esgardat tut un pendant,
> Le bastun vit, bien l'aparceut,
> Tutes les lettres i conut.
> Les chevaliers que la menoent,
> Ki ensemblë od li erroent
> Cumanda tuz a arester ...   lines 79–83

(The queen goes riding along,/ Meanwhile she looks around,/ She saw the stick, she noticed it,/ She knew all the letters./ The knights who were leading her,/ Who were traveling with her/ She ordered them all to stop . . .)

It is not clear how much of the message Tristan actually managed to squeeze on to that carved stick – or did he just carve his name? Speaking practically – and from the point of view of Iseut as reader – it would presumably have been very difficult to read letters carved around a stick which lay at some distance on the ground. But this scene is not presumably intended as a realistic description of the act of reading – which is an interesting fact in itself. This scene is about the sending of a highly artistic and personalized message – and the fact that its intended "destinataire" is indeed, against all odds, able to receive and decode it.

This passage is in several ways typical of Marie's handling of written messages in the *Lais*. First, the stick itself is intriguing. It is hardly just a handy parchment-substitute. This *bastun* bears a provocative resemblance to the medieval tally sticks discussed by M.T. Clanchy in *From Memory to Written Record: English, 1066–1307* (Plate VIII and discussion) – those long, carved, four-sided sticks used for keeping records in medieval England. They are typical of a period that found purely written records somewhat unsatisfactory: psychologically, even epistemologically, inadequate. Though people increasingly used writing, they also desired something more solid, more clearly symbolic of what was being referred to in the written message. Thus, for example, they tended to attach a clod of earth, or some other "real," and symbolic, object to a written charter. One wonders if there is not something of this sense of the inadequacy of the purely written here and elsewhere in the *Lais*. And the wood chosen for this message-bearing stick is not just any wood, but is of course symbolically significant: it is "une codre," a hazel branch, which cannot live without honeysuckle – "chevrefoil" – wound around it. Neither can live without the other.

Another interesting analogy with the tally stick: one half, one end, of a tally stick is meaningless – invalid – without the other; it is a document, a message, requiring two parts to be complete. In Marie's story, the medium is indeed the message. And the message requires that Iseut (and we) see the hazel branch and then think of the goatleaf: she, and we, are to associate the two. Thus, the

40

stick bears at least as much of the burden of the message as does the written (or carved) text itself.

When Iseut does see the stick, and decodes it – whatever that decoding involves – the function of the message is not to console her in Tristan's absence, or to tell her of his love or his future plans (as are commonly the functions of letters), but, precisely, to alert her to his actual presence. She stops her escort. The lovers meet and talk. And then, to commemorate their meeting – ''Pur les paroles remembrer'' (line 111) – Tristan composes a *lai*, which he later plays on his harp. Marie thus downplays the purely written element of the text, emphasizing instead the unusual writing surface, what the message really means, the way in which the message is sent, the way in which it is perceived, and the musical composition to which it gave rise. Moreover, the event that is being commemorated here is their meeting – their words, their ''paroles'' – not the sending of the message. Tristan, and Marie, don't even entitle the lai ''Codre,'' which might be said to commemorate the written message, but, rather, ''Chevrefoil.'' The ''letter'' is somehow displaced, devalued.

> Por la joie qu'il ot eüe
> De s'amie qu'il ot veüe,
> E pur ceo k'il aveit escrit
> Si cum la reïne l'ot dit,
> Pur les paroles remembrer,
> Tristram, ki bien saveit harper,
> En aveit fait un nuvel lai;
> Asez brefment le numerai;
> *Gotelef* l'apelent Englais,
> *Chievrefoil* le nument Franceis.
> Dit vus en ai la verité
> Del lai que j'ai ici cunté.   lines 107–18

([11]Because of the joy that he had had/ With his lover whom he had seen,/ And because of what he had written/ As the queen had told him to,/ In order to remember the words [that they exchanged?],/ Tristran, who knew how to play the harp well,/ Made a new lai about it;/ I have told it briefly;/ The English call it ''Goatleaf'';/ The French call it ''Chevrefeuille.''/ I have told you the truth about it,/ About the lai which I have told here.)

The way in which Marie seems to diminish or marginalize the written text here in ''Chevrefoil,'' she does quite frequently elsewhere, indeed almost everywhere that written messages are involved in the *Lais*. In ''Laüstic'' (''Nightingale'') when the jealous husband has killed the nightingale and

---

11 The meaning of this passage is obscure, and has been interpreted and translated in a variety of ways. See Rychner, pp. 279–80.

thown it at his wife with the taunt, "Now you won't have to sit up all night!" (lines 107–10), she sends a message to her lover. This message is complex, and revealing, as is the lover's response. Marie accords a curious role to writing in all this. The lady wraps the bird in precious fabric, and hands it to a servant to whom she confides her clearly oral message. He takes the message and the bird to the lover, to whom he shows and tells everything. The lover then makes the extraordinary, and memorable, *châsse* in which he places the bird, which he henceforth carries with him always. Where does writing fit into all this? The cloth – the *samit* – in which the lady wrapped the bird was "A or brusdé e tut escrit" (line 136). It is precious – embroidered with gold and covered with writing – but the writing is not her own writing. Apparently this is just a pleasing design, pleasing but lexically meaningless. (Could the lady have embroidered this cloth herself? Perhaps – but Marie does not provide us with this piece of information.) Marie often inserts some written element into her *lais*, some reference to things "escrites" (see also, for example, the identifying tokens given to the infant Fresne). But she seems to have misgivings about the value and interest of the text *qua* text; of "literature." What she seems centrally preoccupied with is, first, the creation of works of art of various sorts: musical, narrative, and visual, such as the crafting of songs, stories and love-caskets. Second, she emphasizes moments of intense human communication. But purely written things somehow do not seem adequate or compelling in the *Lais*. So, for example, when Milun and his lover manage to send each other letters for twenty years, Marie is not interested in the correspondence anywhere near so much as we might be, or as she is in the swan that they use as their postman. It is the swan that appears to be memorable to her.

Where does all this leave Marie, with respect to oral and written matters? As I noted earlier, it can hardly be doubted that Marie was *literata*: that she was able to read Latin. As we noted at the outset, she makes this abundantly clear, by taking up and then rejecting, in her "general prologue," the possibility of translating from the Latin, by quoting Priscian and speaking of glossing the letter, by referring at various points in the *Lais* to some written sources, by ample use of words like "escrit," "letre," and "lecteure" (according to Tobler-Lommatzsch, she is one of the first vernacular poets to use this word), and so on. Her references to her literacy and to the status of her work as text, as *escrit*, are substantially more striking in the prologue to the *Lais* than in the stories themselves, and become still more insistent in the *Fables*. At any rate, she is at some pains to show off her learning and her eloquence. As to her narrative art itself, her treatment of her material has little of the participatory quality that we found in Béroul, and that is common in the oral tradition. While Marie is not lacking in sympathy for her various lovers, there is something very cool about her treatment of love. In some lais, it is not even clear to the reader whose side to be on: this is the case with "Equitan" and "Eliduc," for example, or with "Bisclavret," where we appear to be against the lovers, on the side of the werewolf. Marie can be remarkably even-handed.

Nonetheless, Marie is heavily in debt to the tradition of oral story-telling and song, from which she claims to have received her stories. In her prologue, she tells us that she decided not to do translations from Latin: "De lais pensai, k'oïz aveie" (line 33: "I thought about lais, which I had heard."). There is, moreover, much here that comes from folklore. But Marie's way of using oral material is virtually always unexpected, as several scholars who have studied the role of folklore in her work have concluded.[12] She hardly ever does with traditional oral motifs the traditional – the standard – thing but shifts the position or meaning of motifs in a frequently disconcerting fashion.

Marie retells traditional stories – how faithfully we cannot say – giving us bizarre and memorable characters, objects, and events like the Bisclavret, the werewolf husband; Yonec, the bird-lover; the untying of the love-knots in "Guigemar"; and the nightingale in the reliquary. But there is something highly innovative in her use of traditional material. But then, Marie *wanted* to be innovative: this was to be her claim to the fame – the praise – that she, explicitly, sought. And it was on these grounds that she decided not to translate something from Latin. "It's been done already" (Prologue, line 32): hardly the attitude of a truly traditional story-teller! Her literary quality – as such – emerges most clearly from the *recueil* taken as a whole, where Marie's distinctive if elusive handling of such themes as love, faithfulness, and adultery emerges slowly.

But not all messages sent are messages received, in life or in literature, and Marie may well have been, as we say, ahead of her time. Her message and her ambitions were substantially more "literary" – in the sense of bookish and reader-oriented – than the audience she had available could accommodate. The fact that our modern editions of Marie's work allow us to read the *Lais* as a collection, with complex patterns of internal intertextuality, does not mean that the medieval public generally received – perceived – it in this way. Of the five manuscripts that bring Marie to us, only one of them is complete, including the Prologue which has solicited so much scholarly commentary. Another manuscript contains three *lais*; the two remaining manuscripts contain one *lai* each. The individual *lais* clearly tended to become detached from the whole in which Marie had set them: that compilation of *Les Lais*, her work of art, that she looked forward to offering as a present to the king. The *lais* circulated individually, in their most traditional, and most strongly oral, form; they were performed by minstrels and amateur harpists. (We have many references to such performances of *lais*; though they appear also to have been read aloud in court. Chapter 6 will return to these issues.)

12 See Mary H. Ferguson, "Folklore in the *Lais* of Marie de France"; François Suard, "L'Utilisation des éléments folkloriques dans le lai du 'Frêne.' "

43

*

These three versions of the *Tristan* vary in their relation to traditions of oral story-telling, on the one hand, and to traditions of learning and textualization on the other. There is every likelihood that Béroul was an analphabetic *conteur*. (He may also have had special performance skills, to which we will return in Chapter 6.) Thomas and Marie de France were, evidence indicates, learned: he almost certainly a clerk, she quite possibly a nun. Both of these poets make it clear that they are writers. But all three versions show the magnetic pull, as it were, of *both* traditions. Both oral and written traditions are perceived as having some measure of "authority" and as containing names worth citing: Bréri and Tristan, maker of lais, are given as oral authorities, and Marie refers to "philosophers," written sources, in her prologue (line 17).

While writing increasingly carried authority, that authority appears to have been felt as somehow humanly deficient. This is suggested by the sorts of additional "documentation," often of a vegetal or other nitty-gritty character, appended to written charters. If this was true even of Latin documents,[13] it was truer still of vernacular works. The written word increasingly enjoyed prestige and conferred credibility, but it was perceived as lacking interpersonal warmth and persuasiveness, and even perhaps as esthetically unsatisfactory. So while writers and poets wanted more and more to draw on the authority of the written word, credibility was *all* that writing had to offer.

Even learned vernacular poets in this early period did not invest writing and "letters" with the great metaphorical dignity that some Latin writers did, or that vernacular writers did starting in the late thirteenth and fourteenth centuries.[14] We do not find in these early narratives the language of writing as a sowing of seed, or other metaphors based on the pen, parchment, reading, or the book.

Béroul, Thomas and Marie are very different sorts of story-tellers. What can we adduce from their works with regard to the issue of audience? All three are likely to have been addressing "courtly" – that is "court" – audiences: Marie, of course, speaks to the king himself, and various scholars have pointed out that both Béroul's and Thomas's versions of the Tristan contain preoccupations characteristic of the medieval court. There are two issues to be considered here, and it is important to keep them separate. One is the issue of sophistication, the other is that of literacy. Thomas and Marie both provide sophisticated and highly refined entertainment. Their works – especially that of Thomas, perhaps – are conceptually demanding. He hardly even bothers to

13 See Clanchy, *From Memory*.
14 See, e.g., Jacqueline Cerquiglini-Toulet, *La couleur de la mélancolie*.
Jean de Meung's *Roman de la Rose* provides highly interesting examples of the use of metaphors based on writing; in particular, sexual intercourse (a topic dear to Jean) is presented as a kind of writing.

tell a story: in his tale nothing much happens, except of course that the lovers die; Thomas's story is short on events. (The work may be fragmentary, but there is enough of it left to see this!) The very fact that Thomas's audience enjoyed – or at least that Thomas had in mind an audience who would enjoy – this highly analytical semi-narrative tells us that his public can only have existed in a sophisticated milieu, in which people were used to sitting around talking about love, and debating its joys and sorrows, and the sin and folly into which lovers fall.

But this does not mean that Thomas's, or Marie's, audience was composed primarily of bookish intellectuals – indeed *few* may have been themselves able to read: "literate" in the modern sense of the word.[15] It may not even mean that their public was used to being read aloud to (more on this in Chapter 6). It only suggests that people there were in the habit of analyzing and discussing the substance of what was presented to them. Again, Finnegan is useful to us: she has rightly pointed out that "even primarily non-literate audiences can consist of initiates and intellectuals, and the circulation of oral poetry may sometimes take place within circumscribed limits."[16] Non-literates can be cultural sophisticates.

And Béroul? His work is anything but subtle and refined. The court audiences that he entertained were perhaps particularly unsophisticated – or perhaps they just sometimes enjoyed crude and unpretentious entertainment. Today as well "high-brows" sometimes like decidedly "low-brow" humor, for example at the movies. (We may also be looking at a work performed in a different sort of social or festive context. Chapter 6 will take up this issue as well.)

There are many different kinds of non-literate – or non-predominantly-literate – audiences. And there were, clearly, many different sorts of courts in twelfth and early-thirteenth century France and England, as well as elsewhere. Some were obviously a great deal tonier and more intellectual than others: it was not for nothing that Henry I of England was called "Beauclerc." Some courts were known for their piety, and piety generally went with some measure of learning: Chrétien certainly gives us this impression of Philip of Alsace, count of Flanders. Other courts had no reputation for piety (the court that gathered around the bawdy poet William IX of Aquitaine would surely be a case in point!). Some courts were heavily involved in discussions of *fin amors*, as appears to be the case of Marie of Champagne's court; others markedly less so: the courts of Louis VII and of his son Philippe Auguste spring to mind.

At any rate, there is no reason to think that anything remotely resembling the majority of the men and women in any of the various courts of twelfth

---

15 See Franz Bäuml, "Varieties and Consequences of Medieval Literacy and Illiteracy." Bäuml argues that in the medieval context, access to what was *in* books was an important kind of literacy – whether one could read for oneself or not.

16 *Oral Poetry*, p. 234.

century France or England could read and write. But the presence in court of literate people, especially clerks who received encouragement from the lord and lady to explain works of learning and to compose works of instruction and entertainment, had clear impact on the sorts of pleasures to which the members of these courts became accustomed. It is to such issues that we will turn in the next two chapters.

The twelfth century – especially the mid- to late-twelfth century – was a major period of transition: early in the century, the world of the vernacular was almost entirely oral; by the close of the century, the impact of writing and the written were strongly felt. From the end of the twelfth century date a good many vernacular manuscripts; from a few decades earlier, we have virtually none. The rapidity of this shift in the oral/written ''economy'' will not again be matched until the introduction of the printed book in the late fifteenth and early sixteenth centuries. But this shift was by no means a total transformation: medieval culture did not simply turn a page and become ''literary,'' filled with books, writers and readers. There are many signs of ambivalence in attitude. Oral and written traditions long continued to compete for authority. Writing, texts, and reading were not yet seen as providing any particular ''pleasures,'' and it does not appear to have been for any esthetic reasons that a poet turned to writing. And there are indications of collaboration between oral and written culture. In particular, clerks and minstrels, in their desire to give delight and to transmit fundamental social and religious values, often borrowed each other's plumage. Thus, the two traditions existed in a symbiotic relationship. To an important degree, of course, they still do – and always do. Or, perhaps we should put this more prudently, noting the lack of symmetry: the oral tradition may, in some periods and some parts of the world, be able to get along nicely without the written tradition in its various manifestations – literacy, the presence of books, and the like. But the written tradition cannot do without the oral: cultures cannot stop talking, or teaching children to talk; we cannot stop telling stories, praying, singing . . .

Be all that as it may, what I hope to have established in this chapter is the complexity of the interplay between oral and written traditions, here at the birth of French ''literature,'' and to have posed some fundamental questions which we will explore further in subsequent chapters.

CHAPTER THREE

The Poet of the *Roman de Thèbes*: *Clerc* or *Ménestrel*?

We now narrow the focus. From this chapter on, we will be concerned almost exclusively with romance, for of the narrative genres regularly composed in octo, romance has the most learned reputation.[1] (I set aside genres which were almost exclusively clerical such as the sermon and didactic discourse.) I will define early romance simply as a long narrative work of predominantly secular subject-matter, composed in octosyllabic rhymed couplets.[2] The birth of romance has been seen as *une affaire de clercs*.[3] The

---

[1] This is perhaps a useful point to make the following general statement: there is an immense bibliography devoted to French medieval romance, and indeed to each of the authors I will be discussing from this chapter on. My purpose is not to do justice to this scholarship (though it contains many excellent and thought-provoking books and articles) but to present an argument. I will only take up studies that are necessary to this argument, and studies related to its possible refutation. Indeed in this latter category, I will often just provide "samples" and what we might call "depth-soundings."

[2] I will not be primarily concerned with prose romance, which is a later development, arising essentially in the second quarter of the thirteenth century. While there are, as we have noted in earlier chapters, a small handful of romances composed in other verse forms (such as the *Roman d'Alexandre*, of which important versions were done in "alexandrine" lines) the octosyllabic rhymed couplet is far and away the rule. Shorter narrative genres in octo include the lai and fabliau.

Perhaps I should add to my definition that a romance is a work of "fiction" – but that is the way *we* see it; medieval poets do not always present matters in this fashion. Thus (for example) many early romances are "about" King Arthur – but he was thought, at least by many, to have been a real person; certainly the Welsh and other Britons claimed he was, and the Plantagenets at least pretended to believe it. One might also add that the typical themes of romance are love, adventure, single combat, and the like. But, while true, such elements are not particularly necessary for our concerns.

[3] Indeed, *all* of medieval culture has been seen in these terms. For example, M.D. Chenu declared in *La théologie au XIIe siècle*: "Pendant le Moyen Age, la mise en route de tout enseignement et tous les cadres de la culture s'organisent par des clercs: la civilisation naît dans l'Eglise, non certes par captation cléricale, mais selon des conditions matérielles et morales que la conjoncture explique fort bien . . . l'initiative et l'inspiration viennent des gens d'église; l'enseignement est polarisé par les fins religieuses, bien mieux il est suscité et confirmé, jusque dans la variété de ses objets (les sept arts de la *disciplina* antique), par la puissance spirituelle d'une conception chrétienne de l'homme et du monde. Il est donc normal que la théologie soit la science suprême, étant la première et suprême curiosité de ces esprits . . . Ainsi, à partir de la théologie, premier savoir constitué, se compose une pédagogie qui, sans aboutir à un autoritarisme de principe, accoutume l'intelligence à

romance genre, like the octo form itself, is thought by many scholars to have been a clerical invention, and to have ushered in the world of vernacular textuality. In his *Histoire de la littérature française*, Gustave Lanson said of "romans en vers" that: "Toutes ces productions sont destinées à être lues: elles ne passent pas par la bouche des *jongleurs*. Ce sont vraiment des nouvelles et des romans, au sens moderne du mot" (p. 51). These were, then, novels, written by writers, for readers.

Similarly, Eugène Vinaver declared, in *The Rise of Romance*:

> The rise of romance was ... the birth of a world in which vernacular writings were to share with Latin texts the privilege of addressing the reader through the medium of visible, not audible symbols; through words intended to be read, not sung, or even recited, and with this went a radical alteration of the very nature of literary experience. (p. 4)

More recently, but largely in the same vein, Paul Zumthor began the chapter entitled "Du roman à la nouvelle" in his *Essai de poétique médiévale*, by speaking of the octosyllabic rhymed couplet. He said that:

> ... la marque du vers, impliquant un dessein proprement poétique et une réflexion sur le texte comme tel, semble bien avoir été employée pour la première fois par des clercs anglo-normands, dans les années 1120–1130, puis sur le continent à partir de 1140–1150. (p. 339)

Thus, for Zumthor romance was essentially "text" and "reflection on text as such."[4]

Though not all scholars would go as far as these, romance is reliably seen as a *fundamentally* "written" genre – not just one that *happens* to have existed in texted form or to have found readers.[5] There is a good deal at stake here, and it concerns not just romance, but virtually all early French literature. If romance

procéder de semblable manière dans les autres enseignements . . ." (pp. 352–53). Thus, for Chenu, medieval culture was not merely Christian, it was fundamentally *clerical*.

4 Similarly, in *Littérature française* (gen. eds., Antoine Adam, *et al.*), Zumthor, who authored the medieval section, wrote of romance that "sa forme – l'octosyllabe à rimes plates – l'apparente à l'historiographie, aux genres didactiques" (I, p. 17). But see Vitz, "Paul Zumthor and Medieval Romance."

5 Paul Guth, in his *Histoire de la littérature française*, stated, speaking of "la femme": "Elle désirait une littérature pour elle, qui parlât de sa spécialité: l'amour . . . Elle brûlait de commencer son apprentissage de muse. Et ce furent les romans que l'on lisait, que l'on ne chantait plus . . . Les clercs s'inspirent de l'étranger, comme chaque fois qu'ils veulent plaire aux femmes et à leur nostalgie pour ce qui vient de loin . . . Ainsi naissent les romans à l'antique . . ."; pp. 22–23. I think I will refrain from comment.

The following seminal studies of romance (among many others) are also based, in varying ways and to varying effect, on the idea that romance-poets were romance-*writers*, and were formed by their clerical training: Claude Luttrell, *The Creation of the First Arthurian Romance*; Eugene Vance, *From Topic to Tale: Logic and Narrativity in the Middle Ages*; Douglas Kelly, *The Art of Medieval French Romance*.

can be shown to have strong and enduring links to oral culture, such connections can be recognized as truer still of such genres as the lai and the fabliau whose debt to orality has long been acknowledged (though these genres often have literary features as well.)

The *Roman de Thèbes* is renowned as the first full-fledged vernacular medieval *roman*. Composed around 1150 (perhaps even somewhat earlier) by an anonymous poet, the *Thèbes* is thought to have been the first of the three romances which, in his *Literary Language and Its Public in Late Latin Antiquity and in the Middle Ages*, Erich Auerbach baptized "the classic triad" (p. 210) – the other two being the *Roman de Troie* and the *Roman d'Enéas*. Some scholars make the list of antique romances a foursome by including the *Roman d'Alexandre* (in its various fragmentary versions[6]). The *Thèbes*, like its antique fellows, is considered unanimously by scholars[7] to have been written by a *clerc*. One quotation can suffice to sum up the scholarly consensus on this question: "De l'auteur, on ne peut rien dire que de vague; c'est, sans doute aucun, un clerc . . ."[8]

In this chapter, I will argue that it is unlikely that the *Thèbes* poet was a clerk. It is also unlikely that he was a "writer": by this I mean not merely that he did not himself write down his work – even many clerical authors dictated instead of writing for themselves – but, more importantly, that he did not conceive his work in written terms; that it was to him a story – no more, no less.

Some definitions: *clerc* and *clergie*; *jongleur* and *ménestrel*

But the time has come to look at the word *clerc* more closely – indeed to problematize this important concept. *Clerc* and *clericus* are terms normally used to refer to a school-trained intellectual, educated under the auspices of the Church. (As noted in an earlier chapter, I frequently use the English word "clerk" to refer to such persons, for simplicity's sake, though I do recognize the peril of anachronism.) A clerk was, if properly trained (and many were *not*!) fully *literatus*: able to read and write Latin. Literacy in the vernacular did not count as "literacy"; it did not qualify one as *literatus*. In the twelfth century – before the rise of the universities – a clerk would generally have been educated in one of the many church schools. ("Masters" were produced in cathedral schools, such as existed in Paris, Chartres, Troyes, and other episcopal cities; similarly in England, at Oxford and elsewhere; there were

---

6   The earliest version of the *Alexandre* (in octosyllabic rhymed couplets, ascribed to Alberic de Pisançon) is even earlier than the *Thèbes*, dating from the first quarter of the twelfth century.

7   See John S. Coley's introduction to his translation of *Le Roman de Thèbes (The Story of Thebes)* for a useful overview of critical positions on this work.

8   *Le Roman de Thèbes*, ed. Raynaud de Lage, I, p. xxxi.

other important schools as well, such as the famed School of St. Victor, in Paris.) His education might, however, have begun at home: in noble house-holds, tutors and chaplains sometimes provided the basis of a clerical education to those needing or wishing it.[9] In school, a student studied grammar, as well as rhetoric and dialectic and the other "liberal arts"; the Bible as well. The curriculum varied somewhat from school to school and in different periods. If he remained in school long enough, the student eventually studied theology, but many, with worldly ambitions or who were unfit for the clerical life, left before they reached the study of theology.[10]

Literary scholars tend to emphasize the learning involved in *clergie*. But of course, historically speaking, the term *clerc* did not refer exclusively, or even primarily, to a person's level of learning or way of having been educated, but to his relation to the Church: a clerk was, simply, a member of the clergy. In the early medieval period, the term *clerici* referred exclusively to priests, and distinguished between them and monks, who were not considered "clergy." Eventually, both groups came to be categorized as clergy: the "secular" and the "religious" clergy. Such was generally the case by the twelfth century.

By this period, to have clerical status normally meant that one was in at least "minor orders." There were in all about seven orders (though lists and numbers varied, and there were marked differences between East and West): priests, deacons, subdeacons, acolytes, exorcists, lectors, and porters (door-keepers). Sometimes bishops and psalmists were included; grave-diggers, those who cared for the graves of martyrs, and interpreters (*hermeneutae*) were sometimes counted as orders.[11] But in the listing of orders as elsewhere (sacra-ments, sins, virtues, etc.) the number seven clearly had strong appeal, and there appears to have been a tendency to "sevenize" lists.[12] In Europe in the twelfth century there were the following minor orders: deacon, subdeacon, acolyte, exorcist, lector, and porter. Presumably, the orders or functions which most called for higher levels of education were those of bishop, priest, reader and

9 Especially valuable on home education is Nicholas Orme, *From Childhood to Chivalry: The Education of the English Kings and Aristocracy, 1066–1530*.

10 On the education of the laity, see Pierre Riché, "Recherches sur l'instruction des laïcs du IXe au XIIe siècle." On cathedral schools, see C. Stephen Jaeger, *The Envy of Angels: Cathedral Schools and Social Ideals in Medieval Europe, 950–1200*. Several works focus primarily on England but are of broad interest, especially Orme, *Education and Society in Medieval and Renaissance England*; still valuable is A.F. Leach, *The Schools of Medieval England*. For the universities, see Helene Wieruszowski, *The Medieval Univer-sity*; Charles Homer Haskins, *The Rise of Universities*; Stephen C. Ferruolo, *The Origins of the University: The Schools of Paris and their Critics, 1100–1215*. My special thanks to M.T. Clanchy on the thorny issues of twelfth century education.

11 *Catholic Encyclopedia*, Vol. X, pp. 332–33; Vol. XI, pp. 279–80.

12 See, for example, Mary Frances Rogers, *Peter Lombard and the Sacramental System*, esp. pp. 71–72.

the like. One rather doubts that doorkeepers and grave-diggers had reliably been through the entire Liberal Arts course.

It is important to note the semantic ambiguity – and potential conflict – here: the clerk as learned vs. the clerk as member of the clergy: as a part of the ministerial functioning of the Church. (And with regard to this latter definition, it is useful to remind ourselves that many members of the clergy were anything *but* learned; some were almost totally illiterate – hence the necessity for the various Lateran reforms of clerical training.)

We will need to reflect further on the clerk and his many roles. But for the moment let us return to our text, and my argument. In my view, the *Thèbes* poet was not a clerk by either definition of the term – literacy or function. I believe, rather, that this poet was a minstrel. Here, too, some definitions are in order. We need to look not merely at the word *ménestrel* but also at *jongleur*. These are words whose exact meaning is hard to pin down, as they were often used interchangeably and could mean a variety of things.[13]

Edmond Faral, in his classic work *Les jongleurs en France au moyen âge*, defined *jongleurs* as professional entertainers; he viewed *ménestrels* as a subcategory of *jongleurs*: "[E]t nous dirons que nous considérons comme des jongleurs *tous ceux qui faisaient profession de divertir les hommes*."[14] But Faral also distinguished between the two. The *jongleur* – from Latin *jocus*, but contaminated with *jangler*, or "bavarder" – engaged in a wide and often unrefined variety of acts. These included musical performances of all types – some with the use of a wide variety of musical instruments and the singing of songs – but also juggling, tumbling and dancing. (It was indeed to the dancing and the bodily contortions that churchmen most reliably objected in the performances of *jongleurs* and similar figures.) *Jongleurs* – they were mostly male but there were *jongleuresses* as well – traveled from place to place, making their living as they went. By contrast, the *ménestrel* – derived from popular Latin *ministerialis*, or "servant" – led a more secure existence, attached to a noble court or patron, and tended to specialize in entertainments of a more refined nature. *Ménestrels* were also sometimes highly rewarded by their masters; some are known to have received substantial fiefs.[15]

We should not perhaps take these theoretical or terminological distinctions too seriously. Both *ménestrels* and *jongleurs* are often referred to as present at court events, and many works do not appear to distinguish between them. The two "minstrels" of the *Deux bourdeurs ribauds*, quoted earlier, would

---

[13] *Jongleur* – more typically *jogleor* – could refer to any sort of performer or acrobat; also to a liar. *Ménestrel* could also mean: *artisan, ouvrier, serviteur, médecin, poète ou musicien, vaurien* (Godefroy, Vol. 5, p. 238); also a watchman or the member of a band: *Dictionary of the Middle Ages* (Joseph Strayer, gen. ed.), Vol. 8, pp. 116–17: Edmund A. Bowles.

[14] Faral, *Les jongleurs*, p. 2. Emphasis in the original.

[15] E.g., Faral, *Les jongleurs*, pp. 113–18; Chambers, *Mediaeval Stage*, Vol. I, pp. 42ff.

probably have technically been *"jongleurs."* But, generally speaking, the term *ménestrel* seems to refer to an entertainer attached to an aristocratic court, and working under the patronage of a noble patron. It is in that sense that I shall use the term.

For Faral – and here again contemporary scholars have largely followed his lead – it was quite possible to be at once a *clerc* and a *jongleur*, as in the case of the "Goliards" or *clerici vagantes*. These were men more or less thoroughly educated by the Church, but officially or unofficially defrocked; out of orders. Thus they had clerical training, even if they were no longer members of the clergy. From the point of view of literacy, they were (more or less) clerks; from that of function, they were not. For Faral, it was also possible to be both a *clerc* and *ménestrel*: a high-culture entertainer trained by, and still in good standing in, the Church. It is thus – as "ménestrels de haut rang" *and* clerks – that Faral sees virtually all the great early romance authors (pp. 199ff).

Faral would have found it impossible even to imagine that a court entertainer of any subtlety or refinement could be other than a *clerc* – and many modern academics are afflicted with the same (arguably narcissistic) blind spot. (One frequently reads that a fine poet "must have been a clerk" because of his skilled handling of the material. The idea, shared by many scholars, that poetic excellence and school learning must necessarily go hand-in-hand is one of the assumptions against which this book will frequently argue.) Faral invariably speaks of what such figures do as "writing." In a word, for Faral these two terms – *ménestrel* and *clerc* – represented, at least in the court setting, essentially overlapping categories. Or more precisely, in a noble court one could be (for Faral) a *clerc* without being a *ménestrel* but one could not be a *ménestrel* without *also* being a *clerc*; this, because court entertainments, such as romances, were seen not merely as refined but as showing the marks of school learning and as the product of writing.

It is an interesting fact that Faral does not address the problem of *vernacular* writing. That is, clerks were trained to read and write Latin. But how and where – and *why* – did people learn to read and write the vernacular? What members of the laity could read and write French? This is an issue for which it is hard to find documentation. Such writing was presumably a skill picked up in a spotty or irregular fashion and for particular purposes, ranging from the keeping of records of business transactions, to the sending of personal messages such as love-letters. (It was precisely to avoid their being in a position to send and receive love-letters that Philippe de Navarre (or Novara) recommended that women not be taught to read and write.[16]) In any event, it can be argued that vernacular writing was a higher-order skill than writing in Latin for the simple reason that there were no "rules"; there was no grammar.

---

16 Philippe de Navarre [Novara], *Les quatre âges de l'homme: traité moral*, Marcel de Fréville, ed., p. 16.

The poet of the *Roman de Thèbes*

What do we know – and *not* know – about the anonymous *Thèbes* poet? He is considered by some to have been a Norman, by others a Poitevin; at any rate to have been a continental Frenchman. It has been thought possible that he was in contact with the Anglo-Norman court, but this connection is a bit problematic since at the time of the apparent composition of this work (c. 1150), there were two warring "Anglo-Norman courts": that of King Stephen and that of the Empress Matilda, and one would assume that both rulers had other things on their minds than romance patronage. After 1154, and the accession of Henry II to the Plantagenet throne, such a connection is possible, though by no means certain. But in any event, not one of our early extant manuscripts is Anglo-Norman, whereas for the *Roman de Troie* (on which more below), we do have a twelfth century Anglo-Norman manuscript. In any event, there are a good many continental courts at which such a work might have been found pleasing and would have received a ready audience.[17]

There are five complete surviving manuscripts of the *Roman de Thèbes*, plus an important fragment. The oldest manuscript is a fragment from Angers – called D – which dates from around 1200. Manuscript C dates from the middle of the thirteenth century. Two others – P and A – date from the end of the century. Manuscript B dates from the mid- to late-fourteenth century. Finally, S dates from the end of the fourteenth century. All but the last of these manuscripts are continental; S is Anglo-Norman. These manuscripts vary quite a good deal, especially with respect to the length of the poem: C and B give a markedly shorter version, A and P a longer one.

The poem was first edited by Léopold Constans in 1890: *Le Roman de Thèbes, publié d'après tous les manuscrits*. His edition has proven controversial because, while basing himself on S, he used all the manuscripts and, to some degree, rewrote the poem, trying to get back to the original work – the "Ur-*Thèbes*." The poem has been reedited by Guy Raynaud de Lage who based himself on C, the oldest complete manuscript. While in general this latter edition has much to recommend it – including (in my view) the editorial principles behind it – this chapter will cite the older Constans edition for two reasons. First, it is on the whole slightly more challenging to the argument presented here, as it contains, if not more apparent references to clerks and clergy, more such references that are genuinely interesting: Constans includes some provocative passages not present in C. For all lengthy quotations I will also provide, in brackets, references to the equivalent passage in the Raynaud

---

17 I do not discuss the *Roman d'Énéas*. My focus is on the *Thèbes* and the *Troie* and on the differences and similarities between them. In my view, each work needs to be studied carefully, and I do not wish to make offhand remarks about the *Énéas*, a work which raises complex issues.

de Lage edition. In general, notes will take up references to *clergie* in the C manuscript which are absent from the Constans edition. The translations provided here are my own since for the purposes at hand it is desirable to stay very close to the original.

We cannot be sure what the original poem was like. We have a number of different versions that reflect various poetic reworkings and in some cases the "commentary" of different scribes. But we do not have access to the original poem itself – and indeed if we are talking about a work composed without recourse to writing and performed from memory, which performance would constitute the "original"? The very term implies a written notion of the "work."

To return to the *Thèbes* poet: it is essential to note that, whoever he was, he *never* refers to himself as a clerk; *never* speaks of his work as written, or of himself as writing; *never* claims to have read anything himself; *never* promises to be faithful to the Latin "letter"; *never* refers to his poem as a "book." This may be "negative evidence," but it is surely worth asking ourselves: just what has made us all so sure that this poet *was* a clerk?

The evidence for *clergie* – and its weaknesses

We have believed that the poet was a clerk essentially for three reasons. First, it has been thought inconceivable – literally unimaginable – that a narrative poet, a poet who was "making" something other than *chansons de geste* or love lyrics, could possibly be anything other than a *clerc*.[18] This assumption itself flowed in large part from the belief (discussed in Chapter 1) that the octo form, used by the *Thèbes* poet, was a clerical invention.

The second consideration has been the category into which the *Thèbes* obviously falls: the "romans antiques." But the fact that one or another of these romances may be the work of a *clerc* does not necessarily mean that it is the case of *all* of them. To make this argument about the *Thèbes* and its poet clearer, it will be useful to compare it and him at some length to the *Roman de Troie*[19] and its poet, whose name we *do* know: Benoît de Sainte-Maure. This latter work is thought to have been composed around 1160, and it is unquestionably Anglo-Norman. Both in the introduction and in the conclusion to his 30,000-line romance, and during the story as well, Benoît refers over and over to writing, books, *clercs* and *clergie*. Here is how he begins:

---

18 In the case of love lyrics, scepticism is in order: a good many troubadours and trouvères have been said to be literate – and "*writers* of poetry" – on very little evidence indeed.

19 Benoît de Sainte-Maure, *Roman de Troie*, ed. Léopols Constans; 6 vols.

Salemon nos enseigne e dit,
E sil list om en son escrit,
Que nus ne deit son sen celer,
Ainz le deit om si demostrer
Que l'om i ait pro e honor,
Qu'ensi firent li ancessor.
Se cil qui troverent les parz
Et les granz livres des set arz,
Des philosophes les traitiez,
Dont toz li monz est enseigniez,
Se fussent teü, veirement
Vesquist li siegles folement . . .
E por ço me veuil travaillier
En une estoire comencier,
Que de latin, ou jo la truis,
Sc j'ai le sens e se jo puis,
La voudrai si en romanz metre
Que cil qui n'entendent la letre
Se puissent deduire el romanz:
Mout est l'estoire riche e granz
E de grant uevre et de grant fait.
En maint sen avra l'om retrait,
Saveir com Troie fu perie,
Mais la verté est poi oïe.   lines 1–12, 33–44

(Solomon teaches and tells us/ And also one reads in his writing,/ That no one must hide his sense [knowledge],/ But one must show it forth/ In order to have profit and honor [from it],/ For so did our ancestors do./ If those who invented [found] the parts/ And the great books of the seven arts,/ The treatises of the philosophers,/ By whom everyone is taught,/ If they had kept silent, truly/ The world would live in madness . . ./ For this reason I want to put myself to work/ To start on a story/ Which, from Latin, where I found it, / If I have the knowledge and if I can,/ I want to put into romance [French]/ So that those who do not understand letters/ May be able to enjoy it in romance [French]:/ The story is very rich and great/ Both of great work[manship] and of great deeds./ In many ways have people told/ Their knowledge of how Troy perished/ But the truth is not often heard.)

Benoît introduces here a number of important themes. The first is the theme of wisdom. Benoît clearly and explicitly associates this theme with books, written works, and reading: "escrit" (line 2), "livres" (line 8), "list hom" (line 2). It is, then, with a tradition specifically of *written* wisdom that he wishes to associate himself; we will return to this important theme.

Benoît also tells us that he is translating this work from the Latin and putting it into the vernacular ("romanz") so that those who do not know letters ("la letre'')[20] will be able to enjoy it in French. It is not certain that he has a concept of specifically vernacular literacy; he is writing this work for those without Latin "letters," and he clearly intends it to be heard, read aloud – presumably by clerks such as himself, to laymen – not read privately. Thus he says "la verté est poi oïe" ("the truth is rarely heard") and he often subsequently refers to listeners and to hearing. In other words, Benoît appears to have a sense of vernacular textuality, with the laity as the intended public, but not to have what today would be a corresponding sense of lay vernacular *literacy*; laymen and men provide an audience of hearers, not of readers, to this text.

In his initial plot-summary, Benoît leaves no doubt whatsoever that he himself is a clerk:

> Ceste estoire n'est pas usee,
> N'en guaires lieus nen est trovee:
> Ja retraite ne fust ancore,
> Mais Beneeiz de Sainte More
> L'a contrové e fait e dit
> E o sa main les moz escrit,
> Ensi tailliez, ensi curez,
> Ensi asis, ensi posez,
> Que plus ne meins n'i a mestier.
> Ci vueil l'estoire comencier:
> Le latin sivrai e la letre,
> Nuile autre rien n'i voudrai metre,
> S'ensi non com jol truis escrit.
> Ne dit mie qu'aucun bon dit
> N'i mete, se faire le sai,
> Mais la matire en ensivrai.   lines 129–44

(This story is not common [used],/ It is hardly found [or "told"?] anywhere:/ Never was it narrated before,/ But Benoît de Sainte Maure/ Has invented and made and said it/ And with his hand written the words,/ Thus [has he] fixed [it], thus taken charge [of it]/ Thus has he set it, thus has he put it down,/ So that it needs nothing more, nothing less./ Here I want to begin the story:/ I will follow the Latin and the letter,/ No other thing do I wish to put into it,/ Except as I find it written./ I don't say that some good saying,/ I won't put in, if I know how to do it,/ But I will follow the subject-matter.)

Benoît thus speaks in undeniably written terms. In this preface, written in that blend of past and future that are generally (even today) the earmarks of

---

[20] The situation of vernacular-only readers in this period is much the same as that for vernacular-only writers, discussed earlier: we have little documentation. But we do have a few references to vernacular readers in medieval romances and other works. We will return to such readers, and their reading practices, in Chapter 6.

prologues written after the rest of the work, he makes it clear that not only is he *literatus* but – something more uncommon – he has set down himself, with his own hand, the words we read. He has found it, made it, told it and written it himself: "L'a contrové e fait e dit/E o sa main les moz escrit." He assures us that as concerns the plot-line he has followed faithfully the letter of his Latin source.

The "epilogue" to the vast romance reads:

> Ci ferons fin, bien est mesure:
> Auques tient nostre livre e dure.
> Ço que dist Daires et Ditis
> I avons si retrait et mis
> Que, s'il plaiseit as jangleors,
> Qui de ço sont encuseors,
> Qu'as autrui faiz sont reprenant
> E a trestoz biens enviant,
> Ne que ja rien n'avra honor
> Qu'il n'en aient ire[21] et dolor,
> Cil se porroient mout bien taire
> De l'uevre blasmer e retraire;
> Quar teus i voudreit afaitier,
> Qui tost i porreit empeirier.
> Celui guart Deus e tienge en veie,
> Qui bien essauce e montepleie.   lines 30, 301–16

(Here we will make our end, it is right:/ Our book has lasted long enough./ The things that Darius says, and Dictis/ We have told and put into it,/ So that, if it pleased *jongleurs*,[22]/ Who are so critical/ That they blame other people's deeds [works],/ And are envious of all good things,/ So that nothing is honored/ Without their being angry and sad about it,/ They might well keep quiet/ Instead of blaming and condemning the work;/ For he who would like to improve it,/ Might easily make it worse./ May God protect and preserve in life,/ Him who exalts the good and makes it fruitful.)

The *Roman de Troie* is, then, unmistakably, undeniably, a book written by a clerk who, as he lays down his pen, attempts to defend his creation against the future criticisms and "improvements" of his envious rivals – and perhaps performers – the *jongleurs/jangleurs*.

But the *Thèbes* poet never speaks this way. He talks invariably like a story-teller – an "I" telling a story "now" to "you" – not like a clerk, not like a

---

21 The base manuscript gives "vie," but a variant reading offers "ire," which alone appears to make sense here. See *Troie*, Vol. 4, p. 386.

22 Some manuscripts of the *Troie* have "jangleors" (often translated as "médisants") here; others "jogleors" (*jongleurs*). Cf. Constans' ed., Vol. IV, p. 386.

writer or scribe. He neither prefaces nor concludes his story with any discussion of his sources. Far and away the most persuasive piece of evidence for his *clergie* has been the simple fact that he knew Statius' story of the *Thebaid* – for it is this classical work which provides the general plot line and a good many of the details of the *Roman de Thèbes*.

Now, there is no scholarly consensus on the poet's precise use of the *Thebaid*, or even on the extent of his knowledge of this work. A number of years ago, Guy Raynaud de Lage, editor of the *Thèbes*, wrote in the *Grundriss*:

> Le *Roman de Thèbes* prend appui sur la *Thébaïde* de Stace, poème et auteur qui étaient assurément placés plus hauts qu'aujourd'hui dans la hiérarchie des classiques latins; mais il importe assez peu de définir ce niveau de notoriété: il ne faut pas attribuer au poète français une attitude d'écolier qui attendrait d'un maître des leçons de style et de composition, qui songerait même à rivaliser avec lui, comme un lettré de l'ère classique française. C'est une garantie d'historicité qui est demandée à Stace, il est chargé d'authentifier un récit qui sera dès lors paré du prestige de l'Antiquité; le romancier procède un peu comme le poète "de geste" qui se réclame de la chronique latine de quelque abbaye. Du même coup, il emprunte à Stace un canevas qu'il étrécira ou distendra à sa guise; l'équilibre du récit est bien différent dans les deux oeuvres . . .[23]

Thus, while Raynaud de Lage almost certainly assumed that the *Thèbes* poet was a clerk, in his discussion he does not emphasize the poet's "learning" nor his close dependency on, or even his knowledge of, the *Thebaid*, but rather his freedom from his source and his use of the classical work primarily to give "authority" to his own poem.

Two recent scholars have, however, argued that the *Thèbes* shows direct dependence on the *Thebaid*. L.G. Donovan, in *Recherches sur Le Roman de Thèbes*, expressed the view that the *Thèbes* poet knew the *Thebaid* well, and that the differences between the two works were intentional. Donovan considered, moreover, that our poet was both more faithful to the spirit of the *Thebaid* and more generally learned than is commonly believed. (Donovan thought that the poet also used the *Mythographus secundus*, or a *Thebaid* glossed with that material.) In my view, Donovan's book is perhaps best understood as an *apologia* for the *Thèbes*. He appears to have felt that to show that our poet was "great," he had to show that he was "learned" – and that the considerable differences between his work and his sources were, then, voluntary. Be that as it may, while Donovan thinks that the *Thèbes* poet "avait [la *Thébaïde*] sous les yeux lorsqu'il écrivit le *roman de Thèbes*" (p. 52), he does not deny that our poet is an adapter (p. 63) and an interpreter (p. 29) rather than a true translator in the modern sense. Donovan says that the *Thèbes* poet has "rewritten"

---

23 Jean Frappier and Reinhold R. Grimm, eds., *Grundriss*, Vol. IV: *Le roman jusqu'à la fin du XIIIe siècle*, p. 171.

the *Thebaid* (e.g., p. 64) and he acknowledges that he is showing "similitudes" (e.g., p. 50) rather than true textual parallels.

Aimé Petit, in his recent *Naissances du roman: Les techniques littéraires dans les romans antiques du XIIè siècle*, groups and studies the antique romances together, though he is primarily concerned with the *Thèbes*. Part of his purpose is to show the relationships between the *Thebaid* and the *Thèbes*, and he lays them out at great length and in massive detail, first in over a hundred pages – I, pp. 28–137 – of facing columns which tell the plot and give important details of the two works (in modern French), and then in extensive discussion.[24]

Petit shows that there are many parallels between the two works. But, in Petit's 119-page demonstration of the parallels, the many blanks on one side of the page or the other also show amply that there are also many hundreds of lines of *non*-parallels: there are 36 pages where one side of the page or the other is entirely empty and another 44 pages where it is at least half-white. Thus, in the *Thèbes* numerous things that were present in the *Thebaid* are absent, and many new elements appear.[25] Like Donovan, Petit believes that all these differences are intentional.

Petit considers, moreover, that, despite the differences, the two works are very close together in spirit. Indeed, he asserts that "le poète de *Thèbes* avait sous les yeux le texte de la *Thébaïde* et s'était pénétré de sa substance: il en avait fait la chair de sa chair et le sang de son sang." But perhaps we need to see the entire context for this last assertion:

> La confrontation des deux oeuvres rend évidentes d'incontestables ressemblances. Celles-ci vont bien au delà d'une simple analogie ne concernant que la trame générale du récit. En effet, l'auteur du *Roman de Thèbes* demeure souvent fidèle à sa source à l'occasion d'épisodes ou de détails dont il aurait pu aisément faire l'économie. Si d'autre part – et nous y reviendrons – suppressions, additions, développements, etc. . . . ne manquent pas, il n'en reste pas moins que la multiplicité des rapprochements établis entre l'épopée latine et le roman du XIIe s. prouvent que le poète de *Thèbes* avait sous les yeux le texte de la *Thébaïde* et s'était pénétré de sa substance: il en avait fait la chair de sa chair et le sang de son sang. La prouve aussi l'onomastique [A note here points out that the *Thèbes* contains proper names in Latin and Greek forms: e.g., Adras*us*, Amphiar*as*.] du *Roman de Thèbes*. Le

---

24 I, pp. 21–242. This two-volume thesis comprises 1,454 pages.

25 Petit says, for example: "L'abrègement de la *Thébaïde* par l'auteur du *Roman de Thèbes* se traduit donc par d'importantes suppressions. On a eu souvent tendance à parler d'un *Stace travesti* à propos de *Thèbes*, mais il y a aussi dans ce roman un Stace dépouillé, comme un Stace condensé, et aussi autre chose que Stace. Mais l'un des aspects les plus intéressants de l'adaptation de l'épopée latine par l'auteur de *Thèbes* se manifeste par certaines synthèses. Nous sommes toujours en présence d'une démarche réductrice, mais celle-ci s'opère à partir de plusieurs fragments identiques ou similaires épars dans la source latine. C'est un procédé de fusion et de recomposition" (I, p. 183).

démontrent encore, en dehors des passages signalés en note, nombre de ressemblances ponctuelles si précises que l'on surprend l'écrivain médiéval sur le chemin de la traduction.

Petit attempts to show that the *Thèbes* poet, from time to time, translates short passages directly from the *Thebaid*. Or rather, Petit comes *close* to saying that, at several points, then backs off from the full assertion that the *Thèbes* poet is actually translating. For example, Petit states: "C'est souvent à l'occasion d'épisodes de caractère guerrier que l'auteur de *Thèbes* s'est essayé à traduire la *Thébaïde* (p. 142); at one point... "le récit de Stace nous semble assez exactement transposé pour que le mot traduction vienne à l'esprit" (p. 144); "... l'auteur médiéval peut modifier, transposer, développer certains éléments, mais en même temps, être parfois tenté de traduire *stricto sensu* (p. 148); "Nous constatons en tout cas que ces sept vers du livre VIII de la *Thébaïde* ont été pratiquement traduits" (p. 150).[26]

There are two reasons why Petit may have hesitated to declare outright that the *Thèbes* poet was "translating" the Latin text, but says only that the poet was "tempted" by translation or that "the word translation comes to mind," etc. First, these are very brief passages that we are looking at: a few lines – typically three or four – here and there. (The longest passage which Petit discusses is a 20-line unit from the *Thebaid*, translated, or "transposed," over the course of 37 lines of the *Thèbes*; I, p. 144.) Nor are there many such passages, but just a handful of them.[27] When one is dealing with such small units, it is hard to be sure that one is looking at full-fledged translation. Secondly, since there are so few passages where the question of translation even arises – since so much of the time the *Thèbes* poet is obviously doing anything *but* translating the *Thebaid*[28] – one cannot help but wonder why at some moments he would choose – "be tempted" – to follow the text with some precision.

But let us assume for the sake of argument that some short passages are indeed close to the original Latin. Is the only – or even the *best* – way to account for this occasional proximity to say that the *Thèbes* poet had the

26 In this last passage, Petit goes on to say that "... une faute de lecture (*Culmes*), très précise, nous met en présence du genre d'erreur que ne peut commettre un adaptateur, mais qui est pratiquement le fait d'un traducteur" (I, pp. 150–51). But this error – "Pulmes" as a "mauvaise lecture" of "Culmes," the name of one of the gates of Thebes – does not, in my view, prove that the poet was truly a translator. It does, however, suggest that there may have been garbling in the passing down of the story of Thebes to a medieval story-teller such as our poet.

27 Petit discusses the issue of translation in a chapter of only 20 (dactylographed) pages – and some of the texts discussed are from other antique romances: I, pp. 139–57; the chapter is entitled "La tentation de la traduction."

28 Whether the *Thèbes* poet is very faithful to the spirit of the *Thebaid* seems to be in the eye of the beholder; it is hard to judge this objectively. In any case, many scholars have thought that the two were not particularly close.

Thebaid "sous les yeux"? Let us turn to another hypothesis. Some scholars, including Constans, have believed that while our poet knew the plot of the *Thebaid*, he did not know Statius' poem itself. Thus, he might have read and used some sort of intermediate work. There have been various theories as to just what the poet read: Might it have been a prose summary? Was it in Latin or in the vernacular? No such intermediary written source has, however, ever been found – a fact that is important to Petit's argument that the *Thèbes* poet must actually have known and read the work of Statius for himself (I, p. 23).

But what has made us so sure that the intermediary source has to have been something the poet read himself – therefore, something that we might be able to find (and read) today? How can we be sure he didn't have an oral source? How do we know that he wasn't told the story of the *Thebaid?* In short, between our poet and the *Thebaid* there may have been, not an intermediary textual source, but a middle-man. The poet indeed speaks of an oral – a living – source, and tells his listeners that he has himself heard what he is telling us. For example, discussing a king's son who came to fight in the war he says "Salemandre l'oï nomer" (line 8796: "I heard him called Salemandre").

Let us note that what the poet heard from his oral source (or sources) might have been uneven in a number of respects, which could help account for the variability in the *Thèbes'* faithfulness to its "source."[29] It could, for example, explain why on the one hand the poet knew that Latin male names typically ended in "-us" and Greek names in "-as," but, as we will see shortly – and this strikes me as a fact of *major* consequence – he does not appear to have understood that the "author" of this great story was, in fact, Statius!

My position is not quite as opposed as it might at first blush appear to that of Donovan and Petit. They both want to show that the *Thèbes* poet produced a first-rate work, that he was not an ignorant and careless clerk, that he knew what he was doing. I too believe that this is a beautiful and well-constructed poem, that the poet was not ignorant or careless, that he had poetic intentionality. The only difference – and one may, or may *not*, think of it as fundamental to the honor of this romance and its "author" – is that I consider this poet to have been an excellent *oral*, rather than an excellent *clerkly*, poet.

It is quite true that there has to have been a clerk back there *somewhere*: someone who had read Statius (or a glossed Statius, or a summary of Statius), and who could tell the story to others, such as minstrels. The *Thebaid* was apparently widely read in schools of the period, and 25 manuscripts dating from before the thirteenth century still survive.[30] There would, therefore, have

---

[29] In the course of his study, Petit also shows the many strong links between the *Thèbes* and the tradition of the *chanson de geste* (I, Ch. 4: "Les romans antiques et la chanson de geste," pp. 251–321). If – as I believe to be the case – our poet was a minstrel or *jongleur*, he may well have combined elements from the epic with a narrative line and details provided to him (probably) by a clerk.

[30] See Faral, *Recherches sur les sources latines des contes et romans courtois du moyen*

been no dearth of clerks familiar with Statius. The poet's source may have been such a clerk. But that does not prove that our poet was a clerk himself, or that he had read (or ever seen) Statius' "book."

It might be argued that to compose a story on the Theban War was so clerkly an idea that only a clerk could have had it – that no minstrel could have entertained such a thought. Is an "antique romance" – a romance based on the plot of a Latin epic – a fundamentally bookish project? Yes and no: while the knowledge of the plot and the characters, names virtually has to have come from a clerk, many a minstrel might have recognized the appeal of the story itself – as well as the attractiveness of having a story to tell that was at once "new" and considered "authoritative"! As we will see, this and other "classical" stories and names soon became part of the minstrel repertory.

Clerks and minstrels in twelfth century courts

How likely is it that court minstrels were in contact with clerks in the mid-twelfth century? It is more than likely; it is, I think we can safely say, certain. Let us stop a moment and look at an extraordinary development of the twelfth century, and reflect upon its ramifications for the study of literature and the other arts as well. In this period, there begins to be present in noble courts what we today might call a "critical mass" of secular clerks. Many noble courts had also long had a relatively close association with churchmen and with religious women through relatives who were bishops, priors and monks, nuns, and the like, but we are looking at something different here: clerks not as clergy but rather as scribes, readers, and archivists. This new trend was particularly marked in the Anglo-Norman court: M.T. Clanchy has noted the fundamental involvement of the Anglo-Norman monarchy with documents, which of course require clerks to produce and handle them.[31]

But even on the continent, outside of the Anglo-Norman ambit, by the mid-twelfth century the presence of clerks in courts had risen to remarkable new levels: the development of new schools was both a cause of and a response to this new demand for archivists, and to the growing interest in texts and documents.[32] Nor were many of these clerks narrow or purely other-worldly in

---

âge, p. 400; Donovan, *Recherches sur le Roman de Thèbes*, pp. 21–22. See also Curtius, *European Literature and the Latin Middle Ages*, pp. 48–52.

[31] Clanchy connects the (new) English involvement in documents – and consequent need for clerks – with the Norman Conquest: *From Memory to Written Record*, pp. 5ff.

[32] See, e.g., Georges Duby, "The Culture of the Knightly Class: Audience and Patronage." In "The Court of Champagne as a Literary Center" John Benton focuses on a slightly later period than that at which the *Thèbes* was presumably composed, but there is no reason to suppose that the role played by clerics and ecclesiastics in the court of Henry the "Liberal" of Champagne and his wife Marie would have been markedly different a decade

their functions: Guibert of Nogent taught *honestas* and *exterior elegantia* at the court of the Lords of Clermont.[33] And, as Elizabeth Salter has said:

> When we find expressions and attitudes common to Latin, English, French, and German poetry, it is only necessary to remember that the contacts between various classes of mediaeval poets and singers were lively and continuous. Minstrel, cleric, and courtier met naturally at ecclesiastical or royal court, at cathedral school or university.[34]

Let us set this issue – this relationship among nobles, clerks and minstrels – into the framework of a current debate. Scholars who study the rise of courtliness and chivalry are in some disagreement as to the relative impact of Christian (in particular, monastic) ideals and classical concepts on older feudal patterns. C. Stephen Jaeger, for example, takes up these issues in his *The Origins of Courtliness: Civilizing Trends and the Formation of Courtly Ideals, 939–1210.*[35] However one wishes to resolve the issue, the point that interests us here is that either Christian/monastic or classical ideas (or a blend of the two) were somehow brought home to the lay nobility, the vast majority of whom could not read. This happened primarily in court, and court minstrels are presumably one of the major conduits for this transmission of lore and values – clerks being the other.

Can our poet have been a vernacular literary author? Thus we might imagine him as a poet/entertainer literate in French who had read, perhaps, a vernacular prose summary of the *Thebaid*. This possibility seems unlikely for two reasons: first, the phenomenon of the literate minstrel – the professional poet/performer able to read (and write) French – is one for which I know of no firm evidence before the thirteenth century, and none as early as this. Moreover, as we saw in Chapter 1, we have every reason to think that vernacular prose in France did not emerge before the very end of the twelfth century.[36] In short, this hypothesis – a vernacular reader *cum* writer – does not appear to be the solution.

But let us raise here another important cultural issue: that of the collaboration in this period between *clercs* on the one hand and, on the other, master craftsmen in the various arts, including the arts of language. Let us shift our gaze to the world of architecture, in particular, to the building of the great

---

or two earlier. Moreover, there is no evidence of *clercs* producing works in the vernacular in this court – only in Latin.

[33] Jaeger, *Envy of Angels*, p. 296. As I noted earlier, some noble households employed tutors or chaplains to teach grammar and other rudiments of clerical knowledge.

[34] "The Mediaeval Lyric," p. 454.

[35] See especially the preface. Other works relating to these issues are Maurice Keen, *Chivalry*; Duby, *The Chivalrous Society*.

[36] See, e.g., Godzich and Kittay, *The Emergence of Prose: An Essay in Prosaics*, pp. xiii–xv.

cathedrals, starting in the mid-twelfth. There is no evidence that the master masons and the other major artisans who constructed these extraordinary edifices were themselves clerks – and on the face of the evidence, it would seem unlikely that they were. (Masons and builders received practical training; school learning is quite a different sort of education.)[37] What is certain is that these builders and sculptors were fed technological, symbolic and iconographic information of one kind or another by the churchmen who acted as their advisors, and often employers.[38] In some cases these master-masons not only worked but also lived in close proximity with *clercs* and churchmen. The master mason at Amiens in the mid-thirteenth century is known to have lived in the bishop's manse.[39] Furthermore, it seems clear that the technology which allowed the extraordinary new developments of Gothic architecture was not clerically generated or dominated. It is clear from the very fact that for the new architectural techniques, such as the growing use of flying buttresses, there are no written records: this new technology was, it appears, transmitted orally, and not through Latin – "clerical" – treatises or manuals.[40]

Granted, the *Roman de Thèbes* is not a literary "cathedral": it was not produced with church patronage and public support to the glory of God. But I think we might envision, here and elsewhere, something of the same sort of collaboration between highly talented artists, such as our poet, and clerical "advisors." Artisans of the word, as well as those who worked in stone, were

[37] In *The Contractors of Chartres*, Vol. 2, pp. 541–56, John James states: "Out of a total of some 1200 identifiable English architects of the middle ages only eighteen could possibly have been clerics. This is why 'the literary sources for that period, compiled almost entirely by clerics, are so uninformative as to architectural methods, however much detail they might give as to the history of the particular building works and architects; the clerks could not tell us the answers because they did not know them themselves.' " (p. 545; the quotation in the text comes from Harvey, *The Medieval Architect*, London, 1972, pp. 81 and 104).

[38] See Jean Gimpel, *The Cathedral Builders*. It does not even seem clear that the famous thirteenth century builder and architect Villard de Honnecourt (whose sketchbooks, full of interesting lore, we still have today) was a *clerc*; Gimpel suggests that "presumably" he learned his science in school (p. 100), but Villard's sketchbooks are written in French, and nothing proves that he attended school. To be literate in the vernacular does not, of course, mean that one is a *clerc*, or that one has been to school. By the thirteenth century, many a minstrel, for example, was apparently able to read, and presumably write, French. For artisans in many professions, by the thirteenth century reading (and writing) had presumably become trade skills. Gimpel himself states: "It cannot be claimed that Villard, or other architects of his time, had a very thorough comprehension of geometry, trigonometry or algebra; learning for these builders must have been above all empirical" (101). And Gimpel considers that although sculptors came into contact with "the intellectual world" it was through personal contact with theologians and through the opportunity of looking at (not reading!) beautiful manuscripts: not by going to school themselves (85).

[39] See Stephen Murray, "Plan and Space at Amiens Cathedral," p. 45.

[40] William W. Clark, lecture at New York University, March 27, 1990: "Notre Dame de Paris: The Rapid Spread of Technology in the Gothic Period."

capable of making innovative use of the knowledge now available to them thanks to the presence of *clercs* in their midst.

But although this scenario is possible, in point of fact we do not need conscious or willing collaboration between a minstrel and a clerk in order to account for the knowledge found in the *Thèbes*: clerkly lore was, by the mid-twelfth century, conceptually available in court settings – there for minstrels to draw upon and use. Surely the longest and richest example of this "availability" comes from the *Flamenca* (early thirteenth century).[41] In this remarkable occitan romance, in a long passage where the performance repertory of minstrels and *jongleurs* is being evoked in the context of an elaborate wedding feast, we find the following:

> Qui volc ausir diverses comtes
> de reis, de marques et de comtes,
> auzir ne poc tant can si volc;
> anc null'aurella non lai colc,
> quar l'us comtet de Priamus,
> et l'autre diz de Piramus;
> l'us comtet de la bell'Elena
> com Paris l'enquer, pois l'anmena;
> l'autres comtava d'Ulixes,
> l'autre d'Ector e d'Achilles;
> l'autre comtava d'Eneas
> e de Dido, consi remas
> per lui dolenta e mesquina;
> l'autre comtava de Lavina,
> con fes lo breu el cairel traire
> a la gaita de l'auzor caire;
> l'us comtet Pollinices,
> de Tideu e d'Etïocles;
> l'autres comtava d'Apolloine,
> consi retenc Tyr et Sidoine;
> l'us comtet de rei Alexandri,
> l'autre d'Ero e de Leandri;
> l'us diz de Catmus can fugi
> e de Tebas con las basti;
> l'autre comtava de Jason
> e del dragon que non hac son. . . .   lines 621–46[42]

(Whoever wished to hear different tales/ of kings, earls and counts/ could hear of them as much as was desired;/ no ear was sleeping there,/ for one told of Priam,/ and another spoke of

---

[41] Also see Chapter 6 for evidence that "antique" material was part of the repertory of the *ménestrel* and *jongleur*.

[42] *The Romance of Flamenca*, ed. and trans. by E.D. Blodgett. I cite Blodgett's translation.

Piramus;/ one told of beautiful Helen,/ how Paris wooed her and took her away;/ another told of Ulysses;/ another, of Hector and Achilles;/ another told of Aeneas/ and of Dido, how she remained/ unhappy because of him and full of grief; another told of Lavinia,/ how she had the letter sent by an arrow/ shot by the watchman on high;/ one told of Polynices,/ of Tydeus and Eteocles;/ another told of Apollonius,/ how he possessed Tyr and Sidon;/ one told of King Alexander;/ another of Hero and Leander;/ one spoke of Cadmus when he fled/ and of Thebes and how he built it; another told of Jason/ and the dragon that never napped. . . .)

There is, then, evidence that "clerkly," "bookish" stories became part of the minstrel repertory. The fact that our poet had acquired considerable familiarity with the story of the *Thebaid* does not appear compelling as an argument for his own *clergie*.

What makes the poet's clerical status still less convincing is the fact that while he does mention the name Statius in the context of a particular description, he seems not to understand that Statius is the author of – or the *auctor* behind – his story as a whole. To quote the passage in question: the poet is describing a marvelous cup presented to Polinices by his prisoner, the young son of Darius the Red:

A tant la cope li presente.
Cil prent la cope, l'uevre mire:
Nus hon n'en sét la façon dire.
Si com dit li livre d'Estace,
Li pomeaus en fu d'un topace:
Onque nus hon ne vit son pér:
Ne si bien assis ne tant clér . . .   lines 7820–26 [7459–66]

(Immediately he gives him the cup/ He [Polinices] takes the cup, and marvels at the work[manship]:/ No man knows how to tell its fashioning./ As the book of Statius says,/ The pommel was a topaz:/ No man ever saw its like:/ Neither so well-set or so clear . . .)

In this description – and piece of name-dropping – several features are of interest. First, this is the only reference to Statius – or rather to "Estace," identical in Old French to some forms of the name "Eustache" – in the 10,000-line romance as constituted by Constans.[43] Moreover, this reference

---

43 In this instance manuscript C, used by Raynaud de Lage, seems a bit more "clerical": it has two other, minor, references to Statius. This is the first: the poet is speaking of some games being played and declares "Si conme Estace le raconte, . . ." (line 2749). The second reference is of a similar nature – except that Statius is called "Huitasses." This is a passage concerning a surprise attack by the Greeks on Thebes (more on this passage later);

occurs in a weak place: neither at the beginning nor at the end, nor yet at the middle (all these points being dear to us literary scholars), but about three-quarters of the way through the romance. Also, the authority of *Estace* is brought in exclusively with respect to the placement of a topaz in the pommel of a cup – a trivial detail – and not in regard to the vast story as a whole. The poet does not say that he personally has read the book of *Estace* (I do not give my solemn oath that I would believe him if he did say so), but only, and more "orally," that Statius' book says this.[44] Finally, this description which draws its authority from Statius, is not in fact *in* Statius. This entire passage was added by our poet, or it came from some other poet or work. Renate Blumenfeld-Kosinski has addressed the curious – and very limited – use to which the *Thèbes* poet puts the name of Statius: that the poet does not mention Statius in his prologue, but only later, and in the context of passages that do not actually come from Statius. For Blumenfeld-Kosinski, the poet is consciously freeing himself from the power of his "auctor." But there is another interpretation: that the poet did not understand – or perhaps care? – that Statius *was* the authority behind this story.[45]

Another important passage that has served to convince readers of the poet's clerical status is the one where he describes the images of the Liberal Arts on, and drops some other prestigious names with regard to, a marvelous chariot belonging to the pagan priest Amphiareus. This passage is worth a careful look. I will also compare it shortly with another, unquestionably learned, discussion of the Arts, and in the next chapter with Chrétien de Troyes's handling of the same material. Our poet has spent many lines describing this

---

the relevant section reads: "... si conmne Huitasses le descrit/ qui le voir en sot bien et dit,/ et je, s'il vous i plest entendre,/ vous en sai bien la cause rendre" (lines 8905–8: ... just as "Huitasses" described it,/ who knew the truth well and told it,/ and I, if it pleases you to hear it,/ know how to give you an account of it).

In any event, the form "Huitasses" appears derived from, or a variant form of, the name "Eustace" rather than "Statius." And "Huitasses" is described as someone who knows the truth and tells things – not as a writer.

44 There is another, similar reference to books in the C manuscript: early in the romance, Oedipus goes to speak to "dant Appolo" (lord Apollo) to ask whose son he is. He goes to the sea of Galilee: there "fu fet un temple par Nature,/ ce nos enseigne l'escriture./ Delfox a non, ce dit la lettre." (176–79; "there was a temple made by Nature,/ writing [Scripture? the written text?] teaches us this./ It had the name Delphos, so says the letter.") But, as I have argued extensively elsewhere (see articles cited above and in the Bibliography), this sort of reference to "written authority" should not be construed as a personal claim that the poet himself has read the "letters" in question (or indeed that he can read). "The letter tells *us*" – the "us" and the "tells" are, I think, important. In a word, such a reference only means that behind this story – *somewhere* behind it – stands written *auctoritas*.

45 Renate Blumenfeld-Kosinski, "Old French Narrative Genres: Toward the Definition of the *Roman Antique*", esp. pp. 153ff.

chariot, covered with marvelous images. He finally reaches the rear of the chariot:

> Et a pierres et a esmaus
> Fu faiz deriére li frontaus,
> Et enlevees les set arz:
> Gramaire i est peinte o ses parz,
> Dialetique o argumenz
> Et Rhetorique o jugemenz;
> L'abaque tient Arimetique,
> Par la game chante musique;
> Peint i est Diatessaron,
> Diapenté, Diapason;
> Une verge o Geometrie,
> Un astrelabe Astronomie:
> L'une en terre met sa mesure,
> L'autre es esteiles a sa cure.
> El curre ot mout sotil entaille:
> Bien fu ovrez, onc n'i ot faille. . . .
>
> lines 4749–64 [4987–5002]

(And with stones and enamels/ Was made the front of the rear part [of the chariot]/ And the seven arts:/ Grammar is painted there with her parts,/ Dialectic with arguments/ And Rhetoric with judgments;/ Arithmetic holds an abacus,/ Music sings through the scale;/ Diatessaron is painted there,/ Diapente, Diapason;/ Geometry with a rod,/ Astronomy, an astrolabe;/ The one measures the earth,/ The other has charge of the stars./ On the chariot was much subtle carving:/ It was well worked, there was no fault in it. . . .)

Just how much does one have to know about the Liberal Arts to produce such a description? In my view, not a great deal, and certainly not a full course of study in the subject – any more than an imaginative science-fiction writer today would need a doctorate in academic science. The poet knows the names of the arts. For each he offers another word or object associated with that art: Grammar has "parts," Geometry has a "rod," and so on. As to Diatessaron, Diapente, and Diapason: they refer, respectively, to the musical consonances (as defined by Boethius and many other writers) of 4 to 3, 3 to 2, and 2 to 1. The simplest way to depict these fairly abstract concepts was to divide a line, representing the string on a monochord. Several kinds of theoretical diagrams of these intervals existed in medieval encyclopedias (such as that of Isidore of Seville, in the Spanish recension) and in music texts, as for the monastic clergy.[46] Such images, like most diagrams, are by no means self-explanatory to

---

[46] See, e.g., Guido Aretinus, *Micrologus*, ed. Jos. Smits van Waesberghe, pp. 129, 166. My special thanks to Edward Roesner for his help in this section.

the inexpert viewer. As our poet gives us neither clear visual image nor explanation, and as it is likely that his audience was for the most part unfamiliar with the terms in question, he seems to be attempting not to enlighten, but rather to impress. This is, then, name-dropping – and it makes perfect sense in the context of the description of a marvel. (The *Thèbes* poet, like many other twelfth century poets, loves to describe marvels; my personal favorite is the horse that is part sea-monster: lines 6005ff.)

It is not at all certain that the poet himself knows what the words in the description provided mean. This impression is confirmed by the verbal association that he provides for Rhetoric: "her judgments." This odd term may point to someone without serious formation in Rhetoric. It is not that Rhetoric is free of judgments, and of course "Judicial Rhetoric" is one of the three great branches of Rhetoric[47] – but judgment, strictly speaking, is not a key term or a major issue in that art. It is however possible that the poet understands Rhetoric – and Dialectic as well – in feudal terms: as providing the discourse for the judgments, and the arguments, offered by powerful vassals to their lord. (We will see such a reference shortly.)

The *Thèbes* poet does, of course, know a number of things: he knows that the "Seven Arts" exist; he knows their names; he can provide one (or more) word or object in association with each. But surely all it takes to "invent" the material for such a description is a brief colloquy – a chat – with a clerk such as I have hypothesized. And it is worth noting that the Liberal Arts were very much in fashion in the twelfth century: more precisely, they had been of interest in clerical circles since Carolingian times, but in the eleventh and twelfth centuries the Arts became attractive as a concept with the laity; Countess Adela of Blois had the Liberal Arts carved on her bed.[48]

In his recent study, *The Envy of Angels: Cathedral Schools and Social Ideals in Medieval Europe, 950–1200*, C. Stephen Jaeger documents the fact that, through the eleventh century and into the early twelfth century, the Liberal Arts were seen primarily in ethical and humanistic terms, but that in the twelfth century a new – scientific, rationalistic, and text-oriented – way of thinking about them emerged, which looked on the previous view as old-fashioned.[49] It is worth noting that, in the representation of the Arts that we find in the *Thèbes*, there is nothing remotely rationalistic or textual; I am not inclined to think of "measuring the earth" as scientific. Insofar as we go beyond purely rudimentary details, we find only ethical concerns ("jugements" and "arguments") and care and governance (Astronomy has the "esteiles a sa cure").

[47] See [Cicero], *Ad Herennium*, pp. 5–153.
[48] Jaeger, *Envy of Angels*, p. 167.
[49] Jaeger, *Envy of Angels*, e.g., pp. 130, 170–71, 177, 236, 325; and *passim*.

This description is only modestly iconographic;[50] on the whole, it seems more verbal and conceptual than visual. While it would not be hard to show Geometry with her rod, or Astronomy with her astrolabe, it is far from clear how one would paint or carve Grammar's "parts," or Dialectic's "arguments," or Rhetoric's "judgments," or Music's "scale" (she holds no instruments here). It is nonetheless possible – from a comment that the poet makes toward the beginning of his description of the chariot – that he had at least some of these things shown to him from illuminated books or other images. After telling us that Vulcan made the chariot and put onto it the moon, the sun and the nine spheres, along with the constellations and the stars, and painted on it the land and the sea, filled with men and beasts, the poet says:

> Qui de fisique sot entendre,
> Es peintures pot mout aprendre.   lines 4729–30

> (He who knew how to learn about the physical world,/ Could
> learn much from paintings.)

This idea that one can learn a great deal about the world from looking at pictures – and perhaps by implication that it is not necessary to be able to read books? – is surely a provocative one: it echoes the important saying, attributed to Gregory the Great, that pictures are the books of the illiterate.

We seem to have two different kinds of "learning" in this work, and a certain tension between them. There are things that seem to have been told or explained to the poet but that he may never have seen (such as the Liberal Arts); and there are things that have been shown him in books but whose full conceptual meaning may elude him. In other words, some of the descriptions here seem largely verbal, others largely visual. The two sorts of description are not in synch, and neither reveals a very thorough mastery of the concepts at hand.

It will be illuminating to compare the handling of the Liberal Arts as we find them here in the *Thèbes* with their treatment in a thirteenth century French translation of the famous mid-twelfth century Latin work commonly referred

---

50 There is, of course, an iconographic tradition of representations of the Liberal Arts. See Emile Mâle, *The Gothic Image: Religious Art in France of the Thirteenth Century*, pp. 77ff; Adolph Katzenellenbogen, *The Sculptural Programs of Chartres Cathedral*, pp. 15ff; see also E.R. Curtius, *European Literature and the Latin Middle Ages*, pp. 36–45. But insofar as there are any iconographic implications in the enumeration we are looking at in the *Thèbes*, they appear to be unrelated to iconographic tradition: for example, on the archivolts at Chartres: "Grammar is teaching two boys, Rhetoric is speaking, Geometry is tracing figures on a tablet, Astronomy is contemplating the sky, and Music is playing instruments. The attribute of Arithmetic no longer exists. Only Dialectic is characterized by symbols of good and evil, a flower and a dragon-like creature with the head of a dog" (Katzenellenbogen, p. 21).

to as the *Pseudo-Turpin*, itself inspired by the *Chanson de Roland*.[51] The narrative context for this description of the Liberal Arts is as follows: after Roncevaux, Charlemagne returns to Aix where he builds a church and has it painted with images from the Old and New Testaments, the battles he won in Spain, and the Liberal Arts.

[ch.] XXXI

Premieremant i est escrite et pointe logique qui est mere de toutes les autres arts, qui anseigne quantes letres sont et qu'elez senefient, et qui aprant a escrivre, et par quantes letres les pars sunt et les sillabes devoient estre escrites, et an quel leu l'an doit metre diptonge, et les deus livres d'ostographe qui sont premerein antre tous les autres et demostrent droit, quar "orto" an grieu, ce est "droit" [. . .], si est a dire ortographi autretant comme droite escriture. Par ce antandent li cher an Seinte Iglise que il lisent; et qui n'a cest et il lit, il n'antant neiant, antreci comme cil qui a la clef de huche fermee et ne set qu'il a dedans.

Musique i fu pointe, qui es sciance de chanter bien et droit, par quoi li services se Seinte Iglise est celebrés et ambelis de que l'an la doit avoir plus chiere, et doit l'an chanter par musique par quatre lignes seulement. Iceste arz fu trovee premierement par la voiz des anges car livres dou sacrement dit: "Ha! sire Dieus, nos te prions que tu reçoives nos voiz avec les vois des anges." An cest art si a molt de grans sacremans et grans sinificacions quar les quatre lignes i sont et les .viii. tonz. Les .iiii. lignes sont les .iiii. principaus vertuz d'ome, et sanz, force, atrampance, jotise; et li .viii. tonz sont les .viii. bones aürtés de que nos ames seront esnorees an jor dou jugement.

Dyalectique i est pointe, qui ansoigne a devisier le voir dou fauz et a desputer de parole et de science.

Rectorique i est poite, qui ansoigne a parler a droit. "Rectos" an grieu ce est an "amparlerz." Iceste arz fist home bien parler.

Gyometrie i fu pointe si com ele aprant les autres a mesurer. "Ge" an grieu c'est "terre" et "metros" c'est "mesure." Iceste ars ansoigne a mesurer toute hautace, toute longor. Par ceste art souloient li hauz homes de Rome mesurer les cités et les liucs d'une cité a autre, et li fillz Israel an mesurerent ja dis la terre, par corde, desirree, de droite livree. Et li vilains en mesuroient lor terres et lor près et lor bois.

Arimatique i est pointe qui parole de tout nombre. Qui bien la sait, s'il veoit un haut mur, il diroit bien quantes pierres il i auroit, quantes gotes il ai an ploin basin d'aue, ou quans donier il aura an un moncel, ou quanz home il aura an un ost. Par cest art font ancore li maçons lor hantes torz, ja soit ce que il n'an saichent rien.

Astrenomie i fu pointe, que l'an apele ancerchement des estoilles, par que l'an set quel bien et quel mal doivent avenir ou sont a venir. Chascune des .vii. ai une fille, c'est un livres qui de lui parole. Nicromance de cui naissent piromance et ydromance, et lou livre neiant sacré mes escomenié ne fu mie

---

[51] *La traduction du Pseudo-Turpin du Manuscrit Vatican Regina 624*, ed. Claude Buridant, pp. 119–20.

pointe por ce que ele est ligiere et de legier la puet l'an savoir; mais nus n'an puet ovrer fors par diauble, por ce est apelee ars avoutre et son non li preuve: "manci" a gris est devinaille, "nigros" ce est noir, si est nigromance a dire autretant comme "noire adevinaille." "Poyros," en gré, ce est adevinaille de feu, "ydromancia" d'eve. Li commancemans de nigromance est tiex: "Ci commance la mort de l'ame."

[ch.] XXXI

First is written and painted there logic, which is the mother of all the other arts, which teaches what the letters are and what they mean, and which teaches how to write, and how the parts are written, and how syllables should be written, and where to put the diphthong, and the two books of orthography which are first before all others and which show what is "right," for "ortho" in Greek means "right" [. . .], so orthography means "correct writing." By this [art] clerks in Holy Church understand what they read, and he who does not have this art, when he reads, he understands nothing, like him who has the key to a locked cupboard and does not know what is inside.

Music was painted there, which is the science of singing well and properly, by which the service of Holy Church is celebrated and embellished, for which one should hold [this art] dear, and one should sing in music with only four lines. This art was first found by the voice of angels, for the book of the sacrament says: "O! Lord God, we pray that you may receive our voices with the voices of the angels." In this art are many great sacraments and great meanings, for there are four lines [of musical notation] and eight tones. The four lines are the four principal virtues of man: sense [reason?], strength, temperance, and justice; and the eight tones are the eight good gifts [lit. "happinesses"] with which our souls will be honored on Judgment Day.

Dialectic is painted there, which teaches how to distinguish the true from the false, and how to argue in words, and with knowledge.

Rhetoric is painted there, which teaches how to speak properly. "Rectos" in Greek means "well-spoken." This art makes men speak well.

Geometry was painted there, and she teaches how to measure. "Ge" in Greek is "earth," and "metros" is "measure." This art teaches how to measure every height, every length. By this art, the men of Rome used to measure their cities and the distance from one city to another, and the sons of Israel measured, in their day, the earth with pieces of rope in proper units. And peasants measured their lands and their fields and their woods.

Arithmetic is painted there, which speaks of all numbers. He who knows this art well, if he saw a high wall, he would know how many stones were in it, how many drops there were in a basin full of water, and how many coins will be in a pile, or how many men there will be in an army. It is by this art that masons still build their high towers, although they don't know it.

Astronomy was painted there, that is called the searching of the stars, because one knows what good and evil must happen or are to come. Each of the seven has a daughter, which is a book which speaks of it. Necromancy from which are born piromancy and hydromancy, and the book in no way sacred but condemned, was not painted there because it is simple and easily may one know it; but no one can open it except by the devil, because it is called an adulterous art and its name proves it: "manci" is Greek for "fortune-telling," "nigros" is black, so necromancy means "black fortune-telling." "Poyros," in Greek, is fortune-telling with fire, "hydromancia" by water. The beginning of necromancy is thus: "Here begins the death of the soul.")

This representation of the Liberal Arts, as translated from the *Pseudo-Turpin*, is even less visual than the images evoked by the *Thèbes* poet, though in both cases we are ostensibly dealing with pictures. But whatever else can be said about this text, it is not only substantially more ample and informed than what we saw in the *Thèbes*, it is genuinely explanatory. It is also a great deal more involved in matters of reading and writing – indeed, in *correct* reading and writing: thus, for example, reading with the proper understanding, and writing with proper spelling.

We return to the *Thèbes* poet, as "trouvère" and "ménestrel." In the elaboration of this hypothesis, I may seem to be abandoning the venerable principle of parsimony, whereby the simplest explanation for a phenomenon is generally the best: if we need a clerk, why not assume that the poet himself is he? But there is not only further negative evidence against our poet's *clergie*, there is significant positive evidence for his non-literate minstrel condition. The hypothesis proposed here is ultimately the most parsimonious, in that it allows us to account, in the case of the *Thèbes* and in a good many other works as well, for all the evidence: for the strange, and otherwise inexplicable, blend of learned and unlearned, "written" and "oral" elements in the work.

Further negative evidence for *clergie*, and internal evidence for minstrelsy in the *Roman de Thèbes*

Early in his *Roman de Troie*, Benoît described Homer as a clerk: "Omers, qui fu clerc merveillos/ E sages e esciëntos . . ." (lines 45–46: "Homer, who was a marvellous clerk/ And wise and full of knowledge"). But for the *Thèbes* poet Homer is a "lord." So are Plato, Virgil and Cicero.

> Qui sages est nel deit celer,
> Ainz por ço deit son sen monstrer,
> Que, quant serra del siécle alez,
> En seit pués toz jorz remembrez.
> Se danz Homers et danz Platon
> Et Vergiles et Ciceron
> Lor sapience celissant,
> Ja ne fust d'eus parlé avant.
> Por ço ne vueil mon sens taisir,
> Ma sapience retenir;

Ainz me delét a aconter
Chose digne de remembrer.
Or s'en voisent de tot mestier,
Se ne sont clerc o chevalier,
Car aussi pueent escouter
Come li asnes al harper.
Ne parlerai de peletiers,
Ne de vilains, ne de berchiers;
Mais de dous fréres vos dirai,
Et lor geste raconterai.
Li uns ot non Ethioclès,
Et li autres Polinicès . . .   lines 1–21 [1–21]

(He who is wise should not hide it./ But for that [reason: his wisdom] should show his good sense/ So that when he will have gone from the world,/ He may always be remembered./ If lord Homer and lord Plato/ And Virgil and Cicero/ Had hidden their wisdom,/ Never would they have been spoken of again./ For this reason I do not wish to silence my sense,/ To hold back my wisdom;/ Rather it pleases me to relate/ Something worthy of being remembered./ Now they should leave right away,/ Those who are not clerks or knights,/ For they [these others] listen/ As the ass listens to the harp./ I will not speak of tanners,/ Nor of peasants nor of shepherds;/ But I will tell you about two brothers,/ And I will recount their deeds./ One had the name Etiocles/ And the other Polynices . . .)

Homer and Plato are, then, "wise lords" – and later, our poet will give the latter as a "cousin" to a particularly wise warrior, Otes: line 3532. Does this emphasis on wisdom and on the duty to speak it forth make it certain that the poet is a clerk: the speaker a scholar, a writer? But oral culture has also had a deep preoccupation with wisdom.[52] It is often said that wisdom is a learned topos,[53] but a variety of "ensenhaments" by *jongleurs* – most particularly, the famous "Abril issi'e" by Raimon Vidal[54] – emphasize heavily and repeatedly, the importance of *sagesse* for *jongleurs*, as well.

Here, unlike the *Troie*, wisdom is not associated with reading, writing, and books. Nor is there any connection here between the desire to be remembered – to tell memorable stories – and writing. True, the poet says that everyone who

52 See, e.g., Ong, *Orality and Literacy: The Technologizing of the Word*. For example, the very "conservativeness" of oral tradition (pp. 41–42) – and the status this accords to old people – connects it fundamentally to wisdom.
Moreover, oral traditions contain many proverbs and various forms of gnomic wisdom.

53 See, for example, G. Hilty, "Zum Erec-Prolog."

54 "Abril issi'e e mays intrava" ("Avril s'en allait et mai arrivait, de Raimon Vidal de Besalù") in Jean-Charles Huchet, ed. and trans., *Nouvelles occitanes du Moyen Age*, pp. 38–139.

is not a clerk or a knight should leave the room, but he is presumably at court where, as regards the male population, only those two groups would be represented. (There were assuredly women present as well; that is not the issue.) We need not therefore imagine tanners, peasants, and shepherds actually being compelled to rise and skulk from the hall. This is a rhetorical flourish – and one that does not prove that our poet was a clerk himself. This statement should be interpreted as an advertisement for this as a high-tone work – and indeed it is one. These words also serve to remind us (if we had forgotten) that *clercs* were present at festivities in French courts; they suggest as well that our poet thought French noblemen would be gratified to be able to share entertainment appropriate to learned men, and that clerks would be pleased to listen to the story. Such are the advantages of telling an epic story with antique material.

Unlettered wisdom and eloquence provide a central theme, and ideal, to this work. Many characters are described as wise and are praised for their ability to speak persuasively. All through the work we are told about men (kings, lords, knights: all warriors) and ladies, not one of whom is said to be able to read, but all of whom are wise and eloquent. A handful of important examples:

— Oedipus, the two brothers' father, was (though he never went to school) "of deep wisdom" (line 293): he answered the riddle of the Sphinx, presented here as a demon.

— King Adrastus, the father-in-law of Polyneices, and a major character in the work, is described thus: "Adrastus est reis de nature,/ Sages de sen et de mesure . . ." (lines 3298–99): "Adrastus is a king by nature,/ Wise of sense and of measure . . ." Indeed, the poet declares at one point: "Plus sage home ne sai del rei" (line 6727): "I do not know a wiser man than the king."

— Jocasta, too, is praised at several points for her wisdom: "Jocaste fu et proz et sage . . ." (line 3779): "Jocasta was both bold and wise . . ." She goes as a wise messenger, with good counsel, to the court of Adrastus (lines 3780ff).

— Creon, one of the great lords in the feudal counsel of Etiocles, is described in these terms:

> Creon li vieuz et li antis
> De jugement fu bien apris:
> En la cort se drece en estant,
> En sa main destre tint son guant.
> De raison fu bien doctrinez:
> "Seignor," dist il, "or m'escoutez. . . ."
>
> lines 8341–46 [7925ff[55]]

(Creon, the old and ancient,/ In judgment was well taught:/ In the court he stands up,/ In his right hand he held his glove./ He

---

[55] In the C manuscript Creon is not called "doctrinez" and the entire development is a bit different.

was well taught in speaking ["reasoning"]:/ "Lords," he said,
"now listen to me. . . .")

Obviously, the "well-taught" and "well-indoctrinated" Creon has not
studied Rhetoric at Paris, Troyes or Oxford; he is not a clerk but a great feudal
baron. What is interesting is that, in the mid-twelfth century, expressions such
as "bien apris," "doctrinez," and the like could be applied to noblemen who
were particularly wise and eloquent.[56]

I am tempted to postulate a general "theorem": works composed by clerks
– and, more generally by literate, written-text-producing poets – tend to
include at least some literate characters. To take the case of Benoît: aside from
presenting himself as a learned *persona*, he also claims that Dares and Dictys
were, both of them, at once great warriors and great "clercs"; indeed he
presents them as his literary sources: lines 91ff; 24,397ff. It is as though such
writers inserted into the text a *mise en abysme* of their own exalted literate
status. The contrary theorem does not, however, appear reliably to hold true:
that is, even non-clerical – and non-literate – poets can throw into their stories a
few literate characters to look good, as it were: to seem *à la page*, once the
status of books, letters, and literacy becomes clear. Thus Béroul puts into his
Tristan story the prestigious and kindly letter-writing hermit Ogrin, as well as
the learned but wicked Frocin. One might perhaps take this pair – the learned
and good hermit and the learned and evil dwarf – as embodying the ambivalence of Béroul (and others?) toward the intrusion of reading and writing into
what had long been an essentially oral vernacular world. At any rate, the total
absence of literates in a story appears to be more telling of minstrelsy than a
handful of *clercs* and *briefs* does of *clergie*.

In this work, not merely are many (apparently) unschooled characters
praised for their wisdom and eloquence. *Not one* important character in this
romance is spoken of as, or praised for being, literate: *no one* ever, at any point,
reads anything or even mentions books. Again, by contrast, in the *Troie* such
references are fairly common. For example, in the *Troie*, at one point we are
told that Diomedes "A sei meïsmes pense e dit:/ "De mei n'iert ja feit bon
escrit/ Ne chantee bone chançon" lines 20237–39 ("He thinks to himself and
says: "About me nothing good will ever be written, nor any good song sung").
Benoît's Diomedes wants to inspire not just heroic songs but heroic books. He
wants at least part of his posthumous reputation to be "literary."

In the *Thèbes* even those figures whom one might normally expect to be
referred to by a medieval poet as literate, are not. This is, in my view, a significant fact. Let's look back at Amphiareus, whose artful chariot was described
above. He is a pagan priest, indeed an archbishop. Here is how he is introduced:

---

[56] On this issue of oral knightly eloquence, see Clanchy, *From Memory*, pp. 248–50.

> Amphiaras manda li reis,
> Un arcevesque mout corteis:
> Cil esteit maistre de lor lei,
> Del ciel saveit tot le secrei;
> Il prent respons et giéte sorz
> Et revivre fait homes morz;
> De toz oiseaus sot le latin,
> Soz ciel n'aveit meillor devin . . .   lines 2025–32 [2055–62]

(The king sent for Amphiareus,/ A very courtly archbishop:/ He was the master of their religion,/ He knew all the secrets of heaven/ He receives answers [from the gods] and casts lots/ And makes dead men live again;/ He knew the language ["Latin"] of all birds,/ Under heaven there was no better seer . . .)

The archbishop Amphiareus is, then, the "master of their law," and an immensely learned man – but the only "Latin" he is described as knowing is that of birds. (Birds are often described in medieval works as singing in "Latin" – which may mean discourse which is meaningful to them but unintelligible to the rest of us.) At no point, here or later, is this impressive pagan cleric referred to as being lettered.

When Amphiareus is swallowed up by the earth (as he had predicted that he would be), the Greeks discuss his possible replacements. The issue is raised by:

> Uns poètes vieuz et antis
> Qui ot en bos esté mainz dis,
> Et de sa lei religious . . .   lines 5081–83 [5313–15]

(A poet, old and ancient,/ Who had been in the woods many a day,/ And [was] a monk in his faith . . .)

We will return to the important word "poète" shortly. In these lines, letters are raised as an issue – but only by one of the candidates, Thiodamas, who says that they should choose someone other than himself: "Home d'aage i deivent metre,/ Sage del siécle et de la letre" (5137–38; "They should put in an older man,/ Wise in the world and in letters"). But it is in fact Thiodamas who receives the stole – and no further reference is made to letters or literacy. Thiodamas, like his holy precedessor, is described as wise, but not specifically as lettered.

There are no literate characters of any consequence here, and no written missives: all messages sent are in fact messengers sent. No documents are ever consulted. Moreover, it is perhaps not necessary to be able to read in order to acquire knowledge: one can learn a lot just from looking at pictures – and pictures were not only in books but also painted on the walls of castles and churches, and sculpted on the facades and other surfaces of buildings of all kinds.

A few references to reading and to the existence of written things – and

apparently to literates – do, however, exist in this work. The first of these references is important and calls for careful examination. We are told that, at the
funeral for the warrior Ates:

> Tuit li poète de la vile
> S'assemblent et sont bien dui mile:
> Vestent daumaires et tuniques
> Et portent chasses et reliques;
> Portent textes et philatéres
> Et encensiers et ardenz céres;
> Ardent encens et titiame.
> Li maistre d'eus comande l'anme;
> Pués a un temple iluec defors
> A grant honor portent le cors.
> Li ossèques grant piéce dure:
> Par ordre font a o grant cure
> Chanter respons et leçons lére,
> Pués l'enterrent el cimetére;
> Mais ainz que fust el sarcueu mis,
> Delivra li reis toz les pris,
> Et ainz que fust li cors coverz,
> Franchi li reis cinz cenz cuiverz.   lines 6453–70 [6145–60]

(All the poets of the city/ Assemble, and there are two thousand
[of them]:/ They put on dalmatics and tunics/ And carry reliquaries and relics;/ They carry Gospel-books [texts[57]] and
amulets/ [with words written inside?]/ And incense-burners and
burning tapers,/ Burning incense and perfume./ Their master
commends the soul [of Ates to the gods];/ Then to a temple
outdoors/ With great honor they carry the body./ The funeral
lasts a long time:/ In order and with great care they have/ The
responses sung and the lessons read,/ Then they bury him in the
cemetery;/ But before he was put in the sarcophagus,/ The king
delivered all the prisoners,/ And before the body was covered,/
The king freed five hundred serfs.)

What are we seeing here? Who are these "poets" and what exactly are they
doing? Léopold Constans, in his notes to the *Thèbes*, states:

L'auteur avait sans doute pour modèle un texte latin qui portait *vates*, mot
qui a eu, comme on sait, la triple signification de "prêtre," de "devin," et
de "poète inspiré." (II, p. 341)

Constans claims that in both the *Thèbes* and the *Troie* the word is clearly associated with literacy: *clergie*. It is true that in the thirteenth and fourteenth

---

[57] Constans gives for *textes* the meaning "textes sacrés inscrits sur des banderoles,"
but according to Godefroy *texte* refers to Gospel-books.

centuries in France, a "poète" meant a writer. It is only in the fourteenth century that composers of lyric verse, previously called *trouvères*, began to be called "poètes": Machaut is apparently the first to be honored with this title. I agree with Constans that in the case of the *Troie* the "poet" is linked with literacy and clergy. But in the *Thèbes* the association of the word "poète" with the literate priesthood seems far from clear. The two words "poète" and "clerc" are never brought together as synonyms (as they are in the *Troie*, e.g., line 16557). It is certainly true that the "poètes" at this funeral procession and service dress and generally behave in a priestly way, wearing dalmatics and carrying reliquaries and Gospel-books.[58] But while lessons are read aloud and responses sung in the service it is not clear that the poets themselves are doing the reading: "they *have* responses read and lessons read." Thus, while the two roles – poetry and learning – are firmly linked in the *Troie*, they remain separate in the *Thèbes*: we do not have explicitly clerkly poets here. The inspired seer-*cum*-holy man may not be understood here to be – represented as – a literate figure. The poet may indeed be subtly proposing as attractive a priesthood without letters. This apparently non-literate priesthood of "poètes" is perhaps all the more curious since on the whole the *Thèbes* poet has a hard time remembering that he is talking about a non-contemporary – a non-Christian – culture; that pagan times were "different."[59] Thus, for example, when her beloved has been killed, Ismene declares that she will become a nun, line 6479; on several occasions the poet or a character articulates concern that certain – pagan – characters die on the battle-field "without confession," e.g., lines 1782; 4435–36.

Another pair of important passages relating to literacy is not found in the Constans edition, but is in the C manuscript (and therefore in the Raynaud de Lage edition). Capaneus, one of the leaders of the Greeks, leads an assault on Thebes. (This lengthy development, ending with a council of the gods and the death of Capaneus by a thunder-bolt, is entirely absent in the Constans edition as he did not believe that it was in the original poem.) Capaneus climbs up on the walls and threatens to tear them down:

> . . . li murs est frainz et aterrez,
> nous osteron toutes les pierres
> que Amphÿon vostre harpierres
> assembla ci par artimaire
> et par la force de gramaire
> et par le chant de sa vïele;

---

[58] These "textes" – and the "philatéres" – are absent from the C manuscript, used by Raynaud de Lage.

[59] This sort of anachronism is found in virtually all medieval *romans*, even in works clearly produced by *clercs*. But it is nonetheless truer of some works than of others, and the *Thèbes* seems more profoundly marked by anachronistic thinking than, for example, the *Troie*.

n'i remaindra tour ne tornele;
nous abatrons tout contre terre
pour faire fin de ceste guerre.   lines 9320–28

(. . . the wall is broken and torn to the ground,/ we will take away
all the stones/ that Amphyon your harper/ assembled here by the
power of magic/ and by the force of grammar [or a magic incan-
tation]/ and by the song of his vielle;/ not one tower or turret will
remain here;/ we will knock it all to the ground/ to make an end
of this war.)

According to legend, the poet Amphyon, with the power of his lyre alone,
built the walls of Thebes. What are we to make of this reference to "artimaire"
(from Latin "artem magicam") and especially to "la force de gramaire"?
Does this mean that Amphyon is understood by our poet to have indeed been a
grammarian – and was the poet one himself? But the idea that "grammar" has
magical power reminds me of an observation by Ong:

> When a fully formed script of any sort, alphabetic or other, first makes its
> way from outside into a particular society, it does so necessarily at first in
> restricted sectors and with varying effects and implications. Writing is often
> regarded at first as an instrument of secret and magic power. Traces of this
> early attitude toward writing can still show etymologically: the Middle
> English "grammarye" or grammar, referring to book-learning, came to
> mean occult or magical lore, and through one Scottish dialectical form has
> emerged in our present English vocabulary as "glamor" (spell-casting
> power) . . .[60]

The point that Ong is making is that when writing and "grammar" are new to a
culture (or part of one), they are seen as having magical power. And indeed, in
Old French the word "gramaire" had as meanings, alongside of "gramma-
irien, savant," the Latin language itself, magician and magic spell.[61] Is that not
precisely what we are seeing here? Whether or not Amphyon is to be understood as "literate," does this passage not suggest to us that the person who
used the word *gramaire* in this "magical" way – our poet – was not himself a
grammarian? (Grammarians know better, alas . . .)

The second passage from the Constans edition in which writing occurs
comes right after the funeral discussed above. Etiocles wears marvelous armor
and "une bone espee":

En Babilone fu trovee;
Trovee fu en Babilone,
En un chier sarcueu de sardone:

---

[60] *Orality and Literacy*, p. 93.
[61] See Glossary of the Raynaud de Lage edition; also Tobler-Lommatzsch, Vol. 4,
column 532.

> Si com dit li briés et la letre,
> Ninus i gést, qui l'i fist metre. . . .

lines 6530–34 [6220–24[62]]

(In Babylon was it found;/ It was found in Babylon,/ In an expensive sarcophagus of sardonyx:/ As the words and the letter said,/ Ninus lies here, who had it put here. . . .)

Such a passage surely shows, along with a high tolerance for repetition, an awareness of the appeal of written inscriptions, especially on "amazing" objects. But this short inscription is the only one in the work; there are, for example, no epitaphs on any of the various tombs. Nor is there mention of who read – deciphered – this inscription: we are simply told what it says. Thus, we find the prestige of the written – but no readers.[63]

An oral ethic – and an oral poetics

What we see in the *Thèbes* is, I suggest, an ethic at once deeply feudal and deeply oral: to the *Thèbes* poet, what lords provide to their vassals, and vice versa, is a strong arm and powerful discourse: wise, eloquent words. Even a priest's strength is seen primarily in these terms. Indeed, this is, throughout, a world of physical action and an oral world: a world in which men swear on their oath (occasionally on relics), but where there is not a written letter or document in sight; where they debate what course of action loyalty and wise strategy require; where they insult their enemies and lament, at great and moving length, the passing of their comrades at arms – and sometimes of their worthy adversaries.

The *Troie* is also largely taken up with epic combats, and its characters too are mostly great fighters. But, as noted earlier, two of the central characters, Dares and Dictes, are presented as literates, and as Benoît's written sources. Moreover, when he gives portraits of all the major characters of the war, Benoît assures us that they are faithful depictions because Dares himself had been concerned with the accuracy of his story:

> Beneeiz dit, qui rien n'i lait
> De quant que Daires li retrait,
> Qu'ici endreit voust demostrer
> E les semblances reconter
> E la forme qu'aveit chascuns,

---

[62] In C the key line reads: "ce dit li livres et la lettre" (6223; "so says the book and the letter").

[63] It might be argued that we do have "implied readers." But such an implication works only in a culture in which it can be assumed that people do *know* how to read. Such an assumption cannot be made in twelfth century France.

Qu'a ses ieuz les vit uns e uns.
Quant cil de Troie et li Grezeis
Aveient triues par dous meis,
O par meins o par plus d'espaces,
En tres, en loges e en places
Les alot Daires reguarder
Por lor semblances reconter:
S'estoire voleit faire pleine
Por ço s'en mist en si grant peine.   lines 5093–5106

(Benoît, who leaves nothing out, tells about/ Whatever Dares relates to him,/ And right here he wants to show/ And to tell the appearance/ And the form that each one had,/ Because with his eyes he saw each one of them./ When those from Troy and the Greeks/ Had a truce for two months/ At a greater or a lesser distance/ In tents, in barracks and encampments,/ Dares went to look at them/ In order to tell their appearance:/ He wanted to make his story full [complete]/ For this reason he put himself to great effort.)

This warrior-clerk was busy documenting himself. Dares was not just a character in the conflict, he was a war-reporter, preparing a book on the Trojan War.[64] Benoît, heir to his book, defers to him.

The world of the *Thèbes* is a world full of music and of the social entertainments provided by *jongleurs*: there are repeated references to such music and such *divertissements* – with none of the hostility towards *jongleurs* found in Benoît de Sainte-Maure. (Indeed, in the *Troie*, there are few references to music and instruments; performers are never, as it were, allowed to entertain.) As to military music – no oxymoron to the Middle Ages! – let's recall this passage in the *Thèbes* where Etiocles, king of Thebes, prepares to receive the enemy:

Li reis fut bien de guerre duéz:
Eschauguaites mist par les murs,
Mil Açoparz et cinc cenz Turs.
Sonent tabors, cornent fresteaus
Et troïnes et chalumeaus;
Grant est la noise que il font
As batailles des murs a mont.   lines 3480–86 [3728–34]

---

[64] See also lines 91ff: from the beginning we are told that Dares, though himself a Trojan, wrote about this important war in Greek; each day he wrote down the events of the day. In another passage, Nauplus avenges the death of his son Palamedes through the use of false documents: lines 27671ff. Ulysses reads one of the letters aloud – lines 27746ff – thus he is shown to be literate. In short, Benoît emphasizes literacy and recourse to documents even on the part of his characters.

(The king was well trained in war:/ He put night-watchmen on the walls,/ A thousand Azopars and five hundred Turks./ They sound the drums, blow the flutes/ And trumpets and bagpipes;/ Great is the noise that they make/ On the top of the battlements of the walls.)

As to the entertainments provided by *jongleurs*, the first such occurrence is at the wedding of Jocasta and Oedipus:

La reïne li ont donée,
En es le pas l'a esposée.
Les nueces font a grant baudor:
La veïssiez maint jogleur,
Qui chantoent o lor vïeles
Et o rotes et o harpèles; . . .   lines 433–38 [475ff[65]]

(They [Laius' lords] gave her to him,/ He married her right away./ They make the wedding with great joy:/ There you would have seen many *jongleurs*,/ Who sang with their vielles/ And with stringed instruments and little harps; . . .)

There are other, similar passages – including a reference "Es quatre eschiéles de Rollant,/ Dont cil jogleor vont chantant . . ." (lines 8827–29: "The four squadrons of Roland,/ About whom *jongleurs* go around singing"). Never, at any point, does any performer read anything aloud.

This is, to be sure, a "courtly" as well as a feudal world – courtly in the sense that the role accorded to women and love is altogether striking. Military realities and relationships between men still do, however, claim the foreground. At any rate, what we find here is love talk – not love letters. (We did see these in the *Lais* of Marie de France, in Chapter 2.) There is no reading and no writing in the world that the *Thèbes* poet shows us.

In this essentially oral world, where men (and women) argue and persuade and praise and blame and weep and woo, our poet seems perfectly at home. His own discourse – the frequent "patter" that accompanies his story – is, as we saw earlier, invariably of an oral sort in that he speaks in the first person, talking "now," to "us," making comments on the story and how he will tell it. To give a few examples among many: at the end of his introduction he says:

Des dous fréres ore a present
Ne parlerai plus longement,
Car ma raison vueil comencier
D'un lor aiuel dont vueil traitier. . . .   lines 33–36 [33–36]

---

[65] This manuscript has a different set of musical experiences and instruments: "la oïssiez meint jogleor,/ meinte gigue, meinte vïele,/ harpes, salterions et roles,/ rostruenges, sonnez et notes." lines 479–82.

(About the two brothers now at the moment/ I will not speak at
greater length,/ Because I want to begin my speech/ About an
ancestor of theirs that I want to talk about.)

He repeatedly assures us that he does not want to make his story longer than
necessary: "Ne vos en quier plus alongier . . ." (line 2909; "I don't want to
make this any longer for you . . ."); "Ne vos en quier faire lonc plait . . ." (line
7399; "I don't want to make my words [too] long for you . . .")

The poet also comments frequently, in the first-person singular, on the characters and their behavior: thus, when both of the daughters of King Adrastus
have lost their beloved husbands, he says:

> Des filles Adrastus le rei
> Ne sai mesure ne conrei:
> N'est merveille se grant duel font . . .
>
> lines 9769–70 [9887–89]

(In the daughters of King Adrastus/ I find no measure or order:/
It is not surprising if they make great lament . . .)

In sum, the scholarship which assumes the *Roman de Thèbes* to be the work
of a cleric stands on a shaky foundation. Internal evidence strongly suggests
that the *Thèbes* is the work of a non-literate, but nonetheless "knowledgeable" court-minstrel. One final comment on the poet: it cannot be argued
(though I have seen it done) that he was at once "not much of a clerk" and yet
– simultaneously – someone who had read Statius' *Thebaid* well enough to
translate and adapt it. There were, to be sure, ignorant clerks (I mentioned them
earlier), but the *Thèbes* poet was *not* one. If in this work we must choose – as
indeed we must – between a clerk trying to sound like a minstrel, and a minstrel
trying to sound like a clerk, I submit that the evidence shows the latter to be the
sounder choice.

I cannot emphasize too strongly the importance of looking carefully at the
internal evidence in the work. We have tended, in the past, to assign "clerical
authorship" in a mechanical way: by reference to the genre, not to the specifics
of the work itself. Thus, if the work in question was a romance, the author
simply had to be a clerk. I submit that we must be substantially more attentive
than we have been to such issues as the poet's self-description; the nature of
references to books, reading, and writing; and the role that written culture is
represented as playing in the work itself. As we have seen here, even two
romances that might seem, at first thought, to be "clearly learned" – and thus
equally clerical – can be shown in fact to entertain markedly different relations
to oral and written tradition.

We do not know why or by whom the *Roman de Thèbes* was written down,
or what the relation was between the earliest manuscript and the performance
of the work. It is perfectly possible that our poet – a minstrel – composed this

story without recourse to writing in order to perform it from memory in a court setting. (We will return to such questions in Part II.)

But if it is indeed the case that the *Thèbes* poet was a minstrel – and the *Troie* poet, Benoît de Sainte-Maure, a clerk – what of *other* early verse romances? How common, and how important, a figure was the court minstrel, teller of romances? We will take up another – and yet more important – early romance poet in the next chapter.

CHAPTER FOUR

Chrétien de Troyes as Minstrel: Further Reflections on Orality and Literacy in Twelfth Century French Courts

We now take up the case of Chrétien de Troyes, who occupies so central a place in the "birth of medieval romance." I need not, I trust, elaborate here on Chrétien's importance in the history of French literature; suffice it to say that he is generally considered the Father of Arthurian romance, if not of medieval romance *tout court*.

We have, concerning this great narrative poet, a good deal more information than on the *Thèbes* poet. Of Chrétien we have, aside from his first name, some association with the city of Troyes: he once – at the start of his first romance – speaks of himself as "de Troyes." We have the following romances: *Érec et Énide, Cligés, Yvain (Le chevalier au lion), Lancelot (Le chevalier de la charette)*, and *Perceval (Le conte du Graal)*. (There are also a few works whose authorship is contested.[1]) From dedications within the works themselves, we also have the names of aristocratic personages whom Chrétien identified as patrons: Marie, countess of Champagne, wife of Henry the Liberal (she is referred to at the beginning of *Lancelot*); and Philip of Alsace, count of Flanders (praised in the opening lines of *Perceval*). Chrétien's association with these two courts is frequently over-interpreted; thus, we are sometimes assured that "Chrétien was Marie's favorite poet," and the like. We know, in fact, almost nothing about Chrétien's precise relation to these courts. But since the prologues (on which more later) do speak in some detail about the character and tastes of both Marie of Champagne and Philip of Alsace, it is probably safe to assume that Chrétien actually knew them and that they were actually his patrons, not just figures whose patronage he sought. We do not know whether Chrétien had other patrons as well, or precisely what forms the patronage took.

The names of Marie of Champagne and Philip of Alsace also provide us with valuable dates: 1165, when Henry became count; and 1191, when Philip of Alsace died, on a crusade to the Holy Land. These dates are generally taken as fixing the period within which Chrétien "flowered": a *terminus a quo* and a *terminus ad quem*. While this use is perhaps arguable – Chrétien may have

1 On this issue, see Daniel Poirion, gen. ed., *Oeuvres complètes de Chrétien de Troyes*. The manuscript tradition of Chrétien's works will be discussed at the end of this chapter.

able one, his learning was not acquired through the school, but at court; that it is altogether likely that, if he had any "letters" at all, he was only modestly literate – and probably only in French, not in Latin (thus he was not *literatus*); that he may not have written works himself, or even *had* them written down; that he may very possibly have composed them without any recourse to writing; and that he may well have performed them himself from memory. In short, I am arguing that Chrétien (like the *Thèbes* poet) was at once a minstrel and a *trouvère*: a verbal "inventor." This argument requires us to reconsider not merely the role and identity of Chrétien, but our understanding of the roles of *ménestrel* and *trouvère*, and the relations between them, for the long-accepted understanding has been that minstrels and *jongleurs* typically performed what other people – writers or literate *trouvères* – made up and "wrote."

This set of interconnected theses – which will in fact overflow from this chapter into subsequent chapters – will require that we examine Chrétien's work in detail. We will also need to have another look at the functioning and the relative status of verbal and written eloquence in the twelfth century; and at the sorts of learning that were present and could be acquired in a late-twelfth century French court.

Preliminary evidence

We might begin – and indeed end – with one basic fact: Chrétien, like the *Thèbes* poet, *never* speaks of himself anywhere as a clerk. (By contrast, Wace, Benoît de Sainte-Maure, and many others do identify themselves explicitly as clerks.) Our long-held and widely-shared conviction that Chrétien was a clerk, and that he had an extensive formal education, is not based on any "hard evidence" whatsoever, but on inferences and assumptions which are at least as open to dispute as those that I will present here. Neither Chrétien's contemporaries, nor indeed anyone in the period immediately following him, ever refers to him as a *clerc*.[6] He is known, through a few surviving *chansons d'amour*, as

---

[6] For example, Godefroi de Leigni, who composed a conclusion to Chrétien's unfinished *Charrete*, identified himself as a *clerc* – but not Chrétien (lines 7102–6); see Chrétien de Troyes, *Le chevalier de la charette*, ed. Mario Roques.

See also Colette-Anne Van Coolput, "Appendice: Références, adaptations et emprunts directs" [à Chrétien] in *The Legacy of Chrétien de Troyes*, ed. Norris J. Lacy, Douglas Kelly and Keith Busby, Vol. I, pp. 333–42, pp. 333–7. There are references by many poets and "writers" to Chrétien, but as a *trouvère*; as someone who produced "dis"; no "bouche de Chrétien" produced anything better, etc. Only Wolfram von Eschenbach refers to him as a "master" – "meister Cristjân" (p. 337) – and Wolfram himself was no clerk. Nor – by any means – does the medieval German honorific "meister" refer exclusively to clerical achievement.

a "trouvère."[7] Though Chrétien does use a few "clerical" terms, to which we will return, he never ever refers to himself as "writing" or as a "writer." He generally speaks of himself the way a story-teller does, in the first person: as an "I" speaking "now" to a "you." He never speaks to future listeners, which Thomas, an Anglo-Norman clerk, does at the end of his *Tristan* (p. 162, line 825[8]); nor does he speak of his compiled work as an object to be sent to a benefactor, which Marie de France – also an Anglo-Norman, quite possibly a nun – does in the prologue to her *Lais* (lines 43–56).[9] He does on occasion speak of himself in the third person – as "Chrétien," and, as noted earlier, he identifies himself as being "de Troies" (Troyes, in Champagne) – for example, in *Erec et Enide*, lines 9 and 26. He does this especially at the beginning or end of a work. This self-naming is not uncommon in the tradition of *jongleurs* and similar performers: it is one of the ways in which professional poets attempt to take possession of their discourse. "Oral" does not have to mean nameless,[10] and we have the names of many famous *jongleurs* who (apparently) never actually "wrote" a word.

Chrétien's prologues: proof of *clergie*?

The passages of Chrétien's romances that have most firmly established his "reputation" as a clerk are his prologues, which have functioned as proof-texts for his *clergie*.[11] Two of them in particular are important: those of *Érec et Énide* and *Cligés*.[12] These passages have, I think, been significantly over-interpreted by literary commentators; words – *written* words – have been put into Chrétien's mouth. In the first of these prologues, Chrétien says: ". . . doit chascuns panser et antendre/ a bien dire et a bien aprandre . . ." (lines 11–12; ". . . everyone should think and learn/ to speak well and to learn well . . ."). He declares that:

---

7 See, for example, *Chanter M'Estuet: Songs of the Trouvères*, S.N. Rosenberg and H. Tischler, eds., pp. 172–73.

8 Thomas, *Les Fragments du Roman de Tristan*, ed. Wind.

9 Marie de France, *Lais*, ed. Rychner.

10 See, e.g., Ruth Finnegan, *Oral Poetry: Its Nature, Significance and Social Context*, pp. 209–6. We have many medieval *jongleurs'* names: see Faral, *Les jongleurs en France au moyen âge* and *Mimes français du XIIIe siècle*; in some cases their names are mentioned by others, but many refer to themselves in their compositions or performance.

11 This literary term, "prologue," is ours, not his. It is used by other figures at the time, e.g., Evrat who composed a verse translation of Genesis for Marie of Champagne (see John Benton, "The Court of Champagne as a Literary Center," p. 563, n. 43) – but not by Chrétien.

12 For Chrétien's romances I use the Champion (Classiques français du Moyen Age) series for the following: *Le Chevalier de la Charette*, *Érec et Énide*, and *Le chevalier au lion (Yvain)*, all ed. Mario Roques; *Cligés*, ed. Alexandre Micha. I use the William Roach edition of *Le Roman de Perceval, ou Le Conte du Graal*.

> cil ne fet mie savoir
> qui s'escïence n'abandone
> tant con Dex la grasce l'an done . . .   lines 16–18)

(he does not do wisely/ who does not spread his knowledge [or wisdom] abroad/ insofar as God gives him the grace to do so . . .)

Do such assertions serve to demonstrate *clergie*? Are words and expressions like "bien dire" and "bien aprandre," "escïence" and "savoir" the province of book-learning alone? I think not. Eloquence has never been the property of writers alone, but must be shared with poets and story-tellers, among others. As we saw in Chapter 3, *savoir* and *escience* do not have to allude to book-learning but can also refer to basic human knowledge, wisdom, and common sense.[13] A brief example: the courtly poet Thibaut de Champagne declares at the beginning of one of his famous songs: "De bone amor vient seance et bonté . . ."[14] (VI, line 1). Is he asserting that love teaches things that come from books, or rather that this experience is a source of knowledge and wisdom as well as of goodness, or virtue?

Chrétien speaks of the way in which he has joined things together – his "conjointure" (line 14) – saying that his story is better than that of those *conteurs* who make their living telling stories:

> . . . d'Erec, le fil Lac, est li contes
> que devant rois et devant contes
> depecier et corronpre suelent
> cil qui de conter vivre vuelent.   lines 16–22

(. . . about Erec, the son of Lac, is this tale/ which before kings and before counts/ those who wish to make their living telling tales/ commonly tear to pieces and corrupt.)

"*They* tear the story to pieces and corrupt it." But this sort of affirmation, which has commonly been read by scholars as proving that Chrétien is distancing himself from the *jongleur*esque tradition, and producing a written work, is nothing more than the back-biting common among oral performers and story-tellers. Béroul, as we saw in an earlier chapter, criticizes his rivals in similar terms. To give just one other example from among many: *Le couronnement de Louis* begins as follows:

> Oiez, seignor, que Deus vos seit aidanz!
> Plaist vos oïr d'une estoire vaillant
> Bone chançon, corteise et evenant?

---

[13] Again, the best references here are to the "ensenhamens," or "teachings," of various troubadours, such as Guiraut Riquier's "Supplicatio" in Jean-Charles Huchet, ed. and trans., *Nouvelles occitanes du Moyen Age*.

[14] *Les Chansons de Thibaut de Champagne, Roi de Navarre*, ed. Axel Wallensköld.

Vilains joglere ne sai por quei se vant
Nul mot en die tresque on li comant.
De Looïs ne lairai ne vos chant
Et de Guillelme al Cort Nés le vaillant,
Qui tant sofri sor sarrazine gent;
De meillor ome ne cuit que nuls vos chant.   lines 1–9[15]

(Listen, lords, may God help you!/ Does it please you to hear a
worthy story/ A good song, courtly and pleasing?/ I don't know
why the low-born *jongleur* boasts,/ He can't say anything until
you command him to./ I will not fail to sing to you about Louis,/
And about William of the Short Nose, the valiant,/ Who suffered
so much from the sarazin people;/ About a better man I think no
one can sing to you.)

Are we to assume that Chrétien was a clerk, just because he criticized
jongleurs? But such remarks prove nothing with respect to the written status of
a work or the *clergie* of its "author." And the word "conjointure," used in
regard to the story as a whole, resonates with one of the central themes of the
romance: marriage. This is a "well-joined" or "unified" story about
"union" or "joining." Words from the "conjoindre" family are not necessarily, as one may be given to think, learned – literary, grammatical, or astro-
nomical – but can have erotic and, in this context surely, conjugal
implications.[16]

Does Chrétien claim specifically literary immortality for himself in lines
23–26? He says that he will begin a story that will always remain in memory as
long as Christianity lasts:

Des or comancerai l'estoire
qui toz jorz mes iert an mimoire
tant con durra crestïantez;
de ce s'est Crestïens vantez."

(Now I will begin the story/ which will always remain in
memory/ as long as Christianity lasts.)

But what he is claiming here is by no means necessarily a literary topic.
Chrétien declares what many an oral *conteur* has said (or hoped): that his story
will be remembered. He makes his claim stick to our minds and tongues by the
pun on his name: Chrestïens/ crestïantez.

Cligés is even more famous than *Érec et Énide* for its expression of themes

---

[15] *Le Couronnement de Louis; chanson de geste du XIIe siècle*, ed. Ernest Langlois.
[16] See Tobler-Lommatzsch.
   In this context, one is reminded of Villon's clearly sexual use of the verb "conjoindre" in
the *Testament*: he gives a gift of ginger (thought to be an aphrodisiac) "pour conjoindre culz
et coetes/ Et couldre jambons et andoulles . . ." (lines 1122–23). This meaning of "conjoindre" was common in Old French.

of *clergie*. Here, we have believed that Chrétien says he has "written" and "translated" things: that he has translated Ovid in particular. Let's have another look:

> Cil qui fist d'Erec et d'Enide
> Et les comandemanz d'Ovide
> Et l'art d'amors an romans mist,
> Et le mors de l'espaule fist,
> Del roi Marc et d'Ysalt la blonde,
> Et de la hupe et de l'aronde
> Et del rossingnol la muance,
> Un novel conte rancomance . . .   lines 1–8

> (He who made [a tale] about Erec and Enide/ And put into romance the commandments of Ovid/ And the art of love, And made [a story about] the shoulder bite,/ About King Mark and Iseut the blonde,/ And about the hoopee and the swallow/ And about the transformation of the nightingale/ Begins a new tale . . .)

But Chrétien never uses – here or elsewhere – any explicitly scriptorial terms with reference to himself. What he says is that he has made works: the verb is "fist," and, as I noted earlier, there is nothing intrinsically written or literary about this verb; nor is it necessarily "oral": it is a neutral verb with regard to oral/written issues. It could be applied to a wide variety of verbal activities. Many *trouvères* refer to "making" their songs. The verb "faire" could also refer to non-verbal artistic creation, such as the making of a beautiful object. Unlike Benoît, Chrétien does not say he has "written" anything himself. He does not, in fact, say that he has "translated" Ovid, but simply that he has put various things of Ovid "en roman" – and *mettre en roman* does not necessarily mean "translate a text." (This point was discussed at some length in Chapter 1.) It means to put something (a story, for example) into the French vernacular, most commonly into octosyllabic rhymed couplets. As to the possibility that the term *romanz* referred necessarily to a written composition, I will postpone this matter to Chapter 6, which bears on performance. (There, I believe, many references will make it clear that a *roman* was not necessarily thought of as a "written work.") The story that one sets into rhyme may well have been known as such: as a story – orally. In a word, the fact that someone knows stories from Ovid, and retells them in octo, is simply no guarantee that he has read Ovid – nor for that matter that he is able to read and write at all.

In this prologue comes the famous passage whose theme modern scholars speak of as "translatio studii":

> Ceste estoire trovons escrite,
> Que conter vos vuel et retraire,
> En un des livres de l'aumaire   20
> Mon seignor saint Pere a Biauvez;

93

De la fu li contes estrez
Qui tesmoingne l'estoire a voire:
Por ce fet ele mialz a croire.
Par les livres que nos avons
Les fez des ancïens savons
Et del siegle qui fu jadis.
Ce nos ont nostre livre apris
Qu'an Grece ot de chevalerie   30
Le premier los et de clergie.
Puis vint chevalerie a Rome
Et de la clergie la some,
Qui or est an France venue.
Dex doint qu'ele i soit maintenue
Et que li leus li abelisse
Tant que ja mes de France n'isse
L'enors qui s'i est arestee,
Dex l'avoit as altres prestee:
Car des Grezois ne des Romains
Ne dit an mes ne plus ne mains,   40
D'ax est la parole remese
Et estainte la vive brese.
Crestïens comance son conte,
Si con li livres nos reconte, . . .   lines 18–44.

(The story that I want to tell and/ Relate to you we find written/ In one of the books in the cupboard [armor-closet]/ Of my Lord Saint Peter in Beauvais;/ This story was taken from there/ Which is a witness that the story is true:/ For this reason it is good to believe it./ By the books that we have/ We know the deeds of the ancients/ And the world that once was./ Our books have taught us this:/ That in Greece was the first glory/ Of chivalry and of clergy./ Then chivalry and the "summa" of clergy/ Went to Rome./ Now it is come to France,/ May God grant that it may remain here/ And that the place is pleasing to it/ So that the honor which has come here/ May never leave France,/ God had (only) lent it to the others:/ For no one speaks any more/ About the Greeks and the Romans/ About them have all words ceased/ And the live coal has gone out./ Chrétien begins his story,/ Just as the book tells it to us.)

It is often said that these lines show Chrétien's personal involvement in the cultural rebirth of his time: his commitment to letters, to *clergie*. But in point of fact this passage merely shows three things: 1) Chrétien knew that books taught that Greece and Rome had once been "great" in war and learning. 2) He thought they had "chevalerie" and "clergie."[17] 3) He declared that their

17 This view is not quite accurate, of course: there were no armed horsemen in classical

94

former greatness was now in France. This idea was indeed in the air in the twelfth and thirteenth centuries – and the French royalty and aristocracy liked to think that this greatness was now in France, and not (for example) in England or Germany!

These ideas certainly show involvement in the *prestige* of books and learning. What they do not show is Chrétien's own *clergie*. To say, as Chrétien does, in lines 25–26, "Par les livres que nos avons/Les fez des ancïens savons" ("By the books that we have/ We know the deeds of the ancients") does not guarantee that he reads books himself, only that he recognizes the benefits and the knowledge that come to "us" all from books: books tell "us" things (line 44). This sort of reference to reading falls into the category that D.H. Green in his recent book *Medieval Listening and Reading: The Primary Reception of German Literature 800–1300*, calls "ambiguous."[18] Chrétien clearly recognizes the political, as well as the cultural advantages of such a claim, such a theme: the greatness of the past is said to be now in *France*, and not elsewhere.

Moreover – and this seems an astonishing statement for someone of whom it is claimed that he was deeply steeped in *latinitas* – in this famous proof-text Chrétien does not express the great humanist idea that the Greeks and Romans live on in their books, which are monuments to their greatness. For Chrétien, the men of those times have lost their glory: when men have stopped talking about you – as they have stopped talking about Greece and Rome – the ember of your greatness is *out*: "la vive brise" is "estainte" (line 42). This seems an oral concept of fame and immortality. These are fighting words, articulating a modernist position: classical glory and classical art are *over*. This passage can scarcely be taken as proof of *clergie*.

Chrétien's "Rhetoric": proof of *clergie*?

It is not merely themes and topoi in Chrétien's prologues but the very nature of his poetic discourse which is said to identify him as a clerk. His "rhetoric" is considered not merely to shine but to constitute proof that he had received a clerical education. Here too, we need to have a closer look.

There are two large ways of viewing rhetoric. Rhetoric can refer to those Arts of Language and Discourse elaborated by classical theorists, such as Cicero, the author of the *Ad Herenniam*, and Quintilian. These major texts were commented upon by medieval writers, in particular Matthew of

times, and learning was not, then, the affair of churchmen. But Chrétien is by no means the only one to have thought so.

[18] See pp. 115–30: "wir lesen; man liset," etc. By "ambiguous" Green means that further confirmation is called for. For example, "wir lesen" does not necessarily mean that the individual reads to, or for, himself.

Vendôme (who wrote an *Ars versificatoria*, before 1175) and Geoffrey of Vinsauf (whose *Poetria Nova* dates from around 1210).[19] By Rhetoric, as thus defined and understood, we mean not only the classical and learned – thus the latinate, the clerical – tradition of the arts of language. By this understanding of the term – by Rhetoric with a capital "R" – we also mean the firm divisions of discourse, or public speaking, into the deliberative (persuasive), the demonstrative (praise and blame), and the forensic (judicial). We mean the categorization of various tropes and figures, with indications as to their proper use. As concerns the medieval period, we mean the arts of language as defined rhetorically, and as learned and practiced in schools, by schoolmen – but not by other kinds of people.

But rhetoric can also mean something different, and far broader. Let's not forget that Rhetoric (capital "R") is the written and theoretical codification of an oral praxis. Every culture has its rhetoric – small "r" – and its poetics as well. Every culture has not just language, but *arts* of language: poetic genres, such as praise poems, ritual laments, work songs, songs of love or eroticism, and so on. Every culture has rules – which may or may not be made fully explicit – regulating these different uses of language. In all cultures, different genres use (what Rhetoric calls) tropes and figures in different ways. (For numerous examples of the use of such "rhetorical embellishments" in unlearned – oral – poetry, I refer the reader to the poems gathered by Willard R. Trask in *The Unwritten Song*.) And even in cultures in which a learned tradition of Rhetoric exists, there may exist great orators, story-tellers, and preachers who were not formed by book-learning in Rhetoric, but were endowed with a natural gift for eloquence – a talent perhaps honed by an oral apprenticeship which, in turn, may or may not show influence from the Rhetorical tradition.

The fact that Chrétien speaks well – eloquently – does not prove that he has studied Rhetoric. There were in the Middle Ages many people who lived largely by their ability to speak well. One thinks not merely of *jongleurs* and minstrels but also of feudal barons whose discourses of advice and exhortation could make them extremely valuable to their lords, or win for them the firm allegiance of their vassals. Many characteristics of learned Rhetoric would have been just as true of unlearned, or oral, rhetoric; memory would, here as elsewhere, have been the "storehouse" of arguments and ornaments.

Even those who are most firmly persuaded that Chrétien was schooled in Rhetoric have acknowledged that it is not at the surface level that one sees the impact of Rhetorical training on his poetry. For medieval Rhetorical theory and training hardly appear relevant to, still less reflected in, Chrétien's romances. Here is how Charles Sears Baldwin described the substance of

---

[19] See *Les arts poétiques du XIIe et du XIIIe siècle*, ed. Edmond Faral.

Matthew of Vendôme's *Ars versificatoria*, which might theoretically – that is, historically – have influenced Chrétien:

> Matthew's prose manual, though it omits prosody, is otherwise connected even more obviously than the others with the teaching of *grammatica*. Not only is he known to have been *grammaticus* at Orléans; his book is inclined throughout in the direction of such teaching, and it contains specimen school exercises. The grammatical slant is most obvious in those on adjectives in *-alis, -osus, -atus, -ivus, -aris*. The longer examples of descriptive verse may well be such successively revised themes as were seen earlier at Speier [especially by Walter of Speier, discussed earlier by Baldwin]. The use of Horace's "Ars poetica" is so extensive, even for the time, as to suggest that Matthew's book may have begun in his *praelectiones* on that poem. Whatever degree of probability may be attached to these suggestions, there is no doubt of Matthew's intention and preoccupation. His book seeks to further the writing of Latin descriptive verse. The idea behind it is that poetry is mainly description, which in turns proceeds mainly by dilation. Style, which is his only concern, is conceived as decoration. Though his lists of figures for this purpose (III) generally agree with those of the *Doctrinale* [of Alexandre de Villedieu], rhetoric is evident not only in the phrase *colores rhetorici*, but as a constant preoccupation. That *poetics* as style is identical with *rhetorica* he assumes; that it is distinct as composition can hardly have entered his head, but composition in either field is beyond his scope. His sections on beginning (I.3–16) refer not to introducing the subject, but to phrasing the first sentences. The faults then enumerated (I.30–37) are of style. Description is expounded (I.38–1132) as appropriateness of phrase to condition, age, place, etc., and as the seeking of "attributes" in a person's physical and mental habit, his deeds, his speech, or in the cause, quality, and time of an event. Reference to subject, thought, or composition goes no further; the rest of the book is purely verbal.[20]

Could Chrétien really have learned to do what he did – learned his "art" – from studying a work such as this, with Matthew's almost total emphasis on Latin composition, on description, on ornament, and on the verbal level of discourse? I think, rather, that one would be hard pressed to find anything farther from the spirit of Chrétien's romances.

Many of the things that Matthew of Vendôme (and other rhetoricians) said that one should do, Chrétien does not do – or only does occasionally. For example, Matthew placed considerable emphasis on the importance of a character's name, in description (I.60)[21]: *nomen est omen*.[22] Chrétien does occasionally "omen-ize" characters' names. This is certainly the case of his

[20] Baldwin, *Medieval Rhetoric and Poetic (to 1400) Interpreted from Representative Works*, pp. 185–87.

[21] See Faral, *Les Arts poétiques*, pp. 106–93.

[22] See discussion in Douglas Kelly, *The Art of French Medieval Romance*, pp. 198–99, 233.

introduction of the names Soredamors and Fénice in *Cligés*: their names are full of meaning. But he does it only in *this* romance. Nowhere else does he comment on, or draw attention to, the meaning of a character's name. And in one romance, *Yvain*, it is not even clear that he gave his heroine a name: the name "Laudine" appears in just one manuscript, and there it appears only once. *Nomen est omen* could, in medieval Rhetorical theory, have another sense as well: that the name of an individual can be extended to a type: thus, one can refer to "a Galahad," or "a Lancelot." But, again, it is not necessary to have studied Rhetoric to make such use of a proper name: the *chanson de geste* is full of references to people who are, or are not, "as valiant as Roland"; lyrics contain many references to lovers who love as much as, or more than, Tristan; and today children frequently say, without benefit of *clergie*, that someone is "no Superman" or "no Einstein."

Chrétien begins *Yvain* with a *sententia*; this is one of the openings that Matthew recommends (I.16). But none of his other romances begins this way, or with any of the other rhetorical figures recommended for "opening" in the *Ars versificatoria*.[23] This is not to say that his prologues cannot be analyzed in Rhetorical terms – *any discourse can be* – but only that he does not follow the recommendations of Rhetoricians of his time.

It is sometimes said that it is the general level of eloquence and elegance of Chrétien's discourse that shows his clerical training. But clerks in this period did not live exclusively in the cloister or Latin quarter: many of them were present in court, speaking French (and other vernaculars), and impressing laymen and women with their style – and *style* is easily imitable.

Some have argued that it is primarily at the level of the generation of the text itself, rather than at the level of ornament, that one sees Chrétien's Rhetorical training. Chrétien is said to have learned "topical invention" – the ability to produce discourse by amplification from a topos – in school.[24] Two reflections are in order. First, one might indeed learn to make up stories (or speeches) in this way: by studying the art in class and by doing "invention" exercises. But one might very well *not* learn it this way. One might learn to "invent" stories by listening to great stories and story-tellers: by imitation. There are, in short, poets and story-tellers who never studied Rhetoric or "topical invention" (we might mention Homer's name here) who have made up extraordinarily beautiful and complex stories. Yes, they often sewed their great plots together from pre-existant bits and pieces of narrative: they invented "rhapsodically" (a rhapsode "stitches"). In many cases, the basic plot of a long journey or a

---

[23] These others were zeugma (when one verb governs several congruent words or clauses, each in a different way); hypozeuxis (each clause in a sentence has its own subject and verb); and metonymy (substitition of effect for cause or cause for effect, proper name for one of its qualities or vice versa): Matthew I.3–29. Definitions for figures are taken from Richard A. Lanham, *A Handlist of Rhetorical Terms*.

[24] Kelly, *The Art* (and other works as well) and Eugene Vance, *From Topic to Tale*.

great war serves as a vast portemanteau, allowing many minor episodes to be hung upon it. But such works are nonetheless extraordinary achievements of invention. There are also authors who studied topical invention presumably for years, but whose stories are nonetheless tedious and plodding. It is a bit like studying "Creative Writing" in school today: not all those who have taken courses in this subject learn to write as well as other people with a natural gift who never even heard the term "creative writing."

Some, such as Douglas Kelly, have considered that the key to topical invention is the *intention* of the poet. The poet shapes the *materia* (*remota* and *propinqua*) according to his intention or purpose. This is what makes everything fall neatly into place. But is a narrative poet's intention really so clear, as a rule? Here is how, in "Topical Invention in Medieval French Literature," Kelly defined Thomas's "intentio" in his *Tristan*:

> His original intention – his archetypal vision, in Geoffrey of Vinsauf's words – was to make *fin'amors* the subject of a work pleasing and consolatory to lovers. (p. 247)

This is surely a very broad – not to say vague – "archetype." But, broad as it is, it still seems somehow inadequate, even perhaps inaccurate: while Thomas does indeed speak at the end of his work of consoling lovers, most of the time his analysis of love and lovers is (as we noted in an earlier chapter) very cool, even perhaps sarcastic, and his choice of words can seem positively harsh, as when he speaks of lovers as "emvius" (envious) and "purvers" (perverse or perverted). I am far from sure that, had I been a twelfth century lover, I would have found Thomas's story especially consoling or altogether pleasing. Can we really be confident that it was Thomas's primary "intention" to please and console lovers? (The fact that his version survives only in tatters does not prove that his version did find favor with lovers, or others at court, however much we today find it attractive.)

As for Chrétien: who can speak with certainty of his "intentions," especially with regard to *Lancelot* and *Perceval*? (Yet, theoretically, without a clear intention – a firm mental *archetypus* – he could not even have made up these stories.) Many scholars have certainly disagreed on this score. I will confess to having wondered, and more than once, whether Chrétien didn't make up *Perceval* as he went along. His "intention" seems to have wavered: he appears to have changed his mind a number of times in the course of the (unfinished) romance, for example, with regard to the meaning of the grail and its mysteries[25] – just how Christian *is* all this? – and to the nature and degree of Perceval's "sin." I yield to no one in my admiration for Chrétien's art, but let

---

[25] One telling detail: when Perceval meets with his uncle the hermit, he is told that the grail contains a eucharistic host, which nourishes the wounded king (lines 6420ff). This is, then, a eucharistic miracle. But we were told earlier that at each course of the meal the Grail went past Perceval into the room where the wounded king lay (lines 3290ff). Did the king,

me say it out loud: there is something a bit incoherent about *Perceval*, and perhaps *Lancelot* as well. The "archetype" seems wobbly.

In short, though many scholars have been persuaded that Chrétien studied Rhetoric in school – and Dialectic, etc., as well – this cannot be demonstrated. In any case, it does not appear to me that it *has* been. It appears that Chrétien could have done the things he did – *trové* the things he did – without studying Rhetoric in school. He does not use clearly technical rhetorical terms, nor do his works demonstrate any study of Rhetoric: only rhetorical (with a small "r") excellence. Scholars have noted that Chrétien might have benefited from reading the arts of rhetoric composed at his time, or earlier. Who can argue with that? (The authors of those works might also have benefited from hearing him.) But no one has been able to show that he actually *did* study Rhetoric.

The underlying and implicit argument about Chrétien's "rhetoric" seems to have proceeded as follows: "Since Chrétien was unquestionably a clerk, and therefore has to have studied Rhetoric in school, we ought to be able to find its influence on his work." But if we remove the certainty that Chrétien *was* a clerk, the "obviousness" of the influence of school Rhetoric on his work appears to evaporate as well.

Chrétien as a knowledgeable man, but not a clerk

Here we explore the clerical vs. lay dichotomy in twelfth century courts. The point is not that Chrétien was an unlearned or an ignorant man, only that he was not a clerk. There seems little doubt – and the second prologue we examined certainly claims as much – that Chrétien was familiar with narrative and broadly thematic material from Ovid; he seems also to have known stories from Virgil, perhaps material from Martianus Capella, and quite possibly from other classical writers;[26] he may have had a general familiarity with contemporary rhetorical practice. How to account for such knowledge if Chrétien was not a clerk? We have already confronted this issue with regard to the *Thèbes* poet. But perhaps we need to examine more closely issues of "knowledge" and "learning" in the twelfth century. One of our problems may be that we think in terms of a chasm between the clerical and non-clerical worlds in this period:[27] if we glorify the former as not merely written but learned, we dismiss

---

then, receive the host at each and every course – or, rather, has Chrétien changed his mind about the grail and its meaning: its "holiness"?

26 See, for example, Peter Kardon, *Chrétien de Troyes and the Auctores.*

27 This despite the recent work of scholars such as Brian Stock and M.T. Clanchy who have shown the complex forms of interpenetration between oral and written worlds. Their work is not of course primarily concerned with the status or functioning of vernacular literature; see Stock, *The Implications of Literacy: Written Language and Models of Interpretation in the Eleventh and Twelfth Centuries*; Clanchy, *From Memory to Written Record.*

the latter as not merely oral but ignorant. This is one of the self-serving biases of our profession that have, I believe, clouded our objectivity in these matters.

The dichotomy between clerk and lay is still causing us difficulty. As we saw in Chapter 3, the Latin *clericus* could refer either to function (clerical status) or clerical learning (the quality of being *literatus*, and the practice of reading and writing). Both meanings of the term seem to set the conceptual world – and in particular, the discursive practices – of the clergy off clearly from those of the laity. But this dichotomy is not so marked as it might sometimes appear. As a number of scholars have pointed out, the oral tradition (if we define it as the verbal tradition of the laity) was never totally oral in the Middle Ages, because Christian culture can never be said to have been "textless." Any Christian who went to Mass saw liturgical books in use, and saw and heard the Bible opened and read aloud. Chrétien in particular has many references to attendance at Mass and at the liturgical Hours, and a good many biblical echoes, which proves nothing more than that he was a faithful Christian, and had, like many other people, absorbed stories from the Bible and words and thoughts from the liturgy. That *jongleurs* sometimes sang about saints of long ago – such as Alexis about whom Peter Waldo heard, probably in the 1160s, a song that changed his life[28] – makes it clear that there were some people back there with books. Performers unquestionably enriched their repertory, through memorization, with works composed by others – and no doubt some of the works they mastered were originally, or somewhere along the line, written compositions. Many *jongleurs* were only too happy to refer to the story or song they performed as having a book as a source.[29]

If there were written elements embedded in the oral tradition, there were also important oral elements within the clerical and scholastic tradition. Even clerks and churchmen learned the vernacular at the knee of their mother or wet-nurse, and were familiar with oral tales, songs and the like. As adults, they told "popular" stories in Latin – and probably in the vernacular too. They cannot be said to have lived their lives "remote from" oral culture. Moreover, those clerks, such as Wace and Benoît, who worked in the vernacular produced their works primarily for people who did not read. Many such compositions are "written" in one sense, but they were intended to be read (or even recited) aloud, not read privately. All through the Middle Ages, we find learned clerics grafting themselves onto – or rather, expressing their links to – aural, voiced, performed traditions; we see this phenomenon with perhaps special clarity in the theatre, but elsewhere as well.

In another sense, too, many clerical compositions are not quite books as we use the word. Generally, the author was not the actual writer, but rather the

---

28 "Waldenses" *The Catholic Encyclopedia*, Vol. XV, p. 528: "Peter Waldo."
29 See Vitz, "French Medieval Oral Traditions."

voice behind the text. The author dictated to a scribe who took the words down, often on a wax tablet. Frequently, but not always, the dictator reread what was noted, correcting it; then the work was taken down on parchment in a final, or "fair," copy. Thus many works produced even by literate, text-oriented clerics were conceived more orally than scriptorially: they began with a kind of oral performance of the material. Even the Latin books that clerks studied in school, they often learned orally: these books were read aloud to the students far more, it appears, than they were read privately, silently by the student himself. Clerical training thus had a strong oral component. So did clerical practice, with its oral examinations and exercises: its *quaestiones* and *disputationes*.[30] The point is that both the predominantly oral and the predominantly written tradition in this period were in fact blended traditions. Neither existed typically in a pure or unalloyed form. (Indeed, as we noted earlier, there can be no written tradition without the oral, while the opposite – a purely oral culture – *can* exist.)

In the twelfth century, the dichotomy was being eroded in a new way. Because *clericus* often in fact meant *literatus*, the former term was coming increasingly to be applied to educated members of the laity. Thus, the term *clericus* could now refer to anyone who was lettered, literate, able to read (and probably write) Latin; such a layman was learned, a scholar – and the term praised him for being such.[31] Just as there had long been some semi-literate or virtually illiterate members of the clergy[32] – un-clerical clerks, as it were – there were now rising numbers of literate laymen; should we call them "lay clerks"? In any case, we find references to the *miles literatus*: the knight who can read Latin.[33] In this period, such figures were perhaps most often members of the higher nobility: kings and counts; few were ordinary knights – though men who had a role in government, such as bailiffs, stewards and the like, were apt to know some Latin, for official purposes.[34]

In any event, if the alignment among the various dichotomies – clerical vs. lay; literate vs. non-literate; written vs. oral – had never been especially firm, by the mid- to late-twelfth century, it was increasingly unreliable. In particular, not all *literati* were *clercs*.

But the blend of elements is still more complex, as concerns the issue of "literacy" in particular. In the last chapter, we noted the increasing numbers

[30] Ong points out that the ideal of classical education was to produce not the writer but the orator and rhetor: *Orality and Literacy*, p. 113.

[31] See Clanchy, *From Memory*, pp. 226ff; M.B. Parkes, "The Literacy of the Laity."

[32] See J.W. Thompson, *The Literacy of the Laity in the Middle Ages*, e.g., p. 136.

[33] See Clanchy, *From Memory*, esp. "The Question of the Literacy of the Laity," pp. 231ff, and "Knowledge of Latin among Non-Churchmen," pp. 234ff.

[34] See Clanchy, *From Memory*, p. 299. As to the case of ordinary knights: how common was the case of Abelard's family, in which all the sons were apparently taught Latin? As to the peasantry: according to Clanchy, even some peasants knew how to read at least some Latin. (Personal communcation: 9/1995.)

of clerks of various stripe who were, by the mid-twelfth century, pouring into Anglo-Norman and French aristocratic courts. Their presence is increasingly felt – as M.T. Clanchy has pointed out in *From Memory to Written Record*[35] – in the growing recourse to and preservation of documents, in the rise of bureaucracy, and in many other ways. Now, one of the effects of the presence of such clerical figures was clearly to raise the level of learning, of text consciousness, and sometimes – but not always – of literacy, of the ruler. To some degree his entire household was affected. As the proverb goes: "A rising tide lifts all ships." (Many do not in fact think of oral culture as a *low* tide but never mind . . .) Even those who did not learn to read for themselves heard books read aloud, saw documents (charters and the like, official letters) being drawn up, displayed and read publicly. In other words, the presence and prestige of the book and of written things in general far preceded the rise of general literacy itself among the nobility.[36] It far preceded even the perceived need for literacy.[37] The importance of this virtually self-evident fact has, I believe, been inadequately appreciated. As Clanchy has put it: "Documents had to precede widening literacy . . . The gentry were not going to learn to read until documents were available and necessary."[38] And this did not occur before the thirteenth century.

Just who was "learned" in twelfth century courts? Clerks sometimes taught their lay pupils, patrons, or friends at court "letters" and gave them books to read or handsome codices – such as illuminated Psalters – to look at. But many people in court also heard works read aloud; Latin works were

[35] *From Memory*, Part I, Chapter 2: "The proliferation of documents," pp. 44ff, and *passim*.

[36] Mary D. Stanger has documented the fact that several counts of Flanders in this period were unable to read: "Literary Patronage at the Medieval Court of Flanders."

On the "literate" knight, see also Ralph V. Turner, "The *Miles Literatus* in Twelfth- and Thirteenth-Century England: How Rare a Phenomenon?" Turner identifies a number of English noblemen and women, and other non-clerks, of the period who were able to read, and sometimes write, Latin. Such figures were, however, clearly in the minority. Moreover, what they read (and wrote) were theological or devotional works, or documents such as charters.

[37] It is interesting to note that William Marshal – who had an extraordinary chivalric and diplomatic career in England and France in the twelfth and early thirteenth centuries, and who rose in England from the position of a simple (and poor) knight to that of earl and regent of England – does not appear to have learned to read (or write). See Duby, *William Marshal, The Flower of Chivalry*, p. 36; see also David Crouch, *William Marshal: Court, Career and Chivalry in the Angevin Empire, 1147–1219*. In any event, the Marshall's anonymous biographer never mentions such an accomplishment in his verse "life."

[38] Clanchy, *From Memory*, p. 78. Ralph Turner sees it somewhat differently, though both scholars are trying to account for on-going illiteracy among the nobility: Turner closes his article on "The *Miles Literatus*" with a quotation: " 'If men of position were illiterate, it was because they made no effort to learn rather than that provision for their teaching was not available' " (p. 945). Turner is quoting Doris M. Stenton, *English Society in the Early Middle Ages*, p. 251.

loosely translated into, or explained in, French – what we might call "reor-alized." Thus, "books" could be presented *orally* to court audiences, and they might be recast, retold, in a new form. Moreover, people might just be told what was *in* the books. A layman could, then, become "knowledgeable," or "learned," and even perhaps know some Latin, without being able to read. A number of important late twelfth century nobles, while they were not in fact "lettered," were able to talk as though they *were*. One prominent example is Count Baudouin de Guines who astonished the churchmen of his day by being so learned. He seemed lettered – but, in fact, he was not literate.[39] In short, not all laymen recognized or praised as such were really *literati*.

In an important article, "Varieties and Consequences of Medieval Literacy and Illiteracy," Franz Bäuml has argued that the modern dichotomy between literacy and illiteracy does not reflect the complexities of the medieval situation; he points out that what mattered was not whether people could, or did, read for themselves, but whether they had *access* to what was in books – access through others, often clerks. Many learned people in the twelfth and thirteenth centuries were "literate" in this, but only in this, sense: they knew many things that came from books.

What evidence is there for the existence of this sort of impact of learned men on *jongleurs* and other performers? Let us look at an extremely interesting poem by Raimon Vidal, "Abril issi'ei."[40] This Occitan poem, composed in octo, is a dialogue between Raimon and a *jongleur*. (While Raimon was Catalan, and the work dates from a bit later than our period – about 1213 – much of the poem is taken up with reminiscences of twelfth century courts in England, France and Germany.) The poem is also in part an *ensenhamen*, or lesson, for a *jongleur*; Raimon says that:

> Joglaria vol home gay
> e franc e dos e conoissen,
> e que sapcha far a la gen,
> segon que cascus es, plazer.   lines 954–57, p. 92

> (The *jongleurs*' art wants a man who is gay/ and noble, gentle, and knowledgeable,/ and who knows how to please people,/ according to who they are [according to their station in life].)

How does the *jongleur* manage to become knowledgeable, or "conois-sens"? Raimon advises:

---

[39] Discussed by Duby in "The Culture of the Knightly Class: Audience and Patronage," esp. pp. 261–62. Clanchy discusses similar figures, and the complex blends of literacy and illiteracy, in *From Memory*, pp. 234ff.

[40] In *Nouvelles occitanes du Moyen Age*, ed. and trans. Jean-Charles Huchet, pp. 37–139.

... e de terras captenemens
adzautz e d'omes conoiss[ens]
vulhatz saber. E, sobre tot,
gardatz que li dig e li mot
vos venguan d'omes conoissens
per c'al contar entre las gens
no.us en sia vils pretz donatz.   lines 1073–79, p. 98

(... learn the manners of different countries/ and of knowledgeable men./ And above all/ make sure that your expressions/ and
your words come to you from knowledgeable men/ so that when
you tell stories in front of people/ you will not be given low
value.)

This issue of the importance of learning to please "each one" – but especially to please the learned by listening to and imitating their discourse –
comes up repeatedly in Raimon's poem.

One might call this complex and ambiguous phenomenon "court
learning." What we now have is laymen who are not necessarily lettered –
though they may have acquired some rudiments of "letters." They can be
described as *frottés de clergie*. They have come into close and intimate contact
with letters, book-learning; they have rubbed up against it. But reading and
writing are still essentially marginal to their lives. In the twelfth century, it has
not yet even been fully accepted as desirable for ordinary knights – as distinct
from rulers – to know how to read. (Women and members of the merchant
class seem to have learned to read before male members of the nobility.
Members of the bourgeoisie, however, became interested in reading Latin – in
becoming literate in that strict sense – only fairly late.[41] It is not clear that
women ever became particularly involved in Latin literacy.) The kind of life
these people led in the twelfth and early thirteenth centuries, and the kinds of
entertainment they were accustomed to, by no means required that they know
how to read for themselves.

It is not just the rulers themselves and their immediate families who can be
expected to have been touched by this sort of "trickle-down learning" but all
those who were active at court, including minstrels: those vernacular poets and
performers who were regularly present at court, who functioned as part of the
household. Some performers are known to have been on close terms with their
noble masters. To mention just one great name: Henry I had his own *jongleur* –
his *mimus regis* – named Raherus (who later, with the wealth he had acquired,
founded the priory of St. Bartholomew at Smithfield).[42] Literary works give us
the same picture: for example, in his *Roman de la Rose ou de Guillaume de*

---

[41] Duby, "The Culture of the Knightly Class," p. 258; Clanchy, *From Memory*, pp.
188ff.

[42] See E.K. Chambers, *The Mediaeval Stage*, Vol. I, pp. 48–49.

Dole, Jean Renart tells of a king who had deep affection for a minstrel named Jouglet and kept him with him constantly. The king listened to Jouglet before going to bed at night, and every morning had him sing the same song (whose words Jean provides).[43] *Ménestrels – ministeriales –* were after all servants of the lord or lady. Minstrels too may have learned some letters; they too may have acquired some general learning, but without letters. The standard view of Chrétien (and other early *romanciers*) has been that they were the providers of this classical lore to the nobility, but they are just as likely to have been the beneficiaries as the benefactors.

But what court minstrels of the late twelfth century are *certain* to have grasped is the "cachet" of references to writing and books: books now had prestige. By the latter part of the twelfth century the court poet, whether he could read or not, had to "brush up his Ovid"[44] and be able to refer to other classical or to biblical authorities. In one of his poems the twelfth century poet Conon de Béthune has a knight say to a lady who has, too late, offered him her love, that he has heard talk of her beauty, but it is now gone:

> et de Troie rai jou oï conter
> k'ele fu ja de mout grant seignorie;
> or n'i puet on fors les plaches trover.[45]

(and about Troy have I also heard tell/ that it was, in the past, of great power;/ but now one cannot even find the place . . .)

Gace Brulé, another late twelfth century poet, ends a song by saying:

> Gasçoz define sa chançon
> Ha! fins Pyramus que feron?
> Vers Amor ne somes jor fort.[46]

(Gace finishes his song/ Ha! what shall we do, fair Pyramus?/ Toward Love we are not strong.)

This is Gace's only "learned" allusion.

Do these lines show that Conon and Gace have been reading about the Trojan War? Poring over books by Ovid? References to books, to bookish

---

[43] Jean Renart, *Roman de la Rose ou de Guillaume de Dole*, ed. Félix Lecoy, lines 3390–406.

[44] "Brush up your Shakespeare/ Start quoting him now/ Brush up your Shakespeare/ And the women you will wow. . . ." (Cole Porter, "Kiss Me, Kate").

The poet who composed *Floire et Blancheflor*, apparently in the late-twelfth century in the west of France, refers to Paris and Helen – his only "learned" references, aside from one to Adam. It must be said, though, that the line between classical reference and reference to quasi-historical exoticism – e.g., place names such as "Acianon," "Feminie," and "Ocenie" – is a fine, indeed an arbitrary one. See *Floire et Blancheflor: Seconde Version*, ed. Margaret M. Pelan.

[45] Conon de Béthune, *Chansons*, ed. Axel Wallensköld.

[46] *Chansons de Gace Brulé*, ed. Gédéon Huet, Chanson XXI, lines 36–38 (p. 52).

sources, even – especially! – classy classical ones such as Ovid and Macrobius: are these really to be seen as proofs of a poet's *clergie*? Are they not, in many cases, simply part of a new pseudo-clerical court packaging of a still essentially oral product? The same goes for the use of what we might classify as "learned" terms. It is a bit like the prestige today of computer terminology, or, for that matter, references to Derrida or Foucault. The fact that someone can bandy computer words about or speak of Deconstruction does not necessarily indicate genuine "computer-literacy" or the ability to decipher Derrida. Every generation has its buzz-words, and in the late-twelfth century bookish words had become, at least in the world of the court, the new fashion. We must then be far warier than we have been about accepting the claims poets make about their sources, or even the words they toss around, as proofs of literate status, of *clergie*. We have (as I said earlier) been taking as autobiographical truths claims that are more appropriately viewed as part of the poet's *captatio benevolentiae* (to borrow a Latin term from Rhetoric).

When Chrétien declares, in his prologue to *Cligés* (lines 18–23), that "We find this story written in one of the books of the cupboard (*aumaire*) of my Lord Saint Pierre in Beauvais" – and that, since it is St. Peter's book this shows that the story is true – I for one am not sure I believe he had any such book. St. Peter and "his library" seem there in order to give authority to the story. (The cathedral of St. Pierre of Beauvais did have a distinguished library in the twelfth century – though of course there were no vernacular works in it, and certainly no romances.[47]) A similar claim is made in a "lai féerique" of the late-twelfth or early-thirteenth century, "Le lai de l'aubépine." This lai has no clerkly features, but its poet/narrator assures his listeners that the authenticity of the story is assured because the book containing it is located in the church of St. Aaron in Carlion in Brittany.

> Qui que des lais tigne a mençoigne,
> saciés je nes tienc pas a songe;
> les aventures trespasees
> qui diversement ai contees,
> nes ai pas dites sans garant;
> les estores en trai avant
> ki encore sont a Carlion
> ens el moustier Saint Aaron
> e en Bretaigne sont eües
> e en pluisors lius conneües.
> Pour chou que les truis en memore,
> vos vuel demonstrer par estore
> de .II. enfans une aventure
> ki tous jors a esté obscure.   lines 1–14[48]

---

[47] Personal communication: Guy Danoë, 5/1993.
[48] *Lais féeriques du XIIe et XIIIe siècles*, ed. Alexandre Micha, p. 226.

(Whoever may hold lais to be lies,/ know that I do not think them
to be reveries;/ the stories of the past/ that I have told at various
times,/ I have not told without guarantees [of authenticity];/ I put
forth stories/ that are still in Carlion/ in the church of Saint
Aaron/ and are held in Brittany/ and known in several other
places./ Since I find them [these lais] in memory,/ I want to
demonstrate to you in a story/ the adventure of two children/
which until now has always been obscure.)

Reference to prestigious libraries (or to churches containing books) is what
we might call an "authenticity ploy." It can be found in epic prologues as
well, where reference to tomes at St. Denis was particularly fashionable.

Another look at Chrétien's "learning"

Within this framework, let us have a look at the sort of learning that
Chrétien displays. Is it really the sort that would have to have been acquired
from books? I suggest that it could as easily have been picked up from court
talk, or from sustained social intercourse with learned men. (Later, I will
suggest a few possibles – that is, men who are known to have frequented the
court of Chrétien's patrons Henry and Marie of Champagne.)

Like the *Thèbes* poet, Chrétien was interested in the Liberal Arts. And in his
case as well, this depiction has been seen as proof of clergy. But does Chrétien's
use of the Arts show book-learning with any more certainty than that of the
Thèbes poet? Near the end of *Érec et Énide* (lines 6674–728), Chrétien
describes Enide's coronation robe, decorated with images of the Arts. He
speaks of Macrobius and of a book. (This passage has been read and hence
translated in several ways. I quote here from the edition I have taken as
standard, the Mario Roques edition.)

> Lisant trovomes an l'estoire
> la description de la robe,
> si an trai a garant Macrobe
> qui an l'estoire mist s'antante,
> qui l'antendié, que je ne mante.
> Macrobe m'anseigne a descrivre,
> si con je l'ai trové el livre,
> l'uevre del drap et le portret.
> Quatre fees l'avoient fet
> par gran san et par gran mestrie.   lines 6674–83.[49]

[49] The uncertainties in this passage bear primarily on the following issues: first, the
exact role of Macrobius: did his book teach Chrétien to describe this robe, or did Macrobius
teach him the art of description in general? If the latter, then what book is Chrétien speaking
of? And what, exactly, does the word "estoire" mean here: story? history? book? See

(Reading, we find in a story/ the description of the robe,/ and, to show that I am not lying,/ I take as my witness Macrobius/ who put all his understanding into the story,/ and who understood it./ Macrobius teaches me how to describe,/ just as I found it in the book,/ the workmanship of the cloth and the images on it./ Four fairies had made it/ with great skill and with great mastery.)

Thus, Chrétien speaks of "our finding" things in "stories" and also says that he "found in a book" of Macrobius the art of description. It must be said that this is the most decidedly clerical – indeed, in my view, the *only* strongly clerical – claim that Chrétien makes in his entire work. Perhaps it should be taken at face value: as a statement that Chrétien himself has recourse to, and reads for himself, Latin books. But there are other possibilities. Firstly, his claim that *he* has found something in a book is preceded by the more general statement that *we* find things in books; perhaps he has "found" things that were pointed out or told to him by others. If Chrétien is indeed basing his knowledge of Macrobius on hearsay, this might explain the fact that what he says is in Macrobius is, in fact, not there. Secondly, it is altogether possible that Chrétien is simply using the name Macrobius to give authority to his work, and that he knows little or nothing about this great medieval "auctor." Thus, this would be mere name-dropping. Finally, perhaps we should understand this passage as performed with a wink at the audience . . .

Let us turn to the description itself. In this passsage devoted to the Arts, Chrétien never mentions the trivium – the intellectual arts of language: Grammar, Logic and Rhetoric. He takes up only Geometry, Arithmetic, Music, Astronomy: the quadrivium – though he does not use this learned term, or even speak of the "arts." Rather, he calls the four Liberal Arts that he mentions "oevres" ("works"), saying that they were painted on the robe by fairies. But we should review the passage in its entirety:

> L'une i portraist Geometrie
> si com ele esgarde et mesure
> con li ciax et la terre dure,
> si que de rien nule n'i faut
> et puis le bas, et puis le haut,
> et puis le lé, et puis le lonc,
> et puis esgarde par selonc   6690
> con la mers est lee et parfonde,
> et si mesure tot le monde.
> Ceste oevre i mist la premerainne,
> et la seconde mist sa painne
> et Arimetique portraire,

comments of Peter Dembowski in his edition of *Erec et Enide* for the *Oeuvres complètes de Chrétien* (gen. ed. Daniel Poirion), p. 1112.

si se pena de molt bien faire,
si com ele nonbre par sans
les jorz et les ores el tans,
et l'eve de mere gote a gote,
et puis la gravele trestote,   6700
et les estoiles tire a tire;
bien en set la verité dire,
et quantes fuelles an bois a;
onques nonbres ne l'an boisa,
ne ja n'an mantira de rien,
car ele i viaut antandre bien.
Tex ert l'uevre d'Arimetique,
et la tierce oevre ert de Musique,
a cui toz li deduiz s'acorde,
chanz, et deschantz, et sanz descorde,   6710
d'arpe, de rote, et de vïele.
Ceste oevre estoit et boene et bele,
car devant lui disoient tuit
li estrumant et li deduit.
La quarte, qui aprés ovra,
a molt boene oevre recouvra,
que la meillor des arz i mist:
d'Astronomie s'antremist,
cele qui fet tante mervoille,
et as estoiles s'an consoille   6720
et a la lune et au soleil.
En autre leu n'an prant consoil
de rien qui a feire li soit;
cil la consoille bien a droit
de quanque cele li requiert,
et quanque fu, et quanque iert,
l'estuet certainnemant savoir,
sanz mantir et sanz decevoir.
Ceste oevre fu el drap portreite
don la robe Erec estoit feite
a fil d'or ovree et tissue. . . .   lines 6684–731

(One [fairy] portrays on it Geometry/ as she [Geometry] looks at
and measures/ how far the sky and the earth go on,/ so that
nothing is missing –/ both the bottom and the top,/ and the width
and then the length,/ and then she looks to see/ how wide and
deep is the sea,/ and she measures the whole world./ This work
the first one [fairy] put there,/ and the second one took the
trouble/ to portray Arithmetic,/ and she worked to do it right,/ [to
show] how she [Arithmetic] counts, with her sense,/ the days
and the hours of time/ and the water of the sea drip by drip/ and
all the stones/ and the stars, one by one;/ she knows how to tell
the truth,/ and how many leaves there are in the forest;/ never

does she make a mistake in her numbers,/ and she never lies about anything,/ for she wants to understand rightly./ Such was the work of Arithmetic,/ and the third was of Music,/ in whom all pleasures find their harmony,/ songs and descants, without discord,/ of harp, of rote, and of vielle./ This work was good and beautiful,/ for before her speak all/ instruments and pleasures./ The fourth [fairy], who worked after the others/ found for herself a very good work/ for she put into it the best of the arts:/ she undertook [to depict] Astronomy,/ who makes many marvels/ and takes counsel of the stars/ and the moon and the sun./ She does not take counsel anywhere else/ about anything that concerns her;/ he who counsels her certainly has the right/ to whatever she might ask of him,/ however great it was and will be,/ she must certainly know/ without lying and without deceit./ This work was depicted on the cloth/ from which Erec's robe was made,/ worked and woven with threads of gold.)

Thus, for example, the Liberal Art of Geometry is simply the art of measuring everything, Arithmetic that of counting everything – and no complex or written calculations are mentioned. Music is the art – the work: "she" – in whom all the musical pleasures of song and instrument are brought into accord or harmony. Astronomy "takes counsel of the stars, moon and sun." As I noted earlier, what Chrétien says (at least, many have *thought* he said it) that he found in Macrobius is not there.[50]

If we compare Chrétien's image of the Liberal Arts with that of the *Thèbes* poet (discussed in Chapter 3), we can say the following: 1) Chrétien's description is roughly twice as long – which is all the more striking since Chrétien mentions only four of the arts (the *Thèbes* poet enumerated all seven). 2) His amplification is of a purely formal nature: he multiplies nouns, adjectives, verbs, rather than adding content. 3) His basic concept of the Arts is very similar to that found in the *Thèbes*: both are largely taken up with the counting and measuring properties of Arithmetic and Geometry; both have a humanistic and ethical, as opposed to a scientific and rationalistic, emphasis:[51] Geometry does her work diligently, Arithmetic tells the truth, Music brings harmony and resolves discord, Astronomy takes wise counsel, knows the truth and does not lie or deceive. These works are "good": "boenes oevres." And they are "beautiful" – "beles" in themselves, and worked into the cloth with gold thread. Thus, Chrétien introduces an important "esthetic" element into this discussion, one that was not emphasized in the *Thèbes*.

Nothing here is particularly "clerical" or shows any special book-learning

---

50 There is something along those lines in Martianus Capella; see Kardon, *The Wisdom of the Auctores*.

51 See the discussion of the new twelfth century rationalistic treatments of the Liberal Arts in Chapter 3, and Jaeger, *Envy of Angels*.

or school-training.[52] In light of the general interest in the Liberal Arts in this period – and in particular the growing appeal of the concept for laymen and women (discussed in Chapter 3) – it seems likely that a minstrel such as Chrétien would have found it in his interest to be able to speak of the Arts. It is also likely that he would have found it easy to acquire such general information about them in court. But his view of the Arts is somewhat old-fashioned, which may suggest that he got his material not from a "cutting-edge" clerk but from an older, or at least more conservative, figure. Might he even have gotten it from an informed nobleman or noblewoman – or even from his patrons, the Count and Countess – or from another minstrel?[53]

Chrétien knows the Arts as they were "taught" – explained, discussed, chatted about – informally in many a late twelfth century court. And if in different schools the curriculum varied somewhat, the Arts curriculum would have varied even more as offered in court. Here, it would have depended very largely on the personal interests and abilities of the particular "teacher"; the position of this figure with regard to the latest ideas on the Arts (and other matters); the set of people being instructed; the time that teacher and pupils had available, and so on.

It is with the greatest respect that Chrétien speaks of *oevres* such as we see here. By "oeuvres" I mean, however, not the Liberal Arts themselves, but the work of the fairies: "their great skill (*sens*) and mastery" (line 6681). Chrétien expresses a number of times his admiration for beautiful craftsmanship. He does so when he describes Enide's beautiful saddle: lines 5382; and again when he tells about the extraordinary tower (with private chambers) built by Cligés' serf Jean for the lovers: lines 5307ff. Chrétien even has Cligés call this skilled serf of his a "mestre" (line 5314): this peasant is a master builder!

But it is essential to recognize that Chrétien never speaks admiringly of the beauty or verbal mastery to be found in books. He speaks of books only as bearing authority, as conferring credibility. In short, Chrétien's concept of esthetic excellence and accomplishment appears to be not literary, but

---

[52] We should note that there *are* poetic works which show distinctly learned handlings of this material. A work which gives a systematic review of the Liberal Arts is *La bataille des sept arts* by the thirteenth century poet Henri d'Andeli. In the detail of the representations of the Arts, this 462-line poem leaves no doubt that Henri had been formed by the school curriculum, and that he wanted to see a return to the dominance of Grammar. See *The Battle of the Seven Arts: A French Poem by Henry d'Andeli, Trouvère of the Thirteenth Century*, L.J. Paetow, ed. and trans.

[53] It is true – as M.T. Clanchy has reminded me [personal communication] – that it is dangerous to assume that Chrétien *only* knew about the "arts" what he put into his work. One would not know, from reading *Alice in Wonderland*, that Lewis Carroll was an academic logician; clearly, he knew many things that he did not put into this work of fiction. On the other hand, if one did not already know, from other evidence, that Carroll was a professional logician, one could hardly demonstrate it from *Alice*.

"artisanal": workmanlike. His expressions of admiration go, as it were, toward the *il*-liberal, not the liberal, arts.

Further internal evidence that Chrétien was not a clerk

I have spoken of the importance of a careful examination of internal evidence in the text, rather than reliance on blanket judgments, such as that all romances are the work of clerks. (Let's say it for the record: the opposite – to declare that all romances were the work of minstrels – would hardly be better.)

What can we adduce from the representation of learning and literacy in Chrétien's romances themselves? It is, I think, important to note that the court of Arthur, presented – somewhat playfully, to be sure – as the repository of chivalry, contains virtually no reading or writing. The very few scenes that evoke some reading behavior – and not one of them occurs at Arthur's court itself – show the following:

— Women read, as in the famous passage in *Yvain* (lines 5354–67), in which the daughter reads aloud to the parents. The fact that she can read French does not of course mean that, according to the definitions of the day, she is necessarily "literate," since to be so she would have to be able to read Latin. And, as noted earlier, the word *roman* does not necessarily mean "romance," but can refer to virtually any sort of composition in the vernacular. What this reference does show is that there was some reading of vernacular works going on in small groups; we will return to such matters, and to this passage, in Part II, Chapter 6.

— The woman reading may in fact just be holding an illuminated book and reciting her psalms. This is the case of Laudine who, as she grieves for her dead husband, "reads" a Psalter with gold letters.

> Mes iqui remest tote sole,
> et sovant se prent a la gole,
> et tort ses poinz, et bat ses paumes
> et list en un sautier ses saumes,
> anluminé a letres d'or.
> Et mes sire Yvains est ancor
> a la fenestre ou il l'esgarde;
> et quant il plus s'an done garde,
> plus l'ainme, et plus li abelist.
> Ce qu'ele plore et qu'ele lisit,
> volsist qu'ele lessié eüst
> et qu'a lui parler li pleüst.   lines 1415–26

> (But she remains here all alone,/ and often she tries to grab her
> own neck,/ and wrings her hands and beats her palms together/
> and reads her psalms in a psalter/ illuminated with gold letters./

113

And my lord Yvain is still/ at the window where he looks at her;/ and the more closely he looks,/ the more he loves her, and the more she pleases him./ He would have wished that she would leave off/ her weeping and reading/ and that it would please her to speak to him.)

Is this woman "reading," as we understand the word today? Perhaps – and it must certainly be acknowledged that noble women were strongly associated with copies of the Psalter, and vice versa. (Many twelfth and thirteenth century works, from various genres, refer to devout aristocratic women with Psalters.[54]) Eleanor of Aquitaine is shown – pious for eternity – in her funeral effigy at Fontevrault, holding an open book, presumed to be a Psalter.

But it must also be said that many members of the laity, like the clergy, knew psalms and other prayers by heart.[55] Moreover – and it is significant for our concerns – the medieval word "lire," like "rede" and "lesen," did not refer unambiguously, as they do today, to the activity of "reading a text privately." To some degree, then, the verb "lire" is a *faux ami*: we think we know what it means, but we may well be mistaken. "Lire" could also mean "to say" and "to recite." It could mean "to gaze at" and "to look at"[56] – and in this period noble men and women are known to have enjoyed looking at and "meditating on" beautiful books, such as this one was. As paleographer E.A. Lowe has said of Gothic script – the script characteristic of late-twelfth century books such as the one that Laudine is looking at:

---

[54] Epics include *Girart de Roussillon* and *Berte aux grands pieds*; romances include *The Prose Lancelot*, and others.

On the women's association with – and reading of – the Psalter, see Clanchy, *From Memory*, pp. 191–96.

[55] See, for example, Susan Noakes, *Timely Reading: Between Exegesis and Interpretation*, p. 20.

[56] See Adolf Tobler and Erhard Lommatzsch, *Altfranzösisches Wörterbuch*, Vol. 5, p. 507; their dictionary does not address this issue very directly, but see under the headings "vorlesen, verlesen" and "erkennen, blicken." Frédéric Godefroy, in his *Dictionnaire de l'ancienne langue française et de tous ses dialectes, du XIe au XVe siècle*, addresses the complexities of the meaning of the medieval verb "lire" only in his supplement, and here he adds to the standard modern meaning the fact that the verb can mean "prendre connaissance du contenu d'un écrit, d'un livre," without explaining how this might occur. His examples are rather ambiguous; one of them (for example) seems to refer fairly clearly to reading aloud as opposed to silently: "Li premiers livre est feniz./ Retraiz, liz, cuntez e diz" ("The first book is finished./ Recounted, read (aloud?), told and said"; from Benoît de Sainte-Maure); Vol. X: Complement, p. 86.

For medieval English and German, see Albert C. Baugh, "The Middle English Romance: Some Questions of Creation, Presentation, and Preservation," esp. p. 21. For the similar meanings of the German "lesen," see Green, *Medieval Listening*, Appendix: "Middle High German 'lesen' = 'to narrate, recount, tell,' " pp. 316–23.

I will return to this important verb, and this important issue, later in this chapter, and in Chapter 6.

The Gothic script is difficult to read. It has the serious faults of ambiguity, artificiality, and overloading. It was the child of an age that was not bent on achieving the practical, the age of St. Louis and St. Francis. It is as if the written page was made to be looked at and not read. Instead of legibility its objective seems to be a certain effect of art and beauty.[57]

The beauteous Laudine may, then, be looking at her beautiful Psalter and attempting to recite her psalms as she grieves. In any case, it was presumably as difficult then as it would be today actually to read a book while one also tore one's hair and tried to strangle oneself.

A somewhat similar scene – minus the loud grief – occurs in a description of St. Elizabeth of Hungary by Osbern Bokenham in his mid-fifteenth century *Legends of Holy Women*:

> And thou she of lettrure no kunnyng had,
> Yet ful oftyn-tyme she wolde vse
> To han a sauter opyn beforn hyr sprad,
> Where-in she made hyr for to muse,
> And long yt was or she hyt wold refuse,
> As thow she had red euen by & by . . .[58]

Thus, there was a tradition – still practiced late in the medieval period – for non-literate persons engaged in acts of piety to hold the psalter open before them and look at it: to mediate and "muse" upon it. What is interesting is that Chrétien is prepared to use the word "reading"; three centuries later, Osbern is not: the pious but illiterate saint just "muses" before the open book.

In a word, this scene in Chrétien may indicate the lady's pious behavior, and her wealth and nobility – as well as the violence of her grief – more certainly than it does her ability to read. In any case, in the romance she never reads, or even opens, another book.

— A bit of reading goes on in a cemetery, and in this scene, this romance, Lancelot appears to be doing the reading. A monk leads him there:

> . . . Lors l'en maine.[59]
> El cemetire aprés li mainne
> antre les tres plus beles tonbes
> qu'an poïst trover jusqu'a Donbes,
> ne de la jusqu'a Panapelune;
> et s'avoit letres sor chascune

---

[57] E.A. Lowe, "Handwriting," in *The Legacy of the Middle Ages*, ed. C.G. Crump and E.F. Jacobs, Oxford, Clarendon Press, 1926, p. 223.

[58] *Legendys*, ed. Mary Serjeantson, p. 260. My thanks to Joyce Coleman for bringing this text to my notice.

[59] Other manuscripts introduce this passage a bit differently, and shift the sentence break.

qui les nons de ces devisoient
qui dedanz les tonbes girroient.
Et il meïsmes tot a tire
comanaça lors les nons a lire
et trova: "Cil girra Gauvains,
ci Looys, et ci Yvains."
Aprés ces trois i a maint liz,
des nons as chevaliers esliz,
des plus prisiez et des meillors
et de cele terre et d'aillors.
Antre les autres une an trueve
de marbre, et sanble estre de l'ueve
sor totes les autres plus bele.
Li chevaliers le moinne apele
et dit: "Ces tonbes qui ci sont,
de coi servent?" Et cil respont:
"Vos avez les lettres veües;
se vos les avez antendues,
don savez vos bien qu'eles dïent
et que les tonbres senefient . . .   lines 1856–80

(. . . Then he [the monk] leads him [Lancelot] there./ The monk leads him into the cemetery/ among the most beautiful tombs/ that one could have found from here to Dombes,/ or even to Pampelona;/ and there were letters on each one/ which told the names of those/ who would lie in the tombs./ And he himself [Lancelot?] immediately/ began to read the names/ and found: "Here will lie Gauvain,/ here Louis [Leones?], and here Yvain."/ After these three he read many more,/ of names of elite knights,/ the most prized and the best/ both of this land and others./ Among the others he finds one/ of marble, and it seems the work/ among all the others the most beautiful./ The knight calls the monk/ and says: "The tombs that are here,/ what are they for?" And he replies:/ "You have seen the letters;/ if you heard [understood?] them,/ you know very well what they say/ and what the tombs mean.")

In this passage, it is not altogether clear whether Lancelot or the monk is doing the reading. But let us assume that the knight is reading the tombstones. These are are among the simplest sentences possible, and they are in French: "Here will lie Yvain . . ."

— Guinevere and Gauvain get a letter from Lancelot. A messenger arrives at Baudemagus's court:

Unes letres tint an sa main,
ses tant le roi, et il les prant.
A tel qui de rien n'i mesprant

les fist li rois, oiant toz, lire.
Cil qui les lut lor sot bien dire
ce qu'il vit escrit an l'alue,
et dit que Lancelot salue
le roi, come son boen seignor,
si le mercie de l'enor
qu'il li a fet et del servise,
com cil qui est a devise
testoz an son comandemant.
Et sachiez bien certainnemant
qu'il est avoec le roi Artu,
plains de santé et de vertu,
et dit qu'a la reïne mande
c'or s'an vaigne, se le comande,
et mes sire Gauvains et Ques;
et si a entresaignes tes
qu'ils durent croire, et bien le crurent.   lines 5252–58

(He held a letter in his hand,/ he hands it to the king, who takes it./ So that there may be no mistake/ the king has it read in the presence of all./ He who read the letter knew how to tell them very well/ what he saw written on the parchment,/ and he said that Lancelot greeted/ the king, as his good lord,/ and thanked him for the honor/ that he gave him of serving him,/ and [he spoke] like one who wishes/ to obey all his commands./ And [the letter said,] know with certainty/ that he [Lancelot] is with King Arthur,/ who is full of health and virtue,/ and he says to tell the queen/ that she should come to him, for he commands it,/ and my lords Gauvain and Kay too;/ there were signs [on the letter] such that/ thcy had to bclicve it and they did believe it.)

Later, when they return home and find Lancelot absent, they realize that the letter they had heard read was *not* really a letter from Lancelot, but was intended to send them home without him:

Et mes sire Gauvains lors primes
sot que les letres fausses furent,
qui les traïrent et deçurent;
par les letres sont deceü.   lines 5338–41

(And my lord Gauvain then for the first time/ knew that those were fake letters,/ that betrayed and deceived them;/ by the letters they were deceived.)

Several things about this letter are worth noting. The queen and Gauvain do not read it for themselves, but it is read aloud in front of everyone. This was of course standard practice in court: great lords and ladies had *clercs lisants* to do their reading for them. (Such a practice would, however, hardly have promoted literacy on the part of magnates.) Of this nameless and unidentified clerk, we are told only that he was a good reader. Guenevere and Gauvain identify the letter as being from Lancelot on the basis of unspecified "entresaignes," or marks. But of course they are wrong: the letter is in fact a forgery. We seem to have here an expression of an awareness that Clanchy has documented in *From Memory to Written Record: England, 1066–1307*: that letters and other written documents can lie. Written things are not reliably as trustworthy as, for example, real witnesses, such as "jurors" who swear to say what they know – what they remember – about the matter under dispute. In any case, it must be said that such a passage does not redound unambiguously to the glory of *l'écriture*.

In summary, we see very little, and very ambiguous, reading; reading mostly by women, and by clerks; and written documents lie. Arthur, that model ruler, is never mentioned in connection with a book or writing in any way, nor is any knight or lady at his court. The small number of ecclesiastical figures present in Chrétien's romances are not discussed with respect to, or praised for, their learning or literacy.

Moreover, the word "master" – *maistre* – which has a special meaning in a clerical context, is used by Chrétien exclusively with two meanings, neither of which is clerical. As noted above, the word is used to refer to a serf with a great skill in building. And it refers to the men and women who function as close private servants – tutors and governesses – to the main characters. Thus, for example, Tessala is called Fénice's "maistre," e.g., lines 3154, 3156. This is the same meaning the word had in Béroul's *Tristan*, where Governal was Tristan's "maistre" – and it is by no means a clerical meaning.

Nor does Chrétien speak of his audience or his patrons as literate. Even Henry the Liberal of Champagne and Philip of Alsace, who were, as noted earlier, Chrétien's benefactors and who are known to have been in fact literate,[60] are not praised as such, though Chrétien praises Philip effusively and at considerable length at the beginning of the *Perceval*. Chrétien's praise can indeed be seen as the expression of a deeply oral ethic. Thus we are told that Philip does not listen to evil gossip ("vilain gap"); when he does charitable works he does not let his right hand tell his left hand what he has done, and so on (lines 21ff). If Chrétien were himself a learned clerk, is it not likely that he would have praised Philip for *his* learning? If Chrétien were really a clerk, would it not have seemed rude to fail to praise Philip for his "lay *clergie*"?

In short, the nature of the learning displayed or referred to in Chrétien's romances by no means marks this knowledge as necessarily the product of book-learning, and Chrétien's representation of the Arthurian world suggests that he speaks both of and for a court whose members were, personally, marginally involved, at most, in reading and writing. That is, they were appar-

---

60 John F. Benton, "The Court of Champagne as a Literary Center," esp. 575–76; Clanchy, *From Memory*, p. 181.

ently more interested in the prestige than in the reality of these activities. He does have knowledge that comes from books. But that knowledge seems spotty, as the knowledge acquired in a court would be, in all likelihood. There is certainly no evidence that he has been through the official curriculum of a school. He seems eager to use the learning that comes from books – and the authority that flows from them – but he shows no interest in books themselves: in the reading or the writing of them, in the beauty of "letters." The learning he has absorbed, probably by listening to learned men talk, he has digested as an oral *savoir*, not as textual learning. When he drops prestigious names, and it is not very often, it seems primarily because he recognizes their authority and their ability to lend authority to *his* work.

Let me set the position being presented here into the framework of an interesting contemporary argument. A number of scholars, over the past few decades, have argued that literacy is a technology which introduces substantial intellectual and cultural transformations. Such has essentially been the position of Jack Goody, Eric A. Havelock, Albert Lord, Walter J. Ong and others (though almost all of them have nuanced this position in significant ways). Recently, scholars such as Ruth Finnegan, Brian V. Street, Harvey J. Graff, Joyce Coleman, and others have presented the case against what has been termed the "Great Divide" concept of orality and literacy.[61] They have argued that literacy alone does not bring the changes that are often attributed to it. These scholars emphasize that literacy in a society is not ideologically neutral, but is deeply associated with issues of power and authority. Street and Graff also stress the importance of the experience of schooling, more than just the acquisition of literacy.

What we find, I believe, in twelfth century French courts is, first, the remarkable new prestige of reading and writing: a new awareness and appreciation of *clergie* and the power it represents. One sees this, even at the erotic level, in a new competition between knights and clerks for the love of 'ladies'; clerks are now in a position to vie with warriors for female admiration. But far more important culturally is the fact that it is now books and written documents that establish the credibility of discourse. This feature alone makes writing attractive – indeed virtually *necessary* – to those who wish to be taken seriously and listened to. This list includes magnates who will increasingly have documents promulgated under their name and collect archives and libraries; and minstrels who will speak of their "written source," or refer to their own poem or story as a "book." Second, we see a court situation in which a good many people appear to have received many of the benefits of unofficial "schooling" – but without necessarily becoming actually "literate." That is, people learned what is in books without necessarily learning their "letters."

---

[61] See, e.g., Ruth Finnegan, "Literacy versus Non-literacy: The Great Divide? Some Comments on the Significance of 'Literature' in Non-literate Cultures."

French vs. Anglo-Norman courts in the twelfth century

It will be useful at this point to draw some important distinctions between courts in France and in Anglo-Norman England. Benedeit, Wace, Benoît de Sainte Maure, Thomas, and Marie de France, *et al.* – indeed most of the major figures of early "French" literature – were not French but Anglo-Norman.[62] The Anglo-Normans, especially the monarchy, became very early on engaged not merely in literary patronage in the general sense of commissioning works and rewarding poets, but more precisely in the redaction of vernacular compositions. This was a royal court strongly involved in the written historical – and the pseudo-historical! – record. This historical involvement was frequently seen as a way of authenticating Anglo-Norman rule, in particular by associating the monarchy with the anti-Saxon story of King Arthur. There was, moreover, an ancient tradition of vernacular writing in England before the Conquest: Old English literature has a history far older than Old French. At any rate, we do have twelfth century manuscripts (or fragments) of a good many works composed in that century in Anglo-Norman England, such as Benedeit's *Voyage de Saint Brendan*, Benoît's *Chroniques des ducs de Normandie*, Wace's *Brut*, Thomas's *Tristan*, Guernes de Pont Sainte Maxence's *Vie de Thomas Becket*, and so on.[63]

Chrétien, however, was not an Anglo-Norman or someone working in the Anglo-Norman ambit, but was from central France – apparently Champagne. As Woledge and Short put it: "Quand Bédier prétendait que 'nous ne possédons pas un seul manuscrit du XIIe siècle qui ait été écrit dans l'Ile de France, ou en Beauvais, ou en Champagne,' il exagérait très peu."[64] In fact, we have no evidence that vernacular compositions of a secular nature were either composed or preserved *in writing* in France in this period.[65] It is, of course, possible that such manuscripts were produced, but then destroyed later for some reason. But it is surely difficult to argue, in and from the absence of manuscripts, that they were once common.

To take a specific, and important, case: the court of Count Henry "le Libéral" and Marie of Champagne. Whatever else can be said about this court – and John Benton studied it carefully some years ago[66] – there is no hard evidence whatsoever of *writing* in the *vernacular* on *secular topics* going on

---

62 See, e.g., Mary Dominica Legge, "La précocité de la littérature anglo-normande."

63 See Brian Woledge and Ian Short, "Liste provisoire des manuscrits du XIIe siècle contenant des textes en langue française."

64 Woledge and Short, "Liste . . .", p. 1.

65 The level of literacy in France among the upper classes in this period is generally thought to have been lower than in England. See M.B. Parkes, "The Literacy of the Laity," esp. pp. 556ff.

66 See Benton, "The Court of Champagne as a Literary Center."

there, or even associated with it.[67] Patricia Danz Stirnemann has studied the personal libraries of Henry and Marie, and of Philip of Alsace as well.[68] These libraries appear to have contained almost no works in the vernacular, and the very few there were, were of a religious nature: for example, Marie probably owned a copy of Evrat's translation of Genesis, though this manuscript has not survived. Gace Brulé is believed to have composed courtly songs for the court. But there is no reason to believe that he wrote his songs down: the lyric tradition is by no means reliably written, and none of our manuscripts of lyric – our *chansonniers* – dates from earlier than the thirteenth century.

In a word, from this and other twelfth century French courts, unlike the Plantagenet court, we have no secular vernacular manuscripts. This evidence – or rather, its lack – suggests that clerical presence took a different form in France than in England, a difference perhaps best accounted for by Anglo-Norman ambitions.[69] If in England, clerks were actively involved in the composition of secular texts, by contrast, in France clerks and other churchmen (priests and bishops), appear to have functioned more as intellectual leaven – as muses – rather than as, themselves, vernacular authors.

There are some important historical figures whose names are associated with the court of Champagne, and who might have provided Chrétien, and others, with the kinds of knowledge that one finds in romances. One of the most interesting of these figures is Adam of Perseigne: he was born a serf on the lands of the count of Champagne, and received a clerical education in one of the cathedral schools, presumably with the support of Count Henry himself. He eventually became a Cistercian. (His was apparently a thirsty mind and soul: before joining the Cistercians he was a member of a community of canons regular, then joined a traditional Benedictine monastery.) Sometime before 1188 he was elected abbot of the Cistercian abbey at Perseigne in Normandy. But for a number of years before becoming a monk he was a secular cleric – apparently a priest – at the count's court.[70] It has even been said that he was Marie of Champagne's chaplain.[71] As Adam was born in 1145, he might have been serving as a priest (or clerk) for Henry sometime in the late 1160s.

Another possible figure is Hugh, Count Henry's older, illegitimate half-

---

[67] Benton does not say this: I am drawing this inference from his, and other, evidence.

[68] Patricia Danz Stirnemann, "Quelques bibliothèques princières de la production hors scriptorium au XIIe siècle."

[69] Louis VII – educated for the Church (he was not the eldest son but his older brother died before becoming king) – had little interest in vernacular compositions, indeed in secular pleasures, and seems not to have been a patron of the arts; nor is Philippe Auguste known to have engaged in vernacular literary patronage.

[70] Stephen C. Ferruolo, *The Origins of the University: The Schools of Paris and Their Critics, 1100–1215*, pp. 79–86, esp. 80.

[71] *Dictionnaire des lettres françaises: Le Moyen Age*, pp. 13–14.

brother. Ruth Harwood Cline has recently argued that Chrétien de Troyes was in reality this Hugh, who was, to be sure, no less than Adam of Perseigne, quite an extraordinary figure. He served as a knight, in England. After receiving a debilitating wound he became a monk, and was named abbot of Chertsey Abbey. A woman was found in his bed, and he was castrated (he claimed that she was a "plant"). In any event, he was, in the 1160s, the abbot of Lagny near Troyes.[72] I find Cline's argument most intriguing but ultimately unpersuasive, its gravest weakness being the lack of evidence that Hugh of Champagne had any poetic or literary talent. (Of course, in my view, Chrétien was not a clerk at all.) But such a person might well have provided a minstrel, such as Chrétien, with the knowledge and the historic details that can be found in the romances.

Yet another potential source of classical knowledge is Pierre de Celle, a literary churchman who knew the classics well and wrote spiritual works in Latin. He is known to have been sometimes present at the Court of Champagne and may have played a role as leavening agent there. A final possibility is Simon Chèvre d'Or, apparently a canon of St. Victor in Paris, but who was fairly closely associated with Count Henry, and who composed three Latin poems on the Trojan War.[73]

It is interesting to speculate, and the first two men discussed above were remarkable figures in their own right. But in point of fact we do not need "big names" to account for the kind of learning found in Chrétien's romances: any trained clerk of the time could presumably have provided it.

What of the famed hostility of the Church for *jongleurs* and minstrels?

I have hypothesized, in both England and France, a substantial degree of collaboration between clerks and other churchmen, on the one hand, and court minstrels on the other, at the birth of medieval romance. (I do, however, see the form this collaboration took and the balance of power between the two groups as different on the two sides of the Channel.) But what of the famed hostility of churchmen for *jongleurs* and minstrels, the most frequently cited text being the condemnation of *jongleurs* by Thomas Chobham in a Penitential, written around 1216. He said, for example:

> Some [*histriones*] contort and distort their bodies with shameless jumps or shameless gestures, or in shamelessly denuding their body, or in putting on

---

[72] Ruth Harwood Cline lecture at New York University, fall 1992: "A Key to the Identity of Chrétien de Troyes: Abbot Hugh of the House of Blois-Champagne."

[73] On Pierre de Celle and Simon Chèvre d'Or, see Benton, "The Court of Champagne . . ."

[74] Quoted from Christopher Page, *The Owl and the Nightingale*, p. 21.

Thomas does distinguish among performers.

> . . . There is a third kind of minstrel using musical instruments to entertain people, but there are two varieties of these. Some go to public drinking places and wanton gatherings so that they may sing wanton songs there to move people to lustfulness, and these are damnable just like the rest. There are others, however, who are called *ioculatores*, who sing the deeds of princes and the lives of saints and give people comfort either when they are ill or when they are troubled, and who are not responsible for too much shamefulness as male and female dancers are and others who play in deceitful mummings and cause what appear to be certain phantoms to be seen through incantations or in some other way. If, however, they do not do this, but sing the deeds of princes and other useful things to their instruments to give comfort to people, as has been said, then such entertainers may be tolerated.[75]

Thus, Thomas distinguishes between good minstrels – who sing of princes and saints – and bad ones, who move their audiences to sin. But Thomas's text is often taken as a virtually blanket condemnation of *jongleurs* and minstrels.

In any event, I think we should be wary of assuming that any particular text by a churchman automatically carried vast authority: that all other churchmen would have agreed to it, or that it was reliably obeyed. We today tend to be, paradoxically perhaps, more in awe of medieval church authority than medieval men and women were. Moreover (*pace* Thomas), many bishops and other churchmen as well were themselves also feudal lords, and in their own noble establishments they provided entertainment. In a word, they too patronized minstrels and *jongleurs*. The very fact that several epics and romances glorify or are dedicated to bishops makes their patronage certain.[76] There is some likelihood that church dignitaries offered a more refined and higher-class sort of entertainment than secular establishments (one might perhaps like to think so), but nothing guarantees that such was the case. And it may well be that one of the great advantages of King Arthur, and of Charlemagne and his successors as well, is that narrative recourse to him – to his name – tended to get around clerical objections to vernacular, secular subject-matter: even Thomas had allowed that one might sing the deeds of kings!

The entire tradition of conflict (and cooperation) between the Church and what we might call the medieval entertainment industry has recently been reviewed by Christopher Page in *The Owl and the Nightingale: Musical Life and Ideas in France 1100–1300*,[77] and shown to be more complex and

---

[75] Page, *The Owl*, p. 23.
[76] See, e.g., Edélstand du Méril, *Poésies popularies latines du Moyen Age*, p. 198.
[77] Christopher Page, *The Owl*. See also G.K. Chambers, *The Mediaeval Stage*.

nuanced than has commonly been believed. It is worth remembering that no less than Francis of Assisi liked to speak of himself as God's "jongleur."

But whatever the disapproval – probably for a blend of genuine moral concerns and simple envy – that some clerks and churchmen may have had for the world of minstrelsy, I think it clear that, in the second half of the twelfth century, both groups found it in their interest to imitate each other, to borrow each other's plumage: minstrels tried to sound like clerks; clerks, like minstrels. Perhaps they even cooperated in order to provide high-tone entertainment for the cultured courts to which they were attached.

But we cannot avoid the impression that little vernacular writing indeed was occurring in France in the twelfth century. If we are constantly to assert that Anglo-Norman was "precocious," are we not going to have to concede that France was, well, a bit . . . backward? Are we really to assume that there were many manuscripts, but that, alas, they have all have been lost? Better to admit frankly that we have little evidence that such manuscripts ever existed in any substantial numbers.

It is, however, altogether likely that the presence of Latin compositions and books, associated with the birth of prestigious princely libraries, affected the way in which vernacular, secular poets conceived of and told their stories – especially in England, but to a lesser degree in France as well. Even when these poets were not actually "writing" or even "dictating," they began to think of themselves as producing "oeuvres": "livres." And poets and patrons alike may well have started to want these stories to be made into books: to turn performance into publication – and have engaged scribes to make this possible. Much scholarly emphasis has recently been laid on "literacy as power"; but text-production appears also to have been linked to issues of power. I am inclined to think that this is the case of Chrétien: his patrons, who came after all from the very highest reaches of the French nobility, may have found it attractive, for the purposes of their *own* prestige, to have Chrétien's poetic compositions put into, and preserved in, written form. For some idea of how this might have taken place – that is, how we might visualize such a scene – we could turn to the *Cantigas de Santa Maria*, produced under the authority of King Alfonso the Wise, and apparently with him as "troubadour" as well. Several illuminations show Alfonso and other figures dictating to scribes who take down their words.

Was Chrétien, though not a clerk, *literatus*?

If Chrétien was not a clerk, can he have been *literatus* at all, in the narrow sense of the word: could he himself read Latin? It is true that there are more clerical (and semi-clerical) features in Chrétien's romances than, say, in the *Roman de Thèbes*. He declares, in his prologue to the *Perceval* – it is the only time he uses this verb – that he has read words of St. Paul: "Sainz Pols le dist et je le lui." Now the standard modern translation of this line would be: "Saint Paul said it, and I read him [or it]" (line 49). If this interpretation of the verb "lire" is correct, perhaps we are to understand that Chrétien has learned to read a bit from the Bible – ever the great primer.[78] Many scholars have felt that somehow the *Perceval* is "different" from Chrétien's earlier works. Perhaps it is the change of patron and subject matter. Perhaps Chrétien has undergone a conversion experience of some kind.[79] Perhaps he has made significant strides in the domains of learning and literacy. But with regard to this last hypothesis, it is worth remembering that what Chrétien says is in St. Paul is not there: it is in 1 John 4:16 (though Paul says rather similar things in 1 Corinthians 13). It is also worth noting that he might also have read St. Paul in the vernacular, from one of the early verse translations of the Bible[80] (which would make him able to read the vernacular, but not strictly *literatus*). In any event, the opening lines of the *Perceval* resonate with biblical echoes and fundamental Christian messages.

But as I noted earlier, the medieval verb *lire* did not only mean "to read." I have discussed some of the things it could mean, but among them were "to see" and, not merely "to read something aloud," but also "to *hear* something read aloud" (or, apparently, "recited").[81] Deschamps, for example, begins a "chanson royale" by saying:

> A tous ceuls qui lire m'orront
> Et en lisant proffiteront
>   Salut et bonne affection.[82]

> (To all those who will hear me read/ And who by reading will
> gain profit/   Greetings and good affection.)

In short, those who saw a book or a text and those who heard something read

---

[78] As Clanchy notes, many non-clerks learned to read at least a bit: *From Memory*, pp. 240ff.

[79] This seems to be Daniel Poirion's explanation: *Résurgences*, p. 191: "Ce n'est pas dans saint Paul qu'il l'a lu, bien qu'il soit parti de son épître, mais l'important est ce retour à l'Ecriture chrétienne à l'occasion de l'éloge liminaire. Sous la flatterie de circonstance la couleur de l'esthétique traduit une sorte de conversion."

[80] Jean Bonnard, *Les traductions de la Bible en vers français au Moyen Age*.

[81] Tobler-Lommatzsch, Vol. 5, pp. 506–11. As noted earlier, Tobler-Lommatzsch does not give as meanings of *lire* to "hear something read" or "to recite." (Godefroy does not even discuss the meaning of the verb *lire* until his supplement, and even there its meaning is hardly questioned.) But some examples cited by Tobler-Lommatzsch and others show these meanings. "Lire" appears to have been particularly open to the meaning of "hear (something) read" in its present participial form: "lisant."

See also Joyce Coleman's *Public Reading and the Reading Public in Late Medieval England and France*, who takes up in detail occurrences of the verb "read" (*passim*).

[82] Quoted in Crosby, "Oral Delivery in the Middle Ages," p. 99.

could be said to be, themselves, "reading." Thus, Chrétien may either simply have *seen* this passage in the Bible (or the Bible itself), or *heard* it read aloud.

Composition, performance, and redaction of Chrétien's romances

The central preoccupation of these pages has been with Chrétien's status as a minstrel and *trouvère*, not a clerk. But if one of the corollaries of Chrétien's *clergie* has always been that he was therefore also a writer – or at least a "dictator" – one of the corollaries of the idea that he was not a clerk but a *trouvère* and *ménestrel* is of course the distinct possibility, perhaps even the likelihood, that he was not a writer either. What is at stake here is not merely a new vision of Chrétien himself but of the economy of the relations between *trouvère*, performer, and writer in this period.[83]

How did Chrétien compose his work? Let us review our options:

— He may have written his works down himself. He might have been a clerk. Such is the standard view.

— He may have written his works down *without* being a clerk, without clerical training. He might simply have acquired "vernacular letters" and have learned to write – probably in a court-setting.

— He might have dictated his romances to someone else as he composed, or after making them up in his head. He would thus have been technically a "dictator" rather than a "writer." Whether or not he actually thought of his works as written things, and of himself as a writer, would presumably have depended on such matters as whether he could himself read, whether he reviewed and corrected his "text" once it had been written down by the scribe, and the like.

— He might have composed his work in advance – that is, not during performance – but without any recourse to writing. Thus he would have produced and retained his story entirely in memory: in his mind. It is worth noting that, whether or not we believe this to be the case of Chrétien in particular, *it has to have been true* of virtually all poets and story-tellers from oral culture (aside from those who "composed orally" – next item on our agenda). That is, before vernacular writing, something along these lines must have been a, if not the, standard method of composition. It is hard for us to imagine that works of the length and richness of Chrétien's could have been retained totally in memory, but, as we have seen at various points (and will see again later), oral performers in this period, such as the *jongleurs* in the "Deux bourdeurs ribauds" and the *Renart*, claimed to possess vast amounts of

---

[83] D.H. Green, in *Medieval Listening and Reading: The Primary Reception of German Literature 800–1300*, distinguishes firmly between composition, transmission and reception; see in particular pp. 161ff.

narrative material, much of it clearly composed in octo, in memory.[84] Performers speak of mastering their repertory by memory, and they do not refer to the use of books: beyond that, they do not elaborate. Unless we are to believe that all the works these performers sang and told were composed for them by clerks – a view which seems difficult to defend – logic forces us to assume that many of these non-literate, non-writing story-tellers and singers made up their own works.

— Finally, Chrétien might theoretically have "composed orally," in the sense of improvising his work in the performance itself, with the aid of formulas. This has been seen by oral traditionalists as the mode of composition of the *chanson de geste*. Chrétien's romances are not "formulaic," though like almost all verse romances they contain many repeating elements and phrases. Moreover, Chrétien claims – at least of *Erec et Enide* – that he has "trct d'un conte d'aventure/ Une mout bele conjointure" (vv. 13–14) ("drawn from a tale of adventure/ A very beautiful composition"). The artful ordering of the elements of the story was important to him.[85]

Moreover, the manuscript tradition of Chrétien does not suggest – as that of at least some epics does – wide divergences among different versions.

I am inclined to think that the possibility of Chrétien having "composed orally" can be eliminated. I am, however, increasingly sceptical that full-scale oral composition was the sole composition mode for the medieval epic.[86] As we will see in Chapter 6, the similarity in performance between epic and romance is often striking. If the same people performed them, and in similar ways, is it likely that their mode of composition was reliably so different? – especially since at least some *chanson de geste* poets also produced romances (e.g., Adenet le Roy; admittedly, his *chansons* are late works).

The issue of composition is, we can see, strongly related to that of performance. That is, who originally performed Chrétien's romances – and what did Chrétien himself intend? Here we have, it would appear, two fundamental options, with a few sub-options. The first basic possibility is that Chrétien

---

[84] "Les deux bourdeurs ribauds," in Faral's *Mimes français du XIIIe siècle*, pp. 93–111; Branch Ib of the *Roman de Renart* (ed. Jean Dufournet), discussed in detail in chapter 6.

There is, incidentally, no evidence that such works were composed in performance as (many believe) the epic was. And despite the many repeating elements and small vocabulary of early octo discourse, it is not formulaic.

[85] As noted earlier, Chrétien may also be making a conjugal, or even a discreetly erotic, play on the word "conjoindre."

[86] In any event, many *chanson de geste* scholars consider that not all, but only the most oral epics were orally composed. See Joseph Duggan, *The Song of Roland: Formulaic Style and Poetic Craft*, and two subsequent articles in *Olifant*: "La théorie de la composition orale des chansons de geste: Les faits et les interprétations" and "Le mode de composition des chansons de geste: Analyse statistique, jugement esthétique, modèles de transmission."

performed his own works, and "made" them with that in mind. He might either have read them aloud himself – which, again, makes him a reader, and perhaps a literal, physical, "writer." Or he might have performed his own poetic compositions from memory. Thus, he would not have "orally composed" his works – "invented" them during the performance – but would have made them up (more or less) *in toto* in advance, and have learned them by heart. As Finnegan has noted, this is an attested "oral practice."[87] An intermediate view would be that he might have used a text to learn his own works by heart; this would mean that he could read, and presumably write.

The second large option is that Chrétien intended for others to perform them, and wrote/ made them with this in mind. These "others" might have been minstrels and *jongleurs* – entertainers who would generally learn his works by heart and perform them from memory. (We know that some *troubadours* had *jongleurs* perform their works for them.) Or Chrétien may have intended for his works to be read by public, or even private, readers. It is worth noting that this view has been the dominant one, almost the exclusive one. Some scholars have stated (many others have assumed) that Chrétien's romances were intended for readers.

It is important to recognize that Chrétien always implies that he is himself the performer of his own work: that is, the narrative "I" seems to be the speaking – the performing – "I" as well. Thus, Chrétien does say: "Now I will tell you." He does not say "You will hear" but "You will hear *me* . . ." For example, in *Cligés* he says that when the eponymous hero has come of age "M'orroiz adés de lui conter" (line 2350; "You will soon hear me tell about him").[88] He never suggests, as Thomas of Britain does at the end of his *Tristan*, that he himself will be absent when future listeners "hear" his work. Nor does Chrétien ever speak of his audience as including readers.

But if Chrétien never refers to readers, nor to himself as a clerk or writer, he does, once, refer to a work of his as a "livre." At the beginning of the *Lancelot* he says he now "begins his book" ("comance Crestïens son livre;" line 25). Does this word mean that, indeed, Chrétien was about to start writing a book? Chrétien's "now," however, seems reliably to be that of the narrator ("Now I will tell you about . . ."), and to refer to the present of the telling of the story.

Chrétien may be claiming authority – that possessed by books[89] – for the new work which he is about to perform to his audience. A clear example of

---

87 Finnegan, *Oral Poetry*, pp. 73ff.

88 *Chansons de geste* also frequently said, "You will hear me . . ." But there is an important difference between these works and the romances of Chrétien (and many other *romanciers*). Epics were typically given as anonymous – no author's name was mentioned – so the speaking "I" (and "me") could be taken over by *any* performer. But here Chrétien himself speaks in his own voice and claims his own work.

89 Similarly, Guillaume IX d'Aquitaine refers to one of his own poems as "auctor," which doesn't prove that he writes his poetry either – only that he appreciates the prestige of text and *auctores*, and is prepared to play with the concept of "authority": "E puesc ne trair

"livre" used to refer not to a real (a physical) "book" but to a discourse having written authority behind it occurs in the Occitan *chanson de geste* entitled *Ronsasvals*, where Charlemagne's peer Nayme, as he rides along on his horse, offers religious consolation to his Emperor: we are told that he "comensa lo libre dels sermons" – "began the book of sermons."[90] It is also possible that a scribe was copying down what Chrétien said to him – as in the scenes of Alfonso and others dictating to scribes, referred to earlier. And, though Tobler-Lommatzsch does not offer this interpretation as one of its meanings of "livre" (the word is given as simply meaning "book," or "written letter"), some of the examples cited suggest that the word was sometimes simply a synonym for "story." This, especially in the set phrase "roman et livre"; thus, "Signor, oï avez en livre et en romanz . . . " (from the epic *Florence de Rome*) or – from *Le Roman de la Rose* – ". . . La Fontaine d'Amors/ Dont plusor ont en maint endroit/ Parlé en romanz e en livre" and "Ne porroit nus les maus d'amcr/ Conter en romanz ne en livre."[91] Nor in fact did the Latin word *liber* necessarily refer to a codex – a written text – but could also mean "a work," "part of a work" (as when we refer to "Book I" of a larger composition), or a "composition."

At any rate, what Chrétien's use of the word "livre" reveals unquestionably is the rising prestige of books in aristocratic milieux, as well as the eagerness with which secular poets and entertainers associate their compositions with that prestige. Or to put it a bit differently: when scholars (of a Stockian stripe) assert that this is a society dominated by writing,[92] they are jumping the gun in one sense, but they are certainly right that the *prestige*, if not the literal *fact*, of writing is increasingly dominant.

It is, then, distinctly possible that Chrétien's romances were not originally written, by himself or by anyone. But how is it possible for romances that we have today in "unfinished" form, such as *Lancelot* and *Perceval*, to have been performed rather than written works? Surely an incomplete romance is a written work that the poet did not get around to finish writing. But, in fact, it is possible for a non-written romance to be "incomplete." Chrétien may have performed his romances before court audiences in installments, one or two thousand lines at a sitting.[93] But an illness, a death, a fall from the grace of the patron, or a departure might well have interrupted the performance, which was never resumed. Thus audiences never heard Chrétien's conclusion. Alterna-

---

l vers auctor/quant er lassatz" – "and I can take as an authority the verse itself/ when it has been woven"; *Les chansons de Guillaume IX duc d'Aquitaine*, Alfred Jeanroy, ed.

90 In *Roland occitan*, Gérard Gouiran and Robert Lafont, eds., line 1246.

91 Tobler-Lommatzsch, Vol. 5, cols. 531–32.

92 And Stock does indeed consider that by the turn of the millenium *les jeux sont faits*: ". . . after the year 1000, oral discourse increasingly functioned within a framework of legal and institutional textuality." *The Implications of Literacy*, p. 10.

93 Jean Rychner, *La chanson de geste: Essai sur l'art épique des jongleurs*.

tively, Chrétien might have performed his whole work, but no scribe ever took down the ending.

The manuscript tradition of Chrétien's romances

We now turn to the issue of the redaction, and the early manuscript tradition, of Chrétien's romances. (We will return to this issue from a different perspective in Chapter 7.) As we noted earlier, his career is believed to have ended around 1191. The earliest manuscript of one of Chrétien's romances (*Yvain*) – the Annonay Fragment[94] – may date from the late-twelfth century, or from the early-thirteenth century. There are 30 other manuscripts containing one or more of Chrétien's romances,[95] dating from the mid-thirteenth century and later. These manuscripts have proven virtually impossible to group into families, as the variants are many, complex, and idiosyncratic, though generally fairly small-scale. (That is, there are no *major* divergences among manuscripts, as is common in the *chanson de geste* tradition, where there are strongly different versions of the same work.) Alexandre Micha, who attempted to elaborate satisfactory *stemma* for Chrétien's manuscripts – and he succeeded in establishing some pretty sure groupings – occasionally threw up his hands in dismay.[96] Of course Micha's dismay has been shared by many a medieval manuscript editor, and there are numerous works whose manuscript tradition begins far later, in relation to the poet's life, and is more confusing than that of Chrétien. At any rate, there seems to be a growing understanding that "scribal error" cannot explain away the phenomenon of numberless and mysteriously-related variants.

One interesting feature of the manuscript tradition of Chrétien's works is that, in the compilations in which his romances are gathered, they do not appear in a *fixed* order. They do not occur in what we think of as their correct chronological order: that is, *Erec et Enide*, *Cligés*, *Yvain* or *Lancelot*, *Perceval*; nor, for that matter, in any other reliable order. For example, in Bibliothèque nationale 375, two of Chrétien's romances appear in this order: *Cligés*, then *Erec*; in BN fr. 794 – the famous manuscript penned by a scribe named "Guiot" – Chrétien's works are copied in *this* order: *Erec*, *Charrette*, *Cligés*, *Yvain*, *Perceval*; in BN fr. 1420, it is *Erec*, then *Cligés*; in BN fr. 1450 *Erec*, *Perceval*, *Cligés*, *Yvain*, *Charrette*; in BN fr. 12560, *Yvain*, *Charrette*,

---

[94] This fragment contains parts of *Erec et Enide*, *Yvain*, *Cligés*, and *Perceval* (in an order that, because of the fragmentary nature of the manuscript, is unclear). See Micha, *La tradition manuscrite des romans de Chrétien de Troyes*, p. 40.

[95] See Micha, *La tradition manuscrite*, pp. 28ff. On the manuscript tradition of Chrétien's work, also see *Les Manuscripts de Chrétien de Troyes/The Manuscripts of Chrétien de Troyes*, ed. Keith Busby, *et al.*

[96] Micha, *La tradition manuscrite*, pp. 195ff.

Cligés; and so on.[97] The romances do not appear in any fixed order in the manuscripts. And Chrétien's romances are generally – in whatever order – mixed in with romances by other poets. This manuscript tradition suggests several things. First, to the extent that there were early – late-twelfth and early-thirteenth century – manuscripts of Chrétien's romances, they appear to have been manuscripts containing single romances by the poet. No early consensus was formed on the contents or the shape of his entire "corpus." This suggests that neither Chrétien nor his patrons appear to have launched Chrétien as a Writer with an *Oeuvre* (in the masculine sense of that word).

We do not know the exact role played by any of the scribes associated with Chrétien's work: that is, we do not know their relation to Chrétien himself or to possibly earlier written versions of his work. Nor do we understand the relative importance of these manuscripts in the dissemination of Chrétien's stories – as compared with their dissemination by minstrels: their oral transmission. But two interesting points with regard to this issue should be noted. First, Wolfram von Eschenbach refers in his *Parzival* at several points to his source text as by "Kyot." This name, Kyot, appears to be the German pronunciation of the French Guiot, whose important manuscript of Chrétien was referred to above. The fact that this name is rendered not by eye, but by ear – *German* ear – suggests that Wolfram may have heard Guiot's text of Chrétien, or one derived from his, presented (recited or read) aloud.[98] Second, Annalee C. Rejhon has studied thirteenth century Welsh versions of Chrétien's *Yvain*, *Érec et Énide*, and *Perceval*.[99] She notes that – unlike the thirteenth century Welsh version of the *Chanson de Roland* which is clearly clerical, indeed monastic, in origin[100] – these Welsh romances "probably derive from an aural reception of a reading of Chrétien's romances."[101] (Though Rejhon speaks of a "reading," what interests us here is the expression "aural reception," and nothing in fact indicates that the Welsh poets heard Chrétien's works *read* rather than *recited*.) Rejhon says further:

> In fashioning the tale back into Welsh and with no document to keep the French version intact, the adaptor was free to modify the tale for the benefit of his own audience, focusing on those features that had a particular meaning in a Welsh milieu, and eliminating those that he perceived as lacking even an exotic interest.[102]

97 Micha, *La tradition manuscrite*, pp. 28–29.
98 I am indebted to Peter Dembowski for this point. See also Paul Zumthor, *Essai de poétique médiévale*, p. 483.
99 See Annalee C. Rejhon, "Symposium: The Effects of Oral and Written Transmission in the Exchange between Medieval Celtic and French Literatures: A Physiological View."
100 See Annalee C. Rejhon, *Can Rolant: The Medieval Welsh Version of the Song of Roland*, Berkeley, University of California Press, 1984.
101 Rejhon, "Symposium," p. 135; see also p. 139.
102 Rejhon, "Symposium," pp. 135–36.

What the manuscript tradition of Chrétien and a good many other medieval "writers" suggests is a fairly extensive period of at least partial memory and performance transmission. That such is the case is indeed clear both in Jean Renart's *Roman de la Rose* (lines 1745–47) and in *Flamenca* (lines 596ff), where performers are reciting works (presumably) of Chrétien though his name is not mentioned. (We will return to these issues in Chapter 6.)

There were, however, manuscripts of Chrétien's romances from an early date – whether he wrote, or had them written, himself or not. His romances soon acquired some measure of written status and authority: somehow, he "caused" a written corpus under his name. I suggest that this important phenomenon is related to the rise in a new way of thinking about vernacular works: not just as stories but as "compositions." Increasingly, instead of just getting on with the business of telling the story, as most narrators from the purely *jongleuresque* tradition had generally done, romance poets often seem to think of their work as a "thing" – a discursive entity. They often frame their story with introductory and concluding remarks, and tell why and for whom they composed it. This is, for example, the case of *Eracle* by Gautier d'Arras, a contemporary of Chrétien, also associated at least to some degree with the court of Marie of Champagne. Gautier speaks of his story as a "traitié" (line 3) and, toward the end, tells who had him "rimer" the work (lines 6523ff).[103] The relative stability of the manuscript tradition of Chrétien's (and other) romances may result in part from the fact that these works, while not originally written, nonetheless circulated as compositions possessing "integrity." The spread of letters changed the understanding, indeed in important senses the nature, even of nonclerical works – as it did of so many other ideas of the age.[104]

Some conclusions

We need to revise our understanding of the nature of Chrétien's accomplishment. He may very well have been a great courtly story-teller: a *trouvère* and a *ménestrel*, a verbal artisan with a substantial degree of knowledge, but without a formal education. We must be prepared to honor Chrétien and his achievements such as they were – *however* they were – not as we might perhaps like them to have been. But we also need new and more refined criteria for gauging learning and determining *clergie*, and for discriminating between clerkly narrators and *mock*-clerkly narrators. A few suggestions:

---

[103] Gautier d'Arras, *Éracle*, ed. Guy Raynaud de Lage. Paul Zumthor worked on this romance extensively – in particular on its vocal, and even performed, quality; see "L'écriture et la voix: le roman d'*Eracle*," and "Qu'est-ce qu'un style médiéval?"
[104] See Ivan Illich, "A Plea for Research on Lay Literacy," p. 38.

132

— Reference to *auctores* and familiarity with narrative or thematic material and even plot details (such as characters' names) are not enough to demonstrate book-knowledge, school training.

— Quotations from and references to the Bible are also not convincing proofs of *clergie*, except when they concern passages *not* read in the Mass or Hours (therefore not widely familiar), or when they clearly and indisputably demonstrate close textual familiarity with the Bible.

— Claims by a poet that he has used a learned source, or read a Latin book (perhaps in a famous library), or that a clerk or monk originally wrote the work that the poet is now adapting, and the like, should be taken with several grains of salt. Such declarations should not be seen as constituting adequate proof that the poet is a clerk, or can read, or is in any sense literate. Particularly weak places for such assertions are the beginning and the end of works: here is where learned claims are the most routinely made and where they are, for that very reason, the least convincing – that is, the most apt to be rhetorically motivated. Such declarations should be classified as part of the minstrel's persuasive art: as part of the *captatio benevolentiae*[105] of a work composed for a world which increasingly values the authority of the book, and antique authorities, but which still largely maintains its old oral and performed enjoyments and wisdom. Such declarations should not, then, be taken as Gospel, but should be put under careful scrutiny, for they are known to have been common fabrications.

— The claim that the work in question is itself a book should also be examined with care – and with some measure of scepticism. Are there other features in the work which bolster this claim, or do we seem to be dealing with yet another "authenticity ploy"?

Am I too suspicious, too sceptical? Perhaps – but I think not. We need a powerful antidote to the almost-total credulity with which we have long accepted poets' references to books and knowledge of ancient material as incontrovertible evidence that they were clerks. Sometimes "source studies" have been enough to persuade us. But the issue is surely not just *what* someone knows, but *how* and *where* he learned it. We should stop granting automatic posthumous honorary Doctorates in Humane Letters to medieval poets who were most likely non-literate. To raise the possibility that they were not clerks is not in any way to diminish the accomplishment of these *trouvères*: they were, many of them, great and talented artists. The point is not to rip off the clerkly epaulettes from the shoulders of Chrétien and other poets – to degrade them from their clerical state, or diminish their importance. It is our problem, *not* theirs, that we can think of no higher compliment to pay to a poet than to

---

105 I have personally known four-year-olds with a perfect mastery of *captatio benevolentiae*. Use of the technique proves nothing but innate verbal and interpersonal skill and the desire to win favor.

declare him to have been a clerk, to believe that he had read and could quote from Latin books, that he partook of the joys (and frustrations) of "intertextuality."

Let me make it clear, however, that my scepticism is not absolute. There do exist affirmations within texts which strike me as generally trustworthy: most importantly, when a poet names himself and says explicitly of himself that he is a clerk, I think we should be inclined to believe him. (Again – for the record – neither the *Thèbes* poet nor Chrétien ever says such a thing.) The fact of clerical status was something about which it would probably have been difficult to lie to patrons or audiences. In particular, a clerk would normally have been physically identifiable, by his tonsure and his clothing: clerical dress included long (as opposed to short) garments, dark or subdued colors (as opposed to bright hues), and a generally austere (as opposed to a stylish) character.[106] One can readily imagine that some clerks did not wear the austere clothing considered appropriate to their estate (there were some pretty clerks in the Middle Ages!). But a poet or performer who was playing the "clerical card" – at any rate playing it non-ironically – would presumably have had to be dressed appropriately; misrepresentation of oneself on this score would be obvious: visible to the naked eye. Also generally reliable, in my opinion, are *repeated* and *sustained* references to reading or writing, and to bookish sources; references scattered *throughout* a work – thus, not only at the beginning or the end. All these we find in Benoît's *Roman de Troie*. (Metaphors taken from the world of writing are also important, but they barely exist in early romance.[107])

The assumption that all great medieval poets were necessarily clerks has encouraged us in our tendency to subject medieval narrative to sorts of analysis which may well be inappropriate, that is, anachronistic. We speak of these early romances as if they were, truly, originally, books, written by writers for private readers. In fact, these works were intended for performance: to entertain, and sometimes to inspire, to persuade, to have impact. These were

---

106 See François Boucher, *A History of Costume in the West*, pp. 166–69, 185–86.

107 They do *exist* in the twelfth century – just not in romance. For example, the "Eructavit" is a paraphrase and expansion of Psalm 44 made for Marie of Champagne and attributed to that interesting figure discussed earlier, Adam of Perseigne, lines 239ff; it develops the idea that the "tongue is a scribe" – but then that metaphor is at the center of the opening lines of the psalm itself. See *Eructavit: An Old French Metrical Paraphrase of Psalm XLIV Published from All the Known Manuscripts and Attributed to Adam de Perseigne*. On this poem, see also Chapter 6, pp. 223–4.

Such metaphors are certainly to be found in Latin texts of this period. One interesting example: Robert of Molesmes, one of the founders of the Cistercian Order, who died in 1110 at the age of 92, was at one point sent from Cîteaux to Molesmes to reform the monks there. He wrote back to his friends at Cîteaux: "I should sadden you too much if I could use my tongue as a pen, my tears as ink, and my heart as paper [parchment?]." (See *Butler's Lives of the Saints*, ed. Thurston and Attwater, Vol. II, p. 190.)

dramatic stories, recited – and played – to live audiences, sometimes by minstrels as skilled, wise, and entertaining as, I believe, Chrétien de Troyes. It is to such performance issues that we now turn, in Part II. But if, to be the "Father of French literature," it is absolutely necessary for the person in question to have been a clerk and a writer, perhaps we had better think of Chrétien de Troyes as its maternal uncle?

Part II

PERFORMANCE

CHAPTER FIVE

Voice in Medieval Romance:
The Case of Chrétien de Troyes

Part I of this book addressed the oral vs. written status of early romance, and of "octo" narrative in general, on a range of dimensions. In Chapters 1 through 4, our primary concerns were with literary vs. oral form and composition, literacy and its lack, and the like. We now turn, in Part II, to a related set of issues, those bearing on the performance of romance – for no matter who composed these romances, or how, they *all* invite "hearing."[1] Chapters 5 through 8 will explore performance-related issues.[2]

In this chapter, we will examine the importance of "voice" in romance. If today it is generally agreed that romances were typically heard,[3] that means aural, if not purely "oral." For the time being I will beg the question of precisely how romances were performed: whether they were read aloud from a book, recited from memory, etc. I also set aside for now the issue of private reading. We will return to these matters in the next chapter. But since romances were performed aloud, and were presumably composed by narrative poets with this sort of presentation in mind, we should find it useful to examine the nature of the appeal of romance to listeners. There are many aspects of this question that we cannot study today. We cannot "hear" any readers read or minstrels actually recite these works: it is too late for that, alas. Many things remain conjectural, such as the music and other sound effects that may have accompanied the performance of romance in medieval courts (I will, however, speculate on these and related matters in Chapter 6).

What we *can* examine is the ways in which voice is set into the texts that we have: how voice is inscribed into the work; how voice is made to function. An analogy to make this point clearer: let us suppose that we had no recordings of

---

1   On some of the implications of this hearing mode in manuscripts themselves, see the valuable article by Frank Brandsma: "Medieval Equivalents of 'Quote-Unquote': The Presentation of Spoken Words in Courtly Romance." A few texts were apparently annotated or punctuated by scribes to facilitate oral delivery. (The examples Brandsma gives are in Middle Dutch verse – translations from French romances.)

2   In this chapter, as in Chapters 6 and 8, I am particularly indebted to Benjamin Bagby of the group "Sequentia" for his many valuable suggestions.

3   As I noted in Chapter 1, a generation or two ago this would not have been the accepted view. Most scholars spoke in terms of a public of private readers of romance, even for the twelfth century.

anything that had ever been heard on radio. We would be unable to "hear" what radio programs had sounded like. But if we at least had scripts of, say, plays from "radio theatre," we would nonetheless be able to study – imperfectly, to be sure – some of the ways in which writers for radio attempted to make use of the power of radio as an art form and a medium of communication; some of the ways in which radio script-writers invited those who performed and produced their plays to make effective, dramatic, and appealing use of the human voice. In these pages, we will not be straining to hear – or pretending to hear – long-silent voices. Our point, rather, is to try to understand how medieval story-tellers used voice: how they deployed both the voices of the characters whose adventures and amours they recounted, and their own voice, or – let's be more cautious – the voice of the narrative *persona* they created. I will suggest an array of possibilities, though we can have no certainties.[4]

A number of scholars have studied the importance of voice and "vocality" in oral tradition as a whole,[5] and in the medieval period in particular.[6] The late Paul Zumthor, in *Introduction à la poésie orale, La poésie et la voix dans la civilisation médiévale*, and *La lettre et la voix: De la "littérature" médiévale*, and in articles such as "Poésie et vocalité au Moyen Age," increasingly focused scholarly attention on the power, importance, and indeed the "authority," of the voice in medieval culture and "literature." I am borrowing his quotation marks here to draw attention to what is wrong with this latter term in a largely oral – or what he called a "vocal" or "poetic" – culture. I pay homage to him and his extraordinarily important work here.[7]

In one of Zumthor's last articles, "Qu'est-ce qu'un style médiéval?" which appeared in a recent volume entitled *Pour une anthropologie des voix*, Zumthor emphasized the fact of oral/vocal performance of romances (such as Gautier d'Arras' *Éracle*). I will quote him at length as he raises a number of points that are important for our concerns. He said, speaking of this romance as

---

4   Let me be quite clear on one point: I am not arguing that only medieval poets have made powerful or esthetically pleasing use of voice: this is just as true of many story-tellers and of novelists such as Balzac or Dickens. Many of these authors and works deserve similar study; some have already received it. We can, I think, safely assume that most narrators who have made effective or imaginative use of voice imagined a public which would either hear the work read aloud, or vocalize it for themselves: these story-tellers thought in terms of an audience of listeners who would appreciate their use of voice and voices, as well as other stylistic features of their work. Many novels are indeed available, and widely appreciated, on audio cassettes. One only wishes that such catalogues included more medieval works.

5   Among recent ethnographers, anthropologists, and folkloricists who emphasize the importance of voice in performance are Elizabeth Fine, Dell Hymes, and Dennis Tedlock.

6   For example, Bernard Cerquiglini, in *La parole médiévale: Discours, syntaxe, texte*, has emphasized the priority of the "parole" in Old French. As to the oral delivery of works, this was in fact established long ago: see Ruth Crosby, "Oral Delivery in the Middle Ages."

7   See Vitz, "Paul Zumthor and Medieval Romance."

showing "une langue qui restait encore très profondément, fonctionnellement, la langue de la voix" rather than being part of a truly written culture:

> Il y a dans ce roman un grand nombre de dialogues. Certains sont même des polylogues, à trois, quatre personnages. Dans les éditions modernes, ils sont si faciles à lire qu'on n'y fait même pas attention, parce que l'éditeur a pourvu le texte de tirets et de guillemets. Mais si on regarde le texte en lui-même, indépendamment de cette typographie moderne, on constate que très souvent rien dans la langue n'indique le passage d'un interlocuteur à l'autre. Parfois même, un personnage parle, l'auteur fait une remarque sur ce que dit le personnage, et cette remarque est enchâssée dans le discours. Ceci n'est compréhensible que grâce à des jeux de voix. La nécéssité de la performance est inscrite dans l'oeuvre. Il est clair que si l'on appliquait à l'analyse d'une oeuvre de ce type une perspective stylistique convention-nelle, qui se limite au seul niveau linguistique, on perdrait énormément. Nous ne pouvons pas entendre ces jeux de voix, mais du moins pouvons-nous en décéler la place en creux. Ce que j'ai appelé le style de l'oeuvre est, pour une grande part, une trace qu'il s'agit de retrouver cependant, nous ne pouvons pas, simplement par suite du cours irréversible du temps, la restituer. Tout se passe comme si le texte n'était que l'un des enjeux d'une action. En somme, dans le récit écrit, la finalité performantielle est si profondément intégrée au texte que l'on doit, à tout moment, se demander si ce texte livré à lui-même est bien compréhensible, comme il voulait l'être à l'époque. Pour tous les textes que j'ai regardés d'un peu près, la lecture exige un commentaire vocal/tonal, ce qui presque nécessairement implique mimique et gestuelle. En ce sens, le texte que nous lisons ne nous livre qu'une forme vide et sans doute profondément altérée, au sens propre, c'est-à-dire "devenue autre," de ce qu'il devait être dans le dessein de son auteur. En ce sens, le texte nous cache l'oeuvre. (p. 45)

Zumthor thus emphasizes several features of this particular romance and of romance in general: the frequency of dialogue (and "polylogue"); the way in which vocal performance is implicit in the manuscripts, which are largely punctuation-less; and the evident importance of the "play of voices" in romance (the "text" itself is of relatively lesser importance).

My purpose in this chapter will be to point attention toward this "play of voices," the vocal "*creux*" – the gap or hole – in the texts that survive; to suggest something of the vocal performance quality, and to look at the central importance of dialogue, in medieval romances. I will try to show some of the ways in which voice filled and completed the "*forme vide*" which is the surviving text.

I will focus the discussion in this chapter on the romances of Chrétien. A substantial part of the power – and the lasting charm! – of his romances flows from his extensive, varied and, indeed, theatrical use of voice and dialogue. Chrétien's works are not unique in this regard, but here as elsewhere he was such a master of the art of romance that his works provide powerful examples.

His works lent – and still lend! – themselves to oral presentation, such as recitation or reading aloud, and it can hardly be doubted that they were composed
with such performance in mind.

I will also, at least intermittently, use this chapter to lead into another point:
that these works, however appealing to listeners – to auditors – must also have
appealed to spectators as well. Many of the scenes whose powerful vocal (and
generally auditory) interest will be our primary focus here also invite analysis
of their broader visual and dramatic dimensions, such as the recourse to
gesture that they invited, on the part of those who performed them. These
issues will be explored in the next chapter.

To a considerable degree, Chrétien's romances are what I will call "led by
voice." To demonstrate this, voiced/ performed story-telling will be compared
with impersonal or "unvoiced" narrative which is primarily characteristic of
literary prose; it will also be compared with drama. Early verse narratives (in
particular, the romances of Chrétien, but not his alone) tend to use voice,
speaking characters, and dramatic dialogue in ways very close to those which
characterize the theatre – as well as traditions of oral narrative recently studied
by anthropologists such as Dennis Tedlock[8] and others.[9]

But, first, to define what I shall mean – and *not* mean – by "voice."[10] I
mean something quite different from the theoretical metonym that is standard
usage today. When many literary theorists refer to voice, and to its (hypo-
thetical) ontological and epistemological priority over writing and the written,
they seem to mean the voice that we hear only with the mind's ear when we
read silently: the silent echo of an arguably primal, but nonetheless absent,
voice (or Voice). But in speaking of early medieval romances, I mean, quite
literally, the voices of the characters – voices that performers conjured up and
impersonated and made listeners physically hear – voices such as Zumthor
evoked in the passage cited above. I also mean the voice of the performer
himself: a powerful and, as scholars (Zumthor again included) have shown, a
deeply authoritative voice. Thus, the minstrel or *jongleur*, with his authority –
his personal witness to the truth-value of the words he spoke – competed with
the authority of the "learned" tradition. This may, of course, be an assumed
voice: a dramatic construct, adopted for the performance; and it may, or may
not, be the same as that of the poet/*trouvère* himself. But in any event, I mean
voices *heard* by medieval audiences.

8 See, for example, *The Dialogic Emergence of Culture*, "Introduction," by
Mannheim and Tedlock, pp. 1–32; p. 13. In this volume also of interest is Tedlock, "Interpretation, Participation, and the Role of Narrative in Dialogical Anthropology," pp.
253–85. See also Tedlock, *The Spoken Word and the Work of Interpretation* and "On the
Representation of Discourse in Discourse." I will return to Tedlock's work later in this
chapter.

9 I will return in Chapter 8 to the work of other related scholars.

10 For an interesting discussion of the philosophical and metaphysical issue of voice,
see Tedlock, *The Spoken Word*, Chapter 7: "Phonography and the Problem of Time in Oral
Narrative Events," esp. pp. 194–97.

The many voices in Chrétien's romances

Audiences heard many different voices conjured up by the performers of Chrétien's work.[11] Let's call to mind some of the wonderful, memorable voices that lent themselves to such evocation. Let me make it clear that I do not mean simply that there are a great many interesting and appealing *characters*, but that their voices are represented as speaking: they are *heard to speak*, as in the theatre. Issues such as intonation, pitch, and accent are important. Chrétien is not just a teller of stories; he is a master of dramatic characters – characters as presented sensorially: vocally, auditorially, dialogically. True, most of us today have heard these voices only if we are in the habit of reading Chrétien aloud. We can only imagine how medieval performers might have played these voices. But the same is true of the theatre (or, as noted earlier, of radio). The voices are there in the "scripts" that, blessedly, we still have.

Most modern readers have only imagined these scenes silently, and thus have never even heard themselves imitate these voices. But then, some modern readers (of a particularly stay-at-home temperament, perhaps, and with no TV or video) have never heard Shakespeare's characters "speak" either. The fact that modern audiences may not have heard or seen plays such as *Le Jeu de la Feuillée* or *Everyman* or *La farce de Maistre Pathelin* does not keep these works from *being* "plays": meant to be acted out.

As we call up the individual characters for whom Chrétien created highly individualized *personae* and voices, it is hard to know where to begin. With Gawain, perhaps, whose urbane and ultra-courtly tone is so distinctive – that is, who invites the performer to adopt such a mode? (It is not clear how much Chrétien drew on an already-established tradition of Gawain's sophistication and urbanity.) Or with Lunete whose wise and subtle way of speaking has won the hearts of so many? But then there is Kay, whose distinctively obnoxious words – and *tone* – are unforgettable, and frequently an important stimulus to the plot: for example, it is his insulting remarks that impel Yvain to set off by himself to the fountain:

> – Bien pert que c'est aprés mangier,
> fet Kex, qui teire ne se pot:
> plus a paroles an plain pot
> de vin qu'an un mui de cervoise;
> l'en dit que chaz saous s'anvoise.
> Aprés mangier, sanz remüer,
> vet chascuns Loradin tüer,
> Et vos iroiz vengier Forré!

---

[11] I set aside here the issue of whether or not Chrétien was the original performer of his own works – though I think he was.

Sont vostre panel aborré
et voz chauces de fer froiees
et voz banieres desploiees?
Or tost, por Deu, mes sire Yvain,
Movroiz vos enuit ou demain?
Fetes le nos savoir, biax sire,
quant vos iroiz an cest martire,
que nos vos voldrons convoier;
n'i avra prevost ne voier
qui volantiers ne vos convoit.
Et si vos pri, comant qu'il soit,
n'en alez pas sans noz congiez.
Et se vos anquenduit songiez
malvés songe, si remenez!   lines 590–611

(– It is certainly clear that this is after dinner,/ Kay says, who cannot be silent:/ there are more words in a full pot/ of wine than in a barrel of barley beer;/ they say that a drunken cat goes crazy./ After dinner, without moving,/ everyone goes off to kill [Sultan] Nour-Eddin,/ and you will go to bring vengeance on King Forré!/ Is your quilted clothing ready,/ and are your iron leg-pieces rubbed and oiled/ and are your banners unfurled?/ So, by God, my lord Yvain,/ will you be moving out tonight or tomorrow?/ Do let us know, fair lord,/ when you are going off to this martyrdom,/ so that we can lead you thence;/ there is no provost or officer/ who would not wish to escort you./ And so I beg you, however you do it,/ don't go without saying goodbye./ And if tonight you dream/ a bad dream, then stay [home]!)

Here is a *nasty* voice – one that truly drips with sarcasm and irony. Kay is *the* sharp tongue; his words and tone cut through all that courtly palaver. For this very reason his voice is extremely entertaining. And Kay's voice is heard not merely in all of Chrétien's romances but throughout the entire Arthurian tradition: Kay is not merely a "stock character"; he has a particular – and a recognizable – voice and way of speaking.

I happen to be particularly fond of the giant herdsman in *Yvain* who, surrounded by bulls, appears so inhuman that he horrifies Calogrenant and presumably the listeners. But when he is asked "se tu es boene chose ou non" (line 327: "if you are a good thing or not") he speaks, and replies that he is . . . a man: "Et il me dist qu'il ert uns hom" (line 328). (In some manuscripts, the Herdsman says this himself: "Et il me dist: 'Je sui uns hom.' "[12]) In a voice that is clearly at once that of a human being and of a powerful brute, he carries on this conversation with the incredulous Calogrenant:

12 See Bibliothèque nationale MS 1433, edited by David Hult for Lettres gothiques.

– Que fez tu ci? – Ge m'i estois,
et gart les bestes de cest bois.
– Gardes? Par saint Pere de Rome,
ja ne conuissent eles homme;
ne cuit qu'an plain ne an boschage
puisse an garder beste sauvage,
n'en autre leu, por nule chose,
s'ele n'est lïee et anclose.
– Je gart si cestes et justis
que j'a n'istront de cest porpris.
– Et tu comant? Di m'an le voir.
– N'i a celi qui s'ost movoir
des que ele me voit venir,
car quant j'en puis une tenir,
si l'estraing si par les dens çorz
as poinz que j'ai et durs et forz,
que les autres de peor tranblent
et tot environ moi s'asanblent,
ausi con por merci crïer;
ne nus ne s'i porroit fïer,
fors moi, s'antre'ele s'estoit mis,
qu'il ne fust maintenant ocis.
 Einsi sui de mes bestes sire,
et tu me redevrois dire
quies hom tu ies, et que tu quiers.   lines 331–57

(– What are you doing here? – I stay here,/ and shepherd
["guard"] the beasts in this wood./ – You shepherd them? By
Saint Peter of Rome,/ they don't recognize [the authority of] a
man;/ I don't believe that on a plain or in a forest/ anyone can
guard savage beasts,/ nor in any other place, for any reason,/
unless the place is enclosed./ – I do shepherd these beasts and
command them/ not to go out of this field./ – How do you do it?
Tell me the truth./ – There is not one [beast] that dares to move/
as soon as it sees me coming,/ for when I can grasp one of them,/
I grip it so hard by its two horns,/ with my fists, which are so
hard and strong,/ that the others tremble with fear/ and all gather
around me/ as if to cry for mercy;/ no one could trust them/
except me, if he went among the animals,/ he would immediately be killed./ Thus I am the master of my beasts,/ and you
should now tell me/ what sort of man you are, and what you
seek.)

As Zumthor noted above (speaking of *Éracle*), medieval manuscripts do
not offer the textual markers – the punctuation – which would make this
passage comprehensible. It is only by vocal differentiation that this passage
would have made sense to its public: even the manuscripts, then, invited
vocalization. These lines certainly invite strong differentiation: on the one

hand, we have the somewhat bland knightly Calogrenant, and on the other, the "bestial" bull-herder who was most likely represented as speaking loudly and boorishly, but who also reveals himself to be "a man," and who turns Calogrenant's initial question back on him, asking: "And now tell me what sort of man *you* are."

But, whatever one's personal favorite, Chrétien gives us many voices, and many *kinds* of voices: not just those of kings and counts and queens, of lords and ladies – some of them "good," some "evil" – but also those of demons (*nuitons*) and giants as well as of dwarves, of children (the little girl to whom Gauvain gives his sleeve, in *Le conte del graal*), of a fool and a *charbonnier* (both, again, *Le graal*). A high level of dramatic art is called for in the vocalization of Chrétien's romances, for his works contain a wide range of sorts of characters and, clearly, of *voices*.

By contrast, most *chansons de geste* contain very *few* sorts of voice: virtually all the voices that we hear – that *jongleurs* evoked – were: a) male, b) adult c) noble, d) warring, indeed heroic. A few males were "wicked," which may allow for some performance variation, but the range was narrow. Range of voice is generally not sought in the epic, as it clearly is in Chrétien's works and in and other romances. Some (typically later) *chansons de geste* do introduce vocal variability, adding to the noble, heavy male voices the higher and lighter voices of young children and important female characters – but this is rare in early French epic songs.[13]

It is not merely that Chrétien offers us many voices that are, in themselves, varied and striking. He also plays off distinctive voices against each other. In *Yvain*, we hear the unpleasant voice of selfish daughter of the Count of Noires Epines, who will share nothing of her inheritance with her younger sister:

> ... "Sire, Dex me confonde
> se ja de ma terre li part
> chastel, ne vile, ne essart,
> ne bois, ne plain, ne autre chose.
> Mes se uns chevaliers s'en ose
> por li armer, qui que il soit
> qui voelle desresnier son droit,
> si veigne trestot maintenant.   lines 4786–93

> (... "Lord [Arthur], may God confound me/ if ever, of my land,
> I give her/ castle, or town, or clearing,/ or wood, or plain, or
> anything./ But if a knight dares/ arm himself for her, whoever he

---

13 Just as the array of voices evoked by Chrétien is wider than what is generally found in the epic, the array of dramatic situations in which these voices are deployed is more varied, as well. Most epics have powerful scenes in which men – male voices – can be heard insulting each other loudly and vigorously. There are a few other sorts of dramatic monologues and vocal exchanges, such as laments over dead heroes. But the range is narrow: few *chansons de geste* use voice for many different kinds of conflicts or emotions.

is/ who will uphold her right,/ let him come forward right
now.'')

By contrast, we hear the sweet and humble – but determined! – voice of the
''good'' sister:

> Et la pucele en es le pas
> s'an part et vient devant le roi.
> ''Rois, fet ele, je ving a toi
> et a ta cort querre consoil
> ne n'i truis point, si m'an mervoil
> quant je consoil n'i puis avoir
> mes ne feroie pas savoir
> se je sanz congié m'an aloie.
> Et sache ma suer tote voie
> qu'avoir porroit ele del mien
> par amors, s'ele voloit bien,
> mes ja par force que je puisse,
> par qu'aïe ne consoil truisse,
> ne li leirai mon heritage.   lines 4766–79

(And the maiden immediately/ stepped out and came before the
king./ ''King, she says, I came to you/ and to your court to seek
counsel,/ and I don't find any, and I am astonished/ that I cannot
have any counsel/ but I would not do right/ if I left without your
permission./ And know that my sister in any case/ could have
some of my possessions/ for love, if she wanted,/ but never by
force, if I am able;/ if I can find help or counsel/ I will not let her
take my inheritance.'')

But while we are speaking of distinctive voices played off against each
other, we should not forget the voice of Chrétien himself, or – *soyons prudents*
– of his narrative *persona*. A good many scholars have been interested in the
character of his interventions in his works.[14] His voice, as the words of the text
transmit it to us, sounds at once benevolent but cool: his interventions, when
they reflect an apparently personal judgment, are generally rather dry, as when
he says of the young Perceval, and the difficulties that other people have with
him, ''Molt grief chose est de fol aprendre'' (line 1173; ''It is a painful thing to
teach a fool''). Or, for example, when Perceval fails to ask The Question
(''Whom does the Grail serve?''), since he has been told not to talk too much,
Chrétien makes the comment:

> Si criem que il n'i ait damage,
> Por che que j'ai oï retraire

14 See, for example, P.F. Dembowski, ''Monologue, Author's Monologue and Related
Problems in the Romances of Chrétien de Troyes.''

Qu'ausi se puet on bien trop taire
Com trop parler a la foie[e].   lines 3248–51

(I fear that this is a mistake,/ For I have heard it said/ That one
can keep too silent/ Just as one can talk too much.)

Chrétien can sound amusingly rationalistic, as when he argues at length, in
Yvain, as to whether Love and Hate can coexist:

Par foi, c'est mervoille provee
que l'en a ensanble trovee
Amor et Haïne mortel.
Dex! meïsmes en un ostel
comant puet estre li repaires
a choses qui tant sont contraires?
En un ostel, si con moi sanble,
ne pueent eles estre ansanble,
que ne porroit pas remenoir
l'une avoeques l'autre un seul soir
que noise et tançon n'i eüst,
puis que l'une l'autre i seüst.
Mes en un chas a plusors manbres,
que l'en i fet loges et chanbres;
Ensi puet bien estre la chose:
espoir qu'Amors s'estoit anclose
en aucune chanbre celee;
et Haïne s'an ert alee
as loges par devers la voie
por ce qu'el vialt que l'en la voie ...   lines 6015–34

(By my faith, it is a proven marvel/ that one can find together/
Love and deadly Hatred./ God! even in a large house,/ how can
this be the dwelling-place/ for things that are so contrary?/ In a
house, it seems to me,/ they cannot be together,/ they can't
remain/ the one with the other even for an evening/ without
arguments and quarrels,/ once each knew the other was there./
But in a wing with several parts,/ where they make rooms and
chambers;/ Thus can the thing be:/ I hope that Love had closed
itself off/ in a hidden chamber;/ and Hatred had gone off/ to the
rooms in the front/ so that it can be seen ...)

Here we hear Chrétien reasoning with himself, asking himself questions to
which he then provides answers.

Many, perhaps most, of Chrétien's remarks are of a narratorial nature,
bearing on his role as story-teller. He often explains and justifies his brevity. In
his description of Fénice he declares, with a use of hyperbole that we cannot
possibly take seriously:

148

Ne vuel par parole descrivre,
Car se mil anz avoie a vivre
Et chascun jor doblast mes sans,
Si perdroie gie mon porpans,
Ençois que le voir an deïsse.
Bien sai, se m'an antremeïsse
Et tot mon san i anpleasse,
Que tote ma poinne i gastasse,
Et ce seroit poinne gastee.   lines 2697–705

(I don't want to describe her in words,/ For if I had a thousand
years to live/ And every day my wit doubled,/ Still I would lose
my effort,/ Before I could tell the truth [about her]./ I know it
well, if I undertook to do it/ And I spent all my wit on this,/ I
would waste all my pains,/ And it would be wasted effort.)

Chrétien's own voice seems quite consistent throughout his *oeuvre*. It is strik-
ingly and reliably different from the voice and the narrative persona of, say,
Béroul, who frequently speaks (we have seen) in hot and passionate tones,
which most modern editors punctuate with exclamation points.

If Chrétien's voice is a reliable construct, this is not the case of many of the
characters whose voices he evokes for us. That his conception of the voice of a
particular character is not static or simple was already suggested by the
example of the dramatic two-part monologues. Surely the most striking
example of a character with a variable voice is Guinevere in *Lancelot*: her
voice is sometimes cold and vindictive, sometimes that of the loving lady. A
look at the former mode: Lancelot has come to rescue her, and has defeated her
kidnapper Meleagant in battle. He is led by good King Bademagu into her
presence.

Quant la reïne voit le roi,
qui tient Lancelot par le doi,
si c'est contre le roi dreciee
et fet sanblant de correciee,
si s'anbruncha et ne dist mot.
"Dame, veez ci Lancelot,
fet li rois, qui vos vient veoir;
ce vos doit molt pleire et seoir.
– Moi? Sire, moi ne puet il plaire;
de son veoir n'ai ge que faire. . . ."   lines 3739–48

(When the queen sees the king,/ who holds Lancelot by the
hand,/ she stood up in front of the king/ and pretends to be
angry,/ and she acted angry and did not say a word./ "Lady, you
see here Lancelot,/ says the king, [Lancelot] who comes to see
you;/ this must please and suit you greatly./ – Me? Sire, this
cannot please me;/ I care nothing about seeing him . . .")

Her voice, represented here as sharp and hostile, is very different a bit later, when she thinks that Lancelot is dead and repents of her cruelty to him. She begins her lament (and self-accusations) thus:

> "Ha! lasse! De coi me sovint,
> quant mes amis devant moi vint,
> que je nel deignai conjoïr
> ne ne le vos onques oïr!
> quant mon esgart et ma parole
> li veai, ne fis je que fole?
> Que fole? Ainz fis, si m'aïst Dex,
> que felenesse et que cruex;
> et sel cuidai ge feire a gas,
> mes ensi nel cuida il pas,
> se nel m'a mie pardoné.
> Nus fors moi ne li a doné
> le mortel cop, mien escïant. . . ."   lines 4197–209

(Ah! woe is me! For I remember,/ that when my lover came before me,/ I did not deign to enjoy him/ nor even, you see, to hear him./ When my look and my words/ sent him away, did I not act crazy?/ Crazy? Rather I acted, so help me God,/ in a way wicked and cruel;/ and I thought it was a joke,/ but he didn't think so,/ and he did not forgive me./ No one but me gave him/ the mortal blow, it seems to me.)

This monologue goes on for over 60 more lines. Here we hear the voice of a passionate, loving, anguished, not a cold and haughty, Guinevere. The Queen, then, has more than one sort of voice. Chrétien plays her voice off against itself. Her "characterization" includes vocal variability; or perhaps we should say, bipolarity: that is, Guinevere has two, very different, voices, not an entire range of voices.

Chrétien shows variation, though in a different way, with the voice of Perceval in *Le conte del graal*. At the beginning, Perceval is a big, dumb – and very funny – child. He is "nice": naive, silly. In particular, he speaks in an exaggerated, childish manner. For example, first he declares that the creatures (in fact, knights) who are making an infernal racket as they clank through the forest must be devils:

> Molt se merveille et dist: "Par m'ame,
> Voir se dist ma mere, ma dame,
> Qui me dist que deable sont
> Les plus laides choses del mont;
> Et si dist por moi enseingnier
> Que por aus se doit on seingnier,
> Mais cest ensaing desdaignerai,
> Que ja voir ne m'en seignerai,

Ains ferrai si tot le plus fort
D'un des gvelos que je port,
Que ja n'aprochera vers moi
Nus des autres, si com je croi.''
Einsi a soi meïsme dist
Li vallés ains qu'il les veïst . . .   lines 113–26

(He wonders aloud and says: ''By my soul,/ My lady mother
spoke truly,/ Who told me that devils are/ The ugliest things in
the world;/ And she said it to teach me/ That one must cross
oneself against them,/ But I will disdain this sign [of the cross],/
And truly I will not cross myself,/ But I will strike the strongest
of them/ With one of the javelins that I am carrying,/ So none of
the others will/ Come near me, I think.''/ Thus the boy spoke to
himself/ Before he saw them . . .)

Then, when he sees how bright and beautiful these creatures are, he
excitedly proclaims them to be angels, perhaps even God himself.

Et dist: ''Ha! sire Diex, merchi!
Ce sont angle que je voi chi.
Et voir or ai je molt pechié,
Ore ai je molt mal esploitié,
Qui dis que c'estoient deable.
Ne me dist pas ma mere fable,
Qui me dist que li angle estoient
Les plus beles choses qui soient,
Fors Diex qui est plus biax que tuit.
Chi voi je Damedieu, ce quit,
Car un si bel en i esgart
Que li autre, se Diex me gart,
N'ont mie de biauté la disme.
Ce me dist ma mere meïsme
Qu'en doit Dieu sor toz aoarer
Et suppliier et honorer,
Et je aor[e[rai cestui
Et toz les angles aprés lui.''   lines 137–54

(And he said ''Ha! Lord God, mercy!/ These are angels that I see
here./ And truly have I sinned greatly,/ Just now I did wrong,/
When I said that these were devils./ My mother did not lie to me/
Who said that angels were/ The most beautiful things that are,/
Except for God who is the most beautiful of all./ I see here God
himself, I think,/ For one of them looks so beautiful/ That the
others, by God,/ Don't have a tenth of his beauty./ And my
mother herself told me/ That one must adore God above all
things/ And pray and honor him,/ And I will adore this one/ And
after him, all the angels.'')

151

This is a remarkably comic and ironic scene. (It is ironic in that knights are neither devils nor angels; still less are they divine. But Perceval will soon think of knighthood as a virtually angelic state, while his mother will speak of all the complaints that people have about the behavior of knights, who can, then, be thought of as somewhat demonic.) Let's attend to Perceval's voice here, as distinct from his goofy character as described. He is, aside from being an ignorant and impressionable child, a *Welsh* boy: "un gallois." We should probably imagine this extensive monologue, and Perceval's part of the long and funny dialogue with the knights that follows, played with a strong Welsh (or pseudo-Welsh: who cares!) accent. Medieval works frequently contain scenes in jargon, dialect and patois, unquestionably played with accented voices. We have the same phenomenon here. And the performers of these romances – the first was probably Chrétien himself – surely drew on performance skills of a high order in order to imitate or impersonate such voices, such accents. If these works were presented in a monotone, much of the impact would be lost.

Little by little – this is the medieval equivalent of a *Bildungsroman* – Perceval's voice as performed presumably acquires some maturity: moral *gravitas*. After he defeats the "Orgueilleus de la lande" who has been maltreating his lady-friend, Perceval makes the following civilized speech, and his voice, as we are to imagine it – as medieval audiences heard it imitated – is, by now, I think we can assume, no longer that of an ignorant child; his Welsh accent may be either attenuated or gone.

> – "Va dont al plus proçain manoir,
> Fait cil, que tu as ci entour,
> Si le fai baignier assejor
> Tant qu'ele soit garie et saine.
> Puis t'apareille, si le maine
> Bien atornee et bien vestue
> Al roi Artu, sel me salue
> Et si te met en sa merchi . . ."   lines 3950–57

> (– "Go, then, to the nearest manorhouse,/ He says, that you have nearby,/ And have her bathed right away/ Until she is healed and healthy./ Then robe her, and lead her,/ Well adorned and dressed,/ To King Arthur, and greet him from me/ And put yourself in his mercy . . .")

It might be argued that I am confusing voice with characterization, and that what Chrétien has created – narratively *staged* – is an assortment of interesting characters. But Chrétien's characterization is done to a marked degree *through voice*, as in the theatre: through what characters *say* and *how* they say it. We get to know the characters largely through hearing them speak, to others and to themselves.

I have not forgotten Chrétien's excellent descriptions, but his descriptions of people are very much "set pieces." All beautiful women are so essentially in the same ways; the same goes for men. If Chrétien's men and women "came alive," as we might say today, for their audience, it was probably through their voices as heard – as vocally impersonated – not through their faces or physiques as described.

Voice and dialogue

Chrétien devotes a very considerable proportion of his narrative to talking characters: to direct discourse in dialogue and in monologue, which is itself frequently interior dialogue. Dialogues can, in Chrétien's romances, go on for dozens, sometimes even hundreds, of lines without any narrative elements other than an occasional introductory "fait il" or "dist ele." (Zumthor noted the same phenomenon in *Éracle* – and saw that it pointed to vocal perform- ance, to strong interplay of voices.) Sometimes a brief description of what the character is doing as he or she speaks is provided. For example, in *Yvain*, the hero falls in love with the widow of the knight he has mortally wounded. We hear him talk to, and argue with, himself for almost eighty lines, from line 1432 to line 1510, without interruption. The two sides of the argument are only comprehensible if the two voices are heard as *different*: a rational vs. an amorous Yvain. The scene where Lunete consoles her lady and ultimately persuades her to marry Yvain (the man who has killed her husband) extends from line 1601 to line 1728 – over 120 lines. And in this extended dialogue, where the *parole* is passed back and forth many times, there is only one "ele fet"; the rest of the time no lexical marker indicates the shifting back and forth of discourse, that is articulated for us by modern punctuation. Here is a sample, from the beginning of the passage:

> La premiere foiz a consoil
> li dist: "Dame, molt me mervoil
> que folemant vos voi ovrer.
> Dame, cuidiez vos recovrer
> vostre seignor por vostre duel?
> – Nenil, fet ele, mes mon vuel
> seroie je morte d'enui.
> – Por coi? – Por aler aprés lui.
> – Aprés lui? Dex vos an desfande
> qui ausi boen seignor vos rande
> si com il an est posteïs.
> – Einz tel mançonge ne deïs,
> qu'il ne me porroit si boen randre.
> – Meillor, se vos le volez prandre,
> vos randra il, sel proverai.
> – Fui! Teis! Ja tel ne troverai.   lines 1601–16

> (The first time they were alone together/ she said to her: "Lady,
> I greatly marvel/ that I see you carry on in so mad a fashion./
> Lady, do you think you will recover/ your lord by your grief?/ –
> No, she said, but my desire/ is to die of sorrow./ – Why? – To
> follow after him./ – After him? May God forbid it,/ who can give
> you as good a lord/ since he has the power to do so./ – Never did
> you tell such a lie before,/ that he could give me as good a lord./
> – A better one, if you will take him,/ can God give you, and I will
> prove it./ – Go! Be silent! Never will I find such a one again!)

We have here the passionate and imperious voice of Laudine contrasted with
the reasonable and slightly ironic voice of Lunete.

Among these dialogues, we hear many verbal fights and debates. One of the
reasons why Ong and others have emphasized the "agonistic" character of
"oral narrative"[15] is presumably the simple fact that strongly opposed –
antagonistic – voices are more gripping for audiences to hear than irenic
discourse. It could be argued that the two exciting emotions to see and listen to
are love and hate. (This is surely why Soap Operas, and other popular forms of
entertainment today, are completely taken up with these emotions, and why
television viewers are so fond of courtroom scenes, in programs from "Perry
Mason" to "Night Court" to real trials which often hold the public riveted.)
With regard to love, Chrétien is justly famous for his love dialogue and
debates, as in the debate/ conversation in which Lunete persuades Laudine to
accept Yvain, her first husband's killer, as her new husband; I quoted a bit of
this above. Chrétien is a master, as well, of the inner dialogue or two-voiced
monologue, as when characters, such as Soredamors in *Cligés* or Laudine or
Yvain, fall in love against their will and argue with themselves. In the case of
Laudine, she actually impersonates the male voice of her still-imaginary suitor
as she persuades herself – "he" persuades "her" – to accept the love of her
husband's killer (lines 1762ff); in such an internal debate, we are hearing two
clearly distinctive voices.

Dialogue and culture

It is important at least briefly to set the importance of debates and dialogues
in Chrétien's romances (and other medieval works as well) within a larger
conceptual framework. In recent years, a number of anthropologists and
ethnographers have begun to study the importance of dialogue in the development of human culture; the role of dialogue in traditions of oral narrative is
particularly great. One thinks here of work such as that (cited earlier) of Dennis
Tedlock, in particular *The Dialogic Emergence of Culture*, co-edited with

---

15 Walter J. Ong, *Orality and Literacy*, pp. 43–45.

Bruce Mannheim. Tedlock notes, for example, that "Bakhtin (1981) completely ignores ordinary story-telling and credits the development of multivocalic discourse to novelists" (p. 285). Given the tremendous importance of romance in the constitution of medieval vernacular culture, I think that the centrality of dialogue and debate within this genre deserves greater emphasis than it has previously received. It is likely that that romance, both by the dialogues and debates that it contained in its plots and among its characters, and by the discussions that it invited or generated in its audiences, was a significant cultural force: that is, it allowed for a wide array of feelings, opinions, and frames of reference to be expressed, explored, juxtaposed. This is by no means to deny that other genres as well – the epic, for example, and the lyric "tenso" – also contain, and often foreground, dialogue and debate, but I would say that a wider range of things are discussed in romance than in these other genres, the former focusing on matters of war and male (feudal) relations, the latter somewhat narrowly on love.

Dramatic use of voice

It is not merely that Chrétien conjured up for his listeners a whole array of memorable and highly distinctive voices, that speak – and debate! – often at considerable length. What he does with these voices, and the characters whose being they evoke, is often highly dramatic – which is why the analogy with radio theatre is particularly relevant. For example, Énide whispers to herself in a monologue that was private, but not private enough. (Her husband heard her, and was deeply disturbed.)

> "Lasse, fet ele, con mar fui!
> de mon païs que ving ça querre?
> Bien me doit essorbir la terre,
> quant toz li miaudres chevaliers,
> li plus hardiz et li plus fiers,
> qui onques fust ne cuens ne rois,
> li plus lëax, li plus cortois,
> a del tot an tot relanquie
> por moi tote chevalerie.
> Dons l'ai ge honi tot por voir;
> nel volsisse por nul avoir." lines 2492–502

(Alas, she says, woe is me!/ what did I come here to seek, from my country?/ The earth should swallow me up,/ since the very best knight,/ the bravest and the boldest,/ who ever was a count or a king,/ the most loyal, the most courtly,/ has completely given up/ all knighthood, for my sake./ So I have really shamed him, in truth;/ I wouldn't have wanted this, for anything.)

To be dramatically effective, this monologue must be presented in what we call today a "stage whisper." Énide is talking to herself, but nonetheless she speaks loudly enough to be heard by her husband – and by the audience of listeners!

During the long ride and series of adventures on which Énide's angry husband leads her, forbidding her to speak to him for any reason, we continually *wait* for her to speak: *will* Énide speak up as armed bands of men approach to attack Érec – or not? The "arrival" of her voice has been dramatically staged. In other words, Chrétien makes dramatic use not merely of many different modes of speech but also of *silence*. At one point, Énide sees three robbers coming at them, clearly with evil intentions:

> Enyde vit les robeors;
> molt l'an est prise granz peors.
> "Dex, fet ele, que porrai dire?
> Or iert ja morz ou pris mes sire,
> car cil sont troi et il est seus;
> n'est pas a droiz partiz li jeus
> d'un chevalier ancontre trois;
> cil le ferra ja demenois,
> que mes sire ne s'an prant garde.
> Dex! serai je donc si coarde
> que dire ne li oserai?
> Ja si coarde ne serai;
> jel li dirai, nel leirai pas."
> Vers lui se torne en es le pas
> et dist: "Biau sire, ou pansez vos?
> Ci vienent poignant aprés vos
> troi chevalier qui molt vos chacent;
> peor ai que mal ne vos facent . . ."   lines 2827–44

(Énide saw the robbers;/ she is taken with great fear./ "Lord, she says, what can I say?/ Now my lord will be killed or taken,/ for there are three of them and he is alone;/ it is not in the rules of the game/ that one knight should be against three/ this one will strike him right away/ for my lord is not paying attention./ Lord, will I then be such a coward/ that I won't dare to speak to him?/ Never will I be such a coward;/ I will speak to him, I won't hold back."/ She turns toward him right away/ and says: "Fair lord, what are you thinking of?/ Here come, riding hard after you,/ three knights who are chasing you;/ I am afraid that they will do you harm" . . .)

In this scene we first hear Énide talking softly to herself – once again, whispering – trying to screw up her courage to speak, then speaking boldly at least to herself, and then, finally – dramatically – calling out loudly to her husband to warn him. Here, at the end of the passage she must be talking *fast*, as well: the knights are rushing toward him.

156

Another, similarly dramatic staging of the arrival of voice: in *Cligés*, we hear Fénice awaken from her magically-induced – fake, but all too convincing! – "death," and start to moan as she addresses the lover who weeps over her dead body:

> A tant ciele giete un sopir
> Et dit foiblement et an bas:
> "Amis, amis, je ne sui pas
> Del tot morte, mes po an faut.
> De ma vie mes ne me chaut.
> Je me cuidai gaber et faindre,
> Mes or estuet a certes plaindre,
> Car la morz n'a soing de mon gap.
> Mervoille iert, se vive an eschap,
> Car trop m'ont li mire bleciee,
> Ma char ronpue et depeciee.
> Et ne por quant, s'il poïst estre
> Qu'avoec moi fust ceanz ma mestre,
> Cele me feïst tote sainne,
> Se rien i deüst valoir painne.   lines 6182–96

(At that she [Fénice] utters a sigh/ And says feebly and low:/ "Lover, lover, I am not/ Entirely dead, but almost./ I no longer care about living./ I thought I was joking and pretending,/ But now I am to be pitied,/ For death didn't care much for my joke./ It is a marvel if I get out of this alive,/ For the doctors wounded me so much,/ They broke and tore up my flesh./ And nevertheless, if it could be/ That my nurse could be with me,/ She could make me all well again,/ If it seemed worth the trouble.")

She is half-dead when she begins to talk, and she clearly speaks in piteous tones. But, starting from the words "Et ne por quant, . . ." ("And nevertheless . . .") one can "hear" the desire to live, and to love, slipping back into her discourse.

Chrétien varies his approach. In *Érec et Énide*, the lecherous Count of Limors tries to force Énide to marry him (Érec, badly wounded, appears to be dead). Énide resists and the count strikes her several times. She – who had so often hesitated to speak – cries out:

> "Ahi! fet ele, ne me chaut
> que tu me dïes ne ne faces:
> ne criem tes cos ne tes menaces.
> Asez me bat, asez me fier:
> ja tant ne te troverai fier   4810
> que por toi face plus ne mains,
> se tu or androit a tes mains
> me devoies les ialz sacheir
> ou tote vive detranchier."

157

Antre ces diz et ces tançons,
revint Erec de pasmeisons,
ausi come hom qui s'esvoille.
S'il s'esbahi, ne fu mervoille,
des genz qu'il vit an viron lui;
mes grant duel a et grant enui,   4820
quant la voiz sa fame entandi.
Del dois a terre descendi,
et trait l'espee isnelemant;
ire li done hardemant,
et l'amors qu'an sa fame avoit.
Cele part cort ou il la voit,
et fiert par mi le chief le conte
si qu'il l'escervele et esfronte
sanz desfiance et sanz parole;
li sans et la cerbele an vole.   4830
Li chevalier saillent des tables;
tuit cuident que ce soit deables;
qui leanz soit entr'ax venuz.
N'i remaint juenes ne chenuz,
car molt furent esmaié tuit;
li uns devant l'autre s'an fuit
quanqu'il püent a grant eslais;
tost orent voidié le palés,
et dïent tuit, et foible et fort:
"Fuiez! Fuiez! Veez le mort."   lines 4806–40

("Ahi! she says, it does not matter/ what you say or what you do;/ I do not fear your blows or your threats./ Beat me as you wish; strike me as you wish:/ never will I be so afraid of you/ that I will do anything for you,/ even if you now, with both of your hands,/ should tear my eyes out/ or cut me up alive."/ At these words and these challenges,/ Érec came out of his faint,/ like a man who wakes up./ If he was astonished at the people/ he saw around him, it is not surprising,/ but he has great sorrow and distress,/ when he heard the voice of his wife;/ he got down from the table [on which his body had been laid out]/ and quickly pulls out his sword;/ wrath gives him boldness,/ along with the love that he had for his wife./ He runs there where he sees her,/ and strikes the count in the head/ so that he cuts out his brain and cuts off his/ forehead without even defying him and without words;/ he steals from him his blood and his brains./ The knights jump up from the tables;/ they think that he is a devil/ which has come in amongst them./ Not a young or an old man remains,/ for all were completely terrified;/ one faster than another they run away/ with all possible speed;/ they empty the palace,/ and all say, both the strong and the weak,/ "Run! Run! Look, a dead man.")

The first part of this passage (up to line 4814) emphasizes the bold words – and the courageous "delivery" – of the previously timid and largely-silent Énide. In the latter part of this passage, the auditory emphasis is not on the voice of the person who is waking up – apparently rising from the dead: Érec says nothing whatsoever. Rather, the stress falls on the terrified – and unquestionably comic – voices of the people who see the dead man get up and silently grab his sword: "Fuiez! Fuiez! Veez le mort." There is considerable visual drama in this scene as well, as Érec, like a spectre, arises from his stupor at the sound of his wife's voice.[16]

Voice and Chrétien's narrative strategy

We now turn to the issue of how, in the overall structuring of his romances and in his broad narrative strategy, Chrétien uses voice and voices. But we need to broaden the theoretical framework. Literary scholars and narratologists commonly distinguish between two basic kinds of presentation of events in narrative: "showing" vs. "telling."[17] The former consists of representing – verbally "showing" – the events and personal interactions: we seem to see and hear them occur. Thus, the narration is given in the present; battles are recounted blow by blow; we hear the characters speak in direct address rather than being told, in indirect discourse, the essence of what was said, etc. It is worth remembering, though, that in narrative – as opposed to reality, and to drama – we don't actually see people do things, or even see actors pretend to carry out the actions. "Showing" in narrative is generally something of a metaphor.

By contrast, in a "telling" mode, the narrator relates what happened, making use of summary techniques including heavy reliance on indirect discourse, and the casting of events in the past.

Of these two basic narrative strategies, the first, the more vivid, is adapted from drama or at least conceptually related to it. But, used exclusively, this strategy would make for slow going, narratively speaking: a narrator can hardly show everything, especially if he is dealing with a long period of time, a broad set of characters, or a particularly complex plot. Telling is, among other things, a time-saving device, narratively speaking – which is why playwrights as well often have recourse to it: their characters narrate past events to each

---

16 As I noted earlier, this scene, like several scenes mentioned thus far and others below, invites attention to physical gesture as well as to voice on the part of the performer. Zumthor, in the passage cited earlier, made a similar point. We will return to this important issue. For the moment, though, this is *just* "radio."

17 See, for example, Tzvetan Todorov's classic article, "Les catégories du récit littéraire," pp. 144ff; Todorov speaks of "représentation" vs. "narration," "chronique" vs. "drame."

other, and to the audience. Telling also allows an author/narrator to articulate his – and orient our – perspective on the events and situations. For these reasons, telling is perhaps considered the more truly narrative technique: it puts into play many of the features that are peculiar to narrative, as distinct from drama. At any rate, most theorists would, I think, say that most successful narratives contain some of each of these strategies: some telling and some showing.

This basic dichotomy – like so many others – no doubt has its uses, especially for modern literature. But with regard to medieval narrative in general, and Chrétien in particular, a somewhat more nuanced gamut is needed to replace this pair of theoretical opposites. We will also eventually need to de-metaphorize the "showing" component of the pair.

In early vernacular narrative, of straight telling there is rather little, if, as is commonly the case, we insist that the telling – the narrative summary – be given in the past: that is, that it be cast into a network of past tenses. As various scholars have noted, most early French narrative, whether *chanson de geste*, *vie de saint* or *roman*, is told to a substantial degree in the present tense; in any event, the present coexists with the preterit and the imperfect. This is, in particular, true of Chrétien's romances. In other words, we still have a blend of showing and telling: the narration of events is more vivid and representational than in pure telling.

It is as though early vernacular verse narrative were typically halfway between the verbal drama of showing and the distance of telling, and often substantially closer to the former than to the latter. This is perhaps the case precisely because it is what one might term "voiced narrative": the narrator/performer (whether the same person as the author or not) is dramatically present, at the very least through his voice; and we, the listeners, are present. True, this is not full-scale drama; in particular, the characters of the story are not represented – embodied – by separate actors.

But the coolness and the impersonality – the peculiarly literary irony – that are so common in the written tradition of telling are surely almost impossible in a story told aloud by a person, who moreover adopts as his own (as medieval narrators generally did) the "I" of the story: "Now I will tell you . . .," "I think that . . .", "it seems to me that . . .," and so on. Thus, the oral story-telling tradition, with its common recourse to present-tense narration and to a warm narratorial presence, generally has little of the objectivity and coolness characteristic of the telling mode.

Chrétien's romances are also closer to the showing mode, and to drama in the fairly strong sense of the word, because of what he does with voice. That is, he uses the voices of characters – characters' individual speech and their verbal interaction – to provide vivid exposition, and even to tell the story for him; this is precisely what playwrights do.

Let us consider the opening episodes of *Le conte del graal*, from the scene in the forest, where the young Perceval hears the "devils" and sees the "angels," up to the point where he puts on the Red Knight's armor: lines 69 to 1304. It is important to look not merely at short passages, but at the large pattern in which Chrétien handles speech and speeches, and to think in terms of a substantial chunk of narrative. In this passage, there is a substantial amount of direct discourse, accounting for 739 out of 1236 lines – close to two-thirds: 59.79%, to be exact. In this scene, we learn about most of what has happened in the past, and we see, or "hear," things happen in the present, from the point of view of – in the words of – the characters. Thus, for example, Perceval's mother, not Chrétien, tells us what happened to her husband and other sons: the boy's father and brothers; the charcoal-seller, not Chrétien, tells us why Arthur is both happy and sad; it is the fool, not Chrétien, who prophesies that the youth will break Kay's arm, and so on. In other words, Chrétien uses his characters to do the "telling" of past events and to prophesy the future. They tell the stories, give the summaries – and most commonly they tell it as eye-witnesses.

At two points in this part of the narrtive, Chrétien goes over the same episode twice: in the case of the maiden in the tent, first he shows us the scene, almost completely in direct discourse; then he has the maiden tell her lover about what happened, and try to persuade him that her account is true. In the second instance, we are first shown – and we hear, in direct discourse – the combat between Perceval and the Red Knight, and then Yvonet returns to the court and narrates it in his own words to Arthur. Thus, we hear – are aurally "shown" – two versions of these scenes.

Is all this an issue of "point of view"? I think not. The point is not that we "see things" from the intellectual frame of reference of this or that character. There is, as is common in early medieval narrative, a remarkable consensus on what is going on: even "evil" people (when they think about it) know they are bad. (Examples: the lecherous and murderous Count Aloain in *Erec et Enide* when grievously wounded confesses that the fault was his, not Erec's; the "temptress" in *Le conte du graal* knows she is being "bad.") This unanimity of point of view presumably results from a belief in an existence of objective truth.[18] When a character is defeated in battle by a knight such as Perceval, and is sent to the court of Arthur to tell his story, we do not assume that he is going to tell "his" side of the story! Rather he is going to tell the Queen (or whomever) the truth: there is only *one* true story. This is not, then, an epistemological matter – a matter of truth – but one of voice, of *drama*.

Chrétien does not take all these different characters' voices and discourses as an invitation to distinguish between different kinds of speech stylistically.

---

[18] This truth was "guaranteed" by God: by divine Truth. Thus, for example, when knights fought over an important issue, they believed (or claimed to believe) that God would make Right – the Truth as He knew it – triumph. But while this belief in Truth seems to obtain for large ethical issues, it is far less clearly the case in many other matters, such as those concerning emotions, judgments of strategy, and the like. Which is precisely why, as we saw, there are not merely many dialogues but much debate in romance (and in other works).

Men and women, for example, do not speak "differently," prosodically, lexically: they commonly use the same vocabulary, the same sentence structures, and the like. The issue is not, then, one of "point of view," or of the establishment of stylistic differentiation, but one of voice and of emotion. Characters tell of events and people not only in their own voice, but in a mode that expresses the nature and degree of their own involvement.[19] Some characters have an intense personal engagement in the events: Perceval's mother passionately loves her one remaining child; Perceval burns to become a knight, and then to have that beautiful red armor; the maiden fears (rightly so!) her lover's jealousy; Kay is motivated by his nasty temperament, and by the insults he receives; the fool, kicked into the fire, and the laughing girl who has been smacked to the ground have suffered pain and humiliation and look forward to being avenged; Arthur has a strong sense of duty as king and father to his knights. These characters all care very much about what is going on.

Other speakers, by contrast, are essentially amused by-standers: the five knights mistaken for angels (though they are also a bit irritated with the young Welsh fool, as they are in a hurry to be off: they are seeking for some people in the forest); Yvonet who watches the youth prepare to dissect the dead knight in order to remove the beautiful red armor. Events are, then, almost all mediated through emotions, ranging from grief, to desire, to fear, to a sense of duty, to the desire for vengeance, to sheer amusement.

There is an important sense in which Chrétien's romances are "cool": a good many scholars and readers have responded to this aspect of his tales. But in this perception, they are responding primarily to the narrator's voice as the text conjures it up for us: the voice of Chrétien – or, again, his *persona* – as distinct from those of the characters, who are typically very *engagés* indeed. Chrétien's is, indeed, as we noted above, a cool voice: not one that seems emotionally engaged in the events. (In this sense, it can seem a "modern" narratorial voice.) It might also be argued that the very multiplicity of passionately involved voices tends to discourage us from fully and uncritically taking anyone's side; and this is, precisely, what one often finds in drama. Thus, for example, in *Cligés* we may question whether the lovers were, or not, in the right: Fénice was determined to not be like Iseut, but did she really succeed? This is in contrast, for example, to Béroul, who is, and forces us to be, fully and unequivocally on the side of the lovers.

In any event, Chrétien de Troyes uses voices, characters' voices, to tell the story, and to advance the narrative. This is what might be called a technique of "auditory showing": Chrétien shows us what is happening by making us *hear* it happen.

---

[19] Another way of putting this would be to say that these characters – these secondary narrators – are all "Subjects" and they narrate events with respect to their own "Object." See my *Medieval Narrative and Modern Narratology: Subjects and Objects of Desire, passim.*

162

Our literary analyses tend to focus on Chrétien's works as texts – silent texts. (We will return to this issue in the final chapter.) But perhaps we need to make a more heroic effort to put ourselves back into the shoes – the *solers* – of the twelfth century court public, and to try to hear Chrétien's romances: to think of them perhaps as "medieval live radio theatre"?

But the next question – the question that I have been begging, admittedly quite impatiently, in this chapter – is this: exactly *how* were these romances "performed"? Did their audiences only *hear* these romances, or did they also *see* them? Were these works intended for performance of a more fully dramatic sort? Did they invite it – and did they receive it?

CHAPTER SIX

Modalities of Performance:
Romance as Recited, Sung and Played; Romance as Read

We now turn to the "performance" of romance in all the possible senses of the word. I propose that we think in terms of a medieval performance "spectrum" or continuum, ranging from "high" and festive events to "low," ordinary moments. The establishment of this spectrum will constitute the fundamental framework of this chapter, and with regard to it I will be making three major points: 1) At the festive end of the continuum what we find, with regard to romance-performance, is *exclusively* recitation from memory, and romances were performed alongside of *chansons de geste* and other songs and stories. 2) The recitation of romance was often strongly dramatic, as well as musical (I provide examples from Béroul's *Tristan* and from the romances of Chrétien). 3) Some reading of romance did occur – and reading should certainly be thought of as a "performance practice." Public reading occurred, however, largely at the lower and non-festive ends of the scale, and fully private reading of romance was exceedingly rare.

We begin by looking not at romance itself, but at performance situations in twelfth and thirteenth century courts: at the wide array of occasions at which works could be performed, in any sense of the word. We first turn our gaze to one end of a complex spectrum, to whose fuller elaboration I will return in more detail later. At this end, we find events that can be described by adjectives such as: public, festive, highly social, official, elaborate, and costly. These words do not all mean the same thing, but I am painting here with a broad brush. Still, we can differentiate among these adjectives. We have words that concern the nature of the occasion in itself. Thus, we have intrinsically grand occasions: festive, public, etc. We also have terms – elaborate, costly – that relate primarily to the status, wealth and resources of the establishment providing the entertainment.[1]

---

[1] In the final chapter we will also return to the social and performance functions played by romance and other "literary" works in these settings.

The high end of the performance spectrum: Public feasts and official events

As regards the nature of the events, we find at this "high performance" end of the spectrum such great occasions as Christmas, Easter, and Pentecost, in the Christian year, and perhaps certain great saints' feasts; also more predominantly secular occasions as weddings, coronations, dubbing ceremonies, royal entries, and the like. While my primary concern here is with the top of the line – great noble households – what we find here can be transposed and modulated down the line, to modest (and to bourgeois) establishments.

At such court events, in such settings, we find little evidence indeed for reading aloud;[2] we will return later to such fairly meagre references as do exist. But there is a great *abundance* of references to works of all kinds being performed by skilled minstrels and *jongleurs* at such occasions.[3] Romances were clearly performed here, apparently in the same general repertory as *chansons de geste*. This important fact about the performance of romance has been largely unrecognized by scholars, who typically speak of romances as read aloud, or even silently.[4] It is, then, important to emphasize that romance was there *too* – recited and sung *too* – in those court celebrations. This is not to deny that there are significant generic distinctions between romances and *chansons de geste*,[5] but works of both categories are enumerated, as it were, in the same breath.

Sometimes the blend of genres in the performance situation is explicit: in the 1170s, Pierre de St. Cloud begins his story of Renard by saying:

2 D.H. Green's *Medieval Listening and Reading: The Primary Reception of German Literature 800–1300* generally confirms this view, though he is of course looking especially at the picture in Germany. In general, however, German poets of this period seem to emphasize written literacy and reading more than their French counterparts. I am uncertain as to how to account for this difference in emphasis.

3 Such references have been catalogued by Edmond Faral, *Les jongleurs*; Chambers, *The Mediaeval Stage*; Christopher Page, *Voices and Instruments of the Middle Ages: Instrumental Practice and Songs in France 1100–1300*.

4 The quotations provided at the beginning of Chapter 3 provide the consensus both on the bookish nature and the book-based performance of romance. Even Christopher Page, in his valuable *Voices and Instruments*, speaks only of the *chanson de geste* and of the lyric as performed genres. John Stevens, in *Words and Music in the Middle Ages: Song, Narrative, Dance and Drama, 1050–1350*, takes up a very wide range of works as performed, but romance is not among them. Paul Zumthor is perhaps the only scholar to have emphasized the vocal and even physical performance of romance – and he limited his explicit discussion of this question to a very few romances: Béroul's *Tristan* and Gautier d'Arras' *Éracle*. See Vitz: "Paul Zumthor and Medieval Romance."

5 The most important – indeed, the only permanent and reliable – formal generic distinction between verse romance and *chanson de geste* was that the former was composed in rhymed couplets and the latter in laisse-form (generally assonanced, occasionally rhymed). Thematically, romances tended to be concerned with love and adventure, epics with battle and conquest, but no hard and fast distinction can be made.

165

> Seigneurs, oï avez maint conte,
> Que maint conterre vous raconte
> Conment Paris ravi Elaine,
> Le mal qu'il en ot et la paine,
> De Tristan que la Chievre fist
> Qui assez bellement en dist
> Et fabliaus et chançons de geste.
> Romanz d'Yvain et de sa beste
> Maint autre conte par la terre.
> Mais onques n'oïstes la guerre,
> Qui tant fu dure de grant fin,
> Entre Renart et Ysengrin,
> Qui moult dura et moult fu dure. . . .   p. 177, lines 1–13[6]

(Lords, you have heard many a tale,/ Which many story-tellers
tell you/ [About] how Paris stole away Helen,/ The evil that he
had from it and the pain,/ About Tristan, which La Chievre [a
poet] made/ Who told about it very beautifully,/ And fabliaux
and chansons de geste./ The romance of Yvain and his beast/
Many others tell throughout the land./ But you have never heard
about the war,/ That was so extremely hard/ Between Renard
and Ysengrin,/ And that lasted so long and was so hard. . . .)

Here we have clear references to different narrative genres, all of which
have been heard by the audience that Pierre aims to please, and excite, with a
new story. Let's note here that among the works mentioned is the story of
Yvain and his beast – apparently a reference to Chrétien's romance; more on
this later, when we take up in more detail the romance repertory of oral
performers. Let us also note that the words "conte" and "roman" and the like
appear to have been used almost interchangeably; Chrétien in particular uses
both terms to refer to his stories. (In the opening lines of *Érec et Énide* he twice
refers to the story as a "conte.")

In another important passage from the *Roman de Renart* (Branch 1b, end of
twelfth century), the fox disguises himself as a Breton *jongleur*. Speaking with
a strong if apparently inauthentic Breton accent (it sounds rather Germanic)
and in garbled French, he describes his repertory:

> – Ya, ge fot molt bon jogler.
> Mes je fot ier rober, batuz
> Et mon vïel fot moi toluz.
> Se moi fot aver un vïel,
> Fot moi diser bon rotruel,
> Et un bel lai et un bel son
> Por toi qui fu semblés prodom. . . .
> Ge fot saver bon lai Breton

---

6   *Le Roman de Renart (Branches I, II, III, IV, V, VIII, X, XV)*, ed. Jean Dufournet.

166

Et de Merlin et de Noton,
Del roi Artu et de Tristran,
Del chevrefoil, de saint Brandan.

p. 143, lines 2370–77, 89–92

(. . . I were[7] very good *jongleur*./ But I were yesterday robbered,
beaten,/ And my vielle was taken from me./ If me have viel,/
Make me saying a good rotrouance,/ And a beautiful lai and a
beautiful melody/ For you who seem worthy man . . ./ Me know
good Breton lai/ And about Merlin and Noton,/ About King
Arthur and about Tristan,/ About the honeysuckle, about Saint
Brendan.)

Renart, as a *jongleur*, thus declares then that he can perform romance
material along with lyric works (such as *rotrouanges*) and short lyric-narrative
works such as lais. A bit later, he adds *chansons de geste* to the list:

Fotre merci, dist il, bel sir,
Moi saura fer tot ton plesir.
Moi saver bon chancon d'Ogier,
Et d'Olivant et de Rollier
Et de Charlon le char chanu.   p. 160, lines 2851–55

(Pegging your pardon, he said, my lord,/ Me know how to do all
your pleasure./ Me know good song about Ogier,/ And about
Olivant and about Rollier [*sic*: the names are garbled]/ And
about Charles with the white skin [it should of course be white
"hair"].)

It might be argued that if Renart so garbles the heroes of epic, he may be
garbling genres as well. But, as we will see, this sort of mixed-bag list is
common even in completely ungarbled repertories.

Let us look toward the south, toward the Occitan world: the famous troubadour Raimon Vidal, in "Abril issi'e," evokes a *jongleur* who describes his
repertory. Here too the blend is explicit.

"Senher, yeu soy us hom aclis
a joglaria de cantar
e say romans dir e contar
e novas motas e salutz
e autres comtes espandutz
vas totas partz azautz e bos;
e d'en Guiraut vers e chansos
e d'en Arnaut de Maruelh mays,

---

[7] Translation cannot do justice to the original where the verb forms "was" and
"were" are puns on "foutre."

e d'autres vers e d'autres lays
que ben deuri' en cort caber.''   p. 40, lines 38–47[8]

(''My lord, I know as a knowledgeable man/ how to sing with
jonglerie/ and how to tell and recount romances/ and new
melodies and 'love salutes'/ and other well-known stories,/ to all
esteemed and good places,/ and different kinds of songs by En
Guiraut/ and by En Arnaut de Maruelh even more/ and other
songs and lays,/ so that I should find a good place in court.'')

Here too, we see the ''saying and telling'' of romances mixed in with a general
lyric and narrative repertory.

As we saw in Chapter 1, the joking *jongleurs* of the ''Deux Bourdeurs
Ribauds'' speak in much the same fashion. I refer the reader back to the long
citation provided there. In many other works as well the mixing of genres is
clear, but less explicitly spelled out. The late-twelfth century romance *Le bel
inconnu* begins with an evocation of the festivities at King Arthur's coronation.

. . . La veïsiés grant joie faire,
As jogleors vïeles traire,
Harpes soner et estiver,
As canteors cançons canter.
Li canteor metent lor cures
En dire beles aventures. . . .   lines 21–26[9]

(There you would have seen great joy made,/ With the *jongleurs*
taking up their vielles,/ Playing and competing [or, doing their
best] on harps,/ With singers singing songs./ The singers put all
their effort/ Into telling beautiful adventures . . .)

Here we seem to have several different narrative and musical genres, as
well as different instruments, though specific genres are not mentioned by
name. It is commonly assumed that when reference is made to ''singers telling
beautiful adventures'' (or the like), it is the *chanson de geste* that is being
spoken of. But the evidence suggests that while the verb ''dire'' could be
applied, especially in a musical context, to the singing of epics, romances were
sometimes sung. This is surely clear from the quotations from the *Renart* given
above.

To take an example with a slightly different thrust: in the early-thirteenth
Roman des eles, the poet (Raoul de Houdenc) says that when a host is truly
''courtois'':

---

8   ''Abril issi'e'' in *Novelles occitanes du Moyen Age*.
9   Renaud de Beaujeu, *Le bel inconnu*, ed. G. Perrie Williams.

Le set l'en par les menestrex,
Qui es places et es hostex
Voient les honnors et les hontes,
De qui l'en doit dire beax contes . . .
Quant li conteres a servi
Et vient au point del demander,
Larges ne puet contremander
La larguece qu'il a el cors
Quant li conteres a servi
Et vient au point del demander,
Larges ne puet contremander
La largesse qu'il a el cors,
Que la point n'en saille hors . . .
Qu'a chevalier est cortoisie
Qu'il oie volentiers chançons,
Notes, et vïeles, et sons
Et deduit de menesterex . . .[10]

(You know it from the minstrels,/ Who in public places and in residences/ See the honor and the shame/ About which they must tell good stories./ When the story-teller has finished his service/ And comes to the point of asking [to be rewarded]/ A generous [host] cannot deny/ The generosity that he has in himself [in his body]/ So that it doesn't spill forth . . ./ For a knight has courtliness/ If he listens willingly to songs,/ And melodies, and vielles, and tunes/ And minstrels' entertainment . . .)

This passage is not a description of a wedding or coronation, as are most of our examples, but comes from a book on courtliness – "Cortoisie" – for the nobility, produced by a rather self-interested figure. But here too the blend of various kinds of narrative and musical material is apparent: we have here the work of *contere* and *ménestreleurs*; we have *chançons*, *notes*, *vïeles* and *sons*.

Finally, a highly interesting quote from Chrétien himself, from the Bibliothèque nationale BN fr. 1376 of *Érec et Énide*; this passage deals with wedding festivities:

Quanz la corz fu tote assemblee,
N'ot ménestrel an la contree
Qui rien seüst de nul deduit,
Que a la cort ne fussent tuit.
En la sale mout grant joie ot;
Chascuns servi de ce qu'il sot:

[10] Quoted in Faral, *Jongleurs*, p. 293. The text in question (under a slightly different title) has also been recently edited by Keith Busby: *Raoul de Houdenc: Le roman des eles; The anonymous Ordene de Chevalerie*. Busby has, however, edited a manuscript from which a few of the key lines that interest us are absent.

Cil saut, cil tume, cil enchante;
Li uns conte, li autres chante;
Li uns sible, li autres note;
Cil sert de harpe, cil de rote,
Cil de gigue, cil de vïele,
Cil fleüte, cil chalemele
Puceles querolent et dancent;
Trestuit de joie fere tencent.
N'est riens qui joie i puisse faire
Ne cuer d'ome a leesce traire
Qui ne soit as noces le jor.
Sonent timbre, sonent tabor,
Muses, estives et fretel
Et buisines et chalemeles. . . .   lines 2031–50[11]

(When the court was all assembled/ There were not any minstrels in the region/ Who knew how to do anything to give pleasure,/ Who weren't all at court./ In the hall there was great joy,/ Each one served up what he knew how to do:/ One jumps, one tumbles, one does tricks,/ One tells stories, another sings,/ One whistles, another one sings notes,/ This one plays the harp, that one the rote,/ This one the gigue, that one the vielle,/ Girls sing and dance;/ They all try to make joy./ There is nothing that can bring joy/ Nor draw happiness to the heart of man,/ Which was not that day at the wedding./ The tambour sounds, the tamborine sounds,/ Bagpipes, flageolet and panpipes/ And trumpets and flutes. . . .)

Here we have, once again, a multitude of kinds of entertainers and entertainment. Various manuscripts provide variations on this description. For example, BN fr. 1450, which contains Chrétien's romances along with many other works, completely eliminates this discussion of court entertainers and the pleasures they provide. This seems in a number of respects a particularly "bookish" manuscript. (This is in a sense a tautology, but by this I mean that it eliminates the oral and performed character of the work in question. Similarly, certain manuscripts of *chansons de geste* cut out the *jongleurs'* prologues, eliminate references to singing, and the like.) It may have been intended for a private reader: the handwriting is extremely small and difficult to read, and the scribe has made very heavy use of abbreviations. Such a manuscript may invite solitary decoding by a highly skilled reader. Another interesting and curious feature of this large manuscript: Chrétien's works are inserted into the *Roman de Brut*, at the point dealing with King Arthur. They are thus presented as a narrative expansion on the *Brut* and are seen as part of English history.

---

[11] Edited by Jean-Marie Fritz, in *Chrétien de Troyes: Romans*, Michel Zink, gen. ed.

IN fr. 1450
omit drawing
const exteriors.
vit 3.
170

Further examples of performance in festive court settings

I have cited and discussed only a few out of many possible references to the performance of romances, alongside of *contes* and *fabliaux* and *chansons de geste* and other works, in court festivities. Our focus has been almost exclusively on passages taken from romances, and I have by no means exhausted the list of such passages.[12] We could have looked closely at the twelfth century Occitan romance *Jaufré*, where the *jongleur* speaks of his work as a song: "E cel qe rimet la canso . . ." ("he who rhymed this song").[13] He says he learned it by hearing it:

> E cel ditz qe las a rimadas
> Qe anc lo rei Artus no vi,
> Mais tut plan contar o auzi
> En la cort del plus onret rei
> Qe anc fos de neguna lei,
> Aco es lo rei d'Aragon . . .   lines 56–61

> (And he who rhymed these "novas" [or "nouvelles"] says/
> That he never saw King Arthur,/ But he simply heard this told,/
> At the court of the most honored king/ Who ever belonged to
> any religion,/ I mean the King of Aragon . . .   pp. 42–43.)

The poet reasserts this again in lines 85ff, pp. 44–45, and consistently speaks of himself as telling or reciting the work.

We could have examined the early-thirteenth century romance *Joufroi*, where, for example, in a lengthy scene describing *jongleuresque* activity, we are told that:

> Molt ot grant jou davant le conte;
> Li uns note, li autre conte;
> L'autres chante chanços antives, . . .   lines 1159–61[14]

> (There was great play before the count;/ One sings,[15] another
> tells stories;/ Another sings old songs . . .)

---

[12] It may be felt that in providing the following examples I am overloading my discourse. I give all these examples simply because I think that few scholars have recognized the *abundance* of references to romance performance. I wish to make this point amply, even at the risk of redundance.

[13] *Roman de Jaufré*, in *Les Troubadours: Jaufré, Flamenca, Barlaam et Josaphat*, ed. and trans. René Lavaud and René Nelli, p. 44, line 85.

[14] *Joufroi de Poitiers, roman d'aventures du XIIIe siècle*, ed. Percival B. Fay and John L. Grigsby.

[15] "Noter" is sometimes related to writing, sometimes not. It could mean "to perform from a written *nota*" (perhaps from Latin *notare*), but generally simply meant "to sing." Michel Zink has stated: "A tout le moins, on peut soutenir sans risque d'erreur que, pour un lecteur ou un auditeur du XIIIe siècle, l'expression, assez courante, 'noter un chant'

The verb "conter" is, incidentally, a word that the anonymous poet uses to describe his own story-telling activity (e.g., line 18). He also says that he will "dire une estoire" (e.g., lines 83–4) and speaks of his story both as an "estoire" (line 89) and a "roman" (line 4397).

Or we could have examined the continuation of *Perceval le Gallois* by Gerbert, dating from around 1220. Here, in a long scene describing the marriage festivities for Perceval, we are told that:

> Jogleor chantent et viëlent;
> Li. I. harpent et calemelent;
> Chascuns, selonc le sien afaire,
> Vient avant por son mestier faire;
> Cil conteor dient biax contes
> Devant dames et devant contes;
> Et quant assez orent jué,
> Bien sont li ménestrel loé; . . .[16]

(Jongleurs sing and and play the vielle,/ Some play the harp, some the bagpipes/ Each one, according to his skill,/ Comes forth to do his number;/ The story-tellers tell beautiful stories/ Before ladies and counts;/ And when they have played enough/ Well are the minstrels praised.)

References to performance in *chansons de geste* present a similar picture. We could have examined in detail passages from *Aye D'Avignon*, where at the feast celebrating the restoration of a monastery, knights "font ces fables dire et escouter chansons" ("have fables [stories] told and songs heard"). There are also animal acts: "Et esgardent le gieu des ours et des lions" ("And they watch bear and lion acts").[17] This is, incidentally, one of many passages where it is clear that clerical hostility to *jongleurs* can hardly have been complete or unanimous.[18] We could have looked at *Doon de Nanteuil*, where in the context of a discussion of the *jongleur* and his role the poet refers sneeringly to boys with "clerete voix" who sing "D'Audegier qui fu cuens ou de Minier l'ainsné/ Ou de Morgain la fee, d'Artur et de Forré" ("About count Audegier or about Minier the elder/ Or about Morgan the fee, about Arthur, about Forré")[19] – a clear blend of romance with epic subject matter. Or *Les enfances*

---

signifie, d'abord et tout naturellement, 'chanter,' interpréter musicalement en chant . . ." (unpublished paper given at the Newberry Conference, 1991).

[16] *Perceval le Gallois*, ed. Potvin, Vol. VI, p. 203 ; quoted Faral, *Jongleurs*, p. 306.

[17] *Aye d'Avignon*, ed. F. Guessard, lines 2688–89. Though it is not explicitly stated that these acts are performed by professional entertainers, it is safe to assume that such is understood to be the case: few amateurs would be performing with lions or bears.

[18] See the balanced discussion of clerical disapproval of minstrels and *jongleurs* in E.K. Chambers, *The Mediaeval Stage*, Vol. I, pp. 57ff. See also, more recently, Christopher Page, *The Owl and the Nightingale*.

[19] *Doon de Nanteuil*, *Romania*, t. XIII, p. 18; quoted Faral, *Jongleurs*, p. 280.

Godefroi, where at the court of Emperor Otto "Apres mengier, vïelent li noble jogleor,/ Romans et aventures content li conteor,/ Sonent sauters et gigles, harpent cil harpeor" ("After dinner, the noble *jongleurs* come,/ The story-tellers tell romances and adventures,/ They play on psalteries and "gigles" [small stringed instruments] and harpers harp").[20]

In all the occasions that we have been looking at thus far, the stories told and songs sung were not read. No book is ever referred to in these descriptions, and the verb in question is never "read": *lire*.

Should we be sceptical about the accuracy of these representations of oral performance? Some of them come from romance, which is in some respects a fantasy world. This is a useful caution, to be sure. But two points should be made: First, many of the performance evocations of which I have spoken occur not within the story-line but at its edges, when *jongleurs* (and other figures) are speaking of their repertory; in other words, they are not clearly part of the narrative fiction. Second, whatever reservations we choose to entertain about representations of oral performance by minstrels and *jongleurs* in romances, we should retain when we find reading behavior, as well; if romance is unreliable on the issue of performance, it is presumably unreliable *in general* on this issue.

Reading aloud in festive settings

Evidence for reading aloud of romance in "high-performance" court settings in the twelfth and early-thirteenth centuries is limited indeed. A few poets – clearly clerks – are on record as intending that their works be read aloud at feasts. Such is the case of Wace, who declares at the start of the third part of his *Roman de Rou*:

> Pur remembrer des ancesurs
> les feiz e les diz e les murs,
> les felunies des feluns
> e les barnages des baruns,
> deit l'um les livres e les gestes
> e les estoires lire as festes.
> Si escripture ne fust feite
> e puis par clers litte e retraite,
> mult fussent choses ublïees,
> ki de viez tens sunt trespassees.   lines 1–10[21]

(In order to remember/ The actions and words and customs of our ancestors,/ One must read at feasts the books and the deeds/ And the stories./ If writing had not been done/ And had not then

---

[20] *Les enfances Godefroi*, ed. Hippeau, lines 230–32, quoted Faral, *Jongleurs*, p. 284.
[21] *Le Roman de Rou de Wace*, ed. A.J. Holden, Vol. 1.

been read and recounted by clerks/ Many things would be
forgotten/ Which happened in the olden days.)

Perhaps Wace got his wish. But what he wanted for his historical romance is
not necessarily how it was actually performed. The fact that he intended it to be
read aloud at feasts – perhaps by himself, a "clerc lisant"? – is no guarantee
that it *was* so performed. (Wace would not have been the first intellectual or
writer to hope, in vain, for a large audience, perhaps applauding him in
person.) Wace tells us in his closing lines that he has been relieved, by the king,
of the job of finishing the *Rou* (see lines 11419–40). But, as we have noted
earlier, and repeatedly, the Anglo-Normans were involved in the production of
books with a firmly political agenda, and it is not impossible that Henry II, for
example, or his predecessor Henry I, who bore the honorific title "Beauclerc,"
might have had reading aloud done in court for political reasons: the *Rou* is
essentially Plantagenet propaganda. Such performances may well have
existed, but, if they did, they have left remarkably few echoes in the literature
of the time.

Another interesting case is that presented by the late-twelfth century
Anglo-Norman poet Denis Piramus, who in his youth composed secular
works, then, after a religious conversion, a *Vie de Saint Edmund le Rei*.[22] In the
prologue to the latter, Denis makes his confession, which it is worth quoting at
length:

Mult ai usé cume pechere
Ma vie en trop fole manere,
E trop ai usée ma vie
E en peché e en folie.
Kant court hanteie of les curteis,
Si feseie les serventeis,
Chanceunettes, rimes, saluz
Entre les drues e les druz.
Mult me penai de tels vers fere
Ke assemble les puise treire   10
E k'ensemble fussent justez
Pur acomplir lur volentez.
Ceo me fist fere l'enemi,
Si me tinc ore a malbaili,
Jamés ne me burdera plus.
Jeo ai noun Denis Piramus;
Les jurs jolifs de ma joefnesce
S'en vunt, si trei jeo a veilesce,
Si est bien dreit ke me repente.
En autre ovre mettrai m'entente,   20

[22] *La vie saint Edmund le Rei, poème anglo-normand du XIIème siècle*, ed. Hildung
Kjellman.

Ke mult mieldre est e plus nutable.
Deus m'aïde, espiritable;
E la grace Seint Espirit
Seit of mei e si i aït!
 Cil ki *Partonopé* trova
E ki les vers fist e rima,
Mult se pena de bien dire,
Si dist il bien de cele matire;
Cume de fable e de menceonge
La matire resemble sounge,   30
Kar iceo ne put unkes estre.
Si est il tenu pur bon mestre
E les vers sunt mult amez
E en ces riches curz loëz,
E dame Marie autresi,
Ki en rime fist e basti
E compassa les vers de lais,
Ke ne sunt pas del tut verais;
E si en est ele mult loée
E la rime par tut amée,   40
Kar mult l'aiment, si l'unt mult cher
Cunte, barun e chivaler;
E si enaiment mult l'escrit
E lire le funt, si unt delit,
E si les funt sovent retreire.
Les lais solent as dames pleire,
De joie les oient e de gré,
Qu'il sunt sulum lur volenté.
Li rei, li prince et li courtur,
Cunte, barun e vavasur   50
Aiment cuntes, chanceuns e fables
E bons diz, qui sunt delitables,
Kar il hostent e gettent puer
Doel, enui e travail de quer,
E si funt ires ublïer
E del quer hostent le penser.
Kant cil e vus, segnur trestuit,
Amez tel ovre e tel deduit,
Si vus volez entendre a mei,
Jeo vus dirrai par dreite fei   60
Un deduit, qui mielz valt asez
Ke ces autres ke tant amez,
E plus delitable a oïr.
Si purrez les almes garir
E les cors garantir de hunte.
Mult deit hom bien oïr tel cunte.   lines 1–66

175

(Greatly did I use up, as a sinner,/ My life in a mad manner/ And too much have I wasted my life/ Both in sin and in folly./ When I used to haunt the courts of the courtly,/ I used to make "sirventeis,"/ And little songs, and rhymes, and love-salutes/ Among the lovers, young men and young women./ I worked very hard to make verses/ So that I might bring them [lovers] together/ And that they might be joined together/ To accomplish their will./ The Enemy made me do this,/ So now I consider myself unfortunate;/ I will never joke around again./ My name is Denis Piramus;/ The charming days of my youth/ Are going away, and I am drawing on to old age,/ And it is right that I should repent./ I will turn my mind to other work,/ Which is better and more valuable./ May God help me, spiritually;/ And may the grace of the Holy Spirit/ Be with me and give me help./ He who composed *Partonopeu*/ And who made and rhymed the verses/ Worked hard to speak well,/ And he told this matter well:/ How in fables and in lies/ The matter is like a dream/ For it can never really be true./ And so he is considered a good master/ And his verses are greatly loved/ And they are praised in those rich courts./ And lady Mary [de France?] too,/ Who in rhyme made and constructed/ And put together the verses of lais/ Which are not at all true;/ And so [anyway?] she is very much praised/ And the rhymes are loved above all/ For many love them, and hold them dear,/ Counts, barons and knights;/ And so they love this writing/ And they have it read, and they take delight in it/ And they have these things recited./ The lais are pleasing to ladies,/ With joy they hear them, and willingly,/ Because they [the verses] are according to the ladies' will./ Kings, princes and men at court,/ Counts, barons and vavasors,/ Love tales, songs and fables/ And good "dits," which are delightful,/ For they serve to cast out/ Sorrow, boredom, and travail from the heart,/ And they make anger be forgotten/ And remove pensiveness from the heart./ Since you, my lords, love such works and such pleasures,/ If you listen to me,/ I will tell you, in true faith,/ A delightful story which is worth much more/ Than the others that you love so much,/ And more delightful to hear./ And you can heal your souls/ And keep your bodies from shame./ A man should listen to such a tale.)

This prologue eloquently documents the enthusiasm with which courtly works of a wide variety – *serventeis, chanceunettes, rimes, saluz, lais, cuntes,* and *fables* – were listened to in court. Denis refers once to a written text: *l'escrit*, line 43. In line 42 he speaks of lords having things "read," presumably aloud. Denis appears to be referring primarily to the *Lais* of Marie de France, who herself (as we saw in Chapter 2) insisted quite heavily on the written status of her work. Marie's works, and other things as well, may have been read aloud in the Anglo-Norman court (about whose differences from the

French courts I spoke at some length earlier, in Chapter 4). But Denis also says that these works are both read aloud and recited (''E si enaiment mult l'escrit/ E lire le funt, si unt delit,/ E si les funt sovent retreire,'' lines 43–4). There is some suggestion here of a distinction between a female audience – the ''dames'' who liked Marie's lais (line 46) – and a male audience composed of ''cuntes, barun e vavasur'' (line 50), who appreciated ''cuntes, chanceuns e fables/ E bons diz qui sont delitables . . .'' (lines 51–2).

In any case, there does appear to have been some reading aloud as well as recitation from memory in Anglo-Norman courts. It is not clear whether Denis plans to read his Life of St. Edmund aloud or to recite it; it is in any event clear that he is speaking, not to monks – he has not physically left the world – but to nobles: ''Segnur trestuit.'' And it is clear that he intended his work to be *heard*: ''Mult deit hom bien oïr tel cunte'' (line 60).

The case of the *Vie de Saint Edmund* suggests that reading aloud was done for the feasts of saints. A number of other saints' lives explicitly invite being read aloud. Guillaume de Berneville says toward the end of his *La Vie de Saint Gilles*:[23]

> Ki ceste vie funt escrire
> Et ki l'escutent e funt lire,
> Ki l'escutent pur Deu amur
> E en lur quers en unt tendrur,
> Deus lur rende ben la merite
> Et de lur pechez seient quite
> Par devant les pez nostre sire
> Par l'oreisun del bon saint Gire!   lines 3773–80

(Those who have this story written [copied]/ And who listen to and have it read,/ Who listen to it for the love of God/ and in their hearts feel tenderness,/ May God give them merit/ And may they be relieved of their sins/ Before our Lord's feet/ By the prayer of good saint Gilles!)

But there is no guarantee that a work such as this was composed specifically for a court setting, still less for performance at a major festivity. Indeed the latter possibility surely seems rather unlikely: though contrition and the love of God are frequent themes in French medieval literature, they are rarely the *central* themes of ''festive'' works (or at least for feasts *other* than those of the saints). In any event, our focus is on the performance of *romances* in court settings, and saints' lives are not romances.[24]

---

23 *La Vie de Saint Gilles*, ed. Gaston Paris and Alphonse Bos.

24 Some saints' lives, such as the *Vie de Saint Alexis*, were however redone in the twelfth century in romance style, perhaps to make them appropriate for performance at courts. Since hagiography is not, at least in my view, a genre itself, lives of the saints can be given a variety of generic shapes and emphases. See my ''Vie, légende, littérature: traditions orales et écrites dans les histoires des saints.''

Early in the thirteenth century, Jean Renart composed a romance with lyric interpolations, *Le Roman de la rose ou de Guillaume de Dole*, whose charms he proclaims:

> Ja nuls n'iert de l'oïr lassez,
> car, s'en vieult, l'en i chante et lit,
> et s'est fez par si grant delit
> que tuit cil s'en esjoïrent
> qui chanter et lire l'orront,
> qu'il lor sera nouviaus toz jors.   lines 18–23

> (Never will anyone be weary of listening to it,/ for if you like, it
> is sung and read,/ and it is made with such great delight/ that all
> those will enjoy it/ who hear it sung and read,/ and it will be new
> forever.)

Jean clearly intends that all the parts of his romance be performed aloud. Does he really intend that some portions actually be *read* aloud? Perhaps. The verb is indeed "lire," and this may be one of the relatively few romances truly intended for this performance mode. But as we noted in an earlier chapter, the verb *lire*, like the Middle English *rede* and the Medieval German *lesen*, and indeed like the Latin *legere*, did *not* reliably mean what we mean by "read" – or even "read aloud" – but could be used to signify a wide variety of activities including "tell," "recite," "explain," and the like. Manfred Günter Scholz notes in his important *Hören und Lesen: Studien zur primären Rezeption der Literatur im 12. und 13. Jahrhundert* that "lire" and "dire" in this period are virtually interchangeable (e.g., pp. 42–3). As we noted earlier, the word "lire" could also mean "hear something read aloud." (See the discussion of this verb in Chapter 4.) Let us go back to the Latin *lego*. According to *A New and Copious Lexicon of the Latin Language*, "lego," whose fundamental meaning was "to take away piece by piece," with hands, eye, etc., could mean any of the following (and more): to listen attentively, to run over with one's eyes, to see, to observe, to survey, to read or deliver lectures on any thing, to explain, interpret, illustrate, to read aloud, to choose, etc. In *Cassell's New Latin Dictionary*, "lego" could mean: to survey, scan, read, peruse, read aloud, recite, call out the senate roll, etc. In these dictionaries, "to read" (in any mode) is by no means foremost among the meanings of the Latin verb.[25] The meanings that most directly interest us for the moment are "tell" and "recite." Medieval Latin presents a similar picture: the *Novum glossarium mediae latinitatis* offers the following among the meanings for "legere": *ramasser, recueillir, enrouler, aider, parcourir, choisir, traitir, enseigner,*

---

25 *A New and Copious Lexicon of the Latin Language*, ed. F.P. Leverett, p. 482. Also *Cassell's New Latin Dictionary*, ed. D.P. Simpson, p. 341.

être l'élève de – and *lire* (in the modern sense). *Lectus* often meant "aimé" (thus, "chosen").[26]

If such is the linguistic heritage of the French medieval verb "lire," why should we expect this word to provide incontrovertible evidence – a "smoking gun," as it were – for reading behavior in the modern sense of the term?[27]

It is perhaps worth adding, in this context, that the romance of *Guillaume de Dole* tends generally to enhance and glorify the traditions of essentially oral entertainment. One of the main characters is a *jongleur*, Jouglet, of whom it is never said that he reads, or that he can read. Nor does any other character in the romance read, at any time. It may be that the verb "lire" should not be taken *au pied de la lettre moderne*, but simply distinguishes between the "telling" and the "singing" – and "lit" provides an attractive rhyme with "delit" ("delight"). This romance is indeed rather like an expanded "chantefable."

A similar passage occurs in the late-twelfth or early-thirteenth century anonymous romance, *Le chevalier à l'épee*, a work without any particular pretentions to *clergie*. A feast in court is described:

> Quant mengié orent a plenté
> Et li doblier furent osté,
> Cil lecheor, dont mout i ot,
> Monstra chascuns ce que il sot.
> Li uns atenpre sa vïele,
> Cil flaüste, cil chalemele,
> Et cil autres rechante et note
> Ou a la harpe o a la rote;
> Cil list romanz et cist dist fables;
> Cil chevalier jeuent as tables
> Et as eschés de l'autre part,
> O a la mine o a hasart . . .   lines 795–806[28]

(When they had eaten aplenty/ And the table cloths were removed,/ Those lechers (entertainers), who were numerous,/ Showed each one what he knew how to do./ One tunes his vielle,/ One plays the flute, another the bagpipes,/ Yet another sings and plays/ Either on the harp or the rote;/ This one reads romances and that one tells fables;/ The knights play at tables/ And elsewhere at chess/ Or at games of dice.)

We have here a very brief reference to reading aloud: "cil list romanz." But in this context it is, I believe, altogether possible that *list* is simply a prestigious synonym for *dist*, providing an internal rhyme as well. As we saw in the

---

26 Franz Blatt, ed., *Novum glossarium mediae latinitatis*, Vol. L, pp. 86–87.

27 On this large issue see Ulrich Mehler, *Dicere und cantare: Zur musikalischen Terminologie und Auffuhrungspraxis des mittelalterlichen geistlichen Dramas in Deutschland.*

28 *Two Old French Gawain Romances*, ed. R.C. Johnson and D.D.R. Owen.

example given above, the verb *lire*, with its various syntactic permutations, has entered the vernacular story-telling lexicon, providing valuable rhymes and synonyms. It does seem to be the case, however, that when the words from the *lire/ livre* family are used, they tend to be in regard to romances, or sermons, rather than epics or other songs. For example, in the Occitan epic *Ronsasvals* – a version of the Roland – Charlemagne is in deep sorrow after Roland's death; as the army rides along, Nayme, one of Charles' great surviving vassals, "comensa lo libre dels sermons": "begins the book of sermons." That is, Nayme consoles Charles by reminding him that this life has little joy and is soon ended, and other similar thoughts appropriate to sermons.[29] Nayme is not actually "reading" anything as he rides along, but is rather repeating the sorts of things he has heard in church. Such examples from romance and epic suggest that, whatever the actual performance mode, romances, like sermons, and unlike most epics and lyrics, were commonly considered to have written – *livresque* – authority standing "behind" them.

It is interesting to note that the use of the insulting word "lecheors" in this passage to refer to *jongleurs* has been taken by some scholars as proof that the "author" of this work was a writer, not himself a *lecheor*. But this interpretation denies to the poet/minstrel any sense of humor whatsoever. This romance is largely, and humorously, preoccupied with themes of chastity and lechery, and the poet may just be thumbing his nose at moralists' objections to the art of the *jongleur*.

Such are the sorts of references we find to reading aloud in festive settings. In the great majority of cases, there is no reference to books or reading at great events in court – which presumably means that songs and stories were performed from memory. Some of them were no doubt learned in fully oral fashion: from one non-literate story-teller to another. In the *Roman de la rose ou de Guillaume de Dole*, Jouglet is said to have learned all manner of things by listening: "et s'avoit oï et apris/ mainte chançon et maint biau conte"; "and he had heard and learned/ many a song and many a fine tale." As we saw, the *Jaufré* poet makes the same claim. In some cases, works may well have been learned directly or indirectly from a text. The question of how works were memorized is of course interesting and important, but that is not our primary concern here; we will return to this matter in the next chapter.

How were works performed?: Use of gesture and of the body

How were these works performed – and by what definition of the word "perform"? These romances and *chansons de geste* should not be thought of as simply recited. They were performed in a truly physical sense of the term. What Paul Zumthor called the "présence du corps" in orality, and evoked powerfully in his *Introduction à la poésie orale*, should be applied to the

---

29 *Le Roland occitan*, ed. and trans. Gérard Gouiran and Robert Lafont, lines 1246ff.

performance of romance.[30] Zumthor said: les "mouvements du corps sont . . . intégrés à une poétique."[31] He considered that many works, including romances such as *Éracle* and others, invited gesture.[32] As he says of *Éracle*:

> Gautier [d'Arras] parle de son propre ouvrage. Or, il n'emploie pas moins de quatre termes différents, en douze occurrences, et les connotations qui y sont liées dans le texte trahissent un attachement foncier à la vocalité, sinon (indirectement) à la gestualité même, du message.[33]

In *La lettre et la voix*, Zumthor spoke of the "jeu performanciel" and the "réalisation performancielle" implicit in the romance (pp. 306–7).

Another important scholar whose ground-breaking work we should recall in this context is Marcel Jousse, who in *The Oral Style* presented the view that "the oral style" was *fundamentally* gestural and rhythmic – indeed that it represented, or echoed, the rhythm of life itself. He stated: "It is [therefore] certain that the tendency towards rhythm is a primary manifestation of the human brain, a manifestation that is rooted deep in organic life itself . . ." Jousse went so far as to declare: "In the beginning was the rhythmic gesture" (pp. 20–21).

Jousse's view is in some respects deeply compelling, and the romances we are examining are powerfully rhythmic works. But in most cases I think that the performance of medieval romance (and other genres) went substantially beyond this deeply bio-rhythmic – one might almost say, "brain-stem"[34] – mode of oral performance. That is, these performances appear to have been not simply rhythmic or gestural, but "dramatic" in a strong sense of the word. Which suggests that we should begin to think of these works as "theatrical": as part of the history of drama as broadly defined.

It is true that, in the middle of the twelfth century, the theatre is not yet supposed to exist. The theatre's official (re)birth certificate dates from around the end of the century. But while there was no full-fledged theatre at this time, nor were there any theatres – that is, edifices devoted to the showing of plays[35] – no one denies that there were at this time plenty of *performers*.[36] Perhaps the

---

[30] Paul Zumthor, *Introduction à la poésie orale*, pp. 193–205. Zumthor is speaking generally here – of orality throughout the world, throughout human history – not specifically of the French Middle Ages, or of romance.

[31] Zumthor, *Introduction*, p. 193.

[32] See Vitz, "Paul Zumthor and Medieval Romance."

[33] Zumthor, "L'écriture et la voix: le roman d'Éracle," p. 178.

[34] This term is no exaggeration: Jousse refers to studies which show that deeply brain-damaged people generally retain a fundamental – non-cerebral, biologically rooted – involvement in rhythm.

[35] See Dino Bigongiari: "Were There Theatres in the Twelfth and Thirteenth Centuries?"

[36] Aside from Faral, *Les jongleurs*, see for example, E.K. Chambers' still-classic study *The Mediaeval Stage*, esp. Vol. I, Book I: "Minstrelsy." See also William Tydeman, *The*

antique theatre was (still) dead, but entertainers were certainly alive. Such twelfth century figures as John of Salisbury and others speak of entertainers, whom they refer to as *mimi* and *histriones*, and about whose lewd gestures they complain.[37] (In fact, such terminology and such complaints go back for centuries, and there is no reason to suppose that all such passages are merely intertextual references to long-dead Roman mimes and actors.) An early-thirteenth century author of a work on the Seven Sacraments makes the point – one frequently found – that distinctions must be made regarding different kinds of *jongleurs*. The author stigmatizes those who earn their living "cum ludibrio et turpitudine sui corporis, deformantes imaginem Dei" ("by the lewdness and filth of their body, deforming the image of God"). He is prepared to tolerate others: "Sed si cantant cum instrumentis et de gestis ad recreationem et forte ad informationem, vicini sunt excusationi": "but if they sing with instruments and about great deeds for recreation and sometimes to inform, these serve as excuses."[38] One might be tempted to consider that only the *first* group used their body, but it is important to remember that "gestes" didn't only mean "deeds" (and stories about deeds), but also "gestures." The stage-directions of the *Jeu d'Adam* say that the actors should make the appropriate *gestum* (the demons run around the stage "gestum facientes competentem").[39] It seems unlikely that one would have sung of "gestes" without making "gestes."[40]

The vernacular word *joueurs* is also found in the middle of the twelfth century: Wace in his *Roman de Brut* (around mid-century), speaks of a feast in court that is full of all kinds of music and musicians, which he enumerates at some length. He goes on:

> Asez i ot tresgiteors,
> Joeresses et joeors;
> Li un dient contes et fables,
> Auquant demandent dez et tables . . .   lines 2007–10 [41]

> (There were there many *jongleurs* [acrobats? or people who cast spells?],/ Male and female players;/ Some tell stories and fables/ Others call for dice and back-gammon . . .)

The words "joeresses" and "joeors" are often taken to mean instrument-players, but in this broad performance context, these words may very well have

---

Theatre in the Middle Ages: Western European Stage Conditions, c. 800–1576, esp. Chapter 7: "The Performers." Also, Rosemary Wolfe, *The English Mystery Plays*, esp. "Twelfth-Century Knowledge of Plays and Acting," pp. 25–38.

[37] John of Salisbury, *Policraticus*, ed. Cary J. Nederman, Book VIII, Chapter 8, pp. 182ff.

[38] Quoted Faral, p. 290; also Léon Gautier, *Epopées françaises*, t. II, p. 11.

[39] *Trois Pièces Médiévales*, ed. Robert Harden, p. 15; see also p. 9.

[40] See Tobler-Lommatzsch, Vol. 4, col. 288.

[41] *La Partie Arthurienne du Roman de Brut*, ed. I.D.O. Arnold and M.M. Pelan.

meant dramatic "players." Similarly, the many early medieval images of male and, especially, female performers shown moving their bodies tend to be described as "dancers," but some of them may as likely be dramatic "players."

In any event, what we can assume that Bernard of Clairvaux, John of Salisbury and others meant is that story-tellers and singers of narrative works did not just tell their stories, but that they used their bodies: they acted their stories out, at least in part, with appropriate gestures.

Indeed, it is hardly imaginable that these *histriones – jongleurs –* would not have used gestures. Performers throughout the centuries, around the world, have made reliable and inventive recourse to gesture, as broadly conceived: to use of the body. (On this tradition, see the valuable recent book edited by Eugenio Barba and Nicola Savarese, *A Dictionary of Theatre Anthropology: The Secret Art of the Performer*. Unfortunately, there is little medieval material in this extraordinarily interesting book.)

And why *would* performers have refrained from drawing on so powerful a "communication aid" as the body, as gesture? The works in question were often performed before substantial audiences, but with no amplification system. Moreover, in many situations, some people would have been present whose native dialect or language made it hard for them to understand what was going on in the story or song. (Between crusades and pilgrimages, and journeys of a political and personal nature, medieval nobles seem to have gotten around a good deal – which means that they did not always understand very well what they were hearing in "foreign" courts.) It is highly unlikely that performers unencumbered with codices would have failed to make extensive and fairly dramatic use of gestures just to make themselves understood. And they too were sometimes foreigners: the *jongleur* who speaks at length in Raimon Vidal's "Abril issi'e" (to which I have referred often) is a Catalan who in his youth frequented most of the great courts of France and England.

A further – perhaps even central – motivation for the use of gestures would have been to enhance the entertainment value of their act: providing pleasure was a high priority. What court patrons of this period were paying for was not so much, if at all, a book, but performance. Or perhaps we should say *performability*: a work that could be performed repeatedly on appropriate occasions. (We will return in the final chapter to the powerfully social character of these occasions.)

There is perhaps a stronger reason, historically speaking, to believe that *jongleurs* and *ménestrels* would have made heavy recourse to gesture. Medieval culture was fundamentally involved – far more than our own – in gestures and gesturality. Jean-Claude Schmitt's *La Raison des gestes dans l'Occident médiéval* and François Garnier's *Le langage de l'image au Moyen Age* have made this very clear. In medieval images, figures are reliably shown making the "appropriate" gesture: thus, for example, characters who are in grief are never simply shown looking sad, but grieve actively: they beat their palms together or tear their hair or pull out their beard or rend their garments. To be in grief was to *act* like a mourner. Many human interactions were seen as fundamentally performative: it was the words *plus* the gestures – never the words alone – that constituted the "event." Such is, for example, the case of feudal homage, where the proper linguistic formula had to be accompanied by the proper physical actions. (Nor was the written record any more than that: a record. The text did not perform the action of donation or the like, but only served to remind people of it afterwards.[42]) It seems unlikely that a performer would have merely spoken the words, without making the right gestures. Thus, for example, in a scene in which a woman was shown swearing on relics that she was innocent of some accusation, it would surely have appeared weird (perhaps even perverse, certainly unpersuasive), if the performer merely recited the words and did not raise her right hand.

In this context, an important article by David F. Hult, "The Limits of Mime(sis): Notes Toward a Generic Revision of Medieval Theater," is highly useful. Hult takes the view that in early vernacular literature "theatrical" works were scarcely distinguished from other fictional works, entering into a collective unity which our generic classification tends to obscure (p. 59). Hult argues that:

> Counter to the traditional way of explaining the emergence of a comic theatre ("it appeared from nowhere"), one might boldly suggest a global alteration in the function of various literary works, a de-theatricalization of traditionally performed genres (e.g., lyric, epic, and even romance) having brought about the need for a type of literature whose primary and exclusive aim was the satisfaction of the fundamental human need for group participation and interaction in a context of "play." This is substantiated by Faral's extensive repertoire of performance documents (*Les jongleurs*, pp. 272–327) which contains lists of works performed by *jongleurs* and *ménestrels* through to the end of the thirteenth century, with virtually no mention of the dramatic works we have been considering [works that are clearly "theatrical"]. The twelfth-century counterpart to the widespread farces and *sotties* of late Middle Ages would not therefore be "nothing," an empty box in the generic grid, but rather such works as the *fabliaux* or satirical lyrics (not to mention many works certainly not preserved in writing) which would have been performed in a participatory situation by a *jongleur* in front of a public familiar with the contents and the actions being spoofed. (p. 61)

In short, Hult considers that romances, along with other works, were performed in what one might call the "strong" sense – the dramatic sense – until theatre eventually "detheatricalized" them, by becoming, itself, fully

---

[42] See Clanchy, *From Memory to Written Record*, e.g. pp. 254–55, 262–63.

"theatricalized." But, he notes, this does not happen before the end of the thirteenth century.

Michel Zink has made a similar point, in discussing the work of the famous *trouvère/jongleur* Rutebeuf, whom he edited. Zink states:

> Beaucoup d'oeuvres du Moyen Age sont empreintes d'une théâtralité qui appelle la performance orale, sans relever pour autant du théâtre à proprement parler et sans que les rôles aient été distribués entre plusieurs acteurs. (pp. 20–21)

The hard dichotomy between "oral" and "written" is not, then, the only one that needs to be blurred and nuanced; another is the hard line beteeen "dramatic" and "non-dramatic" (or "theatrical" and "non-theatrical"). Jody Enders has made an argument similar to that of Hult and Zink, though to rather different effect. In particular, in "The Theatre of Scholastic Erudition" (where she discusses the performance of the scholastic debates called "quodlibets") she states:

> A focus on the performance potential of an entire scholastic continuum thus debunks the fantasy of an eternal series of discrete "origins" of drama after periodic and lengthy slumbers, and precipitates instead a conception of early dramatic experience that better reflects the more fluid medieval notions of fictionality, theatricality, and genre. (p. 345)[43]

We must soften, if not erase, the sharp distinction between "dramatic" and "narrative"; this was Hult's point as well. As we saw in Chapter 5, early medieval narrative was deeply involved in "showing," in its very predilection for the narration of past events in present tenses; this is clear in the above quotations as well. Verse narrative also made extensive use of the voice in dramatic ways. And in fact all public performance of a narrative work, whether the latter is recited from memory or read aloud, is a kind of theatrical event: it must be (in some sense of the word) staged, etc. In other words, medieval story-telling was not "purely" narrative, but drew strongly on dramatic techniques.

As for the "theatre": here too we find a blend of "narrative" and "theatrical" elements. Narration often surrounds and invades the medieval dramatic text. There is often a narrator or preacher who speaks. Sometimes he summarizes the story before it is acted out. He may tell the audience about what "they will hear," as in the case of Jean Bodel's *Le Jeu de Saint Nicholas*, in which a "preecieres" (preacher) speaks first, calling out "Oiiés, oiiés, seigneur et dames . . ." (line 1), tells them the plot briefly, and concludes his prologue by saying "Or nous faites pais, si l'orrés" (lines 108–14).[44] On occasion, there is

---

43 See also Enders' *Rhetoric and the Origins of Medieval Drama*.
44 Some scholars have thought that this preacher might be a later addition. But this blend of narrative and theatrical elements is in any case a widely attested phenomenon.

such a figure between the scenes. In short, even spectators to a play are told that they will "hear" things. Yet another example is *Courtois d'Arras*, which contains both dramatic and narrative elements, though the former certainly dominate, and have caused this work to be grouped with "early theatre."

We should not forget that the medieval liturgical theatre was apparently born from dumb-show accompanying the reading of Scripture and from dramatic amplification of biblical narrative, as well as from the dramatic possibilities implicit in antiphony itself. In medieval theatre, then, narrative is often there, right in the midst of, mixed in with, the dramatic "play."

In other words, in this period, performers (and poets) appear to have moved back and forth a good deal across that semiotic line that separates narrative from theatre, story-telling from dramatic mimesis. (See Anne Ubersfeld, *Lire le théâtre*.) Indeed, they appear often to have worked right at the edge, right *on* the line – and to have positively relished that spot.

Are these romances "theatrical"? Yes and no. They are not fully dramatic in the sense that the dramatic space does not appear to have been defined or demarcated. (And, as Hult argues in the passage cited above, once that space was defined, it may have largely excluded romance.) It is not clear whether a single minstrel typically "played" all the voices and roles himself, or whether there were other players working with him; the fact that minstrels appear often to have worked in groups – semi-"theatrical troupes"? – means that some division of roles is possible, though by no means certain. Nor is it clear how "illusionistic" such representations were. There is no clear evidence as to the use of costumes, props, sets and the like. (Of course, in much of modern theatre, there has also been a move away from extensive use of such elements, but many would consider that this has made modern theatre more intensely "theatrical"; the absence of these trappings may thus be seen as heightening rather than diminishing the dramatic quality of a play.)

What we appear to have in many romances is frequent and more-or-less prolonged dramatic scenes and episodes, embedded in a primarily narrative work. The ratio of scene and dialogue to story-telling can, however, vary quite a good deal – and, for example, over a third of the thirteenth century romance *Floriant et Florete* is devoted to dialogue.[45] Such a figure is a crude indicator of a theatrical tendency, even perhaps of a generic move toward theatre.

The blend of story-telling, drama, music, and dance

But there is another major feature of court festivities that we need to address: they were clearly either themselves musical, or they were surrounded by and suffused with song and melody; they were not just rhythmic and gestural, they were musical. Perhaps the most reliable feature of descriptions of festive occasions in courts is that they are invariably described *as* musical:

---

45 According to Harry F. Williams: about 36%. *Floriant et Florete*, ed. Williams, p. 39.

the names of instruments and the kinds of performers present generally receive key emphasis. Whatever other sorts of entertainment are present, music seems to predominate.

This fact blurs still further the sharpness of the dichotomy between theatre and narrative. We are dealing with at least a three-way tension and esthetic symbiosis: story-telling, dramatic acting, and music: singing and instrument-playing. And at least sometimes, there was a fourth term: dancing was present as well. We have seen numerous references in quotations given above to the presence of dance in these events. In *Jaufré*, at the end of a great feast at which everyone, including *jongleurs*, ate from silver plates, we are told:

> Li joglar sun en pes levat,
> E cascun pres sun estrument,
> E comenson tan dousament
> Per meg lo palais a dansar.
> Adonx viratz en pes levar
> Donas, qu'anc neguna tener
> No s'en poc, per negun saber
> Del dous son que fan li strument,
> E cascuna mout s'i entent.   lines 10788–96

(The *jongleur* gets to his feet,/ And each one takes up his instrument/ And they begin so sweetly/ To dance in the middle of the palace./ Then you would have seen the ladies/ Get to their feet, no one could hold/ Them back, for any reason,/ From the sweet sound that the instruments make,/ And each one puts her whole will into it.)

The romance *Joufroi* (among many others) presents a similar picture. At a feast – part of whose description I quoted earlier – the poet says:

> [Si] sonent muses et estives,
> Harpes, sauters, guigues et rotes;
> Molt oïsez voutes et notes,
> E vieoler dances et lais.   lines 1159–65

(There were pipes and bagpipes,/ Harps, psalterions, gigs and rotes (stringed instruments);/ There you would have heard jumping ("vaulting") dances and instrumental music,/ There were dances played with vielles, and lais.)

We must assume that different performers, on different occasions, perhaps in combination with other performers present, gave the priority to one or another of these entertainment modes: story-telling, acting, singing, dancing.

In any event, that these performers fully deserved the insult of being called *mimi* and *histriones*, there can be little doubt.

Comparing performance of romance and epic

I think that we should understand both epic and romance as being – at least in the twelfth and early-thirteenth centuries – performed genres, in a dramatic and a musical sense of the word. But there are, it would seem, some important differences between the basic dramatic "performability" of epic and of romance.

The most obvious difference is that the *chanson de geste* is an intrinsically musical genre in two senses of the word. Not merely is it "sung" – and it is always called a "chanson" – but the *jongleur* who sings it traditionally accompanies himself on a "viele," a bowed instrument that takes two hands to play. The *jongleur* who is performing is therefore rather limited in his ability to act out the events he is recounting: about which he is singing. It is not easy to act out roles in any extensive fashion if one is also not just singing but carrying a fiddle and playing it with a bow. (A performer might put the bow down, or even the fiddle, from time to time, but there is a physical impediment here.) It is, of course, possible that in some cases the *jongleur* was accompanied by someone else playing the vielle. Images of *jongleurs* seem generally to show the *jongleur* carrying his own vielle, but this is perhaps not a compelling argument in itself: such images may simply define the nature of the art, not the way it was actually practiced. The *chanson de geste* singer does not appear to have been involved in the sort of vocal elegance that characterized the lyric, so perhaps the combining of singing, playing and representing was not necessarily so difficult.

But *chansons de geste* themselves commonly acknowledge, in the very way they are composed, that the performer cannot fully act them out: the action is, truly, "epic in scope." The *jongleur* could act out certain of the moments – for example, the intense dialogues, such as those between Roland and Ganelon, and Roland and Oliver in the *Roland*. With his bow arm he could imitate a sword-thrust without too much difficulty. Gifted actors can suggest extraordinary things even with their little finger, or just by raising an eyebrow. (Marcel Marceau and Jean-Louis Barrault, among others, can remind us of this!) But much of the art of the *jongleur* would presumably have consisted of evoking for his listeners and viewers – conjuring up in their mind's eye – through his voice, his physical presence and actions, and his words, the vast panorama that he was describing: a whole great battlefield, a vast army, with the sun shining on armor, blood on the grass . . .

The situation is quite different in romance – though these works were also performed by *jongleurs* and minstrels. Though romance appears also to have been surrounded by music in the festive performance situations that our literary and historical texts describe for us,[46] a romance is almost never

---

46 See, for example, recent work by Linda Marie Zaerr, in particular, "Fiddling with the Middle English Romance: Using Performance to Reconstruct the Past."

referred to as a "song" (the rare exception being the *Jaufré*). That is, romances may occasionally be listed among the works that are sung by performers, but they are not defined as *being* songs. (The same is true of *contes* and *fabliaux*.) Performers do not speak of vielles in any intrinsic connection with romance. Which means that the performer who recites romance is not required by any convention actually to sing; perhaps more importantly still, he has his hands free: no vielle, no bow.

Romance, unlike epic, is, moreover, full of small-scale gestures – of wooing, of welcoming and bidding adieux. Romances contain many gestures of piety: people cross themselves and fold their hands in prayer. These are all highly conventional actions that it would have been very easy for a performer to carry out or imitate. But precisely for this reason, it would have been hard – culturally difficult – to *avoid* enacting them. We might, however, want to differentiate among the kinds of gestures: some, such as raising the hand when swearing on relics or putting one's hands out together when praying, or bowing before the lord in a gesture of feudal submission, can be seen as virtually obligatory; others might have been more optional.

The romance performer was, then, substantially freer than the performer of *chansons de geste*: that is, he was free – indeed he was invited – to exploit and to develop the dramatic potential of the material he was presenting to his audience. True, this is, strictly speaking, "narrative" material. But, as we saw earlier, many verse romances are full of long scenes of dramatic dialogue – and by this I do not just mean words, but dramatic scenes.

It appears likely that the words and gestures, along with the narrative itself, were generally performed by one person, who was thus at once a *conteur* and an actor (Latin *histrio*). But it is also possible that sometimes the narrator was accompanied by a player. There is some evidence of *jongleurs* being accompanied by their female counterparts[47] whose function it would presumably have been to play female roles. Or the narrator might have been accompanied by a mime, in the narrow sense of the Latin *mimus*: that is, along with the story-telling went "dumb show," performed by an actor, or perhaps even several of them. This kind of spectacle was, we know, popular in the medieval period, and records indicate that a number of royal "entries" were celebrated with pantomimed scenes. Moreover, some classical theatre was performed in the medieval period by being read aloud by one person while one or several mimes acted it out.

Béroul's Tristan *as a dramatic work*

We need to look at some particular texts. Let us return to Béroul's *Tristan*. Our one surviving but fragmentary manuscript begins with a wonderful scene

---

47 They are generally referred to as "jongleresses." In the *Jaufré* they are "sòudadeiras" (line 158); this term emphasizes that the women performers are paid for their

where Mark is up in a tree to spy on the lovers' tryst. But the lovers spot him up there as they arrive, and they talk to each other as though they weren't lovers, as though they didn't know Mark was there. It is a long scene, almost 300 lines long – and the first part of it is missing. It is also a highly dramatic scene.[48] It begins (as we have it) with Iseut speaking ''angrily'' to Tristan and pretending to cry with dismay. She reproaches him for having called her to this dangerous meeting and says she is going to leave: ''Tristrans, vois m'en, trop i demor'' (lines 1–78[49]).

> – Dame, por amor Deu, merci!
> Mandai toi, et or es ici:
> Entent un poi a ma proiere.
> Ja t'ai je tant tenue chiere!''
> Quant out oï parler sa drue,
> Sout que s'estoit aperceüe:
> Deu en rent graces et merci.
> Or set que bien istront de ci.
> ''Ahi! Yseut, fille de roi,
> Franche, cortoise, en bone foi,
> Par plusors fois vos ai mandee,
> Puis que chambre me fut veee,
> Ne puis ne poi a vos parler.
> Dame, or vos vuel merci crier,
> Qu'il vos membre de cel chaitif
> Qui a traval et a duel vif,
> Quar j'ai tel duel c'onques le roi
> Out mal pensé de vos vers moi
> Qu'il n'i a el fors que je muere . . .''   lines 79–98

(– Lady, for the love of God, pity!/ I called for you, and you are here:/ Listen a little to my prayer./ I have held you so dear!''/ When he had heard his lover speak,/ He knew that she had noticed [the king]:/ He gives thanks to God for this./ And now he knows that they will get out of this fix./ ''Oh Iseut, daughter of a king,/ Noble, courtly, of good faith,/ Several times I have called for you,/ Since I saw you in the chamber,/ I have been unable to speak with you./ Lady, now I wish to cry out for mercy,/ May you remember the miserable person/ Who has pain and sharp sorrow,/ For I have such grief that the king/ Ever thought ill of

services; according to Lavaud and Nelli, the term may suggest that they are ''courtisanes.'' See *Les troubadours: Jaufré, Flamenca, Barlaam et Josaphat*, ed. and trans. René Lavaud and René Nelli, p. 48.

48 Zumthor (among other scholars) noted the dramatic quality of this work. In *La lettre et la voix*, he said of Béroul's *Tristan*: ''Je ne doute guère que nous ne soyons là en présence d'un 'roman' joué, au sens quasi scénique du mot . . . comme le fut, selon mon interprétation, l'*Éracle* de Gautier d'Arras . . .,'' pp. 306–7.

49 Quotations from the Muret (Champion) edition of Béroul's *Tristan*.

you concerning me,/ So that there is no answer but that I must die'' . . .)

This goes on at considerable length, but we can stop here. The points of particular interest are, first, that Tristan has three audiences: Iseut, there before him; Mark up in the tree; and his listeners. We can assume that Béroul (or the performer) must have played to all three audiences, and have played them off one against the other. For example, he might have blown kisses to Iseut, with his back turned to an imaginary Mark, and so on: to fail to exploit such possibilities would surely have been to miss a golden opportunity, dramatically speaking. Secondly, Tristan is pretending to speak to Iseut, not as his lover but as his queen, his lord's wife: he throws himself on her mercy and begs her to help him. Can we conceive that, as he pronounced these piteous works of supplication, he would *not*, for example, have thrown himself on his knees before her and held his hands clasped before him? The point is not to let our imagination run wild, but to recognize the intrinsically theatrical character of such a scene.

Iseut alternates between acting arrogant and pretending that she fears for her life if caught with Tristan:

> – Par foi, sire, grant tort avez,
> Que de tel chose a moi parlez
> Que de vos le mete a raison
> Et de s'ire face pardon.
> Je ne vuel pas encore morir,
> Ne moi du tot en tot perir!
> Il vos mescroit de moi forment,
> Et j'en tendroie parlement?
> Donc seroie je trop hardie.
> Par foi, Trisran, n'en ferai mie,
> Ne vos nu ne devez requerre.
> Tote sul sole en ceste terre.
> Il vos a fait chambres veer
> Par moi: s'il or m'en ot parler,
> Bien me porroit tenir por for fole.
> Par foi, ja n'en dirai parole;
> Et si vos dirai une rien,
> Si vuel que vos le saciés bien:
> Së il vos pardounot, beau sire,
> Par Dieu son mautalent et s'ire,
> J'en seroie joiose et lie.
> S'or savoit ceste chavauchie,
> Cel sai je bien que ja resort,
> Tristran, n'avreie contre mort.
> Vois m'en mais ne prendrai some.
> Grant poor ai quë aucun home
> Ne vos ait ci veü venir.

S'un mot en puet li rois oïr
Que nos fuson ça assemblé,
Il me feroit ardoir en ré.
Ne seret pas mervelle grant.
Mis cors trenble, poor ai grant.
De la poor qui or me prent,
Vois m'en, trop sui ci longuement.   lines 142–75

(– By my faith, lord, you do me a great wrong,/ When of such a thing you speak to me/ That I might make peace with the king for you/ And that I should arrange a pardon from his wrath./ I do not want to die yet,/ Or completely perish./ He strongly mistrusts you on my account,/ And I would talk to him about this?/ I would be too bold./ By my faith, Tristan, I will not do it,/ And you should not ask./ I am all alone in this land./ He had his chamber refused to you/ For me; if now he hears me speak about it/ He could really consider me a fool./ By my faith, I won't say a word;/ And I will tell you one thing,/ Because I want you to know it well:/ If, my lord, he forgives/ You his displeasure and his wrath,/ I would be happy and delighted./ If he knew of this meeting,/ I know well that no protection/ Tristan, would I have against death./ I am going away but I will not sleep./ I am very much afraid that some man/ May have seen you come here./ If the king hears a word of it,/ That we have been together here,/ He would have me burned in a fire./ It is no great surprise,/ If my body trembles, I am so afraid./ For the fear that takes me/ I am going away, I have been here too long.)

We can so readily imagine the player milking the irony of such lines as ''S'un mot en puet li rois oïr'' (with the king, of course, hearing every word) that we cannot imagine this scene *not* played to the hilt.

The king himself is crouched uncomfortably up in the tree.

> . . . Li rois qui sus en l'arbre estoit
> Out l'asenblee bien veüe
> Et la raison tote entendue.
> De la pitié qu'au cor li prist,
> Qu'il ne plorast ne se tenist
> Por nul avoir: mout a grant duel.
> Mot het le nain de Tintaguel.
> ''Las, fait li rois, or ai veü
> Que li nains m'a trop deceü.
> En cet arbre me fist monter.
> Il ne me pout plus ahonter.
> De mon nevo me fist entendre
> Mençonge por qoi feraia pendre.
> Por ce me fist metre en aïr,
> De ma mollier faire haïr.

Je l'en crus, et si fis que fous.
Li gerredons l'en sera sous.
Se je le puis as poinz tenir,
Par feu ferai son cors fenir.
Par moi avra plus dure fin
Que ne fist faire Costentin
A Segoçon, qu'il escolla
Qant o sa feme le trova.
Il l'avoit coroné a Rome
Et la servoient maint preudomme.
Il la tint chiere et honora.
En lié mesfist, puis en plora.''
Tristan s'en est pieça alez.
Li rois de l'arbre est devalez.
En son cuer dit or croit sa feme
Et mescroit les barons du reigne
Qui li faisosient chose acroire
Qu'il set bien que n'est pas voire.
Et qu'il a prové a mençonge.
Or ne laire qu'au nain de donge
O s'espee si sa merite:
Par lui n'iert mais traïson dite.
Ne jamais jor ne mescroira
Tristran d'Iseut, ainz lor laira
La chambre tot a lor voloir.
"Or puis je bien enfin savoir:
Se feüst voir, ceste asenblee
Ne feüst pas issi finee.
Sil s'amasent de fol' amor,
Ci avoient asez leisor:
Bien les veïsse entrebaisier.
Ges ai oï si gramoier,
Or sai je bien n'en ont corage.
Por qoi cro je si fort outrage?
Ce poise moi, si m'en repent.
Mot est fous qui croit tote gent . . .''   lines 234–84

(. . . The king who was up in the tree/ Had seen the meeting/ And
had heard the discussion./ From the pity which seized his heart/
He would not keep from crying/ For anything; he is so sad./ He
hates the dwarf of Tintaguel./ "Alas, says the king, I have seen/
That the dwarf has deceived me./ He made me climb into this
tree./ He could hardly put me to greater shame./ He made me
hear, about my nephew,/ Lies for which I would have had him
hang./ For this, he made me put myself up in the air,/ He made
me hate my wife./ I believed him about all this, and I behaved
like a madman./ He will soon have his reward./ If I can get my
hands on him,/ I will finish him off with fire./ He will have a

harder end [death] because of me/ Than Constantine gave to/ Segoçon, whom he castrated/ When he found him with his wife./ He had crowned her in Rome/ And many worthy men served her/ He cherished and honored her./ He did wrong to her, and then he repented with tears."/ Tristan has now left./ The king has gotten out of the tree./ In his heart he says that now he believes his wife/ And mistrusts the barons of the kingdom/ Who made him believe this thing/ That he knows well is not true./ And he has proven it is a lie./ Now he cannot wait to give the dwarf/ What he deserves, with his sword./ By him treason will never be told./ And never again will he disbelieve/ Tristan and Iseut, but will let them/ The room, just as they wish./ "Now can I finally know:/ If it were true [that they were lovers], this meeting/ Would not have ended in this way./ If they loved each other with a guilty love,/ They had the opportunity here:/ I would have seen them kiss each other,/ I heard them carry on such grief here,/ That I now know that they don't love each other./ Why should I believe such an outrage?/ I am sorry, and I repent of this./ It is a foolish man who believes everyone . . .")

The king reflects on what he has heard and seen – and *not* heard and seen: Tristan and Iseut did not kiss, as they assuredly would have (so he reasons) had they been lovers: "Bien les veïsse entrebaisier . . ." Thus Mark is referring back to the words he has heard and the scene as he has seen it played. As he reflects, his mood changes several times: for example, he realizes that he has done something very undignified – very unregal – in climbing up into a tree. He grasps the shame of his position, and is suddenly mortified to be up a tree. He gets angry with the dwarf and carries out in his imagination the punishment he will inflict on Frocin, when he can get his hands on him. He thinks tenderly of the wrongly accused lovers . . . Here, Béroul could have drawn from Mark's "discovery" of the innocence of the lovers all the irony, in playing the scene toward us, the listeners and viewers – for we too, like Mark, saw that scene, but we saw a good deal more than he.

There are other long scenes of dramatic dialogue and action in this work – for example, when Tristan, pretending to be a leper and a beggar, carries Iseut piggy back across the swamp (lines 3932ff); she can then take her oath of innocence: that no man except Mark and the beggar has ever come between her thighs (lines 4205–16). This is, in many respects, a crude work, and one can hardly doubt that such a scene was acted out with gestures.

Speaking of Béroul's *Tristan* as a work performed in a "strong" sense of the word, we should note in some of the most important and memorable scenes of the poem the key references to "jumping": to the verb *sauter*. Tristan leaps from his bed to that of Iseut to make love to her:

Dedenz la chanbre n'out clartez,
Cirge ne lanpë alumez.

194

Tristran se fu sus piez levez.
Dex! porqoi fut? Or escoutez!
Les piez a joinz, esme, si saut,
El lit le roi chaï de haut. . . .   lines 725–30

(In the room there was no light,/ No candle or lamp lit./ Tristan
got up on his feet./ God! Why was he there? Now listen!/ With
his feet together, he jumped,/ On the king's bed he landed from
above. . . .)

After they have made love, Tristan hears the king coming and leaps back.

. . . Live du lit, tot esfroïz,
Errant s'en rest mot tost salliz.
Au tresallir que Tristran fait,
Li sans decent (malement vait)
De la plaie sor la farine.   lines 745–49

(He gets up from the bed, all afraid,/ Immediately and very fast
he jumped back./ From the jump that Tristan did,/ The blood
flows (things are going badly)/ From his wound onto the flour.)

Later, he leaps out the church window to save his life – an amazing and
miraculous leap that lives on in legend:

 Tristran ne vait pas conme lenz,
Triés l'autel vint a la fenestre,
A soi l'en traist a sa main destre,
Par l'overture s'en saut hors.
Mex veut saillir que ja ses cors
Soit ars, voiant tel aünee.
Seignors, une grant pierre lee
Out u mileu de cel rochier:
Tristran i saut mot de legier,
Li vens le fiert entre les dras,
Quil defent qu'il ne chie a tas.
Encor claiment Cornuelan
Cele pierre le Saut Tristran.
La chapele ert plaine de pueple.
Tristran saut sus . . .   lines 942–56

(Tristan does not go slowly,/ He went to the window next to the
altar,/ He pulls it toward himself with his right hand,/ From the
opening he jumps out./ He prefers to jump rather than that his
body/ Should be burned, before such a crowd./ Lords, a great
broad stone/ Was there in the middle of the cliff:/ Tristan leaps
very lightly,/ The wind catches his clothes,/ And keeps him from
landing heavily/ The Cornish still call/ This stone "Tristan's
Leap."/ The chapel was full of people./ Tristan jumps up . . .)

There is yet another memorable jump – but let's set the scene up a bit. Mark finds the lovers asleep in the forest. He is about to kill them – his sword is raised, about to fall on the lovers – when, seeing Tristan's sword lying between them, he stops in mid-blow. He interprets the sword lying between the lovers as meaning that they are not sleeping together. (Wrong again!) He removes his ring from the queen's finger, exchanges his sword for Tristan's, sets a glove in a tree to keep the sun from shining in Iseut's face – and leaves them asleep. Iseut, dreaming that two lions are trying to eat her, screams.

> Tristran, du cri qu'il ot, s'esvelle,
> Tote la face avoit vermelle.
> Esfreez s'est, saut sus ses piez,
> L'espee prent com home iriez,
> Regarde el brant, l'osche ne voit:
> Vit le pont d'or qui sus estoit,
> Connut que c'est l'espee au roi . . .   lines 2077–84

(Tristan, from the cry that he heard, wakes up,/ His whole face was bright red./ He is startled, he jumps up on his feet,/ He takes his sword like an angry man,/ He looks at the blade, he doesn't see the notch in it./ He saw the golden pommel that was on it,/ He recognizes that it was the king's sword.)

All in all, this is a very dramatic scene, full of powerful gestures – and again Tristan performs one of his dramatic jumps.

I have not exhausted the list of Tristan's *sauts*, but the point is surely clear. There is a strong likelihood that Béroul was himself not merely a story-telling actor (a *jongleur* and a *histrio*), but also a *sauteour* or *tombeor* – an acrobat – which was a recognized and popular kind of performer. This story would certainly make effective use of such a speciality.[50] I am not arguing that every performer who "did" Béroul's version of the Tristan *had* to jump: one might "suggest" leaping without actually making full-scale leaps. The point is that this work, in its fundamental performance conceptualization, includes leaping as an important possibility – and leapers and tumblers were favorites in festive settings.[51]

[50] It is also interesting to speculate on the possible pun between the acrobatic and the erotic meanings of the verb *sauter*: the frequence with which it is into *bed* that Tristan jumps suggests that the modern slang meaning of the verb was operative even then. In this context it is interesting to note that many fabliaux, including, for example, "De la damoisele qui sonjoit," feature lewd leaping and leapers. (See *Fabliaux érotiques*, ed. and trans. Luciano Rossi and Richard Straub, pp. 82–87, esp. 82–83.) Indeed, fabliaux commonly invite a multiplicity of crude semi-acrobatic gestures.

[51] For useful images of acrobats, and other sorts of performers, see Clifford Davidson, *Illustrations of the Stage and Acting in England to 1580*.

The dramatic and the festive qualities of Chrétien's romances

Many will perhaps not find it hard to imagine this sort of performance of Béroul's *Tristan*, where contemporary scholarly investment in *clergie* and in authorial dignity is relatively low. We turn once again to the more challenging case of Chrétien. True, we are not certain who Chrétien was, but it appears virtually certain that his romances were performed along with other romances, with the rest of that *jongleur*esque repertory, from memory. Pierre de St. Cloud, in a quotation given above from the *Roman de Renart*, mentioned the story of Yvain.

Joseph J. Duggan has noted that the Catalan troubadour Guerau de Cabrera, in an *ensenhamen* ("teaching" or instruction), to which a date of before 1165 has been ascribed, reproached a *jongleur* named Cabra for not knowing a number of *chansons de geste*, the poems of certain *troubadours* and the fabliau "Richeut," and for being unable to tell stories about King Arthur, Gauvain, Erec's conquest of the sparrowhawk, and other romance material. Erec and the sparrowhawk, and perhaps Gauvain as well, seem to refer to romances by Chrétien, the clear implication being that a competent *jongleur* would know them. Duggan also discusses an *ensenhamen* by the troubadour Guiraut de Calanso to his *jongleur* Fadet (between 1190 and 1220) in which the poet makes it clear that he expects the *jongleur* to know stories about – *inter alia* – Troy (would Benoît de Sainte Maure be pleased?), Alexander the Great, and Lancelot.[52]

But surely the most striking and interesting example is that of the thirteenth century Occitan romance *Flamenca*. Chrétien's *Yvain* is first evoked in an explicitly musical context:

> Apres si levon li juglar;
> cascus se volc faire auzir.
> Adonc auziras retentir
> cordas de manta tempradura.
> Qui saup novela violadura,
> ni canzo ni descort ni lais,
> al plus que poc avan si trais.
> L'uns viola[l] lais de Cabarefoil,
> e l'autre cel de Tintagoil;
> l'us cantet cel dels Fins Amanz,
> e l'autre cel que fes Ivans.
> L'us menet arpa, l'autre viula;
> l'us flaütela, l'autre siula;
> l'us mena giga, l'autre rota;
> l'us diz los motz e l'autre.ls nota;

52 Joseph J. Duggan, "Oral Performance of Romance in Medieval France," *Continuations: Essays on Medieval French Literature and Language, in Honor of John L. Grigsby*, Birmingham, AL, Summa, 1989, pp. 51–61; p. 53.

l'us estiva, l'autre flestella;
l'us musa, l'autre caramella;
l'us mandura e l'autr'acorda
lo sauteri ab manicorda;
l'us fai lo juec dels bavastelz,
l'autre jugava de coutelz;
l'us vai per sol e l'autre tomba,
l'autre balet ab sa retomba;
l'us passet sercle, l'autre sail;
neguns a son mestier non fail.
Qui volc ausir diverses comtes
de reis, de marques et de comtes,
auzir ne poc tan can si volc;
anc null'aurella non lai colc,
quar l'us comtet de Priamus,
e l'autre diz de Piramus;
l'us comtet de la bell'Elena
com Paris l'enquer, pois l'anmena. . . .   lines 596–628[53]

(Then the minstrels stood up;/ each one wanted to be heard./ Then you would have heard resound/ strings of various pitches./ Whoever knew a new piece for the viol,/ a song, a descort, or lay,/ he pressed forward as much as he could./ One played the lay of the Honeysuckle, /another the one of Tintagel;/ one sang of the Noble Lovers,/ and another which Yvain composed [or "another tells what Yvain does"]./ One played the harp; another the viol;/ another, the flute; another, a fife; / one played a rebeck; another, a rote; one sang the words; another played notes;/ one the sackbut; another, the fife;/ one, the bagpipe; another, the reed-pipe;/ one the mandora and another attuned/ the psaltery with the monocord;/ one performed with marionettes,/ another juggled knives;/ some did gymnastics and tumbling tricks;/ another danced with his cup;/ one held the hoop; another leapt through it;/ everyone performed his art perfectly./ Whoever wished to hear different tales/ of kings, earls and counts/ could hear of them as much as he desired;/ no ear was sleeping there,/ for one told of Priam,/ and another spoke of Piramus;/ one told of beautiful Helen,/ how Paris wooed her and took her away. . . .)

This list goes on for many lines. Don't miss the tumblers and leapers! We pick it up again almost fifty lines later:

. . . l'autre comtava de Galvain,
e del leo que fon compain
del cavallier qu'estors Luneta;

---

[53] *The Romance of Flamenca*, ed. and trans. by Blodgett.

l'us diz de la piucella breta
con tenc Lancelot en preiso
cant de s'amor li dis de no;
l'autre comtet de Persaval
co venc a la cort a caval;
l'us comtet d'Erec d d'Enida,
l'autre d'Ugonet de Perida;
l'us contava de Governail
com per Tristan ac griu trebail,
l'autre comtava de Feniza,
con transir la fes sa noirissa. . . .   lines 669–82

(. . . another told of Gawain/ and of the lion who was the friend/ of the knight whom Lunete delivered;/ one spoke of the Breton girl/ who held Lancelot in prison/ when he did not return her love;/ another told of Perceval,/ how he went into court upon a horse;/ another told of Erec and Enide,/ another of Ugonet of Peride;/ another told of Governail,/ how for Tristan he suffered grievously,/ another spoke of Fénice,/ how her nurse made her appear dead. . . .)

Several comments are in order here. In the first part of this passage, the emphasis is on the musical, and generally entertaining, character of the occasion – though the words being sung and played are all narrative. Some of the works were unquestionably written works originally; such is the case of Marie de France's lai "Chevrefoil" (here referred to as "Cabarefoil"). In the second part, the emphasis is on the extent of the narrative repertory being performed, rather than on the music. It is hard to believe that at any historical event so many works were actually performed; there is presumably hyperbole here. But that at festive occasions many works were performed, by many entertainers, is, as I hope to have shown,[54] certain. (We will return to such matters and to their importance for the study of medieval romances in Chapter 8.) And the longer festivities lasted – sometimes they went on for days, even weeks – the greater the number of performance events possible.

In both parts, reference is made to works by Chrétien, though his name is never mentioned – nor, for that matter, is the name of *any* "author" referred to. Chrétien's known works are all represented here – *Yvain* (mentioned twice), *Lancelot*, *Perceval*, *Érec et Énide*, *Cligés*. His works are for the most part grouped together, though an unknown work (about a certain Ugonet de Perida) and a Tristan story[55] separate *Cligés* from the others. (It is also worth reiterating here what we noted earlier, in Chapter 4: Chrétien's romances are not in

[54] See also Faral, *Jongleurs, passim.*

[55] Chrétien does, however, say that he "made" a Tristan story – a story which has not survived. Perhaps this is his – though it is worth noting that Chrétien refers to his story as being "Del roi Marc et d'Ysalt la blonde" rather than "about" Tristan. See *Cligés*, line 5.

what we think of today as their chronological order.[56]) Finally, given the fact that *Flamenca* is an Occitan romance, it is possible that Chrétien's works are to be imagined as being performed here not in French but reworked in Occitan, or a sort of Franco-Occitan (like the epics in Franco-Venetian).

It is no accident that Chrétien's works are performed in such a setting: at a splendid court wedding. Indeed, his works may well have been composed with just such festive performances in mind. It may well be that one of Chrétien's innovations was social – one might almost say calendrical – rather than literary: Philippe Walter has studied, in his rich and dense book, *La mémoire du temps: Fêtes et calendriers de Chrétien de Troyes à la Mort Artu*, the multiple reflections and refractions of the festive year in the works of Chrétien and others.[57] It seems to me altogether possible (though this is not Walter's point) that Chrétien composed his works, and his patrons paid for them, with the express purpose of providing the entertainment for such festive occasions. Earlier works, such as *chansons de geste*, Wace's romances, the *romans antiques*, and Béroul's *Tristan*, do not seem tied to specific feasts or great occasions.[58] Chrétien's romances are virtually all (all but one, to which we will return) deeply festive, ceremonial, social, official works, lending themselves to great social occasions. Thus, *Érec et Énide*, where the hero and heroine must learn to balance the demands of marriage with those of chivalry, lends itself extraordinarily well to a marriage feast; so does *Cligés*. *Érec et Énide* is also appropriate for a coronation, as the couple are both crowned at the end. *Perceval* might originally have been composed for – it is perhaps most appropriate for – the festivities surrounding a dubbing ceremony. After all, what Perceval learns is what it means to be a knight; and Gawain provides another model of knighthood here.

Lancelot is the exception to my rule: its central theme is an adulterous affair – hardly appropriate, one is inclined to think, for a wedding, a dubbing ceremony, or any other ceremonial affair. But Chrétien begins the romance by saying that his lady, Marie of Champagne, commanded him to tell the story and gave him the plot; he says he intends to obey her; and, apparently, he doesn't finish the story – which many scholars have taken to signal his disapproval of, and ultimate disengagement from, the story. But we should note that even this work is mentioned along with the other works whose performance is evoked at the wedding festivities in *Flamenca*: "L'us diz de la piucella breta/ Con tent Lancelot en preiso/ Cant de s'amor li dis de no." (One tells of the

---

[56] That is, *Érec et Énide*, *Cligés*, *Lancelot* and *Yvain* (the chronological relationship between these two romances is complex, as the latter appears to refer to an episode in the former: some scholars have thought Chrétien worked on them simultaneously), and finally *Perceval*.

[57] References to great feasts become a topos in later romances – but one that continues to link the work to a fiction of communal rejoicing.

[58] There are a few exceptions: *Le voyage de Charlemagne à Jerusalem* seems to have had as its purpose to provide entertainment for "Lendit," the official fair of St. Denis.

Breton maid/ who held Lancelot in prison/ when he did not return her love). Perhaps our understanding of what was considered appropriate at a wedding is too narrow and moralistic? This is possible (and see Chapter 8). On the other hand, *Flamenca* itself takes adultery as its major theme, and the poet seems far from opposed to the love affair that he is recounting. As *Flamenca* is unfinished, we do not know how the affair was ultimately resolved, if indeed it was.

Chrétien's *Yvain* begins at Pentecost and contains a number of references to that feast and to the Holy Spirit. Chrétien begins by speaking of "cele feste qui tant coste, qu'an doit clamer la Pantecoste" (lines 4–5; "that feast that costs so much, that it should be called Pentecost"). Along with other references to God, the Virgin and the saints, there are several specific mentions of the Holy Spirit (as in lines 273, 4462, 4986, 5450). Near the end of the romance, when the hero has finally won back the love of his wife:

> – Dame, fet il, .v c[ents] merciz,
> et, si m'aist Sainz Esperiz,
> que Dex an cest siegle mortel
> ne me feist pas si lie d'el.   lines 6785–88

> (– Lady, he says, five hundred thanks,/ and, so help me the Holy Spirit,/ God in this mortal life/ could not make me so happy with anything else.)

In short, this work may well have been composed specifically for the Feast of the Descent of the Holy Spirit, which closed the long and festive Easter season. (By way of comparison, in *Lancelot* I find only one fairly minor reference to the Holy Spirit; in *Érec et Énide*, none.) This romance would also have been appropriate for the celebration of a marriage, or to a dubbing ceremony, since like *Érec et Énide* its central theme is the balancing of the duties of marriage and of knighthood.

Moreover, this work, like all of Chrétien's romances, invites performance in quite a strong sense of the word. There are many dramatic dialogues in this work, such as the scene where the charming Lunete persuades her rather difficult if beautiful mistress, the Lady of the Fountain, a) not to die but to remarry, and b) to marry the man who killed her husband, on the grounds that if one knight kills another in combat, the one who won must logically be the better knight (lines 1609ff). In this wonderful scene, the performer, whether Chrétien or someone else, must have changed not just his voice but his physical presence – his entire *persona* – to suggest these two very different women.

> La premiere foiz a consoil
> li dist: "Dame, molt me mervoil
> que folemant vos voi ovrer.
> Dame, cuidiez vos recovrer
> votre seignor por vostre duel?

– Nenil, fait ele, mes mon vuel
seroie je morte d'enui.
– Por coi? – Por aler aprés lui.
– Apres lui? Dex vos an desfande
qui ausi boen seigor vos rande
si com il an est posteïs.
– Einz tel mançonge ne deïs,
qu'il ne me porroit si boen randre.
– Meillor, se vos le volez prandre,
vos randra il, sel proverai.
– Fui! Teis! Ja tel ne troverai.
– Si feroiz, dame, s'il vos siet . . ."   lines 1601–17

(The first time she spoke with her she [Lunete]/ says to her "My lady, I marvel greatly/ that you are carrying on in such a foolish way./ Lady, do you think to recover/ your lord by your grief?/ – No, she says, but I want/ to die of sorrow./ – Why? – To go after him./ – After him? God forbid,/ [God] who can give you just as good a lord/ as he has the power to do so./ – You should never tell such a lie,/ he couldn't give me as good a one./ – Better, if you want to accept him,/ God can give you, and I will prove it./ – Leave! Be quiet! if it suits you . . .")

And the lion! This figure is clearly one of the central characters in the romance, also known as *Le chevalier au lion*. But this lion has no lines. Are we really to believe that the performer who recited and played this romance didn't ever roar? When we first meet the lion he *is* roaring: that is how Yvain knows he is there: the beast has been attacked by a serpent:

Mes sire Yvains pansis chemine
par une parfonde gaudine
tant qu'il oi en mi le gaut
un cri molt dolereus et haus.
Si s'adreca lors vers le cri
cele part ou il l'o oi,
et, quant il parvint cele part,
vit un lyon, en un essart,
et un serpant qui le tenoit
par la coe, et si ardoit
trestoz les rains de flame ardant . . .   lines 3337–47

(My lord Yvain rides alone pensive/ in a deep ravine/ until he hears in the middle of the forest/ a loud cry of pain./ He went toward the cry/ in the direction where he had heard it,/ and when he got there,/ he saw a lion, in a thicket,/ and a serpent which held it/ by the tail, and burned/ its flanks with burning flame . . .)

Would a medieval minstrel worth his salt have failed to produce the appropriate yelps of leonine pain: that "cri molt dolereus et haus"? Moreover, the lion has all kinds of wonderful gestures, actions that could easily be acted out. He kneels in feudal homage to Yvain, from deep gratitude:

> Oez que fist li lyons donques,
> con fist que preuz et deboneire,
> com il li comanca a feire
> sanblant que a lui se randoit,
> que ses piez joinz li estandoit
> et vers terre encline sa chiere;
> si s'estut sor ses piez derriere
> et puis si se ragenouilloit,
> et tote sa face moilloit
> de lermes, par humilite.   lines 3388–97

(Listen to what the lion did then,/ how he acted in a worthy and noble fashion,/ when he began to give Yvain/ the impression that he was surrendering to him,/ and with his feet together he stretched out toward him/ and toward the ground he bent his face;/ and he stood up on his back feet/ and then he knelt,/ and wet all his face/ with tears, from humility.)

The lion falls into wild despair when he thinks his master is dead:

> Li lyons cuide mort veoir
> son conpaignon et son seignor;
> einz de rien n'ot ire graignor,
> qu'il comanca tel duel a fere,
> n'oi tel conter ne retrere,
> qu'il se detuert et grate et crie
> et s'a talant qu e il s'ocie
> de l'espee, qu'il li est vis
> qui ait son boen seigneur ocis . . .   lines 3500–08

(The lion thinks he sees dead/ his companion and his lord;/ never did he have greater anger about anything,/ and he began to carry on grief,/ such as I have never heard told or described,/ so that he turns and scratches and cries out/ and wants to kill himself/ with the sword, because it seems to him/ that it has killed his good lord . . .)

The lion scratches his way out from under a door when he has been locked up so that he cannot help his master fight:

> Or a son cuer dolant et troble
> li lyeons qui est an la chanbre,
> que de la grant bonte li manbre
> que cil li fist par sa franchise,
> qui ja avroit de son service
> et de s'aide grant mestier;
> ja li randroit au grant serter

et au grant mui ceste bonte;
ja n'i avroit rien mesconte
s'il pooit issir de leanx.
Molt vet reverchant de toz sanz
ne ne voit par ou il s'an aille.
Bien ot les cos de la bataille,
qui perilleuse est et vilainne,
et por ce si grant duel demainne
qu'il anrage vis et forsene.
Tant vet cerchant que il asene
au suil, qui porrissoit pres terre,
et tant qu'il l'arache et s'i serre
et fiche jusque pres des rains . . .   lines 5588–607

(Now the lion, who is in the room,/ has a sad and troubled heart/ because he remembers the great kindness/ that he [Yvain] did to him, of free will,/ who now would have of his service/ and of his aid great need;/ now he [the lion] would pay back/ many times over this kindness;/ now he [Yvain] would have no problem/ if he [the lion] could get out of there./ He goes looking around in every direction/ but he cannot see any way to get out./ He hears the blows of the battle,/ which is perilous and ugly,/ and for this reason he carries on great grief/ so that he is mad and wild./ He looks so hard that he fixes himself/ at the doorway, which was rotting near the ground,/ and so much does he pull it and squeeze it/ and gets himself in, up to his hips . . .)

These dramatic actions of the lion are narrated, and there is no dialogue here: again, the lion cannot, does not speak; this is not then a situation of "dramatic dialogue." In this sense, then, this is not a "theatrical" work. But in a work performed from memory – as this one clearly was, at least some of the time – it is, I submit, impossible to believe that the performer would have failed to act out the lion's complex role: this creature is at once noble and bestial, fierce and friendly. This lion is not, then, just a "character in a story," but a figure who belongs in a list of "dramatis personae."

It is important to recognize that Chrétien's romances hardly ever invite what medieval moralists would have called "lewd" performance. The subject matter is invariably noble and high-toned, though not without humor. Moments of what moral writers called "turpitude" and "the deforming of the image of God in man" are few. Probably only an austere Cistercian would have taken offense at such works as they were probably performed in court – and few such Cistercians are apt to have been present there. In short, this was refined entertainment for court events of the highest order.[59]

---

[59] A Middle English work with a similar character is *Sir Gawain and the Green Knight*; it offers entertainment at once delightful, refined and appropriately devout, suitable for the Christmas season.

The middle range on the performance spectrum

The fact that romances were often performed in a more-or-less strongly dramatic sense of the word does not deny the reality or the importance of medieval romance-reading.[60] As I have said repeatedly in the course of this book, romance is not simply or purely oral. We now broaden our perspective on the modalities of medieval performance. If in the first part of this chapter, I used the word "performance" primarily in its narrow and familiar sense – the playing or singing of a dramatic or musical work – here, I will use the word in a wider sense and mean by it *any* mode in which a work can be "executed" or "carried out": in French, *réalisée*. Such a definition includes the act of reading.

We return to our performance spectrum. We have now looked at one end of it: at public, official, social, festive, expensive events. These are special occasions celebrated lavishly, and with a large budget. I called this the "high" end of the scale. We will soon look at the "low" end: events that can be called intimate, private, ordinary, simple, inexpensive, unofficial, off-the-record. This is "ordinary time": not so much celebration as passing the time, and at the low-budget end of the scale.

But before sliding all the way to the "private" end of the scale, we would do well to look at some of the many sorts of performance situations that lie between the two ends of this continuum. For example, with regard to princely or royal courts, it is worth remembering that in such places effort is expended, and money spent, to make even "ordinary" occasions handsomely entertaining, at least to the lord or lady and their intimates. Here, we can profitably cite yet again Jean Renart's *Le Roman de la Rose ou de Guillaume de Dole*. The emperor, you recall, has his own *jongleur*:

> – Un sien vïeleur qu'il a
> q'on apele a la cort Juglet,
> fist apeler par un vallet.
> Il ert sages et de grant pris
> et s'avoit oï et apris
> mainte chançon et maint biau conte.   lines 637–42

---

60 For an excellent general discussion of medieval reading, see Clanchy, *From Memory to Written Record*, esp. Part II, pp. 185–96, 215–20, 246–52.

D.H. Green, in *Medieval Listening and Reading: The primary reception of German literature 800–1300*, documents many references to reading. Aside from being interested primarily in the German world, Green does not break down the data in the same way that I do: I am particularly interested in pleasure reading, especially the reading of romance, as distinct from other kinds of reading and the reading of other kinds of works. But the picture we are painting is in many ways similar. There do, however, appear to be more early references to private reading in Germany than in France.

(– The vielleur that he has,/ whom they call at the court Juglet,/ he has a servant boy call./ He [Juglet] was wise and of great worth/ and he had heard and learned/ many a song and many a fine tale.)

The emperor says to Juglet: "Aucun conte dont ge m'esveil/ me conte, fet il, biaux amis" (lines 653–4; "Tell me," he said, "fair friend,/ Some story that will wake me up"). Juglet tells the emperor a story that makes him fall in love (with a maiden whom, after assorted vicissitudes, he marries at the end). This was, then, a decidedly stimulating and effective story.

At another point, Juglet, asked to entertain the emperor and his entourage, sings a bit of the *chanson de geste* of Gerbert de Metz: "cest vers de Gerbert [de Metz]" (lines 1334ff).

But even in princely establishments, entertainment was not always provided by professional entertainers. In another early-thirteenth century romance by Jean Renart, *Escoufle*, the heroine, Aélis, the emperor's daughter, is skilled at entertaining:

Ml't par sot bien amis aquerre
Par biau parler et par largece
Bele Aelis. He! Diex, en'est ce
La plus prex et la plus cortoise?
Tuit cil a cui ele s'envoise
En sont ml't lié, que c'est raisons;
Ml't lor sot bien chanter chançons
Et conter contes d'aventure.
Ml't lor sot en une chainture
Portraire l'ami et l'amie; . . .   lines 2052–61[61]

(She knew how to make friends/ By beautiful speaking and by generosity,/ Belle Aélis. Oh, God! Is she *not*/ The most noble and the most courtly among them?/ All those whom she finds delightful/ Are very happy about it, and they are right;/ She knew how to sing them songs very well/ And how to tell adventure stories./ With [in? in any case, wearing] a belt, she knew how/ To portray the boyfriend and the girlfriend; . . .)

Thus here we have an amateur female entertainer, who successfully combines different genres, including story-telling. One intriguing detail here: Aélis "portrays" – apparently she acts out – the roles of the lovers. What is this *ceinture* (*chainture*) that she is wearing? Could this "belt" or "girdle" refer to some sort of rudimentary, iconic, costume worn by secular performers – especially of love stories. It would, then, parallel the ecclesiastical vestments (stoles, albs, dalmatics, and the like) worn in liturgical drama,[62] and draw on

61 Jean Renart, *L'Escoufle (roman d'aventure)*, ed. Franklin Sweetser.
62 See David Bevington, *Medieval Drama*, e.g., pp. 36, 45, 80, and *passim*.

the venerable tradition of belts given and worn as love tokens (the green girdle in *Sir Gawain and the Green Knight* is the most famous example). Thomas Chobham in his "Penitential" refers to the "horribiles lorcas vel larvas" of *histriones*. Page translates these as "garments" and "masks,"[63] but the word *lorca* primarily meant "corselet" or "girdle." It is perhaps worth adding that Aélis is an excellent seamstress and in particular sews belts very well. Later in the romance, after running away from home and being separated from her *ami*/future husband, she has to live for a while on her own resources and makes a living sewing belts and selling them to wealthy friends.

In lesser establishments it was even more common for the people gathered together to entertain each other and themselves by dancing and playing games, by singing songs and telling stories – as Juglet and Aélis did. Many people at court appear to have taken considerable pride in their ability to perform songs and stories. Among the favored accomplishments of noble amateurs were the singing of lyric songs and of snatches of epic (*Le roman de la rose ou de Guillaume de Dole* provides numerous examples) and the playing of the harp which was known to be a magical instrument – one of astonishing virtuosity – in the hands of some aristocratic players; here, one thinks first perhaps of young Tristan playing for King Mark. By contrast, the playing of the vielle and the recitation of long romances appear to have been the work of professional minstrels; indeed, I have thus far found no evidence for amateur vielle-players.

It is interesting to note that, while we certainly find minstrels in this middle position on the spectrum, we do not appear to see the full-scale professional-minstrel performances of romance such as I described earlier.

The low end of the performance spectrum: Informal domestic settings

We turn now to the "low" end of the spectrum. Here we have small gatherings of an informal character in more modest noble (and some bourgeois) establishments: for example, evenings at home in non-festive, intimate, or small court settings. We hear echoes of such gatherings in many medieval works.

Public reading

The evidence suggests that in the twelfth and thirteenth centuries, and indeed, for quite a long time in the Middle Ages, it is almost exclusively at this – the private, non-festive, ordinary, unofficial and inexpensive – end of the spectrum, that public reading took place. And even here, reading aloud was far from the only means of entertainment: people played instruments such as harps, and of course they sang alone and to small groups. We have many refer-

---

63 Page, *The Owl*, p. 21.

ences to such private, even solitary, entertainment: for example, in Thomas's *Tristan* Iscut sings to herself the "lai of Guiron":

> En sa chambre se set un jor
> E fait un lai pitus d'amur:
> Coment dan Guirun fu supris,
> Pur l'amur de sa dame ocis
> Qu'il sur tute rien ama,. . .
> La reïne chante dulcement,
> La voiz acorde a l'estrument.
> Les mainz sunt beles, li lais buons
> Douce la voiz, bas li tons.
> Survint idunc Cariado, . . .   pp. 64–5, lines 781–5; 791–5[64]

(In her chamber [Iseut] sits one day/ And makes [sings] a piteous song [lai] about love:/ How lord Guiron was surprised,/ And killed for the love of his lady/ Whom he loved more than anything else. . . ./ The queen sings very sweetly,/ Harmonizes her voice with the instrument./ Her hands are beautiful, the lai is good,/ Sweet is her voice, the sound is low./ Then Cariadoc came in. . . .)

Where *did* reading aloud take place? There is no better place to start this inquiry than with the famous scene in Chrétien's *Yvain*, where the hero sees a young girl reading aloud from a *roman* to her parents. (Let us remember that if we are going to be sceptical of representations of performance in romance, we must be sceptical about this scene as well.)

> Et mes sire Yvains lors s'en antre
> el vergier, aprés li sa rote
> voit apoié desore son cote
> un riche homme qui se gisoit
> sor un drap de soie, et lisoit
> une pucele devant lui
> En un romans, ne sai de cui;
> et por le romans escoter
> s'i estoit venue acoter
> une dame; et s'estoit sa mere,
> et li sires estoit ses pere,
> si se porent molt esjoïr
> de li bien veoir et oïr,
> car il n'avoient plus d'anfanz;
> ne ot mie plus de seize anz,
> et s'estoit molt bele et molt jante . . .   lines 5354–68[65]

---

[64] Quotations from the Wind edition of Thomas's *Tristan*.
[65] *Yvain*, ed. Roques. I discussed this scene briefly in Chapter 4.

(And my lord Yvain then enters/ into the garden, and after him his companions/ he sees leaning on his side/ a rich man who was lying/ on a silken cloth, and there was reading/ a maiden before him/ in a romance [or work composed in the French vernacular],/ I don't know about whom[66]/ and to hear the romance/ a woman had come there too, and it was her mother/ and the lord was her father/ and they must have greatly rejoiced/ to see her and hear her,/ for they had no other children;/ and she was no more than sixteen years old,/ and was very beautiful and noble . . .)

This young girl, this only child, reads aloud to her proud parents (one is reminded of rather similar Victorian images of girls playing the piano before doting mothers and fathers). This is, in the familial sense of the word, an "intimate" scene. But this passage is also unusual: short as it is, this is the only full-fledged reading scene in Chrétien's romances.

But precisely because it *is*, in Chrétien's work, virtually unique, this scene invites further speculation. First, while we today think of such a reading scene as "normal," it is perhaps in the context of Chrétien's work to be understood as "exotic" or at least unusual, for there is no evidence – other than this one scene – that at this time it was common for young women to read to their family, or indeed for laymen or women to read to anybody. This is *the* scene that is always provided by scholars to show that such things were "common."[67]

Moreover, there may be something decidedly "wrong" with this picture. This father and his family are the hosts of the "Pesme Aventure" – the final and the "worst" adventure of the romance. And precisely what these people are guilty of is selfishness and exploitation: they are the managers of the sweatshop where 300 half-naked maidens are forced to work their fingers to the bone day in and day out. Is it not likely that we are – or rather that Chrétien's audience was – invited to find something just a bit off in this family's nice "private" relaxation? Robert Hanning has made a similar observation. Of this scene he says:

---

[66] The Old French reads "de cui," which theoretically could mean either "about whom" or "by whom." The strong likelihood is that it means the former: romances are generally identified by their protagonist(s) rather than by their "author." Thus we hear of the story "of" (*de*) Erec and Enide; Yvain; Perceval. When the poet/*trouvère* is identified, it is by some other formula, e.g., the story that this or that story-teller "fist."

[67] See, for example, Andrew Taylor's "The Myth of the Minstrel Manuscript": ". . . there is some evidence, admittedly scanty, for lay literacy in the twelfth century. Chrétien de Troyes, writing in about 1160, provides evidence to suggest that reading romances had become a social habit among the courtiers of his day. In a much-cited passage in *Yvain* he describes how the hero enters a garden and sees a noble maiden reading to her parents" (p. 51). This "social habit" is, however, apparently based on this text alone.

The scene is idyllic and intimate, but Chrétien includes it, I think, less as a documentary or ornamental touch than as a shocking contrast with the scene Yvain has encountered just outside the garden . . . The escapist quality of the family group, and the unmemorable nature of the *romans* they are enjoying while others suffer at their hands, is part of Chrétien's comment on the kind of amoral (and, by implication, immoral) literature of pleasure and entertainment which stands opposed to the vein of moral seriousness in romances of his own making, like *Yvain*, in which the hero, to atone for his wronging his wife, must defend women from various kinds of masculine aggression, including commercial exploitation. One can, then, well believe that romances were enjoyed under conditions like those described in this pasage of *Yvain*, but it would be a mistake to generalize overmuch from this programmatic, thematically derived instance.[68]

Hanning underestimates, I think, the entertainment value of Chrétien's romances: these are not *just* works of high seriousness. But his basic point is well-taken: this scene appears to be there for thematic purposes – to emphasize the amoral and selfish behavior of this family – not to document the "typical performance of romance in the twelfth century."

As Joyce Coleman has shown in *Public Reading and the Reading Public in Late Medieval England and France*, people who read privately were long viewed with disapproval, as being anti-social; alternately, they were in poor physical or mental health. As late as Guillaume de Guileville's *Pèlerinage de la vie humaine*, c.1320, Oiseuse is shown as a reader. We seem to be picking up a similar attitude here in Chrétien.

Not all "intimate" reading scenes are of so familial a nature. *Floire et Blancheflor*[69] provides a case in point. In this short (3342-line) early-thirteenth century romance, the lovers are a boy and girl who have been brought up together. They are highly literate: Floire's father had them educated from their infancy by a private tutor – Gaidon, the best there is. We are told:

> En aprendre avoient boin sens,
> du retenir millor porpens.
> Livres lisoient paienors
> u ooient parler d'amors.
> En çou forment se delitoient,
> es engiens d'amor qu'il trovoient.
> Cius lires les fist molt haster
> en autre sens d'aus entramer
> que de l'amor de noureture
> qui lor avoit esté a cure.
> Ensamle lisent et aprendent,

---

68 R.W. Hanning, "The Audience as Co-Creator of the First Chivalric Romances," p. 8.

69 *Floire et Blancheflor*, ed. Jean-Luc Leclanche.

a la joie d'amor entendent.
Quant il repairent de l'escole,
li uns baise l'autre et acole.
Ensamble vont, ensamble vienent,
e lor joie d'amor maintienent. . . .   lines 229–42b

(In learning they had good sense,/ in remembering, even greater
capacity./ They read the books of pagans/ where they heard talk
about love./ In this they greatly delighted,/ in the games [tricks]
of love that they found there./ This reading made them hasten/ in
another sense, to love, themselves [each other]/ because love,
from their infancy/ had been their primary concern./ They read
and learn together,/ they put their thoughts to the joy of love./
When they come home from school,/ one kisses and hugs the
other./ They come and go together/ and maintain their joy of
love.)

The precocious children learn well – a bit *too* well perhaps? They read
together, apparently to each other, and their "pagan books" inspire them to
apply their lessons personally, practically. When they come home from
school, they hug and kiss . . . It is not quite clear where this reading is taking
place. And where is their tutor Gaidon? In any event, their reading and *travaux
pratiques* are to all intents and purposes "private." One wonders if this could
be a humorous reflection on the part of a non-clerk – or would it be a clerk? –
on some of the "advantages" of learning and literacy. Be that as it may, the
reading here is of an intimate and an erotic nature.

The early-thirteenth century short romance of *Floris et Liriopé* by Robert de
Blois presents a similar understanding of the uses of reading:

Ce fu en mai, ou tens serain,
Les .II. conpaignes main a main
S'asirent sous .I. olivier.
Biaus fu li leus por soulacier,
Desous vers, desoure floris;
Li rosignors biaus et jolis
En chantant les somont d'amer.
Or ne doit nuns Flori blamer,
S'il quiert de son mal medecine.
Souef vers la bele s'encline,
Doucement l'estraint a .II. bras,
En mi la bouche par solas
La baise .VII. fois par loisir.
Li grans doucors les fait fremir,
Si sont andui mout abahi
De la dousor k'il ont senti.
.I. romans aportei avoient,
Qu'eles mout volentiers lisoient,
Por ce ke tous d'amors estoit;

Et au comencement avoit,
Coment Piramus et Thyshe
Furent de Babiloine nei,
Coment li enfant s'entramerent,
Coment lor pere destornerent
Les mariaige des enfans,
Coment en avint duez si grans,
Q'en vne nuit furent ocis,
Andui an une tombe mis.
Qant ont ceste aventure lite,
Floris, cui ele mout delite,
Dist: "Dame, certes, se i'estoie
Piramus, ie vos ameroie,
Et si vos jur par toz les sains,
Que ie ne vos aim mie moins
Que cil fist la bele Tysbe;
Or me dites vostre pense . . ."   lines 955–90[70]

(It was in May, in the gentle season,/ The two companions hand in hand/ Sat down under an olive-tree./ It was a beautiful place to take pleasure,/ Under the greenery, under the flowers;/ The beautiful and pretty nightingale/ With his singing calls them to love./ One should not blame Floris,/ If he seeks a remedy to his pain./ Gently he leans toward the beauteous one,/ Gently he holds her tight in his two arms/ On her mouth for delight/ He kisses her seven times now that it is possible./ The great sweetness makes them tremble,/ They are both greatly taken aback/ By the sweetness that they have felt./ They had brought a romance with them,/ That they read willingly,/ Because it was all about love;/ And it had at the beginning/ How Piramus and Thisbe/ Were born in Babylon,/ How the children loved each other,/ How their father refused/ the marriage of the children,/ How so great a grief came of this/ That one night they were killed/ They were both put into a single tomb./ When they have read this adventure,/ Floris whom it greatly delighted,/ Said: "Lady, if I were/ Piramus, I would love you,/ And I swear by all the saints,/ that I do not love you less/ than he did the beautiful Thisbe;/ Now tell me what you think" . . .)

Liriopé feels the same way and is soon pregnant with a child whom they name Narcissus. In short, reading provides lovers with amorous, erotic, models of behavior.

In this context, how can I resist recalling that very famous scene, early in the *Inferno*, where Dante meets Francesca da Rimini, who tells him how she and Paolo ended up in hell:

[70] *Floris et Liriopé*, ed. Wolfram von Zingerle.

But if you so desire to know how fell
   The seed whose first root in our bosoms fed,
   I'll tell, as one who can but weep and tell.
One day together, for pastime, we read
   Of Lancelot, and how Love held him in thrall.
   We were alone, and without any dread.
Sometimes our eyes, at the word's secret call,
   Met, and our cheeks a changing colour wore.
   But it was one page only that did all.
When we read how that smile, so thirsted for,
   Was kissed by such a lover, he that may
   Never from me be separated more
All trembling kissed my mouth. The book I say
   Was a Galahalt to us, and he beside
   That wrote the book. We read no more that day.
While the one spirit spoke thus, the other cried
   So lamentably, that the whole life fled
   For pity out of me, as if I died;
And I fell, like a body falling dead.   Canto V, lines 121–42

Francesca blames the book and its author as matchmakers (Galehalt was the go-between between the queen and Lancelot in the *Prose Lancelot*). The reading of the story invited imitation by its readers: it provided, as it were, an "exemplary" story of the joys of sexual union. Interestingly enough, the reading lessons in *Floire et Blancheflor* and *Floris et Liriopé* imply the same thing, but the consequences in these cases are not catastrophic.

There are other settings in which groups of people are read to apparently without deleterious effect. In the early-thirteenth century romance *Li chevalier as deus espees*,[71] a messenger comes to a group sitting on a hot day by a fountain in a shady meadow. A woman reads aloud to them:

> . . . et si tenoit
> Un romant dont ele lisoit
> As chevaliers et as pucieles.   lines 8951–53

> (. . . and she was holding/ A romance from which she read/ To the knights and the maidens.)

In this passage we seem to have reading aloud as a low-key pastime in hot, "ordinary" time. But we note with interest that the reader is none other than Queen Guinevere, renowned at once as "mother" to Arthur's court and as an adulterous lover.

A brief reading scene occurs in another thirteenth century (second quarter of the century) romance: the anonymous *Hunbaut*. Kay and Sagremor, repre-

---

[71] *Li chevalier as deus espees*, ed. Wendelin Foerster.

senting King Arthur, arrive at a castle. They approach the lady of the castle, who is a "pucele."

> La pucele est contre els levee
> Si tost conme venir le[s] voit.
> O li sis puceles avoit
> Et chevaliers desi a dis;
> D'un roumant oënt uns biaus dis,
> La pucele le faissoit lire.   lines 3048–53[72]

> (The maiden stood up before them/ As soon as she saw them coming./ With her she had six maidens/ And around ten knights;/ From a romance they are listening to a beautiful speech,/ The maiden was having it read.)

It is not clear who is doing the reading here: the maiden "had the romance read" by an unidentified reader; one of the group or a clerk? The scene itself may have no particular thematic importance, but it is interesting to note that this unnamed *pucele* who "has the book read" is in love with Gawain and keeps a statue of him in her bedroom. (Kay and Sagremor mistake it for Gawain himself.) We may have here another eroticized female reader.

I have quoted a handful of fairly well-known passages that show reading aloud. It is important to recognize that these do not represent a small sample from a large category, but that they are virtually *the only such passages that exist*. This is why scholars who write about the medieval practice of reading aloud quote repeatedly from the same handful of lines. By contrast, there are dozens of passages, rarely cited, in which we find reference to the performance of romances, along with other works, by *jongleurs* and *ménestrels*.

There are also a very few references to reading aloud in less pleasant contexts: in *loci* not so *amoeni*. For example, in the epic *Florence de Rome* (first quarter of the thirteenth century), Milon, a major character, is held prisoner in a castle, but is well treated:

> Milles fut tot par lui, noblement comme sire,
> En la plus haut tor que l'en peüst eslire;
> Fables et chansonettes la font devant lui dire,
> Harper et vieller, conter romans et lire.[73]   lines 3051–54

> (Milon was all alone, but was treated nobly, like a lord,/ in the highest tower that could be found;/ they [his captors] have fables and songs told/ to [or before] him,/ and harped and vielled, and romances told and read.)

---

[72] Margaret Winters, ed., *The Romance of Hunbaut: An Arthurian Poem of the Thirteenth Century*.
[73] *Florence de Rome*, ed. A. Wollensköld.

Milon is thus sometimes read to in his solitude? Perhaps. But the entertainment provided to him is apparently performed by minstrels. Once again the word "lire" should perhaps not be taken at face value, and may be a synonym for "dire" – a synonym which presents the added advantage of providing a "prestigious" rhyme. (We have noted at many points the power of the *cachet* of the book and reading.) The verb "lire," like "dire," falls at the end of the line, and this epic is composed not in assonance but in rhyme – which means that in this 24-line *laisse* the poet had to come up with 24 words ending in "-ire"; "lire" was, then, all the more attractive.

Performance skills in public reading

Even public readers – "prelectors" – made use of at least some gestures. The recourse to appropriate, if restrained, gestures had ever been part of rhetorical "delivery" – technically termed "pronunciatio" or "actio" – and remained part of the art of public reading, as practiced by professional or trained readers. While rhetorical theoreticians primarily emphasized issues of voice, such as tone, they did leave room for a certain amount of physical gesturing. For example, the author of the influential *Ad Herennium* (this work was long attributed to Cicero) expressed his ambivalence about theatrical – "histrionic" – gestures on the part of orators when he stated:

> Physical movement consists in control of gesture and mien which renders what is delivered more plausible. Accordingly the facial expression should show modesty and animation, and the gestures should not be conspicuous for either elegance or grossness, lest we give the impression that we are either actors [*histriones*] or day laborers [*operarii*]. It seems, then, that the rules regulating bodily movement ought to correspond to the several divisions of tone comprising voice. To illustrate: (1) For the Dignified Conversational Tone, the speaker must stay in position when he speaks, lightly moving his right hand, his countenance expressing an emotion corresponding to the sentiments of the subject – gaiety or sadness or an emotion intermediate. (2) For the Explicative Conversational Tone, we shall incline the body forward a little from the shoulders, since it is natural to bring the face as close as possible to our hearers when we wish to prove a point and arouse them vigorously....[74]

The author is prepared to tolerate a modest amount of gesturing – one can move his right hand or bend the body a bit from the shoulders – to add "plausibility" ("greater probability") to the delivery. But he does not want the rhetorician ever to seem like an actor: a *histrio*. Decorum and professional dignity take precedence over dramatic verisimilitude.[75]

---

[74] [Cicero] *Ad Herennium*, ed. and trans. Harry Caplan, Book III, XV, 26, p. 203.

[75] In *Rhetoric and the Origins of Medieval Drama*, Jody Enders emphasizes the intrinsically dramatic character of rhetorical performance, or "actio," more than I do. Enders

Geoffrey of Vinsauf makes much the same sort of point in his early-thirteenth century *Poetria Nova*, stating:

> These languages should be heard in reciting: first, that of the mouth; next, that of the speaker's countenance, and, third, that of gesture . . . So tame your voice that it is not at odds with the subject, nor let it be inclined down a path other than that which the subject matter intends; let both go together: some particular tone of voice will be the perfect reflection of the subject matter.
>
> As the subject behaves, so let the speaker behave . . . If you represent the person of [the] angry man, what, as a speaker, will you do? Imitate true rage. Yet be not yourself enraged; behave partially like the character, but not inwardly. Let your behavior be the same in every detail but not to such an extent; and suggest wrath becomingly. You can also present the gestures of a rustic character and be humorous. Your voice may suggest the character's voice, your face his face, and your gestures his gestures – through little clues. This is a disciplined charm; this technique of oral recitation is appealing and this food is flavorful to the ear.
>
> A voice decently moderated, and one seasoned with twin flavors of face and manner, should therefore be so conveyed to the ears that it may feed the hearing. Power comes from speech, since life and death rest in its hands; however, language may perchance be aided, in moderation, by both expression and gesture. So, therefore, all combine: apt invention, fluent speech, sophisticated construction, steadfast memory. Read poorly, compositions have no more glory than has, read charmingly, a composition without reference to the principles that herein have gone before.[76]

This quotation demonstrates that with regard to the "pronunciation" of works, Geoffrey is primarily interested in the eloquence of a speaker or reader: in the excellence of the voice. But he is prepared to make room – just a bit of room! – for gesture: gesture "in moderation." Geoffrey wants "little clues," nothing more than that: one should "suggest wrath *becomingly*." Here again, decorum takes priority over full imitation of the emotion being evoked. One cannot help but wonder, however, if prelectors did not learn their skills in part by watching professional minstrels and other entertainers.

For untrained or amateur readers, it may not have been easy both to handle the medieval codex – hardly as *maniable* as our typical book today – and to carry out any but the simplest gestures: even when a book was placed on a lectern, both hands would typically be required to hold it open and turn the pages. Still, any skilled reader could provide the appropriate tone of voice, facial expression and the like. In any event, public reading as a performance mode deserves to be examined more thoroughly. Medieval public reading was

does, however, acknowledge the disapproval, on the part of many rhetoricians, of "show" seen as excessively dramatic.

76 "The New Poetics," in *Three Medieval Rhetorical Arts*, ed. J.J. Murphy, pp. 105–6.

often "staged," in the sense that the reader might stand or sit at an impressive lectern, which signified "authority"; it also provided a *physical* "stage": a separate space, typically higher than floor level. The lectern often had a "tester" or little roof over it, primarily, it would appear, for acoustical reasons, but this roof would also have enhanced the stage-like character of this piece of furniture.[77]

Semi-private and private reading

The rise of more-or-less private reading (including romances) appears to be correlated with the emergence of what we might call "private space" in castles, starting around 1200.[78] Until around the end of the twelfth century (and of course in some places, well beyond), castles had, as living and sleeping areas, only large halls, and almost all living appears to have been essentially communal. A case in point: the palace of the Counts of Champagne was, in the twelfth century, still of this basic design: a large hall, with few if any private apartments.[79] Typically, even the lord and lady often slept in the communal bedchamber. This feature allows for various scenes of adultery in medieval romance where a lover such as Tristan or Lancelot can leap into the queen's bed from his own bed, sometimes with other people also clearly sleeping in the same room. The only private spaces (and they weren't all *that* private!) appear to have been in gardens: *vergers*. It is there that lovers commonly seek their rendezvous, as in Béroul's *Tristan* or *Floris et Liriopé*. Small groups also gather around the hearth or in the space around windows (though Narcissus would presumably not have been conceived in such a setting).

But from the thirteenth century on, it becomes increasingly common – fashionable? – to construct private sleeping and living quarters for the key figures in the court. Originally, it would appear, only the lord and lady had such "apartments" (an interesting word, etymologically). Then such private "chambers" become more frequent.[80] One also finds references to

---

[77] See Coleman, *Public Reading*, e.g., figures 1, 7, 8, 9, 11.

[78] D.H. Green has an extremely interesting discussion of privacy and private reading in *Medieval Listening and Reading*, pp. 303ff. In general, Green seems to see more opportunities for privacy in the twelfth and thirteenth century castle than I. See also Tom McNeil, *Castles*, esp. pp. 51ff.

[79] My thanks to the archivist of the municipal library of Troyes, M. Joël Plassard, for showing me old engravings of the early palace of the Counts of Champagne, long since destroyed.

[80] Was this innovation the result of architectural innovations (the rise of Gothic construction, whose arches divided the spaces below them into smaller units)? Of social considerations, such as the desire for privacy? Or a blend of these, and perhaps other, considerations? It may be related to changes in fortification: Margaret Wood states, "The great residential tower, or 'keep,' of the Norman castle became out of date in the 13th century, at least in the south, owing to the growth in defensiveness of the curtain walls, which could guard less confined and more comfortable quarters within" (*The English*

"parlours." (It is in such a room that Pandarus finds Creseyde and two other women listening to a girl read from the siege of Troy.[81]) Truly private gardens emerge as well.[82] This is certainly an architectural and a sociological development of major importance, and one whose impact on literature, and on performance practice, has yet to be carefully explored.

What are we to make of the manuscripts containing romances (and other works) that began to become popular in the thirteenth century? Whom were they for? Who read them? First, we should note that not only laymen but apparently clerks and even monks were readers of romance: some of the manuscripts that used to be thought of as minstrel or *jongleur* manuscripts (because they were fairly inexpensively made or in poor condition) can be identified as having belonged – as Andrew Taylor has shown – to clerks, even to monks.[83]

It is also a mistake – though, again, one surely natural to those of us in literature departments – to think that a book's purpose is necessarily or exclusively to be read.[84] To be read is, one can assume, what a scribe intended (or at least to have the quality of his calligraphy admired); poets speak or write to be heard or read. But many a handsome codex was paid for by its patron primarily to compete with another book-patron and perhaps to further the constitution of a princely library "collection," or to give "authority" to the contents of the book as being true and important (such is the case of the history of great dynasties). In any case, books were, and often still are today, given as gifts. Many such gifts may in fact never have been been opened by the recipient. (Such is frequently the sad lot of books received as Christmas or birthday presents.)

But manuscripts containing romances (frequently along with other works) do begin to be common from the mid-thirteenth century on. Here, the research of Sandra Hindman is relevant. First in an article entitled "King Arthur, His Knights, and the French Aristocracy in Picardy," then in a full-length study, *Sealed in Parchment: Rereadings of Knighthood in the Illuminated Manu-*

Mediaeval House, p. 166). Wood also speaks of partitions and screens (pp. 139–47) but these too appear to post-date the twelfth century.

See *The History of the King's Works*, Vol. II: *The Middle Ages*, ed. R. Allen Brown, *et al.* In "The King's Houses 1066–1485," Brown and H.M. Colvin speak at many points of chambers being added to preexistent residences, virtually all of them from the thirteenth century on; see, e.g., pp. 896–97 (on Banstead, Surrey), pp. 902–3 (on Brill, Buckinghamshire), pp. 903–4 (on Burstwick, Yorkshire), pp. 910–18 (on Clarendon), etc.

81 *Troilus and Criseide*, Book Two, line 82; quoted from *Chaucer's Poetry*, ed. E.T. Donaldson. On parlors, see Wood, *The English Medieval House*, pp. 81ff; they did not exist in the twelfth century.

82 E.g., McNeil, *Castles*, p. 58.

83 Taylor, "The Myth," e.g., pp. 47–48, 66, 70.

84 The dangers of assuming that books offer a reliable indication of the reading habits of their owners has been discussed by R. Chartier and D. Roche in "Le livre: changement de perspective," esp. p. 123.

scripts of Chrétien de Troyes, Hindman has carefully examined the late-thirteenth and fourteenth century illustrated manuscripts which contain Chrétien's romances. Several of her points are worth setting out in detail here. First, manuscripts containing Chrétien's romances are, to a remarkable degree, Picard in origin, and, in their iconographic programs, they speak to the particular political concerns of the Picard aristocracy in this period.

Second, these manuscripts show clear signs of wear; they were unquestionably used: read. Several of the manuscripts, however, valorize oral performance or recitation of romance. Hindman speaks frequently of a "culture of orality" evoked by most of the manuscripts. That is, some of the romance manuscripts may have been read aloud;[85] the pictures would have been shown and explained to listeners. That a few of the manuscripts show food stains may suggest that they were read at mealtime.[86] (Medieval people do not appear to have done much "snacking" or solitary dining: eating was a communal activity.) These romances were most likely read by an amateur reader – or in any event, by a reader who partook of the meal and handled the book carelessly.

Hindman also, however, suggests that some manuscripts appear to function as *metaphors* for oral culture: the book is "no longer dependent on an external performer" (p. 195). She believes that some manuscripts, such as Paris, BN MS fr. 24403, invited reading and seeing, rather than hearing (p. 162). She thinks that the romances may sometimes have been read fully privately and silently (p. 44). But we should note that the manuscripts she discusses date from the late-thirteenth and early-fourteenth centuries; the Paris manuscript, which in Hindman's view the most clearly invites seeing and reading, probably dates from around 1300. For the earlier period – the late-twelfth and early-thirteenth centuries – we have seen no evidence at all of private or silent reading of romance or other works of entertainment.[87] In this context it is worth noting that Hindman sees the manuscripts she discusses not just as offering the text of romances but as presenting them in the framework of a strongly political and historical agenda: thus these romances may not have functioned primarily *as* entertainment.

From the late-thirteenth century on, public reading (what Coleman calls "prelection") becomes increasingly common.[88] From here on, references to this performance mode become more frequent. The best-known case in French literature is that of Froissart (1337–1404), who read aloud from his (octo)

---

85 *Sealed*, pp. 91, 94.

86 Hindman, *Sealed*, p. 3, for reference to the food-stains, but she does not make the association with mealtime-reading.

87 See, for example, Noakes, *Timely Reading*: "Only in the mid-fourteenth century did the nobility of France begin to accept silent reading. The consequences of this fact are . . . far-reaching . . .," p. 26.

88 See Coleman, *Public Reading*.

romance *Méliador* to Gaston Phébus, Comte de Foix, at night after supper (Gaston, apparently what we would call a "night-person," typically had supper at midnight), in the winter of 1377–78.[89]

Much of this public reading, especially in great courts, appears to have been of an edifying, informative or "improving" nature: for example, from works given as providing ethical exempla or as "historical." Often such works glorified the aristocratic house in question. We have already seen this phenomenon with regard to the Plantagenets; Hindman suggests something along these lines for the Picard aristocracy. In the fourteenth and fifteenth centuries, such is also the case of the Court of Burgundy. (One sees this, for example, in the interest of the Burgundian dukes in their "ancestor," the epic hero Girart de Roussillon, who was a great feudal baron in revolt against his lord, the King of France. The *chanson de geste* starring Girart was translated into "modern" French for the Duke,[90] and also put into prose for him.[91]) Much public reading in France had a rather "official" character.[92] But – and the point is capital – there seems to be no evidence that reading aloud was ever practiced at great festive occasions in French courts in the Middle Ages[93] – or, for that matter, at *any* period.

What we have still to examine, in the gamut of performance modes, is fully private – that is, solitary – reading. But it is hard to examine because there are hardly any references to it. Indeed, of truly private reading of vernacular, secular works of entertainment in the twelfth and thirteenth centuries I have been unable to find more than one or two mentions. Gautier d'Arras' *Éracle* contains a brief reference to solitary romance-reading. Against the advice of the eponymous hero, the Empress Athanaïs was imprisoned in a tower by her jealous husband, the emperor, before he went away to war. He left her in the company of twenty-four knights and their wives, but, bitter and indignant, she spends her days in angry monologues and in private reading.

> La dame sist sor un tapis
> en sus des autres, auques loing;
> de lor socïeté n'a soing,
> il ne li torne a nus delit.
> Un livre tient et si i list.   lines 4240–44[94]

---

[89] See Froissart, *Chroniques*, Vol. XII, ed. Léon Mirot, pp. 75–76, and "Le Dit du Florin," in *"Dits" et "Débats"*, ed. Anthime Fourrier, pp. 183–84; also Peter Dembowski, *Jean Froissart and his Meliador*, pp. 54–56. Coleman discusses this extended prelection in *Public Reading*, pp. 110–12.

[90] *Girart de Roussillon, poème bourguignon du XIVe siècle*, ed. E.B. Ham.

[91] See *Girart de Roussillon ou l'épopée de Bourgogne*, annotated by Marcel Thomas and Michel Zink, trans. into modern French by Roger-Henri Guerrand.

[92] Coleman *Public Reading*, esp. pp. 141ff.

[93] See Coleman, *Public Reading*, esp. Ch. 5, "Aural History."

[94] Gautier d'Arras, *Eracle*, ed. Guy Raynaud de Lage.

(The lady sits on a rug/ below the others, rather far from them;/ she has no interest in their company,/ it gives her no pleasure./ She holds a book and reads in it.)

This is not simply innocent solace (such as many modern readers have practiced when vexed or depressed). This private reader has already met and fallen in love with the man with whom she will soon begin an adulterous affair: Paridés. We have here then a rather special – clearly anti-social and immoral – sort of private reading. The way in which the Empress has turned her back on her companions prepares her future sinful (so it is presented here) behavior.

If the private reading of works of entertainment existed as a general phenomenon, it was not much discussed. One does find the solitary reading of love letters, or the decoding of other love missives sent by one lover to the other, like the inscribed hazel branch in Marie de France's "Chèvrefeuille." But this is not, strictly speaking, "entertainment reading" (at least not to true lovers).

Yet again, it is with Froissart, in the mid- to late-fourteenth century, that we see changes: it is in his work that we first find references in any quantity to solitary reading of romance. In *L'Espinette amoureuse* (c.1370) the poet tells how as a young man he liked to read romances:

Et quant li temps venoit divers
Qui nous est appellés yvers,
Qu'il faisoit laid et pouvieus,
Par quoi je ne fuisse anoisus,
A mon quois, pour esbas eslire,
Ne vosisse que rommans lire.
Especiaument les traitiers
D'amour lisoie volentiers,
Car je concevoie en lisant
Toute cose qui m'iert plaisant; . . .   lines 309–318[95]

(And when the season was unstable [or unpleasant]/ Which we call winter,/ And it was ugly and rainy,/ So that I would not be bored [or irritated],/ In my leisure, to find enjoyment,/ I wanted nothing but to read romances./ Especially treatises/ Of love did I read willingly,/ For I conceived in reading/ Everything that was pleasing to me; . . .)

Froissart tells how he came upon a young woman reading a romance, *Cléomadés* (by Adenet le Roy) to herself:

Droitement sus l'eure de prime
S'esbatoit une damoiselle

95 Jean Froissart, *L'Espinette amoureuse*, ed. Anthime Fourrier.

Au lire .I. rommanc. Moi vers elle
M'en ving et li dis doucement:
"Par son nom ce rommanc comment
L'appellés vous, ma belle et douce?"
Elle cloy atant la bouce,
Sa main dessus le livre adoise;
Lors respondi comme courtoise
Et me dist: "De *Cléomadés*
Est appellés. Il fu bien fes
Et dittés amoureusement.
Vous l'orés, si dirés comment
Vous plaira dessus vostre avis."   lines 696–709

(Right at the hour of prime/ A young lady was enjoying herself/ Reading a romance. I toward her/ Came and I said to her gently:/ "How by its name do you call/ This romance, my beautiful and sweet one?"/ She closed her mouth then/ She placed her hand on the book;/ Then she answered me in a courteous [courtly] fashion/ And said to me: "About Cléomadés/ Is it called. It was well done/ And spoken lovingly./ You will hear it, and will tell [me] how/ It pleases you, in your opinion.")

This young woman is reading to herself, not silently but aloud: she closes her mouth when Froissart interrupts her. (Such a scene tends to confirm what Paul Saenger has argued: that silent reading in the vernacular came in only very late in the medieval period.[96]) Moreover, while this young lady reads "alone," she is nonetheless reading a romance in a place which is not truly private: the garden in which Froissart sees her. As noted earlier, while gardens offered some privacy, they were not as fully private as lovers or conspirators might have liked. Perhaps such an activity should be construed as one designed, precisely, to attract the attention of young gentlemen, and not as the action of one determined to maintain her privacy. To read a romance, understood perhaps as a narrative "art of love," in public was perhaps like publishing a discreet "Personal Ad." In fact, virtually all the romance-reading that Froissart refers to seems to have as its purpose to feed the "amorous" (and erotic) fantasy life, and to prepare the solitary reader to become, in the near future, half of a couple.

These are, then, references to solitary reading of romance, though all seem to show readers who hope soon not to *be* alone. These texts date from the mid-fourteenth century or later. From the earlier period (the twelfth and thirteenth

---

[96] Paul Saenger argued that silent reading became fairly common in the late medieval period: "Silent Reading: Its Impact on late Medieval Script and Society." In *Public Reading*, Coleman finds little evidence for medieval vernacular silent reading; see, e.g., pp. 20ff.

centuries), I have found only the single, and ethically unprepossessing, reference from *Éracle*.[97] It is of course theoretically possible that private reading was popular, but that writers didn't want to talk about it and readers didn't care to read about it. But this would itself be an interesting fact – one pointing presumably to a sense of discomfort, even of guilt, about private reading. In any case, Joyce Coleman has argued compellingly that public reading of works of entertainment was the dominant mode of *réalisation* throughout the medieval period; solitary reading of such works was rare. Books of Hours, and other forms of pious or "improving" reading, were of course different.[98] One tends to think that *mises en prose* and prose compilations were also handled differently from verse romances; such may be the case. But prose romances (and other prose works) continue to speak primarily in terms of audition: that is, they too speak to listeners, though the narratorial "I" is generally gone; it is the book itself which speaks. And – again, according to Coleman's evidence – many of the works read aloud in Burgundian and other French courts were in prose.

Some kinds of works were, nonetheless, in all likelihood sometimes read privately. The list includes: scientific and didactic works, such as lapidaries; historical works, as well. It also includes biblical texts, such as the Psalter; religious works such as saints' lives, inspirational texts; in the later Middle Ages, Books of Hours. With regard to the Psalter we may recall the scene in *Yvain* where the widow (soon to be the hero's wife) is described as reading from a gold-lettered Psalter; this scene was discussed in some detail in Chapter 4. Whether or not it shows full literacy, this scene certainly shows private book *use*.[99] But as regards biblical and devotional works, it is striking that some "texts" – especially early ones – speak explicitly in terms of audition. For example, the "Eructavit," a twelfth century psalm paraphrase, composed – significantly, for our concerns – for Marie of Champagne (and attributed to Adam of Perseigne[100]), says at various points things like: "Qui bien orroit et antandroit/ Que cist vers conte ci androit,/ Toz li cuers li devroit esmuevre/ A

---

[97] Lady Constance, the wife of Ralf Fitz Gilbert and patroness of the mid-twelfth century Anglo-Norman poet Geffroi Gaimar does seem to have been a private reader. Geoffrey refers to a book by a certain "Davit"; "Dame Custance en ad l'escrit,/ En sa chambre sovent le lit/ E ad pur l'escrire doné/ Un marc d'argent ars e pesé" (lines 6489–92; Lady Constance has a written copy of it,/ She reads it often in her chamber/ And for the writing she gave/ One mark of silver burned and weighed). It is highly unlikely that the book that Constance read in her room was a romance: it has been hypothesized that the author referred to here was David, bishop of Bangor, and his book was probably written in Latin; it could also well have been the Psalter, ascribed to King David. See Geoffroi Gaimar, *L'Estoire des Engleis*, ed. Alexander Bell, pp. 205, 278.

[98] See Clanchy, *From Memory*; Green, *Medieval Listening*.

[99] On these issues, see also Clanchy, *From Memory*, esp. pp. 185–96, 217–18, 251–52. See also Green, *Medieval Listening*, esp. pp. 204ff.

[100] See Adam of Perseigne, *Eructavit*, ed. T. Atkinson Jenkins. This interesting figure was discussed in Chapter 4.

bien penser et a bone oevre'' (''He who listens to and hears well/ What these verses tell here,/ His whole heart should be moved/ To think good thoughts, and to good works''; lines 1687–90). Marie is said to be someone who willingly ''hears'' the word of God: ''Mout met son cuer a bone escole,/ Qui volantiers ot sa parole,/ Et vos, dame, estes toz jorz preste/ De öir et d'estre an anqueste'' (''He puts his heart very much to a good school/ Who willingly hears His word,/ And you, my lady, are always ready,/ To hear and to be seeking for God''; lines 2093–6).

Another sort of private reading that existed, presumably from a fairly early period, was what Coleman calls ''professional'' reading, which could be literary or scholarly in nature: professional poets and writers read, at least sometimes to themselves, the works of other writers, for inspiration and to stay abreast of the latest fashions and developments: to be *à la page*.[101]

And of course private letters – especially love letters – were read privately. (Sometimes they were read aloud by a clerk in a private setting, if the recipient was illiterate, but that is not what I mean by ''private reading.''[102]) The earliest reference in French romance to the reading – and the writing – of love letters is, I believe, in the *Énéas*, where Lavinie herself writes a letter to Énéas to declare her love for him and shoots it to him wound around an arrow. (This detail may well be somewhat lacking in verisimilitude: an arrow would not be apt to fly straight with a letter tied around it; never mind!) Énéas is presented as literate: he ''sees'' what is in the letter for himself.[103] It is interesting to note that the actual words of the letter are not quoted; the poet is apparently less concerned with what the letter says in detail than with a) Lavinie's amorous initiative, b) her ability to write, and Énéas' to read, and c) the arrow as vehicle for the post.

A number of scholars have listed the kinds of reading and literacy that existed in the Middle Ages. Clanchy (for example) distinguishes between ''learned,'' ''sacred,'' ''bureaucratic'' and ''vernacular'' literacy. But if we put together the reading of romance by lovers (and would-be lovers) and the reading of love-letters, it seems that we need to carve out from ''vernacular literacy'' a major sub-category: ''erotic'' or ''amorous literacy.''[104] But what we have *not* yet found – at least in the period under consideration here – is what can truly be called ''*literary* literacy'': that is, a literacy that springs from a love of vernacular letters in and of themselves; a love of the pleasures derived from the reading of literature. This kind of vernacular literacy may indeed be, in the Middle Ages, as rare as a black swan.

---

[101] *Public Reading*, pp. 88ff: ''A typology of late medieval English literacies''; and *passim*.

[102] See Green, *Medieval Listening*, esp. pp. 308ff.

[103] *Énéas*, Salverda de Grave, ed., Vol. II, lines 8775ff.

[104] See Clanchy, ''Looking Back from the Invention of Printing,'' p. 18.

Conclusions

A number of conclusions can be drawn from this cursory examination of the performance spectrum, the first of course being that there is much to be done to refine and elaborate it. In particular, it would be interesting to examine carefully the "shape" of a festive court event, insofar as we can reconstruct it. What do we know about the different kinds of entertainment – literary, musical and choreographical performances – that took place? Which sorts of perform-ances took place during the meal, which after? Was there a progression, such as one might perhaps expect to find, from relatively sedate or serious works to more comic and irreverent works? And so on.

But we can already see that a fundamental belief appears to be in need of serious revision. This belief goes something as follows: "Chrétien (et al.) may well have had, as his original public, mostly people who listened to his romances. But, very soon, he had the audience his works deserve: readers – that is, private readers; readers such as ourselves." There are several things wrong with this picture. Those "listeners" also probably saw Chrétien's works performed, in some semi-dramatic fashion. And there is no reason *not* to think that Chrétien himself was the original performer of his own works. He does not just say that we will hear "stories" – this is common in all kinds of works, just as it is common to be told that we will hear "about" someone or something – but that we will hear *him*. For example, in *Cligés*: "Einçois *m*'orroiz dire . . ." (line 563; "Thus you will hear *me* tell . . ."), and "*M*'orroiz adés de lui conter" (line 2350; "You will soon hear *me* tell about him [Cligés]"). It would be easy to multiply such examples.

Very soon, other performers were clearly "doing" Chrétien's romances. (*Flamenca* shows this.) But his romances, when they *were* read, were in all likelihood read aloud to groups, and only rarely – by no means typically – by solitary readers. His only private readers may have been other narrative poets and writers.

By the time non-professional solitary readers did emerge, in the late Middle Ages, Chrétien's works would have become virtually unreadable: linguisti-cally incomprehensible, as well as out of fashion stylistically. To be under-stood and appreciated, they had to be not merely *mis en prose* but also to have their French updated, from *Ancien* to *Moyen*. In short, Chrétien de Troyes may have had few medieval readers.[105] In any case, for every private reader he had,

---

[105] It is perhaps worth reminding ourselves, one last time, just how uncommon the ability to read *was* in medieval and early-modern Europe. For example, in *Literacy and the Social Order: Reading and Writing in Tudor and Stuart England*, David Cressy has stated: "Evidence from the seventeenth century . . . shows that England was massively illiterate despite an epoch of educational expansion and a barrage of sermons. More than two-thirds of the men and nine-tenths of the women were so illiterate at the time of the civil war that

225

there must have been scores who "knew his work" by hearing it recited or sung, or read aloud, or retold in a different form – perhaps in a shorter form, or a different tongue.

The literacy or illiteracy of the poet, patrons, and audience, while unquestionably important, appears not to have been, by any means, the overriding consideration in determining the mode of performance. At least three factors counted more: 1) The intrinsic nature of the event and the magnitude of the celebration that it was considered to command. 2) The financial and other resources available in the establishment in question. 3) The social or interpersonal functions the performance was intended to fill. (We will return to several of these issues in the final chapter.) As Joyce Coleman has shown, public reading had a strongly social role: many of the people who were read to throughout the medieval period were themselves fully literate; they just liked being read aloud to, and believed (as many still do today) that reading aloud and being read to were a Good Thing.

It is often said that references to "orality" – for example, to listeners and listening – are, even in the twelfth and thirteenth centuries, merely "nostalgic," echoes of a bygone oral era. I submit that the evidence from a variety of sources, both literary and historical, suggests that such is anything but the case. Medieval people, certainly those in twelfth and early-thirteenth century France, heard and saw romances performed far more often than they read them for themselves. In France and Anglo-Norman England,[106] audiences did not even begin to hear romances read to them with any frequency until well into the thirteenth century, probably even later. These numerous references are not to a "fictive orality," but to an oral and performance *reality*.

The evidence suggests that medieval romances were frequently performed in a strongly physical, indeed a dramatic, fashion. The evidence also suggests that the performance practice of medieval romance allowed for a good deal of variation: the range goes from fairly sedate prelection, modestly enlivened with intonation and gestures, all the way to virtually theatrical performance. Some performances of romance appear to have contained substantial admix-

---

they could not even write their own names" (p. 2). Such statements must surely give one pause. If such was the case after the Reformation – after the Bible had become readily accessible in the vernacular – what was it like four and five centuries earlier? Most people, unless they were read to, simply had no access to books – nor did they necessarily feel that they needed such access.

106 The situation in England may well have been different, and in advance of France, in terms of reading habits. More early references to reading seem to come from England than from France. As to Germany: Wolfram von Eschenbach, who was a knight, not a clerk, appears to have produced his *Parzival* to be read aloud to noble audiences; one piece of evidence for this is that his romance survives in manuscripts which appear to have circulated in fascicles. (See *Parzival*, Penguin ed., intro by A.T. Hatto, p. 11.) On listening vs. reading in Germany, see D.H. Green, "On the Primary Reception of Narrative Literature in Medieval Literature" and, more recently, *Medieval Listening and Reading*; see also Scholz, *Hören und Lesen*.

tures of music, and of dance and acrobatics as well. But what we hardly find, if at all, is the kind of performance we all would have expected to find typical, precisely because it is second nature to us: private, solitary, silent reading.

But one thing seems clear: nostalgia for orality will have to wait.

CHAPTER SEVEN

On the "Memory-Friendliness" of Verse Romance

The last chapter reviewed the considerable evidence that romances were commonly recited – indeed, played and even sung – without a text: thus, from memory. It is, however, difficult for us today to understand how *jongleurs*, minstrels and other professional and amateur entertainers managed to learn romances and other long works by heart. It will be the purpose of this chapter to lay out and discuss important ways in which verse romances invited being learned "by heart." It is not enough simply to declare – or even to demonstrate – that romance had, to a substantial degree, an oral existence; we need to examine how romances, like so many other works, *functioned* as part of oral culture.

Scholarship in the humanities has focused considerable attention on the ways in which artificial memory systems were, in past centuries, brought to bear on all manner of material – much of this material being powerfully recalcitrant to memorization. Among the major books that have been devoted to such issues are Frances A. Yates' classic *The Art of Memory*, and Mary Carruthers' recent and extremely influential study, *The Book of Memory*.

Our concerns are rather different. Our problem is to try to understand how medieval romances (and to some degree, other works, though our focus is on romance) were geared to making the work of memory *easy*. We will be looking at the phenomenon I call "memory-friendliness." Among the scholars from whom I will draw general inspiration is Marcel Jousse, who argued in *The Oral Style* that poets made considerable recourse to "mnemotechnical devices" in order to make:

> . . . the memorisation and re-memorisation of his . . . composition easier for himself and his "repeaters," [the poet] makes use of certain devices the function of which is to assist in the initial triggering, or the original linking-together, of the propositional gestures of a recitative, and to keep the recitatives of recitation in their proper order.[1]

A surprisingly small amount of attention has been paid to this issue, in

---

[1] Pp. 164–65. Jousse considered this use of mnemotechnics to be conscious, which may or may not be the case. Jousse was also almost entirely concerned with fully oral poets, and with improvised compositions, which are not our concerns here.

particular with regard to medieval vernacular literature: to the ways in which medieval works invited memorization.[2] It is quite true that "formulas" – those partially prefabricated chunks of words with which many of the lines of epic are constructed – have received a great deal of attention. (It must, however, be added that the emphasis has tended to be more on the processes of oral composition through formulas than on memory itself.) In any event, I have argued, at various points in this book, and with regard to a variety of issues bearing on orality and literacy, that it is important to move away from an exclusive preoccupation with the epic: focus on the *chanson de geste* can give us only part of the oral/written picture in the twelfth century. There has been a tendency to think of the epic, and only the epic, as "oral," which leaves romance (and other genres) holding the literary bag. But this dichotomy – in any event, in its simple form – does not hold up. In particular, it cannot be argued (at least not cogently) that only epics and formulas have been "remembered" by oral performers; people have learned many other kinds of works as well.

The general question is this: what makes a performed "literary" work intrinsically easy to remember: memorable? By "performed," I mean recited or played to a live audience. By "memorable": easy to remember both for performers and listeners. A *trouvère* who works within the oral, performed tradition has a stake in making his work memorable for both performers and audiences: the more people tell and re-tell, sing and re-sing, his creations, the greater his reputation – and presumably the rewards for his compositions and, perhaps, public appearances. We are concerned here with a wide range of memory practices, from full-scale, verbatim "memorization" to more general recall.

My basic argument – to some degree it is surely self-evident – is that works composed with performance in mind[3] are set up to require a minimum of effort on the part of those who wish to learn them "by heart." Their poets make it as easy as possible for performers to master them in their entirety, and for listeners to recall both the essence of the story – *memoria ad res* – and at least parts of the actual "text": *memoria ad verba*.

Our primary examples will come from Chrétien's *Yvain*, though we will have a look at other romances of his. We have already examined Chrétien's

2   Carruthers has studied such issues in a number of important recent articles, including "Inventional Mnemonics and the Ornaments of Style: The Case of Etymology"; a number of chapters in *Jeux de mémoire: aspects de la mnémotechnie médiévale*, ed. Bruno Roy and Paul Zumthor, address issues that are close to mine.

3   Many writers have also known how to make their works "memorable" in a variety of ways: by creating unforgettable characters, scenes, and the like. What I am discussing here is not "peculiar" to the oral tradition. It is, however, worth remembering that some of the more-or-less modern writers whose creations are the most unforgettable, such as Dickens, often gave (or anticipated giving) public readings of their works: these works were thus, in an important sense of the term, "performed."

work from a variety of perspectives bearing on oral culture.[4] *Yvain* provides an excellent example of the ways in which both romance form and content can solicit memorization – and thus function as part of "oral tradition," in this sense of the term.

I do not claim that this romance (or any of Chrétien's romances) is unusual with regard to memory-friendliness. I take *Yvain* as providing a familiar and attractive example of the ways in which memorability is set at the heart of a verse romance in general, rather than because I see his work as unique in this regard.

There can be little doubt that Chrétien wanted his works to be not just successful in some vague sense, but remembered. He said of *Érec et Énide*: this is a story "qui toz jorz mes iert an mimoire/ tant con durra crestïantez;/ de ce s'est Crestïens vantez" (lines 24–26: "which will forever be in memory/ as long as Christianity lasts;/ this is what Chrétien has claimed"). There is, of course, a venerable classical *topos*, often termed the "aere perennius topos," which bears on the enduring quality of great literary "monuments." But in this period – before the emergence of a French manuscript tradition – for a vernacular poet, a *trouvère* who does not call himself a clerk, to express his hope of being "remembered," means that he hopes people will literally remember his stories.

We begin with *memoria ad res* and with the characters of the romance. The hero is identified by the name "Yvain," but also – and in a mnemonically far more powerful way – by his association with the lion who is his companion for the entire second half of the story: he is "the knight with the lion." And as though it were not already memorable enough just to have an ordinary lion as a companion, this is an altogether amazing – as Ong would say, a very "heavy" – lion. As we saw in the previous chapter, he kneels and performs feudal gestures of homage; he attempts suicide; he tears the limbs off demons; he follows his master like a faithful dog. This lion is a truly memorable creature. We will return at various points below to criteria of memorability, but one should be mentioned in this context: the color red in general, and blood and gore in particular are considered by virtually all memory theorists to be "memorable": violence, like sex, is what human beings seem to remember best.[5] This lion is repeatedly associated with blood, his own and that of others.

To return to Yvain himself: he exemplifies the way in which story-tellers have traditionally made a central character memorable: by combining the

---

[4] I have argued that the form in which Chrétien and other *romanciers* worked – the octosyllabic rhymed couplet – was originally an oral form; that Chrétien himself may well have been a minstrel rather than a clerk (and thus that he was perhaps not a writer at all); that he conceived his work with voiced performance in mind, and indeed that his poems were intended for full-scale performance, perhaps by him in person. The issue of their intrinsic memorability is yet another part of the overall picture.

[5] See Yates, *The Art*, e.g., pp. 52, 66, 68; Carruthers, *The Book*, pp. 134ff.

"stock" and the bizarre. That is, Yvain is in many respects a standard, or stock, hero: perfectly handsome, noble, chivalric, etc. As such he is easy to remember precisely because he is like all the rest. This is what psychologists call "redundancy": that which is repeated, predictable, reliably present – redundant – is easy to recall, thus memorable. But, in another sense, the standard hero is also unmemorable – again, precisely because he is like virtually every other romance hero. It is hard to tell such heroes apart.

But the constructors of memory systems generally emphasize a different principle of "memorability": it is that which is extreme – indeed the bizarre – that is memorable.[6] It would be useful to look systematically at the ways in which medieval heroes and heroines (of romance and epic as well) constitute a combination of stock and bizarre elements, both in a different sense "memorable." I cannot undertake that large task here, but let us recall at least a few great names, with their titles of perfection and their eccentricities: Tristan, perfectly handsome (though in the surviving text never described in detail), who "loved more than anyone else ever did," and to whom all other lovers are compared; he is also harpist and dog-trainer *extraordinaire* (he trains Husdent to hunt without barking, so as not to draw attention to the lovers). Iseut, of perfect beauty, with hair brighter than gold. True, these details aren't especially bizarre, but there is generally a limit to how strange a poet of romance or lai can make his heroes and heroines, without making them violate medieval canons of beauty and perfection – and that would never do. One of the ways in which poets handled this issue is by making a character alternately superlatively perfect, and deviant: for example, Marie de France's werewolf hero, Bisclavret, who most of the time is a handsome and devoted husband; or Mélusine, the famous heroine of the eponymous romance, who is perfectly lovely – except on Saturdays, when she turns into a serpent. Each of these stories turns on the impact of an alarming, and certainly memorable, physical attribute of the character's spouse. Mélusine's marriage, incidentally, produces memorable children, each with a remarkable feature/defect: "Geoffroi a la grant dent," *et al.* Probably the classic way in which romance poets combined the stock and the bizarre was by having bizarre things happen to fairly standard (handsome/beautiful, etc.) figures. Poets and story-tellers working in a comic or folkloric framework have had their hands a good deal freer and could make even their central figures as weird as they wished. *Chanson de geste* heroes tended to be more physically bizarre than those of romance, presumably because their identity – their perfection – was not dependent on their beauty. Thus, for example, Guillaume d'Orange – the central figure of a vast cycle, with numerous poems – is reliably described as extremely, even disproportionately, large, with an ugly nose, part of which was cut off by a Saracen giant, Corsolt, who then made fun of Guillaume. One

---

6 See Yates, *The Art*, e.g., pp. 13, 68, 77, 92, 95–97; Carruthers, *The Book*, e.g., pp. 71, 80, 87, 134–35.

might suspect that this nasal amputation is sufficiently similar to castration to be particularly memorable to most of the members of an epic audience. Guillaume declares that, though his nose is now diminished, his name will become longer: he will now be called not just "Guillaume" but "Guillaume au cort nes." More than one pagan princess falls in love with him subsequently; Orable, in particular, converts to marry him, changing her name to Guibourc.

But to return, yet again, to Yvain: before pairing him up with the lion, Chrétien had already made of his hero a temporarily bizarre figure: a naked wildman, driven insane from grief at the loss of his wife's love and humiliation at his dishonor. And the wildman was both one of the most popular and one of the most bizarre iconographic figures of the medieval period, often used emblematically.[7]

Other characters of lesser importance to the plot are also rendered memorable by the strange visual images they conjure up: for example, the giant herdsman, whose massive frame and unbelievable ugliness – and his ability to herd bulls (he takes them by the horns and knocks their heads together) – are described for us in some detail (lines 292ff). Carruthers says of memory images: "The stranger, the better."[8] The author of the *Ad Herennium* said: "[I]f we see or hear something exceptionally base, dishonourable, extraordinary, great, unbelievable, or laughable, that we are likely to remember a long time."[9] (The strangeness criterion is also, as we noted earlier, relevant to the lion, who is in many respects a very abnormal lion; therefore memorable.) Yvain's phase as a wildman also echoes the wildness of the herdsman. We are also invited to visualize the Giant ("Harpin de la montagne" – line 3851), though what is primarily memorable here is that he kills sons and rapes daughters. The 300 half-naked maidens in the "ouvroir" (lines 5188ff) also invite such visualization. Once again, sex and violence.

Another principle is operative here as well. Chrétien's characters generally fall into three groups: 1) Those whose names were apparently already familiar from tradition – known, thus already remembered – such as Arthur, Yvain, Gauvain, and the like. 2) Those whose names are of virtually no importance, and who are often referred to by some other feature or title: thus, as noted, Laudine is never named in most manuscripts and is simply Yvain's "lady" or the "lady of the fountain." 3) Those whose names Chrétien attempts to anchor in the memory of his audience. Here we find "Lunete," the etymology of whose name Chrétien emphasizes – "lune" – and who is paired up briefly

---

7 Timothy Husband, *The Wild Man: Medieval Myth and Symbolism*; Richard Bernheimer, *Wild Men in the Middle Ages: A Study in Art, Sentiment, and Demonology*.

8 Lecture at New York University, March 1994: "Literacy, Orality, Memory: Reconsidering 'The Ornaments of Style.' " See also *The Book*, pp. 134ff.

9 See, e.g., *Ad Herennium, III*, XXII, p. 219.

with Gauvain, that "sun of chivalry."[10] Thus, the moon and the sun are brought together – in a paradoxical but appropriate meeting.

De la joie assez vos contasse
se ma parole n'i gastasse;
mes seulemant de l'acontance
voel faire une brief remambrance
qui fu feite a privé consoil
entre la lune et le soleil.
Savez de cui je vos voel dire?
Cil qui des chevaliers fu sire
et qui sor toz fu reclamez
doit bien estre solauz clamez.
Por mon seignor Gauvain le di,
que de lui est tot autresi
chevalerie anluminee,
come solauz la matinee
oevre ses rais, et clarté rant
por toz les leus ou il s'espant.
Et ce celi refaz la lune
dom il ne puet este que une,
de grant foi et de grant aïe.
Et ne poroec, je nel di mie
seulemant par son grant renon,
mes por ce que Lunete ot non.   lines 2395–416

(I would tell you a lot about the joy,/ if I wouldn't be wasting my words/ but I only want to make a brief remembrance/ of the acquaintanceship/ which took place in a private meeting/ between the moon and the sun./ Do you know whom I mean?/ He who was of knights the lord/ and who above all others was renowned/ must be called the sun./ I say it of my lord Gauvain,/ because by him is in the same way [as the sun]/ all chivalry illuminated,/ just as the sun lights the morning,/ works his rays and gives brightness/ to all the places where he extends himself./ And with it [the light] he restores the moon,/ of which there can only be one,/ with great faith and great aid./ And I do not say it only/ for his great renown,/ but because her name was Lunete.)

Chrétien has thus made Lunete and her name memorable by attaching them to the famous Gawain, and to his identity as the sun of chivalry.

In the same category belong both the heroines of *Cligés*. The first, Soredamors, delivers quite an elaborate etymological – or we might say "semiological" – discourse on her own name, in lines 953–80. She must love, she says – her name proves it. (I will return to this passage shortly, and quote it in full.)

10 See Carruthers, "Inventional Mnemonics."

233

Such a passage certainly anchors the heroine's name, Soredamors, firmly in our memory. (I am not of course arguing that this is Chrétien's sole purpose here.) The same is true of Fénice, the heroine of the second part of the romance. When she is first introduced to us, we are told:

> Fenyce ot la pucele a non:
> Ce ne fu mie sanz reison,
> Car si con fenix li oisiax
> Est sor toz les autres plus biax,
> Ne estre n'an pot c'uns ansanble,
> Ice Fenyce me resamble:
> N'ot de biauté nule paroille.
> Ce fu miracles et mervoille
> C'onques a sa paroille ovrer
> Ne pot Nature recovrer. . . .   lines 2685–94

(The girl had the name Fénice [Phoenix]:/ And it wasn't without reason,/ For just as the bird the phoenix/ Is, in comparison with all others, the most beautiful,/ And there can only be one of them,/ Here Fénice seems to me similar:/ In beauty she had no equal./ It was a miracle and a marvel/ That never, to make her equal,/ Was Nature able to do it. . . .)

The description of Fénice's great beauty goes on for a good many more lines. But what is particularly interesting here is that Chrétien uses etymological concepts quite fully and elaborately to anchor this heroine and her story in our memory. Fénice is, as we saw in this first etymological passage, "unique" in beauty. But Fénice is also, precisely, the heroine who will – as her name implies – arise from her own ashes: come back to life. (She wasn't really dead, but never mind. A "fausse morte," she was buried in her tomb – her idea: all this to get away from her husband, and be able to marry the man she loved, Cligés.) In other words, her name helps us – who have of course heard stories from "bestiaries" – to remember her story, as distinct from that of various other heroines. At the end of the romance, Chrétien uses yet another sort of mnemonic anchor of an etymological character: a story of origins. We are told that Fénice and Cligés lived (essentially) happily ever after.

> Et chascun jor lor amors crut,
> Onques cil de li ne mescrut,
> Ne querela de nule chose:
> N'onques ne fu tenue anclose,
> Si com ont puis esté tenues
> Celes qu'aprés li sont venues;
> Einz puis n'i ot empereor
> N'eüst de sa fame peor
> Qu'ele nel deüst decevoir,
> Se il oï ramantevoir

234

Comant Fenice Alis deçut,
Primes par la poison qu'il but,
Et puis par l'autre traïson.
Por ce einsi com an prison
Est gardee an Costantinoble,
Ja n'iert tant haute de tant noble,
L'empererriz, quex qu'ele soit:
L'empereres point ne s'i croit,
Tant con de celi li remambre;
Toz jorz la fet garder en chanbre
Plus por peor que por le hasle,
Ne ja avoec li n'avra masle
Qui ne soit chastrez en anfance.
De ce n'est criemme ne dotance
Qu'Amors les lit an son lïen.
Ci fenist l'uevre Chrestïen.   lines 6639–64

(And every day their love grew,/ Never did he distrust her,/ Nor did he chide about anything;/ Never was she kept locked up [enclosed],/ The way that, every since, are kept/ Those who came after her [Fénice];/ Ever since then, there was no emperor/ Who wasn't afraid of his wife,/ That she would deceive him,/ If he hears it recalled/ How Fénice deceived Alis,/ First by the poison that he drank,/ And then by the other treachery./ For this, as though in prison,/ Is kept in Constantinople,/ No matter how high-born or noble,/ The empress, whoever she may be:/ The emperor does not believe in her,/ As long as he remembers that other woman [Fénice]/ He always keeps her [the empress] in her chamber/ More out of fear than for the harsh weather,/ Nor will there ever be a male with her/ Who is not castrated from infancy./ For this reason there is no fear or alarm/ That Love may bind them in his bond./ Here ends Chrétien's work.)

So the story of Fénice is what makes Byzantine emperors – who remember it well – keep their empresses locked up. Chrétien ends on a final pun on the name Fénice: "Ci *fenist* l'uevre Chrestïen" – "Here finishes [*fenices*] Chrétien's work."

Yet another mnemonic aid helps us to remember characters (though of course character and plot cannot be fully dissociated). The second half of the *Perceval ou le conte du graal* stars Gawain. Here, virtually every new character introduced has a name that begins with (or contains) a "g" sound – which of course resonates both with Gawain and the word "Graal": Guinganbresil, Grégoréas, Guiromelant; and Ygerne.[11] And we should not forget that Perceval comes from the "Gaste forest," the man who taught and knighted

---

11 There is one interesting exception: Gauvain's sister, named of Clarissans, introduced and named in line 8269 – and "C" is just a non-aspirated form of "G."

him was Gornement de Gohort, Gauvain's horse is named Gringalet and his brother Guerrehés, the queen is Guinievre, and so on. One might entitle this: "The romance in G."

We have looked at issues of character and characterization, as related to memorability. We turn now to the plot, of *Yvain* in particular. This story-line is not without its subtleties, in which many modern scholars have revelled. But the basic plot of this romance is a very simple one indeed: boy gets girl, boy loses girl, boy gets girl back – on which is superimposed another virtually identical plot structure: man gets glory, or honor; man loses honor; man regains honor. This is, then, at two levels, a stock plot.

Moreover, this romance (like almost all romances) is organized episodically, by short segments. The segments are also standard – highly predictable – including "hospitality" sequences, wooing scenes, scenes of combat, etc: such passages are found not merely in all of Chrétien's romances but in virtually every single medieval romance, period. One might say – indeed it has been said, repeatedly – that the adventures in medieval romances are hackneyed.[12] In a word: as far as the *memoria ad res* goes, the attentive listener – the performer as well – has an easy time remembering the basic features of this romance.

Frederic C. Bartlett's classic study *Remembering: A Study in Experimental and Social Psychology* may be able to help us understand why many of the episodes of medieval romance were particularly memorable to twelfth century (and early-thirteenth) century audiences. Bartlett demonstrated that people remember best those things that are relevant to them as a group. For example, members of the Swazi tribe of Africa recall with extraordinary accuracy details that relate to cattle – and "most Swazi culture revolves around the possession and care of cattle" (p. 249). Bartlett showed that people remember things that they care about, or that remind them of their own situation: things that have affective importance to them (esp. pp. 79ff). Now among the large issues around which twelfth century French aristocratic culture revolved were battle and war, knighthood and military conflict. The more superficial manifestations of these large themes were swords, horses, armor, tournaments, and the like. Other large concerns were marriage and love, and the difficulties surrounding both, and at the surface level weddings and the attendant festivities, conflicts between connubial bliss and the love of tournaments, etc. Still further dominant preoccupations were religious imperatives such as the responsibilities of Christian faith, and social imperatives such as hospitality, etiquette, elaborate clothing, and the like. All these were dominant cultural concerns and things that people cared about. Chrétien's romances are,

---

12 E.g. (one example from *many*) George Saintsbury, *A Short History of French Literature*, p. 98 and *passim* – though Saintsbury in general admires and appreciates these romances.

precisely, *full* of such themes and details, which were of deep personal and affective interest to a contemporary aristocratic audience: conflicts between knightly honor and love; recovery from dishonor of one sort or another; marriage, and the threat of forced marriage, and the working out of a happy marriage; the ways in which young men can make a name and a place for themselves in society; and so on. Thus, for example, the scene evoked above, where the Giant Harpin threatens either to kill all the sons of a lord, or to rape his daughter – in fact, Harpin proposes to give the maiden to his vilest servants to rape – was for nobles of the time surely an intensely memorable sort of dilemma.

The sort of work done by Bartlett has been extended by subsequent scholars in a number of ways, some of which are relevant to us. Psychologists have shown that what is termed "pragmatics" is significantly related to recall. By this word is meant the "communicative situation, the temporal position of the utterance in the communication, and various types of information about the speaker."[13] Many medieval works were performed in contexts that were themselves memorable – for example, at the wedding or coronation of an important person (or a person important to the listener). Moreover, these works were at least sometimes performed by well-known performers (we have the names of a good many famous *jongleurs*), who may also have interacted with the people present in the hall. Raimon Vidal's *ensenhamen* (or "lesson in conduct" for a *jongleur*), "Abril issi'e," discussed at various points in this book, clearly shows such interaction between *jongleur*, audience and patron, as does the "Supplicatio" of Guiraut Riquier to Alfonso the Wise of Castile.[14] (We will return to such issues from a different perspective in the next chapter.) Thus the general "communicative situation" was itself often conducive to recall. By contrast, most of us today read books in situations that are anything but intrinsically memorable, for example, day after day, in the reading room of a library or alone in our room. In my own experience, works that I have read in "extraordinary" circumstances – for example, at the time of some significant event in my life, or in the company of someone who mattered to me, or in an unusual place – stand out particularly well in my memory.

Similarly, psychologists have studied the importance of what is termed "arousal" in learning: apparently heat, noise, and incentives of various kinds (along with other factors) stimulate memory arousal, which affects recall to a

13 Janice M. Keenan, *et al.*, "Pragmatics in Memory: A Study of Natural Conversation," pp. 315–24, esp. p. 317. The same general phenomenon has been called "context" by other psychologists, and has received similar emphasis. See, for example, *Memory in Context: Context in Memory*, ed. by Graham M. Davies and Donald M. Thomson, in which issues of context (including environment, mood, and the like) are shown to enhance learning and recall.

14 *Les Epîtres de Guiraut Riquier, troubadour du XIIIe siècle*, ed. Joseph Linskill.

significant degree.[15] The medieval performance situation, as described in Chapter 6 (and we will return to it in Chapter 8), appears to have been very noisy indeed (Jean Renart says of a performance situation that the instruments were so loud that "if God had thundered, one wouldn't have heard").[16] It was almost certainly hot: ventilation was poor; people wore bulky clothing; guests were apparently packed quite closely together at long tables, etc. And among the medieval memory "incentives" was surely the fact that the members of the audience often themselves performed, or at least "reported," the works they heard to other people later.

Chrétien's stories are also rendered memorable by the way in which he ties together important episodes, themes, names, and the like, into what one might call "mnemonic bundles," and fastens them to the romance in question. In *Érec et Énide*, when the couple are on the road together, there is a set of episodes in which they are attacked: the episodes are all similar to each other, and different from episodes in any other of Chrétien's romances: twice the couple meet counts who try to force Énide to marry them: lines 3223ff and 4636ff. In the second instance, the count is named: "Limors" – "the Dead Man" – which can serve as a reminder that Érec appears dead here and this count is killed by Érec when he recovers consciousness. Énide's unwillingness to accept a new husband is of course strongly related thematically to the central thrust of the plot. Some episodes are also graduated in an upward pattern: that is: Érec and Énide, on the road, are first accosted by three brigands (lines 2791ff), then by five (lines 2921ff). In their final "adventure" – "la joie de la cort" – they meet a couple who are not only in themselves memorable (she is unutterably beautiful, he is enormous) but the woman is Énide's cousin.

We see the same mnemonic bundles in the *Perceval ou le conte du Graal*. In the first part, there is a series of episodes tied together thematically, and rendered mnemonically powerful, by the fact that in each case the hero misunderstands something he has been told by an authority figure (his mother or Gornement de Gohort), and therefore makes a serious error. As was the case in *Érec et Énide*, this particular sort of episode occurs only in this particular romance.

Chrétien also makes effective use of "places" as mnemonic anchors, which raises a number of interesting questions.[17] All the great rhetorical theorists emphasize the use of memorable *loci* or backdrops for the memorization of

15 See Michael W. Eysenck, *Human Memory: Theory, Research and Individual Differences*, pp. 162–90.

16 *Le roman de la rose ou de Guillaume de Dole*, lines 2351; Chrétien says almost the same in a passage quoted below; I am familiar with other citations as well. This appears to have been a commonplace.

17 I am indebted to a paper by B. Christopher Wood: "Lieux cachés de la mémoire: Chrétien de Troyes," written for a graduate class in the French Department at New York University, fall 1992.

material; indeed, the construction of powerful places is perhaps *the* fundamental memory technique.[18] Theorists encourage orators (and others) who
wish to learn by heart large quantities of material to put them into permanently
constructed "places" in their minds, such as theatres, palaces, and streets.
These places are the constructs of what is termed "artificial memory." But the
theorists agree that artificial memory builds on "natural memory": the art
builds on what is natural to human beings.[19] Both memory places and the
images placed in them build on this principle. What I suggest we find in
romances such as *Yvain* (and many other vernacular works) is that the poet first
"constructs" for his audience powerfully stimulating "places" – places
which the performance of the work sets into the mind of his audience. Then the
poet puts into these places important scenes and characters. Thus, vernacular
poets do, presumably intuitively – or perhaps they know perfectly well what
they are doing, but most do it apparently without Rhetorical training – what
trained orators and mnemonists do: they set characters and other events which
are to be remembered within places which are themselves memorable.

Yvain offers an important example. In this romance, an amazing fountain –
a dazzling, storm-producing fountain, with a golden basin on a golden chain,
and with a beautiful chapel to one side and a large emerald to the other –
functions as a strong memory place. Here is its first description, as given by the
giant herdsman whom Calogrenant begged to send him toward some "adventure":

> La fontainne verras qui bout,
> s'est ele plus froide que marbres.
> Onbre li fet li plus biax arbres
> c'onques poïst former Nature.
> En toz tens sa fuelle li dure,
> qu'il ne la pert por nul iver.
> Et s'i pant uns bacins de fer
> a une si longue chaainne
> qui dure jusqu'au la fontainne.
> Lez la fontainne troverras
> un perron, tel con tu verras;
> je ne te sai a dire quel,
> que je n'en vis onques nul tel;
> et d'autre part une chapele
> petite, mes ele est molt bele.
> S'au bacin viax de l'eve prandre
> et desus le perron espandre,

---

18 See, in particular, Frances Yates, *The Art, passim*.
19 The *Ad Herennium* author framed a quote given above in this way: "[I]f we see or
hear something . . . we are likely to remember [it] for a long time." Rhetoric builds on
ordinary human experience.

la verras une tel tanpeste
qu'an cest bois ne remanra beste,
chevriax ne cers, ne dains ne pors,
nes li oisel s'an istront fors;
car tu verras si foudroier,
vanter, et arbres peçoier,
plovoir, toner, et espartir,
que, se tu t'an puez departir
sanz grant enui et sanz pesance,
tu seras de meillor cheance
que chevaliers qui i fust onques.   lines 380–407

(You will see the fountain that boils,/ and it is colder than marble./ The most beautiful tree that Nature ever could have formed/ makes shade for it./ At all times [of year] its leaves last,/ and it does not lose them in the winter./ And there is hanging an iron basin/ by a long chain/ which hangs down to the fountain./ Next to the fountain you will find/ a stone, as you will see,/ I do not know how to tell you what it is like,/ for I have never seen one like it;/ and on the other side there is a chapel,/ small, but it is very beautiful./ And if you wish to pour water/ and to spill it on the stone,/ there you will see such a storm/ that in the forest no beast will remain,/ neither stag, neither deer nor boar/ even the birds will fly away;/ for you will see it make such thunder and lightning/ and the wind blow, and trees get blown to pieces,/ rain, thunder and lightning/ that, if you can get away/ without great difficulty and suffering,/ you will have more luck/ than any knight ever had before.)

This is a remarkable fountain – and it is therefore memorable. It is redescribed, in more or less detail, several more times. In this particular description, the giant herdsman is represented as not recognizing the chain as golden or the stone as an emerald. When the fountain is re-described by Yvain's cousin Calogrenant, he as a noble does recognize these precious substances. The fountain and its properties are described yet again when Yvain himself arrives there, etc. In short, Chrétien anchors this fountain powerfully in the memory of the audience.

The fountain is also a place to which characters return over and over: for example, it is here that Yvain almost dies of sorrow and the lion almost commits suicide from grief; here, that Lunete is to be burned at the stake; here, that Yvain returns at the end to be, with Lunete's help, reconciled with his wife.

Against the background of this *locus* Chrétien also places important objects and themes: many important events are associated with, or set near, the fountain. In the light of memory systems' reliable predilection for images of sex and violence, we note with interest that virtually all the scenes set at the fountain are violent (the violence of nature and that of men), and that (as

Eugene Vance noted some years ago[20]) there is a decidedly erotic quality to the fountain's mysterious behaviors.

As I mentioned earlier, the heroine, Yvain's lady, is not even named in most manuscripts (when her name is provided, it is Laudine). Proper names, modern psychological research suggests, are typically very un-memorable: forget-table.[21] But she is identified as the "lady of the fountain." Memorable persons, animals, and things are placed in – projected into – the minds of listeners (or readers). An interesting question arises: where are memory systems located – in the mind of the memorizer or in the work itself? What I am suggesting is that, in markedly memory-friendly works, a system – a pattern, a structure – has been set into the composition, rather than having to be constructed, generally with considerable effort, by the would-be memorizer.

Interestingly enough, Chrétien uses the fountain as a mnemonic place outside of *Yvain*, as well: in *Lancelot*, Guinevere's comb, which, as a small object might escape both initial notice and subsequent recall, is placed on the fountain. Moreover – and this strikes me as very interesting indeed – we may be invited to "recognize" this fountain as the same one as in *Yvain*; for example, it too has a stone sitting next to it.

> La fontainne est enmi uns prez
> et s'avoit un perron delez.
> sor le perron qui ert iqui
> avoit oblie ne sait qui
> un peigne d'ivoire dore.   lines 1347–51

> (The fountain is in the middle of a field/ and had a stone next to it./ On the stone which was there/ someone, I don't know who, had forgotten/ a comb of gilded ivory.)

Thus, Chrétien seems to take a memory place from one work and use it to the same effect in another. As various scholars have noted, there is another echo between the two stories: when in *Yvain* a young woman is seeking for Gawain to protect her interests, she is told that he is off trying to rescue the queen – which seems to refer to the *Lancelot* story. Chrétien appears to be attempting to tie the two romances together mnemonically.

We have looked at a variety of features that would tend to make the plot of a romance (this one or others) easy to remember.[22] A larger look at the plot of *Yvain*, from a mnemonic perspective, will be useful:

20 Vance, "Le combat érotique chez Chrétien de Troyes: de la figure à la forme."
21 Bartlett, *Remembering*, p. 172.
22 The features – the patterns – we have been looking at here are, of course, true of a great many stories. As I said at the outset, *Yvain* is by no means unusual in its use of such patterns. Some medieval romances do not, however, contain such features. In particular, many long prose romances are so intricately interlaced that they defy, at least to a great

Court of *Arthur* – standard opening gambit
Calogrenant's tale:
Herdsman (*giant cum wildman*)
    Fountain
Yvain wants to avenge his cousin
    Kay insults him.
Yvain
    Herdsman
    Fountain
    Combat – knight wounded to death
    Meeting with Lunete
Funeral of dead knight [Esclados – name mentioned only once – ergo unimportant]
Yvain falls in love with beautiful widow of the man he killed [Laudine – name not mentioned in Guiot text, and rarely elsewhere: name clearly unimportant]; Lunete persuades her mistress [Laudine] to marry husband's killer: Yvain
Marriage of Yvain and Laudine
Arthur comes
    Kay is punished
    Gauvain (the sun) meets Lunete (the moon)
Yvain and Gauvain leave
Yvain forgets to return *in time* – becomes *wildman*
Yvain *helped* by hermit
Yvain *helped* – healed – by dame de Norison [name mentioned only once];
    Yvain *refuses marriage*
Yvain *helps* – saves – *lion* from serpent; *lion* becomes his companion and
    helper
Return to *fountain*; finds Lunete in chapel: *maiden oppressed*
Giant [Harpin de la Montagne – name mentioned only once] threatens
    Gauvain's relatives: *woman in danger*; *Lion's help*
Yvain returns to *fountain*; arrives *in time* to *rescue* Lunete; *lion's help*
Noire Espine sisters: younger *sister oppressed* by elder in the "Pesme
    Aventure:" (the "Worst Adventure"): *oppressed women* in "sweatshop"; Yvain kills Netun's *giant* sons; *lion's help*; women liberated.
    Yvain *refuses marriage* with daughter
Yvain arrives *in time* to *help oppressed* sister
Yvain and – vs. – Gauvain, court of *Arthur*
Yvain's final return to *fountain: storm*
Wife *persuaded by Lunete* to be reunited with husband.

extent, memory-mastery. Presumably, no one was intended to remember the over-arching plot of such works.

242

The elements of this plot are bound together by patterns of repetition and recapitulation of important themes and motifs: returns to the fountain; the role of giants and wildmen; refusals of marriage on the part of Yvain (who has to prove that he really does love his wife); Yvain's getting places on time (after failing to come home on the agreed-upon date); themes of help and assistance – and, in particular, Yvain's rescuing of women in distress; helping the lion, and then help from the lion; the relationship between Yvain and Gauvain – both friendship and combat; Lunete as a persuader of the lady of the fountain. Sometimes there is reversal or opposition: thus, funeral vs. marriage, which is in this case perhaps particularly striking (thus memorable) because the funeral of the dead man is hardly over before the marriage of his widow takes place – and this almost happens a second time. Even the frequent, though not fully systematic, repetition of the initial sound "n" (Norison, Noire Espine, Netun) is a mnemonic aid – and Yvain, Gauvain, lion, fountaine, and Harpin all have final "n" sounds (the nasal vowels did not yet exist).

Thus far we have been looking at two kinds of features of this romance. First, those that are "standard" and are therefore easy to remember, since they reduce what psychologists call "memory load" by being predictable. Second, those that draw on the principles underlying artificial memory systems: the construction of bizarre and unforgettable images. Both of these kinds of features, bearing as they do on *memoria ad res*, are by no means peculiar to works from oral tradition. As we noted earlier, even fully literary writers can want – historically they often have wanted – their readers to be able to remember their stories, indeed to be unable to forget them. Many a writer has, by a masterful blend of the stock and the bizarre, anchored characters and plots so firmly in the memory of his public that they stayed put.

But this romance, like virtually all early medieval romance, contains features which make its memorability one geared specifically to listeners, and to performance from memory. Again, the issue here is not so much how the work was composed – with or without substantial recourse to formulas,[23] with or without the use of writing – as the ways in which it invites memory-mastery by performers and listeners. (And as we will see in the next, and final, chapter the blurring of the line between performers and public was one of the most significant elements of medieval court performance.)

Here, at the level of the learning of words (vast quantities of words), the centrality of visual images largely drops out. It would, after all, be massively

---

[23] My emphasis here is on the learning of works as more or less set pieces. Many *chansons de geste* were quite probably composed through the process called "oral composition." But the strong likelihood is that many such works were, like romances, performed in a relatively fixed form. And some *chansons de geste* – especially but probably not exclusively those "made" by clerks – were also composed as set pieces, and not by oral composition.

inefficient for performers to learn not just the *res* but every single *verbum* of a work from a distinct visual image.[24] And there is little evidence that performers have ever done so. Other mnemotechnical principles come into play here, in particular those by which one puts together the pieces of poetry and narrative. As Marcel Jousse said:

> Similar assistance [similar to the use of rhythm] was offered by "block memorisation" of a certain number of rhythmic schemas closely related in meaning. "Precise experiment has in fact shown that one can more easily and rapidly memorise a piece of poetry by repeating it several times in its entirety, without breaking the natural associations of words and phrases, than by taking up the lines one by one, or in [too small fragmentary] groups, which interrupts the associations and movement. Just as 'reintegration' has to do with ensembles to be recalled, so 'integration' must have to do with ensembles to be remembered."[25] (p. 197)

That is, one learns poetry not by taking the pieces apart but by repeating it in its entirety, by maintaining the flow, by keeping the words and lines together.

The rhetoricians and scholars who constructed the great memory systems seem to have been, on the whole, largely uninterested in, even sceptical about – sometimes hostile to – the *ad verba* memorization of large quantities of words: song or poetry. (Perhaps their attitude flows from the fact that the verbatim learning of large amounts of verse, etc. was simply not their problem; they needed only short-term storage of variable material for punctual use.) The *Ad Herennium* author makes this statement – and it is one of the more favorable:

> Now, lest you should perchance regard the memorizing of words either as too difficult or as of too little use, and so rest content with the memorizing of matter, as being easier and more useful, I must advise you why I do not disapprove of memorizing words. I believe that they who wish to do easy things without trouble and toil must previously have been trained in more difficult things. Nor have I included memorization of words to enable us to get verse by rote, but rather as an exercise whereby to strengthen that other kind of memory, the memory of matter, which is of practical use . . .[26]

In other words, the memorization of words is much harder than that of "things," and less useful.[27] The author does not "disapprove of it" but one does it just for practice. Moreover, we saw in the previous chapter the general antipathy of rhetorical theorists such as the *Ad Herennium* author toward *histriones*; presumably it is they who memorized (and acted out) long passages of verse by rote. In short, the somewhat antipathetic silence of rhetoricians

---

24 See, e.g., Yates, *The Art*, pp. 14–15.
25 Jousse is quoting from the French psychologist Baudin here.
26 [Cicero] *Ad Herennium*, ed. by Harry Caplan, p. 223.
27 See Carruthers, *The Book*, p. 74.

appears to result from the fact that it was actors, not orators or rhetorical theorists, who cranked out from memory, and acted out before eager audiences, those thousands upon thousands of lines of story and song.

We return yet again to *Yvain*. This romance is composed in verse, that is, in a rhythmic form – and Jousse was particularly eloquent concerning the powerful mnemonic properties of rhythm (pp. 109ff). He focused particularly on parallelisms, rhyme, alliteration (Part II, chapters XV–XVIII); all of which will be taken up below. Other scholars as well have discussed the mnemonic properties of verse. James A. Notopoulos, in his classic article "Mnemosyne in Oral Literature," pointed out that "The oral poet as a mnemotechnician preserved the useful by binding it in verse, by forging a metrical pattern which facilitated and guarded against mistaking the information to be preserved" (p. 469).

Yvain is composed in octo, as is (we have noted) the case of virtually all early romance and indeed of the vast majority of early medieval discourse and narrative (aside from the epic). Octo is typically described (by those relatively few scholars who have looked at it carefully) as a form at once rigid and regular, leaving little room for variation, even beset by "monotony and sing-song"; also as "fluent," "facile," and "limber," inviting recitation; and, finally, "pedestrian."[28] It also happens that the eight-syllable line is a powerful mnemonic line for lengthy discourse or narrative. Research of various kinds has shown that the human mind can perceive, and short-term memory retain, units of up to eight items – but not much longer.[29] Thus, an eight-syllable line is remarkably well suited for discourses which contain a substantial amount of information – as a long story inevitably does – but which still aim for retention with some precision by memory.

A number of historians of versification have taken the position that the octo-syllable is hardly even an independent line of verse. That is, an eight-syllable line has to be – is only perceived as, and presumably learned as – one in a sequence of lines; it has no identity or strength on its own. (This is perhaps one reason why the octosyllable tends to be treated as part of the *pre*-history of versification, and generally receives very skimpy treatment.) For example, Maurice Grammont stated in *Le vers français*:

Un vers de douze syllabes isolé est un vers; il a son rythme complet et son harmonie forme un tout. Un vers de dix syllabes isolé n'est un vers que dans

---

28 "Monotony and singsong" comes from Saintsbury, *A History of English Prosody*, Vol. I, p. 67; see also p. 71. Also of Saintsbury see *A Short History of French Literature*, e.g., p. 37. See also G. Lote, *Histoire du vers français*, Vol. II, pp. 58–59.

29 Benoît de Cornulier, *Théorie du vers*, pp. 32ff. See also the classic, and highly influential, piece by psychologist George Miller, "The Magical Number Seven, Plus or Minus Two: Some Limits on Our Capacity for Processing Information."

certaines conditions. Les vers qui n'ont que huit syllabes ou moins de huit syllabes ne sont des vers qu'à condition de ne pas être isolés.[30]

My point is, precisely, that the octosyllabic line was not perceived as "isolé" but was felt to be part of a larger poetic entity.

The octo form is made up of rhymed couplets.[31] This form, like the octosyllabic line itself, has not been very thoroughly studied by historians of versification.[32] Rhymed couplets present the peculiar feature that, as they are spoken, the ending of every second line is highly predictable: again, "redundant." The exact lexical item may not be forseeable – though it often is – but the syllable, the sound, on which the line is going to end is predictable: this is what rhyme is, after all.[33] And the rhymed couplet is rhyme in one of its very simplest forms, where predictability is at its most striking, since it hits the very next line. The stress on memory is at its very slightest. (By contrast, in a more complex rhyme scheme, such as that of the sonnet, the intervals are farther apart, and they change over the course of the poem: the pattern is thus harder to

---

[30] Maurice Grammont, *Le vers français*, p. 438. Despite the general-sounding title, the earliest examples of French verse discussed by Grammont date from such sixteenth century poets as DuBellay.

[31] On the mnemonic properties of rhyme, see David C. Rubin, *Memory in Oral Traditions: the Cognitive Psychology of Epics, Ballads, and Counting-out Rhymes*, which came out as I was completing this manuscript. Rubin states, for example: ". . . rhyme limits choices and cues recall, thereby increasing the stability of genres of oral traditions that employ it" (p. 84). Rubin also discusses the mnemonic importance of rhythm.

[32] They tend to be more interested in later periods of French literature. Their concerns are also most typically with issues of male vs. female rhymes, rhyme-richness, and the like, and with normative issues such as "good" vs. "bad" rhymes, and by their criteria octo provides more examples of the latter than of the former. While Lote's classic *Histoire du vers français* is very useful for the large picture of the history of French versification, his focus is primarily on lyric; he speaks relatively rarely of narrative verse, and he has very little to say about the octosyllabic rhymed couplet – of which, moreover, he seems to take a rather dim view, speaking for example of the "maigres octosyllabes" at the beginnings of French literature (vol. II, p. 51).

Few historians of versification seem interested in the very phenomenon of rhyme itself. An important exception is the great Georges Saintsbury, who wrote the history of a quite a number of things, including French literature, English literature, and English prosody. Unfortunately, Saintsbury did not study the history of *French* versification and prosody; his remarks on the octosyllabic couplet come only in the context of English verse and are not particularly useful for us.

Another important and thought-provoking exception is Clive Scott's important study, *The Riches of Rhyme: Studies in French Verse*. Unfortunately, Scott discusses no texts earlier than Racine.

[33] Rhyme can be, and has been, defined in a variety of ways. Henri Morier in his *Dictionnaire de poétique et de rhétorique* defines "la rime" as "*un accent phonétique*" (p. 349) – and he has only about five words to say of the rhymed couplet (p. 352).

The question of whether or not rhyme is "essential" to French poetry, and why, has been much debated. Here, I am speaking from the point of view of predictability and learning. What we can count on – what is predictable – reduces memory load.

remember and to predict.)[34] All of which means that the audience is invited to furnish – to speak aloud or to murmur *in pectore* – the ending to half the lines of the work. The first time through may be said to invite collaborative improvisation, the second time to anchor *memoria ad verba*.

The rhymed couplet as a form is strongly dialogical or "responsorial." I mean this in two ways. First, the couplet form itself was conducive to the articulation of the "back and forth" of dialogue, and romance contains a great deal of dialogue. But the rhymed couplet is responsorial in another sense as well. Anyone who has had the experience of reading aloud to a child from a book of nursery rhymes, which are commonly composed in rhymed couplets, will know what I am talking about: if given half a chance, the child invariably furnishes the ending (or *an* appropriate ending) to the second line of the couplet. Often when one is reading or reciting such rhymes to a child, one waits – one pauses – so that the child can supply the rhyme-word: "Humpty Dumpty sat on a wall/ Humpty Dumpty had a great . . . fall . . ."; "There was a little girl/ And she had a little . . . curl . . ." In any event, this form, being so strongly predictable, reduces memory load and simplifies the work of *ad verba* memorization. (It would be interesting to do a study of predictable vs. unpredictable rhymes in medieval romance – as well as a history of rhymes for the ear vs. those for the eye – but such projects would take us too far afield here.)

In short, the octosyllabic rhymed couplet – whatever its deficiencies from the point of view of sophisticated versification and poetic theory – is a markedly memory-friendly form. The octo's dialogic or responsive character, combined with its ease of learning makes it doubly unsurprising that, as medieval theater develops from the late-twelfth century on (or at least as it begins to be preserved in written form), it too is regularly composed in octosyllabic rhymed couplets, thereby facilitating more-or-less exact memorization of lines by performers only some of whom could read; others, drawn from among ordinary townsfolk, apparently could not.

The intrinsic mnemonic properties of the octosyllabic rhymed couplet may

---

[34] Another way of conceptualizing this – one suggested by Clive Scott in *The Riches of Rhyme* – is to think of rhyme as occurring *between* the rhymed elements, but *at* neither: "Rhyme reminds us that the semantic activity of the poetic text takes place not so much within the words of the text as they occur, in sequence, but in the spaces opened up by anticipation and reopened by retrospection. French terminology is in the habit of referring to the first rhyme in a rhyme pair as the *rime d'attente* and of its partner as the *rime-écho*. These very terms leave us with the question: where does the phenomenon of rhyming actually occur? If the *rime d'attente* presents a syllable *to be rhymed with* and the *rime écho recalls* a syllable *to be rhymed with*, where exactly do we hear the rhyme? Perhaps the truth of the matter is that we do not, we only project it and remember it. Like the meaning of the poetic text, rhyme takes place in an elusive elsewhere, in the protean collisions of desire and memory, so that rhyme, like poetic meaning, is constantly glimpsed and missed . . ." (p. 140). By such a standard, octo can provide only shallow pleasures – and, as it were, shallow disappointments: the "space" opened up between the expectation and the echo is exceedingly short.

show up in greater relief when set against those of the *chanson de geste* line.[35] The classic French epic presents the following poetic features:

– It is most commonly composed of ten-syllable, or decasyllabic, lines.
– The lines are invariably set into "laisses" (or "tirades": stanzas) of varying length.
– The lines of a given laisse are generally assonanced: they end with the same vowel sound but not the same consonant. Georges Lote's definition is as follows: "L'assonance consiste dans l'identité de la voyelle tonique qui termine le mot par lequel s'achève le vers, tandis que les consonnes dont est suivie cette tonique sont différentes."[36] Thus, assonanced lines do not actually rhyme. (There is, however, in many epics a significant proportion of actual rhyme. There are, as well, fully rhymed *chansons de geste*.)
– The contents of the lines and of the poem as a whole, are strongly stereotyped, with many recurring groups of words or "formulas." The proportion of formulas varies from work to work – and according to the definition of the formula that one adopts.
– The work is traditionally sung, to the accompaniment of a vielle, or occasionally a harp.

The mnemonic strengths of such a line and form are clear: memory load is greatly reduced not only by the predictability of the subject matter, story-line and general treatment, but also by the fact that the poet/minstrel, and the audience, can predict, to a highly significant degree, how each and every line within a laisse is going to end; that is, they know what will be the final vowel, but not what final consonant. To put it differently, the vocality but not the lexicality of the line-closure is predictable.

The exact sequence of lines within a laisse, and of the laisses among themselves, is not predictable, though laisses that need to stay together often begin with more or less the same line, or begin by recapitulating the same material: these are called "laisses similaires."[37] In any case, the laisse provided a major bonding unit.

Another mnemonic advantage of the *chanson de geste* – though it may perhaps seem paradoxical – is the very fact that it did not have to be learned "perfectly." As a genre, the French epic had a high tolerance for improvisation and variation in *res*; different versions of the same song often vary substantially. Variations in sequence and on other dimensions appear not to

---

[35] It would be interesting to look at the English alliterative line as well, but that too would carry us too far afield. There are many other powerfully mnemonic forms, as well, in other cultures and linguistic matrices.

[36] Lote, *Histoire du vers français*, Vol. I, p. 95.

[37] In a few *chansons de geste* the last line of a laisse is repeated in the first line of the following laisse – obviously a memory-aid.

have bothered performers or audiences. So performers could "mis-remember" – reinvent – the song as they wished, to a substantial degree.

If we look at the memorability of octo, we see disadvantages and advantages to this form. First intrinsic disadvantage: in octo, only half the lines end predictably: the second line in each couplet. But there is an advantage here as well. In octo we know what the entire final syllable will be: the final vowel, plus the final consonant; only the precise lexical choice remains uncertain. Second disadvantage: whereas a laisse could be learned in its entirety, as a rythmic and poetic unit, works composed in octo cannot normally be broken down into the same sort of natural segments. (We will however return shortly to the way in which Chrétien connects up series of lines.)

The fact that an eight-syllable line is easier to learn than a ten-syllable one was an important plus for the octo, surely helping to assure its vast popularity. As to the issue of story-line predictability and attendant memory-load reduction, this varies from genre to genre. (Octo, as noted, is used in many genres, whereas the decasyllabic assonanced laisse is the exclusive property of the epic.) But within the particular genres such as the romance, the fabliau, the rhymed sermon – subject matter is often as predictable as in the *chanson de geste*. And while the term "formula" is not commonly applied to romance, such works certainly contain an abundance of clichés and repeated line-filler of one kind and another.

One important factor which would have aided *jongleurs* and minstrels in the memory-mastery of some long octo works, as well as of *chansons de geste* was recourse to a melodic line. For while romances are not called "songs," they too appear often to have been sung or at least intoned by *jongleurs*, as we saw in Chapter 6. And of the usefulness of melody as an adjuvant to memory, there can be, of course, no doubt – though the *Ad Herennium* author and others of that ilk never take up such considerations, as they are speaking to orators. Tom Lehrer made even the "Periodic Table" of chemical elements memorable by putting it to a patter song from Gilbert and Sullivan. However the minstrel performed a particular romance – and this mode may have varied – he may have learned the work with a musical support.

As to the matter of romance length, Chrétien's *Yvain* is about 6,500 lines long. (Many romances are substantially longer.) Some modern scholars have been sceptical that performers could know such works by heart. To some degree, this scepticism has come from the oral theorists themselves, who have tended to think that only formulaic works could be performed from memory; thus it was memory combined with – bolstered by – re-creation on the spot. But we know today, from considerable amounts of ethnographic and other research, that there is virtually no limit to the amount of material that performers and other professional mnemonists are able to store in their memory.[38] Various

---

[38] Bartlett, *Remembering*; A.R. Luriia, *The Mind of a Mnemonist: A Little Book about a Vast Memory*; Ulric Neisser, ed., *Memory Observed: Remembering in Natural Contexts*.

scholars have discussed performers such as *guslars* who knew 100,000 lines of poetry (see, e.g., Jousse, p. 125) – and that figure is nowhere given as an outer limit. The human memory is not like that of a computer, with just so many ''K'' of capacity, which can get used up. The mind apparently never says, as my rather weak computer does, ''Out of Memory.'' Rather, human memory appears to be almost infinitely expandable. In any event, references to performance and performers in such works as *Le Roman de Renart*, and ''Les Deux Bourdeurs Ribauds,'' all of which have been referred to repeatedly earlier, clearly indicate that *jongleurs* and *ménestrels* knew many romances by heart. The key question may well be, not ''how long a work can a performer learn?'' but ''how long a work will audiences *tolerate*?'' We assume – safely, I think – that long works were performed in several sessions, not just one. But even in this performance setting, at what point does the audience cry, ''Enough!'' – or just wander away? Be that as it may, a romance, such as *Yvain*, of under 7,000 lines offers, in terms of its sheer length, no special strain to the mind of a poet/ performer/ mnemonist of any skill or training whatsoever.

We saw earlier some of the ways in which the plot of Chrétien's *Yvain* is easy to retain. A related question is how a performer might have learned long strings of actual octo couplets from Chrétien's romances. Though groups of lines are not bound in a laisse, they are generally quite strongly fastened together in a variety of ways. A few examples may be useful. We could hardly do better than to go back to the passage in *Cligés* where Soredamors talks about her name, and examine it more closely from a mnemotechnical perspective.

> Amors ne m'aprant se bien non.
> Por neant n'ai ge pas cest non
> Que Soredamors sui clamee.
> Amer doi, si doi estre amee,
> Si le vuel par mon non prover,
> Qu'amors doi an mon non trover.
> Aucune chose senefie
> Ce que la premiere partie   960
> En mon non est de color d'or
> Et li meillor sont li plus sor.
> Por ce tieng mon non a meillor
> Qu'an mon non a de la color
> A cui li miaudres ors s'acorde
> Et la fine amors me recorde:
> Car qui par mon droit non m'apele
> Toz jorz amors me renovele;
> Et l'une mitiez l'autre dore
> De doreüre clere et sore   970
> Et autant dit Soredamors
> Come sororee d'amors.

Doreüre d'or n'est si fine
Come ceste qui m'anlumine:
Molt m'a donc Amors enoree,
Quant il de lui m'a sororee,
Et je metrai an lui ma cure,
Que de lui soie doreüre,
Ne ja mes ne m'an clamerai.
Or aim et toz jorz amerai ...   lines 953–80

(Love teaches me nothing if not good./ Not for nothing do I have this name,/ That Soredamors am I called./ I must love, and must be loved,/ And I want to prove this by my name,/ That I must find love in my name./ It means something/ That the first part/ In my name is about the color of gold/ And the best [golds] are the most "sor" [yellow-gold]/ For this I consider that my name is the best/ Because in my name is the color/ Which is in accord with the best gold,/ And courtly [fine] love recalls me:/ For he who by my proper name calls me/ Every day renews love in me;/ And the one half [of my name] gilds the other/ With a light and "sor" gilding,/ And whoever says Soredamors/ Says gilded by love./ Gilding with gold is not so fine/ As the one that illuminates me:/ Thus has Love greatly honored me/ When he gilded me with himself,/ And I will put all my care in him,/ Since by him am I gilded,/ Nor will I ever complain about him./ So I love and will always love ...)

Patterns of repetition, meaning and sound – especially end-rhyme and internal rhyme – bind this passage together powerfully. The words and sounds "nom" (generally spelled "non" but meaning "name" as well as "not"), "amor" ("love") and "or" ("gold") are woven together throughout and dominate the passage. "Nom" rhymes with "mon": this is "*mon* non" (lines 957, 958, 961, 963, 964, 967). "Nom" ("name") is also played off against "non" ("not"), "neant" and other negatives – which may serve to remind listeners that Soredamors had originally strongly intended *not* to love: only after she falls in love, against her will, does she "discover" her name; Love "teaches" her what her name means. Her name is thus in strong and memorable contrast to the person she had planned to be. Thus, we have "Amors ne m'aprant se bien *non*./ Por *neant n*'ai ge pas cest *non*" (lines 953–54), "*Si le vuel par mon non* prover,/ Qu'amors doi an mon *non* prover." (lines 957–58), "... la premiere partie/ En mon *non* est de color d'or ..." (lines 960–61), "Por ce tieng mon *non* a meillor/ Qu'an mon *non* a de la color ..." (lines 963–64), "Car qui par mon droit *non* m'apele ..." (line 967), etc.

Into these plays on "name" and "not" are woven a whole set of puns and repetitions of "love" and "loving." We begin with lines accentuating her new-found identity as lover and love-object: "Por neant n'ai ge pas cest non/ Que Sore*damors* sui clamée./ *Amer* doi, si doi estre *amee* ..." (lines 954–56). We move on from there: "Si le vuel par mon non prover,/ Qu'*amors* doi an

251

mon non trover'' (lines 957–58). Soredamors will, indeed, find love in her name: ''Et la fine *amors* me recorde:/ Car qui par mon droit non m'apele/ toz jors *amors* me renovele . . .'' (lines 966–68). Soredamors finds ''love'' everywhere in her name partly through the very word ''*or*'' (''gold'') which is part not merely of ''s*or*'' (yellow-gold), but, being precious, of love itself: am*or*. Thus, for example:

> Aucune chose senefie
> Ce que la premiere partie
> En mon non est de col*or* d*or*,
> Et li meill*or* sont li plus s*or*.
> Por ce tieng mon non a meill*or*
> Qu'an mon non a de la col*or*
> A qui li miaudres *ors* s'acor*de*,
> Et la fine *amors* [am*ors*] me recor*de*:
> Car qui par mon droit non m'apele
> Toz j*orz* *amors* [am*ors*] me renovele;
> Et l'une mitiez l'autre d*ore*
> De d*ore*üre clere et s*ore*,
> Et autant die S*ore*dam*ors*
> Comme soror*é* d'*amor*.
> D*ore*üre d'*or* n'est si fine
> Come ceste qui m'anlumine:
> Molt m'a donc *Amors* eno*ree*,
> quant il de lui m'a soro*ree*,
> Et je metrai en lui ma cure,
> que de lui soie d*ore*üre,
> Ne ja mes ne m'an clamerai.
> Or *aim* et toz jorz *amerai*.   lines 959–80

This passage is a mnemonic as well as a poetic *tour de force*. All the key words and concepts are inextricably, and memorably, interwoven. I have cut the strands here, a bit arbitrarily, at line 980 – but the weaving pattern continues. For example, the next few lines keep the ''love'' thread going, along with the use of negatives, but move into a series of rhetorical questions:

> Cui? Voir, ci a bele demande!
> Cestui que *Amors* me comande,
> Car ja autres m'*amor* n'avra.
> Cui chaut, quant il ne le savra,
> Se je meïsmes ne li di?
> Que feroie, se ne li pri?
> Qui de la chose a desirrier
> Bien la doit requerre et proier.
> Comant? Proierai le je donques?
> Nenil. Por coi? . . .   lines 981–90

(Whom? In truth, there is a nice question!/ Him that Love
commands me to love,/ For never any other one will have my
love./ What does it matter to him, since he won't know it,/ If I
don't tell him myself?/ What shall I do, If I don't ask him?/
Anyone who desires something/ Must ask for and pray to have
it./ How? shall I beg him then?/ No. Why? . . .)

I would not wish to argue that Chrétien's romances are all, or everywhere,
so tightly woven. But many passages do contain this sort of dense poetic and
mnemotechnic patterning. I do not see that this sort of mnemonic weaving
makes it necessarily any more likely that Chrétien composed his works in
written form: this only means that he "made" them with care and with verbal
artistry, and who has thought otherwise?

How does Chrétien handle the fountain, mnemonically speaking? The
question that interests us here is this: are we simply to remember the fountain
as a "place"? Thus, are we just dealing with *memoria ad res*? Or does
Chrétien facilitate *memoria ad verba* in the description of the fountain? To put
this a bit differently, is it only the story that is memorable here, or the words as
well? First, we meet the ugly herdsman who knows nothing about adventure:

> Mes se tu voloies aler
> ci pres jusqu'a une fontainne,
> n'en revandroies pas sanz painne,
> se ne li randoies son droit.
> Ci pres troveras or en droit
> un santier qui la te manra.
> Tote la droite voie va,
> se bien viax tes pas anploier,
> que tost porroies desvoier:
> il i a d'autres voies mout.
> La fontainne verras qui bout,
> s'est ele plus froide que marbres.
> Onbre li fet li plus biax arbres
> c'onques poïst former Nature.
> En toz tens sa fuelle li dure,
> qu'il ne la pert por nul iver.
> Et s'i pant uns bacins de fer
> a une si longue chaainne
> qui dure jusqu'an la fontainne.
> Lez la fontainne troverras
> un perron, tel con tu verras;
> je ne te sai a dire quel,
> que je n'en vi onques nul tel;
> et d'autres part une chapele
> petite, mes ele est molt bele.
> S'au bacin viax de l'eve prandre
> et desus le perron espandre,

253

la verras une tel tanpeste
qu'an cest boi ne remanra beste,
chevriax ne cers, ne dains ne pors,
nes li oisel s'an istront fors
car tu verras si foudroier,
vanter, et arbres peçoier,
plovoir, toner, et espartir,
que, se tu t'an puez departir
sanz grant enui et sanz pesance,
tu seras de meillor cheance
que chevaliers qui i fust onques.   lines 370–407

(But if you want to go/ nearby to a fountain,/ you will not come back without difficulty,/ and unless you give it its due./ Nearby you will soon find/ A path that will lead you there./ Take the straight path,/ if you want to make good use of your steps,/ since you can easily lose the way:/ there are many other paths./ You will see the fountain that boils,/ and yet it is colder than marble./ There is shade there, from the most beautiful tree/ That Nature could ever have formed./ In all seasons its leaves last,/ so that it never loses them in the winter./ And there hangs an iron basin/ from a long chain/ which goes down to the fountain./ Next to the fountain you will find/ a stone, such as you will see;/ I don't know how to tell you what it is like,/ because I never saw another one like it;/ and on the other side is a chapel/ small, but it is very beautiful./ If you want to take water in the basin/ and pour it over the stone,/ you will see there such a storm/ that in this woods will remain no beast,/ neither goat nor stag nor deer nor boar,/ even the birds will go out;/ for you will see such thunder,/ and wind blowing, and trees torn to pieces,/ and rain, and lightning,/ that if you can leave/ wihout great sorrow and cost,/ you will have better luck/ than any knight that ever was.)

Just a few lines later Calogrenant tells the story himself. His description is longer, and is blended with the narration of his experience. Many words and groups of words that were also found in the herdsman's description recur here: ''l'arbre'' and ''la fontainne'' several times; ''perrons,'' ''tampeste'' and ''vent'' more than once; also ''li plus biax,'' ''basin pandre,'' ''boloit,'' etc.; see lines 410–77.

Calogrenant thus reuses key terms from the herdsman's description, but without repeating any of the actual verse segments. In other words, he does not repeat what the herdsman said word for word. In some cases, he changes the wording, for example, using ''aroser'' rather than ''espandre.'' He also shifts the emphasis in a number of ways, for example, by stressing the precious nature of the substances – the gold, the ruby and emeralds. And he introduces the double focus on joy and on music. In short, as we move from the first to the second passage, the primary mnemonic emphasis seems to be more on *memoria ad res* than *ad verba*.

But Calogrenant's description, which is the longest and fullest description of the fountain and its marvels, must now itself be examined from a mnemonic perspective. I will break the passage into small units, and will mark the two sensations that bind the parts of the narrative together: sight, then hearing. Calogrenant "sees," then he "hears" – both sensations being tied to affectivity, first to a general admiration and pleasure, then to intense *enui* and *repentir*, followed by great *joïe*. Essentially Calogrenant takes up all the key words mentioned earlier by the herdsman – the tree, the basin, the stone, the fountain, the storm – and amplifies them, establishing them, once again, this time in his terms, as "marvelous": bizarre, thus memorable. Then he adds the music – "le chant des oisiaux" – and the joy, in a passage that is densely repetitive.

> Espoir si fu tierce passee,   410
> et pot estre pres de midi,
> quant l'*arbre* et la *fontainne vi*
>
> Bien sai de l'*arbre* c'est la fins,
> que ce estoit li plus biax pins
> qui onques sor terre creüst.
> Ne cuit c'onques si fort pleüst
> que d'eve i passast une gote,
> einçois coloit par desor tote.
>
> A l'arbre *vi* le *bacin* pandre,
> del plus fin or qui fust a vandre   420
> encor onques en nule foire.
>
> De la *fontainne*, poez croire,
> qu'ele boloit com iaue chaude.
>
> Li *perrons* ert d'une esmeraude
> perciee ausi com une boz,
> et s'a quatre rubiz desoz,
> plus flanboianz et plus vermauz
> que n'est au matin li solauz,
> quant il apert en orïant;
> ja, que je sache a escïant,   430
> ne vos an mantirai de mot.
>
> La mervoille a *veoir* me plot
> de la *tanpeste* et de l'orage,
> don je ne me ting mie a sage;
> que volentiers m'an repantisse
> tot maintenant, se je poïsse
> quant je oi le *perron* crosé
> de l'eve au *bacin* arosé.

Mes trop en i verssai, ce dot;
que lors *vi* le ciel si derot   440
que de plus de quatorze parz
me feroit es *ialz* li esparz;
et les nues tot mesle mesle
gitoient pluie, noif et gresle.
Tant fu li tans pesmes et forz
que cent foiz cuidai estre morz
des foudres qu'antor moi cheoient,
et des arbres qui peçoient.
Sachiez que molt fui esmaiez,
tant que li tans fu rapaiez.   450
Mes Dex tost me rasegura
que li tans gaires ne dura,
et tuit li vant se reposererent;
des que Deu plot, vanter n'oserent.

Et quant je *vi* l'air cler et pur,
de *joie* fui toz asseür;
que *joie*, s'onques la conui,
fet tot oblier grant enui.
Jusque li tans fu trespassez
vi sor le pin toz amassez   460
oisiax, s'est qui croire le vuelle,
qu'il n'i paroit branche ne fuelle,
que tot ne fust covert d'*oisiax*;
s'an estoit li *arbres* plus biax;
doucemant li *oisel chantoient*,
si que molt bien s'antr'acordoient;
et divers *chanz chantoit* chascuns;
c'onques ce que *chantoit* li uns
a l'autre *chanter* ne *oï*.
De lor *joie* me res*joï*;   470
s'*escoutai* tant qu'il orent fet
lor servise trestot a tret;
que mes n'*oï* si bele *joie*
ne ja ne cuit que nus hom l'*oie*
se il ne va *oïr* celi
qui tant me plot et abeli
que je m'an dui por fos tenir . . .   lines 410–77

Chrétien repeats certain words, such as ''joie'' and ''chant,'' over and over, and frequency of repetition is of course strongly correlated to ease of learning. He makes strong use of patterns of recapitulation and repetition to anchor the fountain in memory both of ''things'' and of ''words'' – and he links things to words, for example, by the ongoing rhymes between joy and the hearing of music: ''joie'' and ''oie.'' He also connects the fountain up with themes which were, we know, of intense interest to medieval 'high culture': jewels and precious substances; and music and song.

We have examined a wide variety of elements that would have contributed to facilitating the *ad verba* learning of Chrétien's romances. These factors are by no means peculiar to his works. Psychologists Wanda T. Wallace and David C. Rubin have studied a number of works from poetic traditions, and state:

> Our studies of counting-out rhymes, epic poetry, and ballads have led us to the view that multiple constraints play large roles in keeping oral traditions stable over time. In ballads, the multiple constraints are based on music, poetics, narrative structure, and imagery. These constraints limit the possible choices for any one word or phrase and thereby reduce the memory load. That is, the constraints, plus a minimum of detailed information, can be transmitted instead of the exact words. This view of multiple constraints is much the same as Bartlett (1932) suggested for the single constraint of meaning. Here, however, we assume that singers display not only effort after meaning but also effort after all the forms of organization present in the ballad tradition. The combination of these forms of organization, or constraints, in oral traditions leads to a much more stable transmission than Bartlett observed in material that lacked forms of organization other than meaning.[39]

It is precisely such a set of multiple constraints – musical, poetic, narrative, and the like – which characterize the romances of Chrétien, and many other works as well, making them what I have termed memory-friendly.

But we must not forget another important factor bearing on romance memorability and memorization:[40] recourse to gesture and other physical action. Though classical and medieval rhetoricians and memory-theorists do not discuss this particular mnemonic aid, a number of modern psychologists have studied the importance of "somatic" or "motoric" activity in memory work.[41]

The simplist physical actions with mnemonic relevance are body movements such as rocking and swaying, which have been recognized by a

---

[39] Wanda T. Wallace and David C. Rubin, " 'The Wreck of the Old 97': A Real Event Remembered in Song," pp. 283–310, in *Remembering Reconsidered: Ecological and Traditional Approaches to the Study of Memory*, p. 285.

[40] They also bear on epic memorability, and indeed on that of fabliaux and many other sorts of works. My point is, precisely, that the differences between epic and romance (and other performed genres as well) are not so very marked and have tended to be overemphasized.

[41] See, e.g., A.A. Smirnov, *Problems of the Psychology of Memory*, esp. p. 35. See also the extensive work on the importance of the body in learning by Bryant J. Cratty – for example, *Perceptual-Motor Behavior and Educational Processes*. This was also the position of Jousse, *The Oral Style*, p. 20 and *passim*. It is, however, interesting to note that, in general, modern American psychology is so strongly "cognitive" in its approach to memory that it allows little room for the role of the body.

variety of scholars as common among oral performers. Other such movements and gestures include rhythmic pacing or more-or-less acrobatic movement about the room, the "bowing" of a stringed instrument such as the vielle, and the rhythmic plucking of the strings of the harp. All of these body movements we know to have been part of the medieval performance situation.

One final, and thorny, pair of question remains. Was it with or without the use of a book – a written text – that octo works such as Chrétien's romances were learned? And were these works learned word-for-word, or not? The two questions are related because it is commonly argued that works "memorized" without recourse to a book are not learned verbatim,[42] but only through a loose process of recall that leaves room for improvisation. Many literary scholars think of the two modes of memorization as markedly different. Psychological research, however, does not sustain so firm a distinction, since "memorization" is not merely a warehousing activity but is a mental reconstitution of the material being learned.[43] That is, the difference is one of degree rather than of kind. We do not have certain answers to either of my two questions, but a de-dichotomization of the issue may perhaps bring us closer to historical realities.

The evidence: the manuscript tradition of Chrétien's romances – as of most other early romances, fabliaux, etc. – shows a great many *variantes*. But they are mostly small: shifts in wording, in rhyme, in the articulation of a few lines; occasionally a pair or two of lines will be added or eliminated, etc. The pattern of *variantes* has made editors throw up their hands over the difficulties in constructing adequate stemma to show affiliations among manuscripts.[44]

An interesting and illuminating example of the manuscript variants is offered by the passage in *Yvain* which describes the reception offered to Arthur upon his arrival in Yvain's new kingdom. This passage has recently been examined from a musicological perspective by Sylvia Huot in an article entitled "Voices and Instruments in Medieval French Secular Music: On the Use of Literary Texts as Evidence for Performance Practice." Here is the way in which a few of the lines read in the Guiot manuscript (BN fr. 794), as edited by Roques:

> Li sain, li cor, et les buisines
> font le chastel si resoner
> que l'en n'oïst pas Deu toner.
> La ou descendent les puceles,
> sont flaütes et vïeles,
> tympre, fretelles et tabor;

---

[42] See, for example, Ian M.L. Hunter, "Lengthy Verbatim Recall: The Role of Text," pp. 207–35, esp. p. 234.

[43] Bartlett, *Remembering*, p. 213.

[44] See Micha, *Tradition manuscrite, passim*. See also Margot Van Mulken, "*Perceval and Stemmata*."

d'autre part refont lor labor
li legier sailleor qui saillent . . .   lines 2350–57

(The bells, the horns and the bagpipes/ make the castle so resound/ that one could not have heard God thunder./ There where the young girls go down [to greet the king]/ are flutes and vielles,/ tambourines, cymbals and tabor;/ elsewhere do their work/ the light jumpers who jump . . .)

Let's focus on just three of these lines, and look at them carefully. Here is how lines 2353–55 read in BN fr. 12603:

Contre lui ivent les puceles
Les flahutes et les fresteles,
Timbres, tabletes et tabors.

(Toward him went the young girls/ The flutes and the freteles,/ Tambourines, cymbals and tabors.)

Very close to this is BN fr. 12560:

Encontre lui vont les puceles
Les flahutes et les fresteles,
Timbres, tabletes et tables.

(Up toward him go the young girls,/ The flutes and the freteles,/ Tambourines, cymbals and "tables" [another kind of cymbals?].)

In this manuscript it is not clear whether or not it is the girls who are playing the instruments (one gets the impression it is not).
But Chantilly, Musée Condé, 472 is quite different. It reads:

Contre lui sonnent les puceles
Et lor timbres et lor vieles
Flahutes, tabletes et tabors.

(Toward him play the young girls/ And their tambourines and their vielles,/ Flutes, cymbals and tabors . . .)

This time it is the girls who are playing the instruments: they are the musicians.
BN fr. 1433 reads:

Et la ou chantent les pucheles,
Sonnent fleütes et freteles,
Timbres, tabletes et tabours.

In this case, the girls are singing and other people are apparently playing the instruments; and, here, they are not clearly in a procession toward the king.

259

As Huot notes, this "single description is thus in reality seven descriptions, no two of them quite alike" (p. 67). Huot's primary concern here is with musical practice; ours is with the issue of memory transmission. And what from our perspective is primarily striking is that, in these three lines, not a single element is perfectly stable except the presence of "puceles" ("girls") at the end of the first line, and the fact that they are associated, in one way or another, to music: they dance to it, they sing it, or they play it on instruments. The girls "vont" or "ivent" or "descendent" or "sonnent" or "chantent"; sometimes it is "toward" – "Contre" ou "Encontre" – Arthur, but not always: "La ou . . ." and "Et la ou . . ." The music produced also varies considerably, and no two descriptions are the same. Two instruments – "timbre" and "flahutes" – are there in each instance, but not reliably in the same place in the line.

These manuscripts – these versions – are all clearly very similar; substantially the same. But there is an extensive, indeed a pervasive, pattern of minor differences between them: every line differs from manuscript to manuscript. And while I would not wish to argue that this pattern is completely "typical" of Chrétien's manuscript tradition taken as a whole, it is by no means unusual.

There are, as I see it, four hypotheses that can account for this general phenomenon: 1) Scribes consulted and selected details from an array of manuscripts. That this sometimes occurred can hardly be doubted; that it accounts for all such differences among manuscripts seems far less likely. 2) Scribes intentionally modified – attempted to improve upon – the text from which they were copying. That this too occurred cannot be denied. Intelligent scribes frequently tried to make texts that they found incomprehensible or "wrong" make sense. (Sometimes, of course, they made matters worse. The scribe was not always as smart as he thought, and the problem was sometimes in his understanding of the text, not in the text itself.) Scribes also occasionally reworded passages of texts that seemed antiquated to update them or make them more relevant to a new audience. 3) Scribes made errors in deciphering the text or in copying the manuscript. Again, this is frequently the case, but cannot, by any means, account for all variants. 4) Finally, scribes sometimes trusted their memory of a work they knew well over against that of their written exemplar. I see this explanation, which is rarely discussed, as accounting for at least some differences among manuscripts.[45]

Let us examine another example of the sorts of *variantes* found in manuscripts of Chrétien's romances. This time we will take a long passage, also from *Yvain*, from the hero's first meeting with the lion. I choose this scene as one that might well have been popular with fans of Chrétien. This time, I will just give two manuscript versions of the scene, as I believe they make the point adequately. (Other manuscripts do confirm the findings.) First, here, is the passage as given in the Guiot edition, as edited by Mario Roques:

---

[45] See Dembowski, "The French Tradition of Textual Philology."

Mes sire Yvains pansis chemine
par une profonde gaudine
tant qu'il oï en mi le gaut
un cri molt dolereus et haut. 340
Si s'adreça lors vers le cri
cele part ou il l'ot oï,
et, quant il parvint cele part,
vit un lÿon, en un essart,
et un serpant qui le tenoit
par la coe, et si li ardoit
trestoz les rains de flame ardant.
N'ala mie molt regardant
mes sire Yvains cele mervoille;
a lui meïsmes se consoille 350
auquel d'aus deus il aidera;
lors dit qu'au lÿon se tanra,
qu'a venimeus ne a felon
ne doit an faire se mal non,
et li serpanz est venimeus,
si li saut par la boche feus,
tant est de felenie plains.
Por ce panse mes sire Yvains
qu'il l'ocirra premieremant;
s'espee tret et vint avant 360
et met l'escu devant sa face,
que la flame mal ne li face
que il gitoit par mi la gole,
qui plus estoit lee d'une ole.
Se li li lÿons aprés l'asaut,
la bataille pas ne li faut,
mes que qu'il l'en aveigne aprés,
cidier li voldra il adés,
que pitiez li semont et prie
qu'il face secors et aïe 370
a la beste gentil et franche.
A s'espee, qui soef tranche,
va le felon serpant requerre;
si le tranche jusqu'anz en terre
et les deux mitiez retronçone,
fiert et refiert, et tant l'en done
que tot le demince et depiece.
Mes il li covient une piece
tranchier de la coe au lÿon
por la teste au serpant felon 380
qui par la coe le tenoit;
tant con tranchier an covenoit
en trancha, c'onques moins ne pot. . . . lines 3337–83

261

(My lord Yvain, pensive, rides along/ through a deep ravine/ until he heard in the middle of a wood/ a very sorrowful and loud cry./ And he went forward toward the cry,/ in the direction where he had heard it,/ and when he got to the place,/ he saw a lion, in a clearing,/ and a serpent which held it/ by the tail, and burned/ its flanks with burning flames./ Yvain did not spend much time looking/ at this marvel;/ he debates with himself [takes counsel of himself]/ as to which of the two he will help;/ then he says that he will hold to the lion,/ for to a poisonous or evil creature/ one should only do ill,/ and the serpent is poisonous,/ fire comes out of its mouth,/ and it is full of wickedness./ For this reason, my lord Yvain thinks/ that he will kill it first;/ he draws his sword and went forward/ and puts the shield before his face,/ so that the flame that it throws from its mouth,/ which is as wide as a cauldron,/ won't hurt him./ If the lion attacks him afterwards,/ he won't refuse the battle,/ but whatever happens afterwards,/ he wants to help him now,/ for pity summons and prays/ that he give succor and aid/ to the noble beast./ With his sword, which cut smoothy,/ he goes to find the wicked serpent;/ he cuts through it down to the ground/ and the two halves chops up some more,/ he strikes and strikes again, and hits so much/ that he cuts it all to pieces./ But he has to cut one piece/ of the lion's tail/ because the head of the wicked serpent/ was holding the lion by the tail;/ he cut what he had to, he couldn't cut any less.)

Here is the same passage as given in BN fr. 1433, as edited by David Hult for "Lettres gothiques." I italicize the differences between the Guiot/Roques edition and this edition, but do not mark differences that are essentially matters of dialect.

Mesire Yvains pensis chemine
Tant qu'il vint en une gaudine;
Et lors oÿ en mi le gaut
Un cri mout dolereus et haut,
Si s'adrecha leus vers le cri
Chele part ou il l'ot oÿ.
Et quant il parvint chele part,
Vit .i. lion en .i. essart
E .i. serpent qui le tenoit
Par le keue, si li ardoit   3350
Toutes les rains de flame ardant.
N'ala mie mout regardant
Mesire Yvains chele merveile:
A lui meïsmes se conseille
Auquel des deuz il aidera.
Lors dit c'au lyon *secorra*.
Qu'a *enuious et* a felon

Ne doit on faire se mal non.
Et le serpens est *enuious*,
Si li saut par la *goule* fus,   3360
Tant est de felonnie plains.
Che se pense Mesire Yvains
Qu'il ochirra premierement.
L'espee trait et vient avant
Et met l'escu devant sa faiche,
Que la flambe mal ne li faiche,
Que il getoit par mi la gole,
Qui plus estoit lee d'un ole.
Se li lions aprés l'assaut,
De la bataille *ni* li faut.   3370
Mais quoi qu'i l'en aviengne aprés,
Aidier li vaurra il adés,
Que pités l'*en* semont et prie
Qu'il faiche secours et aÿe
A la beste gentil et franche.
A l'espee *fourbie et blanche*
Va le felon serpent requerre,
Si le trenche jusques en terre,
Et les .ii. moitiez retronchonne;
Fiert et refiert et tant l'en donne   3380
Que tot *l'emenuse* et depieche.
Mais *de le keuë une pieche*
Li couvint trencier du lion
Por la teste au serpent felon
Qui *engoulee li avoit*.
Tant com tranchier en covenoit
*L'*en trencha, c'onques mais n'en pot. ... lines 3341–87

The two manuscript versions of this passage present a good many quite small-scale differences. The variations do not appear to come at places where a scribe would have perceived a problem that he had to resolve either by looking at a different manuscript, or on which he might have felt invited to use his own judgment. Thus, the differences do not occur at "problem points." Nor do they seem to be simple scribal errors: there are no "sauts du même au même," for example, or mere transpositions. Rather, I suggest that the variants are of the sort that would naturally occur when someone knew the text by heart and trusted his own memory more than his written exemplar. We have a serpent that is *venimeux* vs. one that is *enuious*; fire is coming from the *boche* of one such beast, from the *gole* of the other; we have one sword *qui soef tranche* and one that is *fourbie et blanche*; and so on. These are minor issues of lexical choice – and they constitute a particular sort of "error." (Though of course it is possible that neither choice is an error, but that Chrétien himself performed the work differently on different occasions, and that his *own* variations are recorded into the manuscript tradition.) It is the kind of mistake that most of us have made when learning a poem of, say, Shakespeare or Wordsworth by heart. We have some small syntactic differences which are not accounted for by differences in dialect, such as "Mes sire Yvains pansis chemine/ par une profonde gaudine/ tant qu'il oï en mi le gaut" vs. "Mesire Yvains pensis chemine/ *Tant qu'il vint en une gaudine/ Et lors* oÿ en mi le gaut." We have ". . . fiert et refiert, et tant l'en done/ que tot le demince et depiece./ Mes il li covient une piece/ tranchier de la coe au lïon" vs. ". . . Fiert et refiert et tant l'en donne/ Que tot *l'emenuse* et depieche./ Mais *de le keuë une pieche/ Li couvint trencier du lion*." These are all minor variations that could easily be the result of memorization.[46]

Philologists think – they *must* think – in terms of a base manuscript, designated as the best on some set of criteria (the oldest, the least corrupt, etc.), and they view other manuscripts as variants of this base text. It might, however, be wise, at least in some cases, to conceive of the different manuscripts, with their variants, as reflecting a combination of textual transmission, on the one hand, and memorized, or "memorial," transmission, on the other. That is, textual tradition sometimes bears marks of *semi*-verbatim recall. To put all this a bit differently: the evidence suggests that, indeed, scribes sometimes used more than one manuscript of Chrétien's romances, and that they sometimes took it upon themselves to improve upon the texts they were copying. But the evidence also suggests that written exemplars may have served at once as a mnemonic aid and as a curb to the freedom of performers to "improvise" – or to remember *their* way. (Written copies of works often serve a similar function today: my freedom to recall the poetry of Ronsard, Shakespeare, Hugo, and Browning as I wish is restricted by the general availability of written copies of their works – and by other people's memories of their poems.) While there was a substantial amount of memory-transmission going on in the twelfth and thirteenth centuries, this memory transmission was often rather "imperfect": not absolutely verbatim, not altogether controlled by written exemplars. Many people knew Chrétien's romances pretty well – but only pretty well! – by heart.

Another way of conceptualizing this issue might be to focus on the distinction between *trouvères* (or "troubadours"): poetic "inventors" and makers of verse, on the one hand, and mere performers (*jongleurs*, minstrels and the like), on the other. With regard to the ancient Greek tradition, James Notopoulos distinguished between true "oral poets" and mere "rhapsodes" or performers. In the earlier period, rhapsodes learned the works they sang in a fully oral fashion – from other singers; later, they apparently learned works by heart from a written text.[47] But though in any case the rhapsodes were learning other people's works by memory, in the early phase presumably more lexical

46 On these issues see Linda Marie Zaerr and Mary Ellen Ryder, "Psycholinguistic Theory and Modern Performance: Memory as a Key to Variants in Medieval Texts."
47 Notopoulos, "Mnemosyne in Oral Literature," p. 470.

(and other) leeway was tolerable in performance than at the later period, when many people possessed, or had read, the text of works of Homer and others.

In the fourteenth century, Dante would deal with his twin desires to have people learn his *Divine Comedy* by heart and to have them learn it *right* – that is, absolutely verbatim – by using the very tightly-structured "terza rima" form in hundred-line cantos, producing a work that tried to compel perfect memorization from those who wished to learn it at all.[48]

Thus, in early French literature (and no doubt elsewhere) we may be seeing a third – or rather, an intermediate – mode of "memorization": something in between the two extremes of true verbatim, text-based memorization, on the one hand, and the looser, freer formulaic recall *cum* improvisation, so common in full-scale oral tradition, on the other. Those who recited the stories from memory felt free, within a fairly limited range, to introduce changes as *memoria ad verba* failed them, or to respond to a new performance situation. For example, in the first passage given above, shifts in references to instruments might correspond to the instruments present in the particular court at the time of performance. And those who copied the texts, the scribes, may also have felt free to "remember" the text they were copying differently from what they actually saw on the page.[49] These factors may account for some of the complex patterns of variation and contamination among manuscripts.

One last look at Chrétien de Troyes's romances, and at the manuscripts that contain them, from a mnemonic perspective – but with a new twist. In BN 794 (the famous "Guiot manuscript") an unknown medieval hand wrote the following – assonanced decasyllabic – verses:

> Erec Enyde est a la premiere enseigne,
> Lancelot en Charrete la second tesmoigne,
> Cliget qui welt trover la tierce ensoigne proigne,
> Li chevaliers au lions a la quarte voigne,
> Athis, Profilias la quinte nos donra
> Et lou Romant de Troies la siste ensoignera,
> Estoires d'Eingleterre la setime avera
> Des Empereurs de Rome l'uitime nos dira,
> De Perceval lou viel quant tu en wels oïr
> A la neuvime ensoigne qu'est par soi doïs venir.[50]

[48] See John Ahern, "Singing the Book."

[49] I am by no means the first person to have proposed that this sort of thing occurred. Chaytor, for example, says that scribal error was not always due to carelessness, that "if a scribe was copying a text composed in a dialect not native to himself, he was likely to substitute his own auditory memory of the text for his visual impression of it, and to write *er* for *ar*, *el* for *al*, and the like" (*From Script to Print*, p. 19). My point is simply that we should extend this principle from issues of dialectal form, more broadly to issues of content: scribes may well have trusted their memory of the substance of the line itself over what they saw before them.

[50] Reprinted in Micha, *Tradition manuscrite*, p. 34.

(Erec and Enide is in the first place [literally: "mark"],/ Lancelot in the Cart, the second witnesses,/ Cligés, let him who wishes to find the third place take,/ The knight with the lion, let him come to the fourth,/ Athis, Profilias, the fifth will give us,/ And the Romance of Troy the sixth will teach,/ The Story of England will have the seventh/ About the Emperors of Rome the eighth will tell us,/ About Perceval the Elder, when you want to hear/ To the ninth place which is by itself, you must come.)

This is primarily, it would appear, a "Table of Contents." But by its verse form it appears to be a mnemonic aid as well: its purpose is to allow the owner and user of the volume to remember what is in it. This is, then, *memoria ad res* at the level not of the contents of a work, but of those of a manuscript. But it is intriguing to note that even in this reference tool, the book's user is presented as someone who will "hear" – "*oïr*" – the book, not "read" it. He must come to various "places" to hear what they have to "say" and to "give us."

In this chapter we have been concerned with one of the major implications of the performed status of early French romance. We now turn, in the final chapter, to some of the important social and "literary" implications of this performance reality: to how romances "worked," and were received, in French medieval culture.

CHAPTER EIGHT

On the Advantages of a Performance-Oriented Approach to Medieval Romance

The central argument of this book has been that early French romance had strong roots in oral culture and that it was frequently performed from memory in a way that drew significantly on the resources of both the voice and the body of the performer.[1] This final chapter will attempt to demonstrate the usefulness of a performance-centered, or performance-oriented, approach to medieval romance. The advantages of such an approach are, I believe, especially clear as regards matters of audience response.

I will have, in these pages, three basic points to make. 1) We must focus more scholarly attention on the contexts in which medieval romances were performed. 2) We should consider the impact of the performance situation on audience response to and interpretation of romance. 3) We need to begin not merely to read aloud but to recite and – in strong senses of the word – "perform" medieval romances.

These three points flow from a single underlying contention: it does make a difference that medieval romances were works intended for performance; specifically, it *should* make a difference in the ways in which we approach and study them.

Performance context

Let us move into the large issue of performance context and audience response somewhat obliquely, by asking the question: Why is the verb "read" not an acceptable way to express how medieval audiences experienced, understood and interpreted romances?

First, to take the verb literally. As I have pointed out repeatedly over the course of this book – and I refer my readers to the many scholars who have made similar points[2] – few laymen and women of the late-twelfth and thir-

---

[1] To avoid misunderstandings, I will avoid here expressions like "a strongly dramatic fashion." But that such performances were markedly theatrical, in the medieval senses of the word, can hardly be doubted.

[2] See the work of Bäuml, Clanchy, Green, Illich, Parkes, and others. Cressy emphasizes the still-general illiteracy of Western Europe several centuries later.

teenth centuries could read. Those who could and did read, were rarely reading romances, but rather devotional works or useful things such as documents; most such "written texts" were in Latin. Normally, people *heard* romances recited. Even those persons who possessed copies of romances apparently heard the books read aloud rather than reading them for themselves. Thus, in the literal sense, there were few readers, still fewer romance-readers, and few books of romance *to* read.

But of course the verb "read" is used broadly these days. Many reception critics and others use the terms "reading" and "text" to speak of any and all sorts of works which call for some decoding interpretation[3] – and that excludes few works indeed. A "text" can be almost any sort of verbal or even conceptual structure, or an event, and "read" can refer to any act of interpretation or decoding. Thus, a film can be a "text," and one can "read" a picture.[4]

Yet the literal modern meanings[5] of "reading" and "text" tend to dominate reception-theory discourse. The reader is apt to be conceived as a solitary, silent individual, alone with a text, a text from which the author, indeed any "authority" intrinsic to the work, is absent; a text which may be thought of as ultimately having no meaning of its own – that is, it is up to the reader to construct, or to invent, meaning in and for the text. Reading is fundamentally a private intellectual activity.[6]

Today's solitary reader may well have had his expectations formed by a community, and he may later attempt to persuade, even to coerce, others to accept his interpretation of the work.[7] But the contemporary "interpretive community" is typically a figure of speech in the sense that most members of a given "community" of this sort have never actually met or even spoken to each other; theirs is a meeting only of minds, even of small bits of their respective cerebra. Or one might say that they share sociological features; they do not, however, form a "society."

In short, the reader is generally defined today as engaged in a private, cognitive activity, of which he is largely in control. Interpretive community tends to be an intellectual construct.

The situation of the medieval audience is profoundly different from that of

---

3   See, for example, R.C. Holub, *Reception Theory: A Critical Introduction*, e.g., pp. xii, 82ff, 107ff, 152ff. The audience of a work is reliably referred to as its "reader."

4   Among the scholars who have noted, and been disturbed by, this tendency to generalize the word "text" to all sorts of non-"textual" things is E.C. Fine, in *The Folklore Text: From Performance to Print*, pp. 91ff.

5   The word "read" (as we saw earlier) did not originally mean what we mean by this word today . . .

6   See, for example, Wolfgang Iser, "The Reading Process: A Phenomenological Approach."

7   Stanley Fish, *Is There a Text in this Class?*, e.g., pp. 338–55 ("What Makes an Interpretation Acceptable?") and pp. 356–72 ("Demonstration vs. Persuasion: Two Models of Critical Activity").

this modern reader. The differences are *precisely* those that arise from performance context – and these differences make the words "text," "read," and "reader" unsatisfactory.

The "text" was not experienced *directly* by the audience, but was *mediated*, in several ways. The work, the words, were mediated to them by the performer (or group of performers). Audience understanding of particular romances cannot help but have been affected by the *performers'* interpretation. Indeed, in many cases, audiences could hardly have distinguished between the intentions of the poet and of the performer (assuming that they were in fact different individuals, for the performer tended to adopt the speaking "I" of the former).

Thus, the work was known to listeners not in itself – not as a "text" – but as relayed to them through the performer. Similarly, today, theater audiences may "know" certain plays of Shakespeare primarily through the "interpretation" of these works by actors who have played the key roles: Laurence Olivier, Richard Burton, Kenneth Branagh and others.[8]

But the medieval audience (like theatre and other "live" audiences today) was not merely responding to the work as mediated; it was responding to the mediator himself or herself:[9] to the performer, and to the character and the quality of the performance. The audience responded then (as they still do today[10]) to the physical appearance, the clothing or costume, the charm, the gestures, the voice, and the sheer human presence of the actor or other performer. They were (or were not) taken by his or her talent and appeal. There before the members of the audience stands the performer, alive and present, with the compelling quality – some have termed it "authority" – of that presence: "*I* tell *you* . . .!" (This is a point that Zumthor brought out with great eloquence in almost all of his studies of oral/vocal culture.) This is a powerfully dynamic interpersonal element.

Along with the performer, there are other elements of the performance situation to which audiences would have responded and which would have served to mediate the work. One of the most important of these is music, which we know was invariably present and abundant in festive court settings.[11] We all recognize the power of music to set a mood, to create an emotional

---

8   This is not to deny that Shakespeare has, and has had, many private readers (people who read his plays silently to themselves). But not all audiences of Shakespeare have been, or are, such.

9   For "jongleresses," see Faral, *passim*; also C. Bullock-Davies, *Ménestrellorum multitudo: Minstrels at a Royal Feast*, pp. 55ff; also C. Davidson, *Illustrations of the Stage and Acting in England to 1580*.

10   The situation of film is in some respects similar, aside from the living *presence* of the performer, which is an important phenomenon.

11   As we saw in Chapter 6, romances appear often to have been sung and/or to have been performed with musical accompaniment. More generally, music suffused court events as a whole.

ambiance. If we need a modern analogy: we need only think of the sound track of contemporary films to be aware of the power of this psychological and indeed physiological phenomenon. But the thirteenth century *Roman d'Yder* expresses the power of music well, putting it eloquently if hyperbolically: after listing at length all the kinds of instruments, songs and dances at a great wedding party, the poet says that no one present there could feel sad or angry. One could only be happy, and one would wish to remain in such bliss forever:

> Il ne peust avoir cele ire,
> Ço ne li feist oblier.
> Home qui osast en ço fier
> Qu'il i peust estre a sojor.
> Tote sa vie en cele dolçor,
> Ne quesist ja changier cel estre
> Por avoir parais terestre.   lines 6755–61.[12]

(He could not be angry or sad,/ For it [the music] would make him forget about it./ A man who dared to believe/ That he could stay/ All his life in that sweetness/ Would not want to change his situation/ For the earthly paradise itself.)

In the court hall, there was typically a gay – sometimes even a raucous – assortment of musical noises: vielles and other highly resonant stringed instruments (in the thirteenth century, bowed strings did not yet encompass what we have come to call the "bass register"), flutes, bagpipes, cymbals, drums, trumpets and other horns are the instruments that appear to have predominated in such settings. The various musicians and kinds of music competed with each other. The *Flamenca* poet refers to the noise in the hall when *jongleurs* and minstrels are performing romances and other works: "Per la rumor dels viuladors/ e del brug d'aitans comtadors,/ hac gran murmuri per la sala" (lines 711–13; "Because of the music of the viols/ and the noise of so many minstrels/ there was a great commotion in the hall"[13]).

As this last quotation suggests, there was also lots of just plain noise and commotion: people chatting, flirting and arguing, calling out. That there was often noisy disorder is clear just from the many requests for silence – especially but not exclusively by *jongleurs* in *chansons de geste*. Since performances often took place during a feast, members of the audience might well be eating and drinking. Sometimes entertainment came after the feast was over – which means that some members of the audience would have been sleepy or drunk. It is safe to say that there were thus many full-scale or partial interruptions during the performance. It is also safe to say that the festive event would

---

12 *The Romance of Yder*, ed. and trans. Alison Adams.
13 *The Romance of Flamenca*, ed. and trans. Blodgett.

have been marked both by "courtly manners" (indeed at their most elaborate) and by a presumably increasing loss of decorum as the event "evolved."

Such is the dense immediate interpersonal and sensorial context to which, and in which, audiences were responding. But broader and deeper social contexts were often highly important for audience response, as well. In festive settings, such as we evoked in Chapter 6, a particular work was frequently nested or included in a complex performance event.[14] For example, an evening's entertainment, which might include the performance of romances and many other things as well, was often embedded in a substantially larger social and cultural event, lasting for many days or even weeks. In larger courts, hundreds of people might be present. There was much elaborate food and lavish dress. Rich gifts were exchanged: armor, clothing, horses and the like were often distributed to new knights, and others – including minstrels and *jongleurs*. Many different kinds of performances were presented at such events: there were romances, epics, and other short narrative works, and lyric songs of all kinds; as noted earlier, music was omnipresent. Fools, acrobats, marionnettists, prestidigitators and other entertainers added to the variety (and no doubt the din).

Such occasions were not merely socially and sensorially complex; there was often much at stake in them. Feasts such as Christmas, Easter, and Pentecost were important religious occasions: seasons of spiritual transformation. Weddings, dubbing rituals and coronations had strong religious and political implications: bonds of loyalty were being forged or repaired, and these events all had a more or less strongly marked sacramental character. These festivities were not, then, just big bashes. They were deeply significant rituals and ceremonies: "transforming" events, at which people and their lives were changed. In the works whose performance followed such rituals we can often see the desire to ratify, in a court setting, the religious and political transformation, primarily by the representation and enacting of similar transformations.

Some early performed romances, in their overall plot and central themes, also present to audiences major difficulties that can arise in the transformation process. One might call these difficulties "what if" problems: "What if the desired transformation fails to occur, or goes wrong?" Thus, what if one member of the married couple doesn't feel or act married to the other? or feels married to someone else?: we get Béroul's *Tristan*, or indeed any of the Tristan stories. What if one of the couple forgets to fulfill his conjugal responsibilities?: Chrétien's *Yvain*. Or what if the married couple act *too* married and forget about their other duties?: *Érec et Énide*. What if the knight doesn't get

14 For highly interesting discussions of performance events, see Richard Schechner, *Performance Theory*, especially "Toward a Poetics of Performance" (pp. 153–86). Also of interest is Schechner's *Between Theatre and Anthropology*. I am indebted to Schechner's work at various points below.

his chivalric and religious lessons right?: Chrétien's *Perceval*. And what if the crowned king fails to behave in an ethical fashion, as a true king?: Chrétien's *Cligés*, Gautier d'Arras' *Éracle*. Thus, many romances take up the difficulties that may impede great transformations if individuals either do not wish, or are unable, to be properly transformed. Such works either resolve the problem symbolically – that is, in the story – or at least play the problem through to its, often dire, consequences.[15]

Such stories – both those which presented successful transformations and those which presented failures or catastrophes – provided audiences with what we would call today "role models" and were called at the time "exempla."

One is often aware in romances – such as those of Chrétien – of a dynamic tension between the festive nature of the romance-event and the gravity of the underlying concerns: knighthood, kingship, love, marriage, spiritual renewal.

I believe that we need to study more carefully how the performance of individual works can be understood as fitting into such broad social and cultural events – rather as scholars have recently begun to focus on the ways in which particular works are set into large manuscript compilations from which they draw part of their meaning. Works may be reworked to fit into a new manuscript context for a new reader or set of readers, just as oral compositions were recast for new audiences.

To be sure, not all performance events were so complex, or had such great political, religious, or cultural issues so powerfully at stake. There were, as I showed earlier (Chapter 6), some "ordinary" and fairly quiet performance moments – though the performance of romance was apparently rare in such contexts. We need to study these performance situations as well.

I have evoked a number of elements which mediated and contextualized medieval romances (and other works) for their audiences. One that I have not yet discussed explicitly was the other members of the audience. The performance situation was strongly interpersonal. We can take as a partial analogy the different kinds of performances that people attend today: whether it is an audience of *cognoscenti* attending a high-culture event, or teenagers at the movies or at a rock-concert, often the personal interaction is among the most important parts of the experience. The play, concert, or film itself may even take back-seat to social intercourse. In the late-twelfth century court setting – such as the courts of Champagne and Flanders, to which Chrétien was connected – many of the people present would have known each other very well indeed: they were members of the count's or countess's family, and of the court. Others would have been visitors from nearby courts, and from farther afield. Thus, we would have a blend of strongly familiar faces – with all the

---

15 By contrast, the epic less reliably deals with such situations where the social roles of great nobles intersect with their identity as individuals, at a crisis point: a moment of transformation. They too, however, frequently address large ethical issues, such as, when and in what circumstances should a vassal renounce his feudal allegiance to his lord?, and the like.

in-jokes and ongoing topics of conversation that characterize such settings –
with newer personalities and topics. (For example, the court of Champagne,
under Marie's influence, appears to have been much concerned with "fin
amor"; Philippe of Alsace's court of Champagne was strongly preoccupied
with religious matters.)

The performance situation was, moreover, not merely interpersonal in some
general sense, it was strongly interactive. A quotation from drama-theorist
Ellen Donkin is useful. She argues:

> Th[e] . . . parley between audience and performers mean[s] that the "reception
> loop" of performer to audience back to performer again [is] an extremely
> tight one . . . When a breathing, murmuring, commenting, laughing audience
> respond[s] positively to something new in a performer's work, it cement[s]
> that change on the spot . . . This [is] not the leisurely process of reader-
> response; it [has] more in common with deals being made in the pit of a
> commodities exchange.[16]

In these lines, Donkin is in fact speaking about the role of actresses in eight-
eenth century theatre, but her point is just as applicable to many other performance situations, including the performance of medieval romance.[17] Immediate
response is an interpersonal *loop*, not just a one-way street, and there may be
parleying, even haggling, involved.

The medieval performer was very much part of this interactivity. If in an
important sense he mediated the work to the audience, he also had to respond
to their tastes and desires. He had, for example, to shift subjects if his listeners
were bored. Peter the Chanter (an important late-twelfth century cleric) gives a
wonderful example of this practice – indeed this necessity. In the passage that
interests us – curiously enough, it occurs in a Bible commentary – he is talking
about priests who sing the mass up to the Offertory but begin again, sometimes
over and over, if no one has given any money yet. He goes on to say:

> They are like those who sing fables and stories, who, seeing that the song
> about Landry [the hero of a story which has not survived] is not pleasing
> their listeners, immediately start singing about Narcissus; because if it will
> not please, they sing about something else.[18]

[16] E. Donkin, "Mrs. Siddons Looks Back in Anger: Feminist Historiography for
Eighteenth-Century British Theatre," p. 279.

[17] A similar point has been made by Tedlock and Mannheim: "Ethnographers of
performance argue that verbal meaning does not arise solely from texts, conceived
narrowly. Rather, it is an emergent property of performance, conceived as a fully engaged
social event and constructed jointly through the actions of all participants in the event" (*The
Dialogic Emergence of Culture*, "Introduction," p. 13). In this volume see also Tedlock,
"Interpretation, Participation, and the Role of Narrative in Dialogical Anthropology."

[18] *Verbum abbreviatum*, 27, Migne, *Patrilogia latina*, Vol. CCV, c. 101; quoted, but
with partially-erroneous reference, Faral, p. 288. My translation.

The performer's job was to *please*, and not to bore, irritate, or offend. And, as the quote from Peter the Chanter suggests, he had to follow the audience's lead. I think it is pretty safe to assume that if a minstrel was performing, say, Béroul's *Tristan* in a court where a king was *present*, he would have handled the role of King Mark – and of the adulterers, our "hero" and "heroine" – quite differently than if he was performing the work in the *absence* of a great magnate. If a king is there, the lovers can be made to look – to sound – a bit slimy; they are certainly liars and tricksters. Mark's role as cuckold and fool could be downplayed, and his virtues of loyalty and genuine love emphasized; certain scenes (such as Mark up in the tree looking foolish) might even be omitted. Alternately, the prudent performer might have switched to another, safer, subject . . .

Performance may sometimes have been interactive in yet another way: in *Le roman de Merlin*, an early-fourteenth century prose romance, Merlin, the great shape-shifter, comes to Arthur's court disguised as a blind minstrel, wearing magnificent clothing and a golden crown, and led by a little white dog. Playing a silver, jewel-encrusted harp, Merlin the minstrel goes from table to table, singing to different groups:[19]

> . . . Et li harperes aloit del .j. renc al autre & lor harpoit seriement & cler si le regarderent a merueilles li vn & li autre car il navoient onques oi harper a cele guise. Si lor plot plus & enbeli le deduit del harpeor que de nule cose que li autre ménestrel fisent. (p. 442)[20]

> (. . . And the harper went from one bench to another and harped to them sweetly and clearly so that this and that group looked at him with amazement for they had never heard anyone harp like this. And the delight provided by this harper pleased and ravished them more than anything that the other minstrels did.)

Thus, as he moved around the room, the performer interacted with individuals and small groups in the audience. Cabaret performers today often relate to their audiences in the same fashion, establishing brief moments of intimacy with members of the larger crowd. It is tempting to speculate about other ways in which medieval performers may have interacted with, and made

---

[19] *Le Roman de Merlin, or The Early History of King Arthur*, H.O. Sommer, ed., pp. 438–43.

[20] In this passage the words "a cele guise" could mean either that it is the excellence with which he played that so thrilled his audience or the way he moved around the room. I assume that it is the former, as minstrels may with some frequency have performed in an ambulatory manner.

Just *how* Merlin – and similar harp-playing minstrels – combined their playing/singing and their walking about is not clear. The harp – especially a heavy harp like this one! – is most easily played with two hands, with the harpist seated. It would appear likely, then, that minstrel-harpists moved from table to table, talking perhaps as they went, but that they sat down to play and sing.

use of, their audiences. For example, in romances there are many portraits of beautiful maidens. The performer who was, like Merlin, in a position to move about the hall may very well have made these verbal portraits more real by pointing to – and thus praising – the beautiful blond hair, or the perfect features, or the elegant dress, of young women present in the room; they may of course have praised and drawn attention to males as well.

The impact of performance situation on audience response to romance

We are, then, looking at an intense, interpersonal, heavily-mediated, and strongly interactive situation, rather than at a private reader sitting alone with his book. What is the impact of such a situation on audience response and interpretation?[21]

First, works composed for such performance are very apt to have, among their primary functions, purposes that can be defined as affective, ethical, and esthetic, rather than cognitive or intellectual. Such works are there above all to move the heart and the will, to delight, to entertain.

Let us begin with the appeal to emotions. The late-twelfth century theologian Peter of Blois said, in a work on penance and sorrow for sin entitled *De Confessione*:

> Often in tragedies [sad stories: "tragoediis"] and other songs of poets, and in songs of *jongleurs*, some man who is prudent, handsome, strong, lovable, and in all things gracious, is described. The pressures or injuries cruelly inflicted on him are recited, whether it concerns Arthur or Gawain or Tristan; actors tell these fables, at whose hearing the hearts of the audience are stirred to compassion, and are even moved to tears. You who are moved to pity at the recitation of stories, if you hear something pious read about God which squeezes tears from you, are you not then able because of this to give expression to the love of God? You who are moved to compassion for God will also be moved to compassion for Arthur.[22]

Audiences of the stories of Arthur, Gawain and Tristan are, then, often moved to tears of sadness and compassion. These are not the only tears to which Peter thinks they should be moved, any more than the tears that Augustine had wept centuries earlier over Dido were in his later view those he thought *he* should have been shedding; but that is another story.

Many romances, and other works, inspired tears of sorrow or pity. But what we typically find – even in works that are generally "sad" or generally "happy" – is a *blend* of tears and laughter. In the *Roland*, when the heroes die,

---

21 On these issues, for the later medieval period, see Coleman, *Public Reading*, esp. pp. 27–33 and 85–88.
22 *Patrilogia latina*, Vol. CCVII, c. 1088; quoted in part, Faral, p. 287. My translation.

one by one, and then when Charlemagne arrives to find his beloved nephew and all his peers dead and collapses in grief, we should probably assume a weeping performer and a sobbing audience. But (for example) when Ganelon is captured and slapped around, audiences might have cheered. In Béroul's *Tristan*, when the hero leaps from the queen's bed to his own, leaving tell-tale drops of blood falling onto the floor, audiences might have moaned – with Béroul himself – in dismay. But when, at the "Mal Pas," Tristan, disguised as a leper, makes the "felons" fall into the mud, and then when Iseut exculpates herself through a cleverly-worded oath, audiences would have laughed, probably uproariously – they might even have wept for laughter; this is indeed quite "low" comedy. Listeners and spectators to Chrétien's *Yvain* would have smiled – and perhaps laughed aloud – at the love-debates between Lunete and Laudine, and between Yvain and Laudine; they would have surely groaned with sorrow as the hero realizes he has forgotten to return home in time to retain his wife's love and loyalty, and loses his mind from despair; and, though the pleasures provided by Chrétien are generally refined, audiences might well have crowed with delight as the lion tore demons apart (one rather senses that they were supposed to respond in this fashion).

In many cases the audience was already familiar not merely with the genre or the sub-genre, such as "Arthurian romance," but with the individual work; this is true not merely of the *Chanson de Roland* but of many other songs, stories, and plays, which appear to have been performed with almost ritual frequency. This familiarity can hardly have failed significantly to influence emotional response. Audiences appear to have come to an epic like the *Roland*, as later to Passion Plays, prepared above all to weep – to weep, yet again, as they had in past years! – and to other favorite works ready to laugh. What is being activated is thus not merely the audience's anticipation – their "horizon d'attente" with respect to the kind of work in question – but their memory as well: their emotion-laden recollection, and partial reliving, of evenings, people, melodies, feelings, from their past.

But surely the most important emotion that romances, like minstrels themselves, were intended to provide for their audiences was *pleasure*. Romances gave *joy* – such a frequent word in these works! They made people feel "happy." One could provide an abundance of evidence for this point, but let me offer just two, very different examples: In the "Deux Bourdeurs Ribauds" one *jongleur* says:

> Ge sai des romanz d'aventure,
> De cels de la Reonde Table,
> Qui sont a oïr delitable.   lines 82–83[23]

---

23 Faral, *Mimes français*, pp. 93–111.

(I know adventure romances,/ The ones about the Round Table,/
Which are delightful to hear.)

Jean Renart promises that his *Le Roman de la rose ou de Guillaume de Dole*
will give joy and delight to those who hear it:

Ja nuls n'iert de l'oïr lassez,
car, s'en vieult, l'en i chante et lit,
et s'est fez par si grant delit
que tuit cil s'en esjoïrent
qui chanter et lire l'orront,
qu'il lor sera nouviaus toz jors.   lines 18–23

(Never will anyone be weary of listening to it,/ for if you like, it
is sung and read,/ and it is made with such great delight/ that all
those will enjoy it/ who hear it sung and read,/ and it will be new
forever.)

Romances (and many other stories) did not merely affect feelings in a
superficial and short-term sense, but had more fundamental and enduring
emotional and moral functions as well. To some degree this was implicit in my
earlier discussion of the large religious, ethical and political issues that often
surrounded the performance of a particular romance (or other work). One
might say that romances were intended not merely to give delight but to help
make important things happen. This is what performance-theorist Richard
Schechner would call the "efficacy" of performance events:[24] they are not
there just to entertain but to help produce major social and interpersonal transformations.

Victor Turner also provides us with a way of conceptualizing the social
usefulness of traditional "literature." In the "Introduction" to *From Ritual to
Theatre*, Turner states:

By means of such genres as theatre, including puppetry and shadow theatre,
dance drama, and professional story-telling, performances are presented
which probe a community's weaknesses, call its leaders to account, desac-
ralize its most cherished values and beliefs, portray its characteristic
conflicts and suggest remedies for them, and generally take stock of its
current situation in the known "world." (p. 11)

Romances often perform these functions, asking kings – and queens, and
knights, and others – about the ways in which they exercise their responsibilities; they pose important ethical dilemmas, such as those bearing on conflicts
between love and marriage.

The effectiveness and impact of early romance (and many other works) can

24 See Schechner, *Performance Theory*: he considers that performance events constitute a "braid" of "efficacy" and "entertainment."

be conceived in rhetorical terms. I do not mean the term ''rhetorical'' in the highly cognitive way in which it is often used in literary theory, but in a simpler and quite literal way: I mean the kinds of *effects* intended by poets and performers. Rhetoric was the art by which one affected not merely the understanding, or even the emotions, of one's listeners – how they thought or felt about something – but also their moral judgment and indeed their behavior. Most figures and embellishments had as their goal to persuade people to do something. The ''something'' in question could, and did, range widely from work to work, genre to genre. We see – hear – medieval performers inspire listeners to imitate chivalric, courtly or religious virtues; we hear them try to persuade knights to join a crusade or another holy endeavor; we hear them talk people into falling into love, or rejecting love; we hear them talk patrons and audiences into being generous in gifts of coin or clothing. Most medieval works, deeply rhetorical in their essence, aim at some sort of efficacy.

If the first consequence of the context we have been exploring is that performed romances tend to have affective, ethical and esthetic purposes, a second, and related, consequence is that such romances generally make only limited hermeneutical and cognitive demands on their audiences. The situation for medieval romance is, in fact, similar to that of the theatre. Drama-theorist Marvin Carlson has spoken of the ''conservatism'' that characterizes much of traditional theatre with regard to hermeneutical demands:

> Throughout much of the history of Western theatre, a strong conservatism in subject matter and genre organization has provided spectators with highly predictable psychic models to apply in the reading of new dramatic pieces (or in revivals of older ones). From the Greeks until fairly recent times, the designation of a play as a comedy or a tragedy alerted the spectator to seek a certain emotional tone, certain types of characters, even certain themes and a certain structure of action . . . Since the general structure of tragedy [for example] was given and the stories were drawn from the cultural storehouse, these spectators arrived at the theatre with a good deal of their reading strategy already in place, even when the play had never been presented before . . .[25]

Thus, traditional theatre tends to be stereotyped, and to present situations and characters that are largely familiar, so that only a small number of new features has to be handled conceptually and interpretatively by the audience of listeners/spectators. (This stereotyping also of course makes the work of memory easier: that which is predictable is easy to recall.) What Carlson says of such theatre goes as well – if not better still! – for early romance, and for epic too. Plots were highly conventionalized, strongly predictable, presenting what Carlson calls (speaking of drama) a ''remarkably consistent narrative structure.'' Audiences of both romance and epic – and other genres as well,

---

[25] Carlson, ''Theatre Audiences and the Reading of Performance,'' p. 87.

such as fabliaux and lyric forms – knew very well what was expected of them in the particular genre.

There do exist, in medieval works designed for performance (as in traditional theatre), occasional passages that call for real interpretation – indeed for serious hermeneutical attention.[26] These passages, however, tend to be marked or "tagged": thus, clearly identified as calling for such attention. The medieval listener may be encouraged to "listen carefully" or to "have ears to hear." Something truly puzzling – as distinct from simply "marvelous" or "amazing" – may be presented in the narrative. The audience may be offered elements that cry out for symbolic interpretation.

This is particularly the case of puzzling and mysterious dreams – and they are in general clearly marked as needing interpretation. One thinks immediately of the *Roland* where Charlemagne dreams of a titanic struggle between a bear and a hound, and of many other *chansons de geste*. In Béroul's *Tristan*, Iseut dreams that two lions are fighting over her. In the *Roman de Renart* (Branch II), the rooster Chantecler dreams that he is having to put on a very unpleasant fur coat inside out – a coat with sharp teeth at the collar. The character who has the dream is invariably anxious or worried about its meaning.

The dream or other event to be interpreted is presented to the audience as a hermeneutical puzzle – a *riddle* – whose interpretation may well have been a social game. The riddle, or puzzle, was typically not so simple as to be totally self-evident, nor was it truly obscure: its answer flowed from familiar symbolic meanings, but invited thought and discussion. In some cases (especially dreams) the symbolic or allegorical meaning was resolvable in the sense that there was clearly a "right answer." Thus, if Chantecler dreamed he was putting that sharp-collared fur coat on inside out – this could *only* mean that the fox would try to eat him. Such is indeed the correct interpretation: Renart soon attempts to devour the rooster and comes very close to succeeding.

Some works, and some poets, are a bit more playful in the presentation of hermeneutical puzzles. For example, when we first meet the lion in *Yvain*, Chrétien sets up the "riddle" as follows:

> ... vit un lÿon, en un essart,
> et un serpant qui le tenoit
> par la coe, et si li ardoit
> trestoz les rains de flame ardant.
> N'ala mie molt regardant
> mes sire Yvains cele mervoille;
> a lui meïsmes se consoille

---

[26] By "interpretation" I mean simply thought and perhaps discussion devoted to the meaning of a work; by "hermeneutical attention" I am thinking of something conceptually more strenuous: an attempt to reveal the "secrets" of a text, to elucidate symbolic or allegorical meanings, and the like.

auquel d'aus deus il aidera;
lors dit qu'au lÿon se tanra,
qu'a venimeus ne a felon
ne doit an feire se mal non,
et li serpanz est venimeus,
si li saut par la boche feus,
tant est de felenie plains.
Por ce panse mes sire Yvains
qu'il l'ocirra premieremant . . .
Se li lÿons aprés l'asaut,
la bataille pas ne li faut,
mes que qu'il l'en aveingne aprés,
eidier li voldra il adés,
que pitiez li semont et prie
qu'il face secors et aïe
a la beste gentil et franche.   lines 3344–59, 3365–71.

(. . . he saw a lion, in a clearing,/ and a serpent which held it/ by the tail, and burned his flanks/ with burning flame./ My lord Yvain did not spend a lot of time/ looking at this marvel;/ he takes counsel with himself/ as to which of the two he will aid;/ then he says that he will stay with the lion,/ for to something venomous and evil/ one should only do evil,/ and the serpent is venomous,/ fire leaps from his mouth,/ so full is he of felony./ So my lord Yvain thinks/ that he will kill him first . . ./ If, after the attack, the lion/ does not fail to do battle with him/ but whatever happens afterwards,/ he [Yvain] wants to help him now,/ for pity summons and calls him/ to give help and aid/ to the worthy and noble beast.)

Faced with this dilemma, Yvain easily identifies "evil": the serpent is wicked and felonous, and Yvain knows that he must fight it. But Yvain is far from sure that the lion, while "noble," will in fact be any less dangerous to him than the serpent: it too may attack him. As it turns out, of course, the lion will become his close friend and associate. The lion is, then, not merely noble but good. But, in short, if Chrétien is hermeneutically somewhat playful in this scene, the passage is nonetheless decidedly identified as carrying symbolic value concerning matters of evil and good, and that symbolic meaning is fully resolved within the stories.

It is important to recognize that the hermeneutical puzzles in medieval romances and other works do not offer truly "literary" challenges: they are not part of a purely intellectual exercise or a word game. Rather, the events that call for interpretation generally present life-threatening choices and dangers; this is why the characters themselves are generally represented as eager to understand what the "symbolic" things mean. Interpretation was strongly ethical and practical, with implications within the work itself, rather than being, as it generally is today, a game for readers, without real consequences.

280

In some cases in which interpretation or even hermeneutical activity was called for, there does seem to have been room for dissenting views, indeed for *debate*. We know that medieval court audiences were fond of debates, which were often resolved or "judged" by the king or queen or another high-ranking authority. In such cases, the issue is not what something "means" but rather which character is in the *right*, or which of several characters suffered (or loved) the *most*,[27] or some such question. Occasionally, the decision may bear on which of several versions of a story is the most *beautiful*.

In short, though some interpretation may be called for in early romance, people came to these works, as to many others, with a clear sense of what to expect – and, in terms of interpretation and hermeneutics, relatively little *was* expected of them. (As noted earlier, such was especially the case of works with which the audience was already highly familiar!) Works intended for public performance rather than for private reading rarely make heavy intellectual demands on their audiences.[28] We must be wary of finding in (reading into?) medieval works details so subtle that they would have been imperceptible to audiences – details that may indeed be invisible to any but the most exhaustive re-reader.[29]

When there were interpretive issues to be resolved, the members of the audience did not come to them alone, as "solitary readers." They were, rather, members of an actual interpretive community, as opposed to one that is merely "sociological." I have evoked the dense interpersonal situation in which the medieval audience, like the performers, found themselves. This means that they were, and were fundamentally, together not merely in their immediate response to a work – the "reception loop" of which Donkin speaks – but in their longer-term interpretive activity. There was little *but* "interpretive community."

Such an interpretive situation is perhaps difficult for us to grasp. Today, even when we experience a work in a social setting, we are nonetheless able to form our own judgment and interpretation of the work – though it may not be easy even for us to dissent from the common interpretation. For example, many find it hard to respond to a film or play with reference to a moral,

---

[27] See for example Marie de France, the lai of "Chaitivel"; or "En aquel temps c'om era jays," in *Nouvelles occitanes*, ed. by Huchet, pp. 142–221, esp. pp. 203ff. See also the numerous "jeux-partis."

[28] There are exceptions, one important one being the "trobar clus" or hermetic tradition in the troubadour lyric. But such songs were a) fairly short and b) presented to a highly sophisticated audience, used precisely to this sort of highly stylized and coded game.

[29] The relation of medieval audiences to romances may well have been closer to that of spectators at modern sporting events than to that of readers of contemporary novels: in both of the former cases virtually all the "players" were familiar, the "plot" was standard, the "challenges" well-known. It was less this particular game than the game in general that drew them. And they were surrounded by people who felt the same as they did and were there for the same reasons.

political or religious code different from that which the rest of the audience shares. But this was even harder to do in the Middle Ages. We today have been carefully trained from infancy to have "our own" responses to things; we have been taught – even forced – to "think for ourselves." There was no such cultivation of personal taste, or of idiosyncratic intellectual or ideological systems, in the Middle Ages. Thus, esthetic response and interpretive activity were fundamentally, and from the start, a *collective* construct. It is this powerful social reality – put negatively, this lack of interest in individual freedom, put positively, this sense of community – that made public performance, including public reading, an enduring phenomenon throughout the entire medieval period, and well beyond. We must assume that people valued the experience of group reception: the sense of a truly shared culture. They enjoyed being part of a family.

The need for performance

I would like to close this chapter, and this book as a whole, with the simple thought that we cannot begin truly to appreciate the interpersonal and interactive, nor indeed the dramatic and musical, qualities of medieval romances unless and until we actually perform them, and hear and see them performed.

Fortunately, there have recently been valuable attempts to perform medieval romances and other narrative works. An extremely interesting videotape has been made of Jean Renart's *Le Roman de la rose ou de Guillaume de Dole* by Margaret Switten.[30] Linda Marie Zaerr has made audiotapes and has given live performances of medieval works including *Aucassin et Nicolete* and several Middle English romances.[31] The production of these performances was fueled perhaps primarily by musicological considerations: music is central to most of these works. But these performances have strong dramatic elements as well. In the video of the *Guillaume de Dole*, the dialogue is not delivered exclusively by the narrator, but is spoken and in fact quite strongly acted out by several different actors; there is also a good deal of dancing. These modern performances thus constitute attempts to respond to the dramatic qualities of the romances as well as to their musical elements. And to see Zaerr perform *Aucassin et Nicolete* is not just to listen to the lovely music of our sole surviving "chantefable," but to watch a skilled and charming actress at work. It is an eye-opening experience. Two related performances: Benjamin Bagby of the remarkable musical group "Sequentia" performs

[30] Prof. Margaret Switten of Mount Holyoke College. The video was produced in 1992 with support from the National Endowment for the Humanities.

[31] For further information, contact Prof. Linda Marie Zaerr, The Quill Consort, Department of English, Boise State Universty, Boise, Idaho 83725. See also Zaerr, ''Fiddling with the Middle English Romance.''

substantial passages from *Beowulf*, with an extraordinary sense of drama. I am told that John Fleagle of Boston gives wonderful performances of Old French romances and other works, including *Le Voyage de Saint Brendan*, with harp accompaniment; I look forward to seeing and hearing him. And I recently saw the Italian actor Paolo Pannaro[32] recite from memory long sections of Boiardo's *Orlando Innamorato* and Tasso's *Gerusalemme Liberata*; Pannaro performs these works with a generous use of the body and gesture, acting out all the parts, sometimes virtually simultaneously. Such performances make it possible to imagine what medieval performed romance might have been like.

One hopes that in the future we will see and hear more medieval romances performed by such talented performance artists. But we also need, as teachers – and as lovers of these romances – to get in the habit of reading passages from them aloud and even reciting parts of them from memory ourselves. We should encourage our students to do the same. Romances can be performed either in their entirety or in substantial pieces. Ideally they should be done in Old French, but modern poetic translations may be acceptable as well[33] – not, however, "normalized" modern prose translations, which are often written, one assumes, to please private readers of today.

If at least some of the time an effort is made to reconstitute, from the medieval social setting, at least its festive character and the presence of music,[34] such performances may give us valuable data on the fundamental character of the performability of such works, and on the options open to performers in different works. Such options include: whether or not the romance is best performed by a solo actor or actress, or whether more than one player might be useful; whether or not extensive recourse to gesture or other use of the body, such as acrobatics, seems called for; whether or not props should be used, and if so, which; to what extent the recitation should include singing; and so on. (Such reconstructions have been attempted with interesting and promising results by a number of folklorists and ethnologists.[35])

It may be objected that such performances cannot tell us about medieval

[32] Pannaro performed at New York University's Casa Italiana on October 21, 1996.

[33] Many of the texts quoted and discussed by anthropologists, ethnologists, and folkloricists in the work cited elsewhere in this chapter are also given in English translation, rather than in Zuni and other languages unknown to most modern speakers of English.

[34] As to attempts to reconstitute the original medieval setting more fully: that way, I fear, lies madness.

[35] See, for example, Fine, *The Folklore Text*, Chapter 7: "An Illustration of Performance-Centered Text," pp. 166–203. In this lengthy chapter, Fine discusses the performance of a black "joke" called "Stagolee" in a college class; this was hardly the original setting for such a story, but its performance demonstrated many things about the performance-quality of the work, the nature of the response it elicited from the audience, etc.

See also Tedlock, *The Spoken Word*, Chapter 13: "Ethnography as Interaction: The Storyteller, the Audience, the Fieldworker, and the Machine," pp. 285–301. Tedlock

performances, and to some degree that is true. But we learn a great deal about Shakespeare's plays *qua* plays from seeing them put on today; we learn important lessons from hearing medieval songs played and sung. Similarly, if we can see and hear medieval romances performed, we will understand many new things about their dramatic and interactive capacities: their performance quality. Romances are not *just* "medieval"; not simply works that delighted by-gone audiences. Rather, they have enduring ability to interest and entertain, in performance as in textual form. Our interest in them *need* not be, nor *should* it be, entirely antiquarian – or silent.

In short, we medievalists are not only archeologists but also ethnographers working with beautiful works from the past[36] which survive and can still be performed successfully today.

recounts how he was present at a story-telling session which in some ways – but only some – approximated the traditional context for Zuni narrative. This experience was nonetheless instructive for Tedlock in his study of oral narrative (especially Zuni) traditions.

[36] E.C. Fine and other ethnologists would call these "folklore texts."

BIBLIOGRAPHY

Primary texts

(Only works actually discussed are included):

Adam of Perseigne (?), *Eructavit: An Old French Metrical Paraphrase of Psalm XLIV Published from All the Known Manuscripts and Attributed to Adam de Perseigne*, ed. T. Atkinson Jenkins, Gesellschaft für Romanische Literature, Vol. 20, Dresden, Max Niemeyer, 1909.

Adgar, *Le gracial*, ed. Pierre Kunstmann, Ottawa, University of Ottawa Press, 1982.

Adams, Alison, ed. and trans. See *The Romance of Yder*.

Arnold, I.D.O and M.M. Pelan, eds. See Wace, *La Partie Arthurienne du Roman de Brut*.

Aye d'Avignon, ed. F. Guessard and Paul Meyer, Paris, Wieweg, 1986.

Benedeit, *The Anglo-Norman Voyage of St. Brendan [by Benedeit]*, ed. E.G.R. Waters, Manchester, Manchester University Press, 1928.

Benoît de Sainte-Maure, *Roman de Troie*, ed. Léopold Constans, Paris, Firmin Didot, 1904, 6 vols.

Béroul, *Le Roman de Tristan, poème du XIIe siècle*, ed. Ernest Muret, Paris, Champion, 1966.

Blodgett, E.D., ed. and trans. See *Flamenca*.

Bonnard, Jean. *Les traductions de la Bible en vers français au Moyen Age*, Geneva, Slatkine, 1967.

Boulton, Maureen, ed. See *Evangile de l'Enfance*, Toronto, Pontifical Institute, 1984.

Buridant, Claude, ed. See *Pseudo-Turpin*.

Busby, Keith, ed. See Raoul de Houdenc.

Caplan, Harry, ed. and trans. See [Cicero].

Li chevalier a deus espees, ed. Wendelin Foerster, Halle, Max Niemeyer, 1877.

Chrétien de Troyes. *Le Roman de Perceval, ou Le conte du Graal*, 2nd edn revised and expanded, William Roach, ed., Genève: Droz/Paris: Minard, 1959.

———. *Le Chevalier de la Charrete*, Mario Roques, ed., Paris, Champion, 1963.

———. *Erec et Enide*, Mario Roques, ed., Paris, Champion, 1966.

———. *Cligés*, Alexandre Micha, ed., Paris, Champion, 1970.

———. *Le chevalier au lion (Yvain)*, Mario Roques, ed., Paris, Champion, 1971.

———. *Oeuvres complètes*, gen. ed. Daniel Poirion, Paris, Pléïade, 1994.

———. *Le chevalier au lion*, ed. David Hult, Poche/ Lettres gothiques, 1994.

———. *Romans*, gen ed. Michel Zink, Paris, Poche, 1994.

[Cicero] *Ad Herennium*, ed. and trans. Harry Caplan, Cambridge, MA, Harvard (Loeb Library), 1981.

Cohen, Gustave. *La vie littéraire en France au moyen âge*, Paris, Taillandier, 1953 edn.

Coley, John Smartt, trans. See *Le Roman de Thèbes (The Story of Thebes)*, New York, Garland, 1986.

Conon de Béthune, *Chansons*, ed. Axel Wallensköld, Helsingfors, Imprimerie Nationale, 1891.

Constans, Léopold, ed. See *Roman de Thèbes*; Benoît de Sainte-Maure, *Roman de Troie*.

Le Conte de Floire et Blancheflor, ed. Jean-Luc Leclanche, Paris, Champion, 1980.

Le Couronnement de Louis; chanson de geste du XIIe siècle, ed. Ernest Langlois, Paris, Champion, 1984.

Denis Piramus, *La Vie Saint Edmund le Rei, poème anglo-normand du XIIIème siècle*, ed. Hildung Kjellman, Geneva, Slatkine, 1974.

Donaldson, E.T., ed. See Geoffrey Chaucer

Dufournet, Jean, ed. See *Le Roman de Renart*.

Edelstand du Méril, M., ed. *Poésies populares latines du Moyen Age*, Paris, Firmin Didot Frères, 1847.

Énéas, roman du XIIe siècle, ed. J.J. Salverda de Grave, Paris, Champion, Vol. I, 1973; Vol. II, 1983.

Évangile de l'Enfance [Old French Évangile de l'Enfance], ed. Maureen Boulton, Toronto, Pontifical Institute, 1984.

Fabliaux [Twelve Fabliaux], ed. T.B.W. Reid, Manchester, Manchester University Press, 1958.

Fabliaux érotiques, ed. and trans. Luciano Rossi and Richard Straub, Paris, Poche, 1992.

Faral, Edmond, ed. *Mimes français du XIIIe siècle*, Paris, Champion, 1910, pp. 93–111.

———. *Les arts poétiques du XIIe et du XIIIe siècle*, Paris, Champion, 1924.

Fay, Percival B. and John L. Grigsby, eds. See *Joufroi de Poitiers*.

Flamenca [The Romance of Flamenca], ed. and trans. E.D. Blodgett, New York/London, Garland, 1995.

Floire et Blancheflor: Seconde Version, ed. Margaret M. Pelan. Paris, Phyrys (University of Strasbourg), 1975.

Floire et Blancheflor. See also *Le Conte de Floire et Blancheflor*.

Florence de Rome, ed. Axel Wallensköld, Paris, 2 vols.: 1907, 1919.

Floriant et Florete, ed. Harry F. Williams, Ann Arbor, University of Michigan, 1947.

Floris et Liriope. See Robert de Blois.

Foerster, Wendelin, ed. See *Li chevalier a Deus Espees*.

Gace Brulé, *Chansons [de Gace Brulé]*, ed. Gédéon Huet, Paris, Firmin Didot, 1902

Gaselee, Stephen, ed. *The Oxford Book of Medieval Latin Verse*, reprinted, corrected edn, Oxford, Clarendon, 1937.

Gautier d'Arras, *Eracle*, ed. Guy Raynaud de Lage, Paris, Champion, 1976.

Geoffrey Chaucer, *[Chaucer's] Poetry*, ed. E.T. Donaldson, Glenview (Illinois), Scott, Foresman and Co., 1975.

Geoffroi Gaimar, *L'Estoire des Engleis*, ed. Alexander Bell, Oxford, Blackwell, 1960.

Girart de Roussillon, poème bourguignon du XIVe siècle, ed. Edward Billings Ham, New Haven, Yale University Press, 1939.

Girart de Roussillon ou l'épopée de Bourgogne, annotated by Marcel Thomas and Michel Zink, trans. into modern French by Roger-Henri Guerrand, Paris, Philippe Lebaud, 1990.

Goldin, Frederick, ed. and trans., *Lyrics of the Troubadours and Trouveres*, Doubleday/Anchor, 1973.

Gouiran, Gérard and Robert Lafont, eds. See *Roland occitan*.

Guessart, F. and Paul Meyer, eds. See *Aye d'Avignon*.

Guido Aretinus, *Micrologus*, ed. Jos. Smits van Waesberghe, Nijmegen, American Institute of Musicology, 1955.

Guillaume IX, *Les chansons [de Guillaume IX duc d'Aquitaine]*, ed. American Institute of Musicology, 1955.

Guillaume de Berneville, *La Vie de Saint Gilles*, ed. Gaston Paris and Alphonse Bos, Paris, Firmin Didot, 1881.

Guiraut Riquier, *Les Epîtres [de Guiraut Riquier]*, *troubadour du XIIIe siècle*, ed. and trans. Joseph Linskill, Liège, Marche Romane, 1985.

Ham, Edward Billings Ham, ed. See *Girart de Roussillon*.

Harden, Robert, ed. *Trois Pièces Médiévales*, New York, Appleton-Century-Crofts, 1967.

Harrington, K.P., ed. *Medieval Latin*, University of Chicago Press, 1962.

Hatto, A.T., trans. See Wolfram von Eschenbach.

Henri d'Andeli, *The Battle of the Seven Arts: A French Poem by Henry d'Andeli, Trouvère of the Thirteenth Century*, ed. and trans. Louis Jean Paetow, Berkeley, University of California Press, 1914.

Huchet, Jean-Charles, ed. and trans. *Nouvelles occitanes du Moyen Age*, Paris, Garnier-Flammarion, 1992.

Huet, Gédéon, ed. See Gace Brulé, *Chansons*.

Holden, A.J., ed. See Wace, *Le Roman de Rou*.

Hult, David, ed. See Chrétien de Troyes, *Le chevalier au lion*.

Hunbaut [The Romance of Hunbaut]: An Arthurian Poem of the Thirteenth Century, ed. Margaret Winters, Leiden, 1984.

Jean Froissart, *Chroniques*, 15 vols., Paris, Société de l'Histoire de France, 1865–1975. Vols. I–VIII, ed. Siméon Luce and Gaston Raynaud. Vols. IX–XI, ed. Gaston Raynaud. Vol. XII, ed. Léon Mirot. Vol. XIII, eds. Léon Mirot and Albert Mirot. Vols. XIV–XV. ed. Albert Mirot.

———. *"Dits" et "Débats" avec en appendice quelques poèmes de Guillaume de Machaut*, ed. Anthime Fourrier, Geneva, Textes Littéraires Français, 1979.

———. *L'Espinette amoureuse*, ed. Anthime Fourrier, Paris, Klincksieck, 1972.

Jean Renart, *Le Roman de la Rose ou de Guillaume de Dole*, ed. Félix Lecoy, Paris, Champion, 1962.

———. Video of *The Romance of the Rose or of Guillaume de Dole*, by Margaret Switten, with support of National Endowment for the Humanities, South Hadley, MA, Mt Holyoke College, 1992.

———. *L'Escoufle (roman d'aventure)*, ed. Franklin Sweetser, Paris, Droz, 1974.

Jeanroy, Alfred, ed. See Guillaume IX.

John of Salisbury, *Policraticus, or the Frivolities of Courtiers and the Footprints of Philosophers*, ed. and trans. Cary J. Nederman, Cambridge, Cambridge University Press, 1990.

Johnson, R.C. and D.D.R. Owen, eds. *Two Old French Gawain Romances*, Edinburgh, Scottish Academy Press, 1972.

Joufroi de Poitiers, *Roman d'aventures du XIIIe siècle*, ed. Percival B. Fay and John L. Grigsby, Geneva/Paris, Droz/Minard, 1972.

Kjellman, Hildung, ed. See *La vie saint Edmund le Rei*.

Koopmans, Jelle, ed. *Recueil de sermons joyeux*, Geneva, Droz, 1988.

Kunstmann, Pierre, ed. See Adgar.

Langlois, Ernest, ed. See *Le Couronnement de Louis; chanson de geste du XIIe siècle*, Paris, Champion, 1984.

Lavaud, René and René Nelli, ed. and trans. *Les Troubadours: Jaufré, Flamenca, Barlaam et Josaphat*, Declée de Brouwer, 1960.

Lecoy, Félix, ed. See Jean Renart, *Le Roman de la Rose*.

Leclanche, Jean-Luc, ed. See *Le Conte de Floire et Blancheflor*, Paris, Champion, 1980.

Levy, Brian, ed. See Nicolas Bozon.

Pelan, Margaret M., ed. See *Floire et Blancheflor*.

Marie de France, *Les Lais*, ed. Jean Rychner, Paris, Champion, 1977.

Micha, Alexandre, ed. See Chrétien de Troyes, *Cligés*.

————. *Lais féeriques des XIIe et XIIIe siècles*, Paris, Garnier-Flammarion, 1992.

Muret, Ernest, ed. See Béroul.

Murphy, James J., ed., Jane Baltzell Kopp, trans. *Three Medieval Poetic Arts*, Berkeley, University of California Press, 1971.

Nederman, Cary J., ed. See John of Salisbury.

Nicolas Bozon, *Nine Verse Sermons by Nicholas Bozon: The Art of an Anglo-Norman Poet and Preacher*, ed. Brian Levy, Oxford, Oxford University Press, 1981.

Osbern Bokenham, *Legendys of Hooly Wummen*, ed. Mary Serjeantson, London, Oxford University Press, 1938.

Paetow, Louis John, ed. and trans. See Henri d'Andeli.

Paris, Gaston and Alphonse Bos, eds. See Guillaume de Berneville.

Peter of Blois, *De Confessione*, in J.-P. Migne, gen. ed., *Patrilogia cursus completus. Series latina*, Paris, J.-P. Migne, 1844–82; Vol. CCVII, c. 1088.

Peter the Chanter, *Verbum abbreviatum, 27*, in J.-P. Migne, gen. ed., *Patrilogia cursus completus. Series latina*, Paris, J.-P. Migne, 1844–82; Vol. CCV, c. 101.

Poirion, Daniel, ed. See Chrétien de Troyes, *Oeuvres complètes*.

Pseudo-Turpin: La traduction du Pseudo-Turpin du Manuscrit Vatican Regina 624, ed. with introduction, notes and glossary, Claude Buridant, Geneva, Droz, 1976.

Raby, F.J.E., ed. *The Oxford Book of Medieval Latin Verse*, Oxford, Clarendon, 1959.

Raoul de Houdenc, *Le roman des eles; The anonymous Ordene de Chevalerie*, ed. Keith Busby, Amsterdam, John Benjamins, 1983.

Raynaud de Lage, Guy, ed. See *Le Roman de Thèbes* and Gautier d'Arras.

Reid, T.B.W., ed. See *Fabliaux*.

Renaut de Beaujeu, *Le Bel Inconnu, roman d'aventures*, ed. G. Perrie Williams, Paris, Champion, 1983.

Robert de Blois, *Floris et Liriope: altfranzösischer roman [des Robert de Blois]*, ed. Wolfram von Zingerle, Wiesbaden, Dr Martin Sandig, 1892 (reprint 1968).

Roques, Mario, ed. See Chrétien de Troyes, *Le chevalier de la charrete* and *Erec et Enide*.

Roland occitan, ed. Gérard Gouiran and Robert Lafont, Paris, 10/18, 1991.

Le Roman de Merlin, or The Early History of King Arthur [from French MS Add. 10292, British Museum], H. Oskar Sommer, ed., London (privately printed), 1894.

Le Roman de Renart (Branches I, II, III, IV, V, VIII, X, XV), ed. Jean Dufournet, Paris, Garnier-Flammarion, 1970.

Le Roman de la Rose ou de Guillaume de Dole, ed. Félix Lecoy, Paris, Champion, 1962.

Le Roman de Thèbes, publié d'après tous les manuscrits, ed. Léopold Constans, New York, Johnson Reprint, 1968 (orig. Paris, Firmin Didot (SATF), 1890, 2 vols.).

Le Roman de Thèbes, ed. Guy Raynaud de Lage, Paris, Champion, 1969, 2 vols.

[Le] Roman de Thèbes (The Story of Thebes), trans. John Smartt Coley, New York, Garland, 1986.

The Romance of Yder, ed. and trans. Alison Adams, Cambridge, D.S. Brewer, 1983.

Rosenberg, S.N. and H. Tischler, eds., *Chanter M'Estuet: Songs of the Trouvères*, London, Faber and Faber, 1981.

Rossi, Luciano and Richard Straub, ed. and trans. See *Fabliaux érotiques*, Paris, Livre de Poche, 1992.

Rutebeuf, *Oeuvres complètes [de Rutebeuf]*, ed. Michel Zink, Paris, Bordas, 1990.

Rychner, Jean, ed. See Marie de France.

Salverda de Grave, J.J. ed. See *Énéas*.

Serjeantson, Mary, ed. See Osbern Bokenham.

Sommer, H. Oskar, ed. See *Le Roman de Merlin*.

Spitzmuller, Henry, ed. *Poésie latine chrétienne du Moyen Age, IIIe–XVe siècles*, Bruges, Desclée de Brouwer, 1971.

Sweetser, Franklin, ed. See Jean Renart, *L'Escoufle*.

Switten, Margaret. See Jean Renart, *The Romance of the Rose*.

Thibaut de Champagne, *Les Chansons [de Thibaut de Champagne, Roi de Navarre]*, ed. Axel Wallensköld, Paris, 1925.

Thomas, *Les Fragments du Roman de Tristan: poème du XIIe siècle*, ed. by Bartina H. Wind, Geneva/Paris, Droz/Minard, 1960.

Trask, Willard R., ed. *The Unwritten Song: Poetry of the Primitive and Traditional Peoples of the World, Edited, in Part Retranslated, and with an Introduction*, New York, Macmillan, 1966.

[La] vie de Saint Gilles. See Guillaume de Berneville.

Wace, *Le Roman de Rou [de Wace]*, ed. A.J. Holden, Paris, Picard, 1970–73, 3 vols.

———. *La Partie Arthurienne du Roman de Brut*, ed. I.D.O. Arnold and M.M. Pelan, Paris, Klincksieck, 1962.

Wallensköld, Axel, ed. See Conon de Béthune, *Florence de Rome* and Thibaut de Champagne.

Waters, E.G.R., ed. See Benedeit.

Williams, G. Perrie, ed. See Renaut de Beaujeu.

Williams, Harry F., ed. See *Floriant et Florete*.

Wind, Bartina H., ed. See Thomas, *Les Fragments du Roman de Tristan: poème du XIIe siècle*, ed. by Bartina H. Wind.

Winters, Margaret, ed. See *Hunbaut*.

Wolfram von Eschenbach. *Parzival*, ed. and trans. A.T. Hatto. London, Penguin, 1980.

Wolfram von Zingerle, ed. See Robert de Blois.

Zink, Michel, ed. See Rutebeuf.

Scholarly works

Adam, Antoine, Georges Lerminien and Edouard Morot-Sir, gen. eds. *Littérature française*, Vol. I, Paris, Larousse, 1967.

Ahern, John. "Singing the Book: Orality in the Reception of Dante's *Comedy*," *Annals of Scholarship* 2, 1981, pp. 17–40.

Auerbach, Erich. *Literary Language and Its Public in late Latin Antiquity and in the Middle Ages*, trans. Ralph Manheim, New York, Random House/Bollingen, 1945.

Badel, Pierre-Yves. *Le sauvage et le sot: Le fabliau de Trubert et la tradition orale*, Paris, Champion, 1979.

Bakhtin, M.M., *The Dialogue Imagination*, trans. C. Emerson and M. Holquist, Austin, University of Texas Press, 1981.

Baldwin, Charles Sears. *Medieval Rhetoric and Poetic (to 1400) Interpreted from Representative Works*, Gloucester (MA), Peter Smith, 1959.

Barlett, Frederic C. *Remembering: A Study in Experimental and Social Psychology*, Cambridge, [Cambridge] University Press, 1950 (1932)

Baugh, Albert C. "The Middle English Romance: Some Questions of Creation, Presentation, and Preservation," *Speculum*, Vol. XLII, No. 1, January 1967, pp. 1–31.

Bauman, Richard. *Verbal Art as Performance*, Prospect Heights, IL, Waveland Press, 1977.

———. *Story, Performance, and Event*, Cambridge, Cambridge University Press, 1986.

Bäuml, Franz. "Varieties and Consequences of Medieval Literacy and Illiteracy," *Speculum*, Vol. LV, No. 2, June 1980, pp. 237–65.

Bédier, Joseph and Paul Hazard. *Histoire de la littérature française*, Paris, Larousse, 1948.

Beer, Jeannette. *Villehardouin – Epic Historian*, Geneva, Droz, 1968.

———. *Early Prose in France: Contexts of Bilingualism and Authority*, Kalamazoo, MI, Medieval Institute Publications, 1992.

Beissinger, Margaret Hiebert. "Text and Music in Romanian Oral Epic," *Oral Tradition*, Vol. 3, No. 3, October 1988, pp. 294–314.

Benskin, Michael, Tony Hunt and Ian Short. "Un nouveau fragment du Tristan de Thomas," *Romania*, Vol. 113, 1992, pp. 289–319.

Benton, John. "The Court of Champagne as a Literary Center," *Speculum*, Vol. XXXVI, No. 4, October 1961, pp. 551–91.

Bernheimer, Richard. *Wild Men in the Middle Ages: A Study in Art, Sentiment, and Demonology*, Cambridge, MA, 1952.

Bevington, David. *Medieval Drama*, Boston, Houghton Mifflin, 1975.

Bigongiari, Dino. "Were There Theatres in the Twelfth and Thirteenth Centuries?" *Romanic Review*, Vol. 37, No. 3 (1946), pp. 209–24.

Blatt, Franz. *Novum glossarium mediae latinitatis*, Hafniae, Ejnar Munksgaard, 1957– .

Blumenfeld-Kosinski, Renate. "Old French Narrative Genres: Toward the Definition of the *Roman Antique*," *Romance Philology* 34, Nov. 1980, pp. 143–59.

Bonnard, Jean. *Les traductions de la Bible en vers français au Moyen Age*, Geneva, Slatkine, 1967.

Boucher, François. *A History of Costume in the West*, trans. John Ross, London, Thames and Hudson, 1967.

Brandsma, Frank. "Medieval Equivalents of 'quote-unquote': the Presentation of Spoken Words in Courtly Romance," in Evelyn Mullally and John Thompson, eds., *The Court and Cultural Diversity: International Courtly Literature Society, 1995*, Cambridge, D.S. Brewer, 1997, pp. 287–96.

Brown, R. Allen, H.M. Colvin, and A.J. Taylor, eds. *The History of the King's Works* (gen. ed., H.M. Colvin), Vol. II: *The Middle Ages*, London, Her Majesty's Stationery Office, 1963.

Bullock-Davies, Constance. *Ménestrellorum multitudo: Minstrels at a Royal Feast*, Cardiff, University of Wales Press, 1978.

Busby, Keith, Terry Nixon, Alison Stones and Lori Walters, eds. *Les Manuscrits de Chrétien de Troyes/ The Manuscripts of Chrétien de Troyes*, 2 vols., Amsterdam, Rodopi, 1993.

Butler's Lives of the Saints, complete edition, edited, revised and supplemented by Herbert Thurston, SJ, and Donald Attwater, New York, P.J. Kenedy and Sons, 1956.

Bynum, David E. "Oral Epic Tradition in South Slavic," *Oral Tradition*, Vol. 1, No. 2, May 1986, pp. 302–43.

Calin, William. "L'Épopée dite vivante: Réflexions sur le prétendu caractère oral des chansons de geste," *Olifant* 8, 1980, pp. 227–37.

———. "Littérature médiévale et hypothgèse orale: Une divergence de méthode et de philosophie," *Olifant* 8, 1980, pp. 256–85.

———. *A Muse for Heroes: Nine Centuries of the Epic in France*, Toronto, University of Toronto Press, 1983.

Carlson, Marvin. "Theatre Audiences and the Reading of Performance," in *Interpreting the Theatrical Past: Essays in the Historiography of Performance*, Thomas Postlewait and Bruce A. McConachie, eds., Iowa City, University of Iowa Press, 1989.

———. *Places of Performance: The Semiotics of Theatre Architecture*, Ithaca, Cornell University Press, 1989.

Carruthers, Mary. *The Book of Memory: A Study of Memory in Medieval Culture*, Cambridge, Cambridge University Press, 1990.

———. "Inventional Mnemonics and the Ornaments of Style: The Case of Etymology," in *Connotations*, Vol. 2, No. 2, 1992.

The Catholic Encyclopedia, New York, Encyclopedia Press, 1913.

Cerquiglini, Bernard. *La parole médiévale*, Paris, Editions de Minuit, 1981.

Cerquiglini-Toulet, Jacqueline. *La couleur de la mélancolie: La fréquentation des livres au XIVe siècle, 1300–1415*, Paris, Hatier, 1993.

Chadwick, H. Munro and N. Kershaw Chadwick. *The Growth of Literature*, New York, Macmillan: Vol. I, 1932; Vol. II, 1936; Vol. III, 1940.

Chambers, E.K. *The Mediaeval Stage*, 2 vols., Oxford, Oxford University Press, 1903.

Chartier, Roger and D. Roche. "Le livre: changement de perspective," in Jacques LeGoff and Pierre Nora, eds. *Faire de l'histoire*, Paris, Gallimard, 1974; pp. 115–36.

Chaytor, H.J. *From Script to Print: An Introduction to Medieval Literature*, Cambridge, Cambridge University Press, 1945.

Chenu, M.D. *La théologie au XIIe siècle*, Paris, Vrin, 1976.

Clanchy, Michael T. *From Memory to Written Record: English, 1066–1307*, 2nd edn, Oxford, Blackwell, 1993.

———. "Looking Back from the Invention of Printing," in Daniel P. Resnick, ed., *Literacy in Historical Perspective*, Washington, Library of Congress, 1983, pp. 7–22.

Cohen, Gustave. *La vie littéraire en France au moyen âge*, Paris, Taillandier, 1953.

Colby, Alice. *The Portrait in Twelfth-Century French Literature: An Example of the Stylistic Originality of Chrétien de Troyes*, Geneva, Droz, 1965.

Coleman, Joyce. *Public Reading and the Reading Public in Late Medieval England and France*, Cambridge, Cambridge University Press, 1996.

Cratty, Bryant J. *Perceptual-Motor Behavior and Educational Processes*, Springfield (IL), Charles C. Thomas, 1967.

Cressy, David. *Literacy and the Social Order: Reading and Writing in Tudor and Stuart England*, Cambridge, Cambridge University Press, 1980.

Crosby, Ruth. "Oral Delivery in the Middle Ages," *Speculum*, 11, 1936, pp. 88–110.

Crouch, David. *William Marshal: Court, Career and Chivalry in the Angevin Empire, 1147–1219*, London/New York, Longman, 1990.

Curtius, Ernst R. *European Literature and the Latin Middle Ages*, New York, Harper & Row, 1963 (German orig., Bern, 1948).

Davidson, Clifford. *Illustrations of the Stage and Acting in England to 1580*, Kalamazoo, Medieval Institute Publications, 1991.

Davies, Graham M. and Donald M. Thomson, eds. *Memory in Context: Context in Memory*, Chichester/New York, Wiley, 1988.

Davies, Sioned. "Storytelling in Medieval Wales," *Oral Tradition*, Vol. 7, No. 2, 1992, pp. 231–57.

de Cornulier, Benoît. *Théorie du vers: Rimbaud, Verlaine, Mallarmé*, Paris, Seuil, 1982.

De Marinis, Marco. *The Semiotics of Performance*, trans. Aine O'Healy, Bloomington, Indiana University Press, 1993.

Dembowski, Peter F. "Monologue, Author's Monologue and Related Problems in the Romances of Chrétien de Troyes," *Yale French Studies*, 51, 1974, pp. 102–14.

———. *Jean Froissart and his Meliador*, Lexington (KY), French Forum, 1983.

———. "The French Tradition of Textual Philology," *Modern Philology*, 90, 1993, pp. 512–32.

———. *La chronique de Robert de Clari: Etude de la langue et du style*, Toronto, University of Toronto Press, 1963.

Dictionnaire des lettres françaises: Le Moyen Age, new edn, Paris, Fayard/Poche, 1992.

Donkin, Ellen. "Mrs. Siddons Looks Back in Anger: Feminist Historiography for Eighteenth-Century British Theatre," in Janelle G. Reinelt and Joseph R. Roach, eds., *Critical Theory and Performance*, Ann Arbor, University of Michigan, 1992, pp. 276–90.

Donovan, L.G. *Recherches sur* Le Roman de Thèbes, Paris, SEDES, 1975.

Dronke, Peter. "Profane Elements in Literature," in *Renaissance and Renewal in the Twelfth Century*, Robert L. Benson and Giles Constable, eds., with Carol D. Lanham, Cambridge (MA), Harvard University Press, 1982, pp. 569–93.

Duby, Georges. *The Chivalrous Society*, Berkeley, University of California Press, 1977.

———. "The Culture of the Knightly Class: Audience and Patronage," in *Renaissance and Renewal in the Twelfth Century*, Robert L. Benson and Giles Constable, eds., with Carol D. Lanham, Cambridge (MA), Harvard University Press, 1982, pp. 248–62.

———. *William Marshal, The Flower of Chivalry*, trans. Richard Howard, New York, Pantheon, 1985.

Duggan, Joseph J. *The Song of Roland: Formulaic Style and Poetic Craft*, Berkeley, University of California Press, 1973.

———. "La théorie de la composition orale des chansons de geste: Les faits et les interprétations," *Olifant* 8, 1980, pp. 238–55

———. "Le mode de composition des chansons de geste: Analyse statistique, jugement esthétique, modèles de transmission," *Olifant* 8, 1980, pp. 286–316.

———. "Social Functions of the Medieval Epic in the Romance Literatures," *Oral Tradition*, Vol. 2, No. 3, 1986, pp. 728–66.

———. "Oral Performance of Romance in Medieval France," *Essays in Honor of John Lambert Grigsby*, Norris J. Lacy and Gloria Torrini-Roblin, eds., Birmingham (AL), Summa, 1989, pp. 51–61.

Eco, Umberto. *The Role of the Reader: Explorations in the Semiotics of Texts*, Bloomington, Indiana University Press, 1984.

Enders, Jody. *Rhetoric and the Origins of Medieval Drama*, Ithaca, Cornell University Press, 1992.

———. "The Theatre of Scholastic Erudition," *Comparative Drama*, 27, 1993, pp. 341–63.

Eysenck, Michael W. *Human Memory: Theory, Research and Individual Differences*, Tarrytown, NY, Pergamon, 1977.

Faral, Edmond. *Les jongleurs en France au moyen âge*, New York, Burt Franklin, 1970 (orig. 1910).

———. *Recherches sur les sources latines des contes et romans courtois du moyen âge*, Paris, Champion, 1913.

Ferguson, Mary H. "Folklore in the *Lais* of Marie de France," *Romanic Review*, Vol. 57, No. 1, 1966, pp. 3–24.

Ferruolo, Stephen C. *The Origins of the University: The Schools of Paris and their Critics, 1100–1215*, Stanford, CA, Stanford University Press, 1985.

Fine, Elizabeth C. *The Folklore Text: From Performance to Print*, Bloomington, Indiana University Press, 1984.

Finnegan, Ruth. "Literacy versus Non-literacy: The Great Divide? Some

Comments on the Significance of 'Literature' in Non-literate Cultures," in Robin Horton and Ruth Finnegan, eds., *Modes of Thought: Essays on Thinking in Western and Non-Western Societies*, London, Faber, 1973, pp. 112–44.

———. "What is Oral Literature Anyway?", in *Oral Literature and the Formula*, Benjamin A. Stolz and Richard S. Shannon III, eds., Ann Arbor, University of Michigan, 1976.

———. ed. *The Penguin Book of Oral Poetry*, London, Allen Lane, 1978.

———. *Literacy and Orality: Studies in the Technology of Communication*, Oxford, Blackwell, 1988.

———. *Oral Poetry, Its Nature, Significance and Social Context*, rev. edn, Bloomington, Indiana University Press, 1992.

———. "The Poetic and the Everyday: Their Pursuit in an African Village and an English Town," *Folklore* 105, 1994, pp. 3–11.

Fish, Stanley. *Is There a Text in This Class?: The Authority of Interpretive Communities*, Cambridge, MA, Harvard University Press, 1980.

Frappier, Jean and Reinhold R. Grimm, eds., *Grundriss der romanischen Literaturen des Mittelalters*, Heidelberg, Carl Winter; Vol. IV, 1978.

Garnier, François. *La langage de l'image au Moyen Age*, Paris, Le Léopard d'or, Vol. I, 1982; Vol. II, 1989.

Gautier, Léon. *Epopees françaises*, 4 vols., new edn, Paris, 1878–92.

Gimpel, Jean. *The Cathedral Builders*, trans. Teresa Waugh, New York, Harper and Row, 1980.

Godefroy, Frédéric. *Dictionnaire de l'ancienne langue française et de tous ses dialectes, du XIe au XVe siècle*, Geneva, Slatkine, 1982.

Godzich, Wlad and Jeffrey Kittay. *The Emergence of Prose: An Essay in Prosaics*, Minneapolis, University of Minnesota Press, 1987.

Goody, Jack, ed. *Literacy in Traditional Societies*, Cambridge, Cambridge University Press, 1968.

Grammont, Maurice. *Le vers français*, Paris, Delagrave, 2nd edn, 1947.

Green, D.H. "On the Primary Reception of Narrative Literature in Medieval Literature," *Forum for Modern Language Studies*, Vol. XX, No. 4, 1984, pp. 289–308.

———. *Medieval Listening and Reading: The Primary Reception of German Literature 800–1300*, Cambridge, Cambridge University Press, 1994.

Guth, Paul. *Histoire de la littérature française*, Paris, Fayard, 1967, Vol. I: *Des origines épiques au siècle des lumières*.

Guthrie, Stephen. "Meter in Performance in Machaut and Chaucer," in *The Union of Words and Music in Medieval Poetry*, Rebecca A. Baltzer, Thomas Cable, and James I. Wimsatt, eds., Austin (TX), University of Texas Press, 1991, pp. 72–100.

Haidu, Peter. *The Subject of Violence: The Song of Roland and the Birth of the State*, Bloomington, IN, Indiana University Press, 1993.

Hanning, R.W. "The Audience as Co-Creator of the First Chivalric Romances," *Yearbook of English Studies*, II, 1981, pp. 1–28.

Haskins, Charles Homer. *The Rise of Universities*, Ithaca, Cornell University Press, 1957 (orig. 1923).

Hilty, G. "Zum Erec-Prolog," *Philologica Romanica E.Lommatzsch Gewidment*, Munich, Fink, 1975, pp. 245–56.

Hindman, Sandra. "King Arthur, his Knights, and the French Aristocracy in Picardy," *Yale French Studies*, spec. issue: *Contexts: Style and Values in Medieval Art and Literature*, 1991, pp. 114–33.

———. *Sealed in Parchment: Rereadings of Knighthood in the Illuminated Manuscripts of Chrétien de Troyes*, Chicago, University of Chicago Press, 1994.

Holub, Robert C. *Reception Theory: A Critical Introduction*, London, Methuen, 1984.

Howlett, David. *The English Origins of Old French Literature*, Dublin, Four Courts Press, 1996.

Hult, David F. "The Limits of Mime(sis): Notes Toward a Generic Revision of Medieval Theater," *L'Esprit Créateur*, Vol. XXIII, No. 1, spring 1983, pp. 49–63.

Hunter, Ian M.L. "Lengthy Verbatim Recall: The Role of Text," pp. 207–35 in *Progress in the Psychology of Language*, Vol. One, Andrew W. Ellis, ed., London, Lawrence Erlbaum Associates, 1985.

Huot, Sylvia. "Voices and Instruments in Medieval French Secular Music: On the Use of Literary Texts as Evidence for Performance Practice," *Musica Disciplina*, Vol. XLIII, 1989, pp. 63–113.

Husband, Timothy, with assistance from Gloria Gilmore-House, *The Wild Man: Medieval Myth and Sybolism*, New York, Metropolitan Museum of Art, 1980.

Hymes, Dell. *Ethnography, Linguistics, Narrative Inequality: Toward An Understanding of Voice*, London, Taylor and Francis, 1996.

Illich, Ivan. "A Plea for Research on Lay Literacy," in *Literacy and Orality*, ed. David R. Olson and Nancy Torrance, Cambridge, Cambridge University Press, 1991, pp. 28–46.

———. *In the Vineyard of the Text: A Commentary to Hugh's* Didascalion, Chicago, University of Chicago Press, 1993.

Iser, Wolfgang. "The Reading Process: A Phenomenological Approach," in *Reader Response Criticism from Formalism to Post-Structuralism*, ed. Jane P. Tompkins, Baltimore, Johns Hopkins University Press, 1980, pp. 50–69.

Jaeger, C. Stephen. *The Origins of Courtliness: Civilizing Trends and the Formation of Courtly Ideals 939–1210*, Philadelphia, University of Pennsylvania Press, 1985.

———. *The Envy of Angels: Cathedral Schools and Social Ideals in Medieval Europe, 950–1200*, Philadelphia, University of Pennsylvania Press, 1994.

James, John. *The Contractors of Chartres*, 2 vols., Ywong (Australia), Mandorla, 1981.

Jauss, Hans Robert. *Toward an Aesthetic of Reception*, trans. Timothy Bahti, Minneapolis, University of Minnesota Press, 1982.

Jousse, Marcel. *The Oral Style*, trans. Edgard Sienaert and Richard Whitaker, New York, Garland, 1990. (Original French title, *Le style oral rythmique et mnémotechnique chez les verbo-moteurs*, Paris, 1925.)

Kardon, Peter. "Chrétien de Troyes and the Auctores", unpublished University of Chicago dissertation, 1984.

Katzenellenbogen, Adolph. *The Sculptural Programs of Chartres Cathedral*, New York, Norton, 1964 (orig. 1959).

Keen, Maurice. *Chivalry*, New Haven, Yale University Press, 1984.

Keenan, Janice M., Brian MacWhinney, and Deborah Mayhew, "Pragmatics in

Memory: A Study of Natural Conversation," in Ulric Neisser, ed., *Memory Observed: Remembering in Natural Contexts*, San Francisco, W.H. Freeman, 1982.

Kekez, Josip. "Bugarscice: A Unique Type of Archaic Oral Poetry," *Oral Tradition*, Vol. 6, Nos. 2–3, 1991, pp. 200–24.

Kelly, Douglas. "Topical Invention in Medieval French Literature," in James J. Murphy, ed., *Medieval Eloquence: Studies in the Theory and Practice of Medieval Rhetoric*, Berkeley, University of California Press, 1978.

———. *The Art of Medieval French Romance*, Madison, University of Wisconsin Press, 1992.

Kittay, Jeffrey. "On Octo (Response to 'Rethinking Old French Literature: The Orality of the Octosyllabic Couplet,' Evelyn Birge Vitz)," *Romanic Review*, Vol. 77, No. 3, 1987, pp. 291–98.

Lanham, Richard A. *A Handlist of Rhetorical Terms*, Berkeley, University of California Press, 1969.

Lanson, Gustave. *Histoire de la littérature française* (completed for the period 1850–1950 by P. Tuffrau), Paris, Hachette, 1951.

Leach, A.F. *The Schools of Medieval England*, New York, Macmillan, 1915.

Legge, Mary Dominica. "La précocité de la littérature anglo-normande," *Cahiers de civilisation médiévale*, 8, 1965, pp. 327–49.

Leverett, F.P., ed. *A New and Copious Lexicon of the Latin Language*, Philadelphia, Lippincott, 1893.

Lord, Albert B. *The Singer of Tales*, Cambridge, Harvard University Press, 1960.

Lote, Georges. *Histoire du vers français*, 5 vols., Paris, Boivin, 1951.

Lowe, E.A. "Handwriting," in C.G. Crump and E.F. Jacobs, eds., *The Legacy of the Middle Ages*, Oxford, Clarendon, 1962, pp. 197–226.

Luriia, A.R. *The Mind of a Mnemonist: A Little Book about a Vast Memory*, trans. Lynn Solotaroff, New York, Basic Books, 1968.

Luttrell, Claude. *The Creation of the First Arthurian Romance*, Evanston, Northwestern University Press, 1974.

McNeil, Tom. *Castles*, London, B.T. Batsford, 1992.

Mâle, Emile. *The Gothic Image: Religious Art in France of the Thirteenth Century*, New York, Harper & Row (Icon), 1972 (orig. 1913).

Mehler, Ulrich. *Dicere und cantare: Zur musikalischen Terminologie und Auffuhrungspraxis des mittelalterlichen geistlichen Dramas in Deutschland*, Regensburg, Bosse, 1981.

Micha, Alexandre. *La tradition manuscrite des romans de Chrétien de Troyes*, Paris, Droz, 1939.

Miller, George. "The Magical Number Seven, Plus or Minus Two: Some Limits on Our Capacity for Processing Information, *Psychological Review* 63, 1966, pp. 81–97.

Morier, Henri. *Dictionnaire de poétique et de rhétorique*, Paris, PUF, 1961.

Murray, Stephen. "Plan and Space at Amiens Cathedral," *Journal of the Society of Architectural Historians* 49, 1990, pp. 44–67.

Neisser, Ulric, ed. *Memory Observed: Remembering in Natural Contexts*, San Francisco, W.H. Freeman, 1982.

Noakes, Susan. *Timely Reading: Between Exegesis and Interpretation*, Ithaca, Cornell University Press, 1988.

Notopoulos, James A. "Mnemosyne in Oral Literature," *Transactions of the American Philological Association* 69, 1938, pp. 465–93.

Olsan, Lea. "Latin Charms of Medieval England: Verbal Healing in Christian Oral Tradition," *Oral Tradition*, Vol. 7, No. 1, 1992, pp. 116–42.

Ong, Walter J. *Orality and Literacy: The Technologizing of the Word*, London, Methuen, 1982.

Orme, Nicholas. *From Childhood to Chivalry: The Education of the English Kings and Aristocracy, 1066–1530*, London, Methuen, 1984.

———. *Education and Society in Medieval and Renaissance England*, London, Hambledon Press, 1989.

Page, Christopher. *Voices and Instruments of the Middle Ages: Instrumental Practice and Songs in France 1100–1300*, Berkeley, University of California Press, 1986.

———. *The Owl and the Nightingale: Musical Life and Ideas in France 1100–1300*, Berkeley, University of California Press, 1989.

Parkes, M.B. "The Literacy of the Laity," in *The Medieval World*, D. Daiches and A. Thorlby, eds., London, 1973, pp. 555–77.

Poirion, Daniel. *Résurgences*, Paris, PUF/écriture, 1986.

Pope, Mildred K. *From Latin to Modern French with Especial Consideration of Anglo-Norman Phonology and Morphology*, Manchester, Manchester University Press, 1966, rev. edn, 1952 (orig. 1934).

Postlewait, Thomas and Bruce A. McConachie, eds., *Interpreting the Theatrical Past: Essays in the Historiography of Performance*, Iowa City, University of Iowa Press, 1989.

Reinelt, Janelle G. and Joseph R. Roach, eds. *Critical Theory and Performance*, Ann Arbor, University of Michigan Press, 1992.

Rejhon, Annalee C. *Can Rolant: The Medieval Welsh Version of the Song of Roland*, Berkeley, University of California Press, 1984.

———. "Symposium: The Effects of Oral and Written Transmission in the Exchange between Medieval Celtic and French Literatures: A Physiological View," *Oral Tradition*, Vol. 5, No. 1, 1990, pp. 131–48.

Riché, Pierre. "Recherches sur l'instruction des laïcs du IXe au XIIe siècle," *Cahiers de civilisation médiévale*, Vol. V, No. 2, 1962, pp. 175–82.

Rogers, Mary Frances. *Peter Lombard and the Sacramental System*, Merrick, NY, Richwood Publishing, 1976.

Roy, Bruno and Paul Zumthor, eds. *Jeux de mémoire: aspects de la mnémotechnie médiévale*, Montréal/Paris, Université de Montréal, 1985.

Rubin, David C. *Memory in Oral Traditions: the Cognitive Psychology of Epics, Ballads, and Counting-out Rhymes*, Oxford, Oxford University Press, 1995.

Rychner, Jean. *La chanson de geste: Essai sur l'art épique des jongleurs*, Geneva, Droz, 1955.

———. *Contribution à l'étude des fabliaux: variantes, remaniements, dégradations*, Neuchatel, Faculté des Lettres, 1960.

Saenger, Paul. "Silent Reading: Its Impact on Late Medieval Script and Society," *Viator* 13, 1982, pp. 367–414.

Saintsbury, George. *A Short History of French Literature*, 4th edn, Oxford, Clarendon, 1892.

————. *A History of English Prosody, From the Twelfth Century to the Present Day*, 2nd edn, New York, Russell & Russell, 3 vols., 1961 (orig. 1923).

Salter, Elizabeth. "The Mediaeval Lyric," in *The Medieval World*, D. Daitches and A. Thorlby, eds., London, 1973, pp. 445–84.

Schechner, Richard. *Between Theatre and Anthropology*, Philadelphia, University of Pennsylvania, 1985.

————. *Performance Theory*, rev. edn, New York, Routledge, 1988 (orig. 1977).

Schmitt, Jean-Claude. *La raison des gestes dans l'Occident médiéval*, Paris, Gallimard, 1990.

Scholz, Manfred Günter. *Hören und Lesen: Studien zur primären Rezeption der Literatur im 12. und 13. Jahrhundert*, Wiesbaden, Franz Seiner Verlag, 1980.

Scott, Clive. *The Riches of Rhyme: Studies in French Verse*, Oxford, Clarendon, 1988.

Segre, Cesare. "Sermoni in versi" and "Cicli di sermoni in versi" (pp. 60–64), in *Grundriss der Romanischen Literaturen des Mittelalters*, Vol. VI/1 (Heidelberg, Carl Winter, 1968), and Vol. VI/2 [Documentation], pp. 97–110.

Simpson, D.P., ed. *Cassell's New Latin Dictionary*, New York, Funk and Wagnalls,

Smirnov, A.A. *Problems of the Psychology of Memory*, New York, Plenum, 1973.

Southworth, John. *The English Medieval Minstrel*, Woodbridge (Suffolk, UK) Boydell Press, 1989.

Stanger, Mary D. "Literary Patronage at the Medieval Court of Flanders," *French Studies*, XI, 1957, pp. 214–29.

Stenton, Doris M. *English Society in the Early Middle Ages*, 4th edn, Harmondsworth, Penguin, 1965.

Stevens, John. *Words and Music in the Middle Ages: Song, Narrative, Dance and Drama, 1050–1350*, Cambridge, Cambridge University Press, 1986.

Stirnemann, Patricia Danz. "Quelques bibliothèques princières de la production hors scriptorium au XIIe siècle," *Bulletin archéologique du C.T.H.S., nouv. série, fasc. 17–18*, 1984, pp. 7–38.

Stock, Brian. *The Implications of Literacy: Written Language and Models of Interpretation in the Eleventh and Twelfth Centuries*, Princeton, Princeton University Press, 1983.

Strayer, Joseph, gen. ed. *Dictionary of the Middle Ages*, New York, Scribner, 1982.

Suard, François. "L'Utilisation des éléments folkloriques dans le lai du 'Frêne,' " *Cahiers de civilisation médiévale* 21, 1978, pp. 43–52.

Suleiman, Susan R. "Introduction: Varieties of Audience-Oriented Criticism," in *The Reader in the Text: Essays on Audience and Interpretation*, Princeton, Princeton University Press, 1980.

Taylor, Andrew. "The Myth of the Minstrel Manuscript," *Speculum*, Vol. 66, No. 1, 1991, pp. 43–73.

Tedlock, Dennis. *Finding the Center*, New York, Dial Press, 1972.

————. *The Spoken Word and the Work of Interpretation*, Philadelphia, University of Pennsylvania Press, 1983.

————. "On the Representation of Discourse in Discourse," *Journal of Anthropological Research*, Vol. 43, No. 4 (1987), pp. 343–4.

———— and Bruce Mannheim, eds. *The Dialogic Emergence of Culture*, Urbana, University of Illinois Press, 1995.

Thompson, James Westfall. *The Literacy of the Laity in the Middle Ages*, Berkeley, University of California Press, 1939.

Tobler, Adolph and Erhard Lommatzsch, *Altfranzösisches Wörterbuch*, Berlin, Weidman, 1925– .

Todorov, Tzvetan. "Les catégories du récit littéraire," *Recherches sémiologiques: L'analyse structurale du récit, Communications* 8, 1966, pp. 125–51.

Turner, Ralph V. "The *Miles Litteratus* in Twelfth-and Thirteenth-Century England: How Rare a Phenomenon?" *American Historical Review* LXXXIII, 1978, pp. 928–45.

Turner, Victor. *From Ritual to Theatre: The Human Seriousness of Play*, New York, Performing Arts Journal Publications, 1982.

Tydeman, William. *The Theatre in the Middle Ages: Western European Stage Conditions, c.800–1576*, Cambridge, Cambridge University Press, 1978.

Ubersfeld, Anne. *Lire le théâtre*, Paris, Editions sociales, 1982.

Van Coolput, Colette-Anne. "Appendice: Références, adaptations et emprunts directs," in Norris J. Lacy, Douglas Kelly and Keith Busby, ed. and trans., *The Legacy of Chrétien de Troyes*, 2 vols., Amsterdam, Rodopi, 1987; Vol. I, pp. 333–42.

Van Mulken, Margot. "*Perceval* and Stemmata", in *Les Manuscrits de Chrétien de Troyes/ The Manuscripts of Chrétien de Troyes*, ed. Keith Busby, Terry Nixon, Alison Stones and Lori Walters, Amsterdam, Rodopi, 1993, Vol. I, pp. 41–48.

Vance, Eugene. "Le combat érotique chez Chrétien de Troyes: de la figure à la forme," *Poétique* 12, 1972, pp. 544–71.

———. *From Topic to Tale: Logic and Narrativity in the Middle Ages*, Minneapolis, University of Minnesota Press, 1987.

Vinaver, Eugène. *The Rise of Romance*, New York and Oxford, Oxford University Press, 1971.

Vitz, Evelyn Birge. "Vie, légende, littérature: traditions orales et écrites dans les histoires des saints," *Poétique* 72, 1987, pp. 387–402.

———. Review of *The Old French Evangile de l'Enfance* for *Romance Philology*, Vol. XLI, No. 4, 1988, pp. 471–73.

———. "The Impact of Christian Doctrine on Medieval Literature," in Denis Hollier, gen. ed., *A New History of French Literature*, Cambridge, Harvard University Press, 1989, pp. 82–87.

———. *Medieval Narrative and Modern Narratology: Subjects and Objects of Desire*, New York, New York University Press, 1989.

———. "From the Oral to the Written in Medieval and Renaissance Saints Lives," in Renate Blumenfeld-Kosinski and Timea Szell, eds., *Images of Sainthood in Medieval Europe*, Ithaca, Cornell University Press, 1991, pp. 97–114.

———. "The Apocryphal and the Biblical, the Oral and the Written, in Medieval Legends of the Life of Christ: The Old French *Evangile de l'Enfance*," in Ruth Sternglanz and Nancy Reale, eds., *Satura: Essays on Medieval Satire and Religion*, Stamford (UK), Paul Watkins, 1998, pp. 129–55.

———. "Paul Zumthor and Medieval Romance," *Dalhousie French Studies* 44 (1998), pp. 3–11.

———. "Minstrel Meets Clerk in Early French Literature: Medieval Romance as

the Meeting-Place between Two Traditions of Verbal Eloquence and Performance Practice," in Collected Papers of Fordham Conference 1997 [volume
under review].

————. "French Medieval Oral Traditions," in John Miles Foley, gen. ed.,
Teaching Oral Traditions, New York, Modern Language Association, 1998,
pp. 373–81.

Wallace, Wanda T. and David C. Rubin. " 'The Wreck of the Old 97': A Real
Event Remembered in Song," pp. 283–310, in Ulric Neisser and Eugene
Winograd, eds., *Remembering Reconsidered: Ecological and Traditional
Approaches to the Study of Memory*, Cambridge, Cambridge University Press,
1988.

Walter, Philippe. *La mémoire du temps: Fêtes et calendriers de Chrétien de
Troyes à la Mort Artu*, Paris/Geneva, Champion/Slatkine, 1989.

Watkins, Calvert. *How to Kill a Dragon: Aspects of Indo-European Poetics*, New
York, Oxford University Press, 1995.

Wieruszowski, Helene. *The Medieval University*, Princeton, Van Nostrand, 1966.

Woledge, Brian and Ian Short, "Liste provisoire des manuscrits du XIIe siècle
contenant des textes en langue française," *Romania* 102, 1981, pp. 1–17.

Wolfe, Rosemary. *The English Mystery Plays*, Berkeley, University of California
Press, 1972.

Wood, Margaret. *The English Mediaeval House*, New York, Harper Colophon,
1983.

Yates, Frances. *The Art of Memory*, Chicago, University of Chicago, 1966.

Zaerr, Linda Marie and Mary Ellen Ryder. "Psycholinguistic Theory and Modern
Performance: Memory as a Key to Variants in Medieval Texts," *Mosaic* 26,
1993, pp. 21–35.

————. "Fiddling with the Middle English Romance: Using Performance to
Reconstruct the Past," *Medievalia*, Vol. 21, 1996, pp. 47–65.

Ziolkowski, Jan M. *Talking Animals: Medieval Latin Beast Poetry, 750–1150*,
Philadelphia, University of Pennsylvania Press, 1993.

Zumthor, Paul. *Histoire de la littérature française*, Paris, Presses Universitaires de
France, 1954.

————. *Essai de poétique médiévale*, Paris, Seuil, 1972.

————. *Introduction à la poésie orale*, Paris, Seuil, 1983.

————. *La poésie et la voix dans la civilisation médiévale*, Paris, PUF, 1984.

————. "L'écriture et la voix: le roman d'*Eracle*," in L.A. Arrathoon, ed., *The
Craft of Fiction*, Rochester, Solaris, 1984.

————. *La lettre et la voix: De la "littérature" médiévale*, Paris, Seuil/Poétique,
1987.

————. "Qu'est-ce qu'un style médiéval?," in Nicole Revel and Diana Rey-
Hulman, eds., *Pour une anthropologie des voix*, Paris, L'harmattan/ Centre de
recherche sur l'oralité, 1993, pp. 35–47.

————. "Poésie et vocalité au Moyen Age," *Cahiers de culture orale* 36, 1994,
pp. 23–34.

INDEX

Medieval names are listed first name first, in conformity with medieval usage. Proper names since the Renaissance are given last name first.

French proper names are given in their full French form when that is the only fashion in which the person is generally referred to: thus, Chrétien de Troyes and Marie de France, but Marie, countess of Champagne and Philip of Alsace, count of Flanders.

313